BY SEA TO THE
Channel Islands

From packet boats and steamers to ro-pax and catamarans

CONDOR

CONDOR 10

RICHARD KIRKMAN

Ferry
Publications

Published by: Ferry Publications, PO Box 33, Ramsey, Isle of Man IM99 4LP
Tel: +44 (0) 1624 898445   Fax: +44 (0) 1624 898449
E-mail: ferrypubs@manx.net   www.ferrypubs.co.uk

Main front cover view: *Corbière* – the ship that successfully challenged and broke the Sealink monopoly of passenger services to the Channel Islands. Seen here in her BCIF livery. *(Ferry Publications Library)*

Frontispiece: *Condor 10* at speed off the Needles during trials. *(Fotoflite)*

Below: *Earl Harold* shows off the corporate Sealink British Ferries livery, which she wore for the 1985 season. *(Fotoflite)*

Produced and designed by Ferry Publications trading as Lily Publications Ltd
PO Box 33, Ramsey, Isle of Man, British Isles, IM99 4LP
Tel: +44 (0) 1624 898446   Fax: +44 (0) 1624 898449
www.ferrypubs.co.uk   e mail: info@lilypublications.co.uk
Printed and bound by Gomer Press Ltd., Wales, UK +44 (0) 1559 362371
© Lily Publications 2018
Published June 2018

ISBN: 978-1-911268-13-0

Contents

Introduction

Despite their proximity to the French coast, the Bailliwicks of Guernsey and Jersey have long been dependent on their shipping links with England. Their status as offshore British Crown dependencies saw them look north for trade and military support. *By Sea to the Channel Islands* is the story of these vital links. It is a tale of intense and often dangerous rivalry, of war and peace, of rise and decline in passenger business across the twentieth century - repeated in the modern era, of feast and famine in ship capacity, and of technological innovation from the earliest days of packet boats, through the development of steam, to the modern fast craft era. It is also a story of tragedy, as the Islands' dramatic tidal range and their treacherous topography have claimed a disproportionately high number of shipping casualties. Few shipping routes have such a complex history. Long served by a railway monopoly providing stability and continuity of service, frequently at a loss, the mould was quickly broken after the privatisation of Sealink in 1984. The subsequent tale has seen the restoration of a monopoly with a unique dependence on fast craft to sustain the lifeline passenger service. But sea passengers are now only a small proportion of arrivals in the Islands. The importance of the daily arrival of the mailboat has been replaced by the 'just in time' appearance of the Portsmouth ro-ro freight service. The market is now deemed too small to justify sea competition, but in reality this has always been the case.

This narrative focuses on the main passenger routes from England, bringing freight services into the story as necessary. These services were often closely integrated with other routes, particularly those operated by the railway companies from Southampton, Weymouth and the Channel Islands to France, so these are weaved into the narrative where relevant.

Richard Kirkman
Seaford, East Sussex
Liberation Day, 9 May 2018

EARL GR...

Earl Granville was the final vessel acquired by Sealink UK Ltd for Channel Islands service whilst still under railway ownership. *(FotoFlite)*

Exeter
Topsham
Weymouth
Portland Bill
Torquay
Berry Head
Plymouth
Start Point
Eddystone

Channel Light Vessel

Alderne

Casquets

Platte Fougère
Guernsey
Herm
Les Hanois
Sark

La Corbière
Noi

Roches Douvres

Les Courtis

Ports
Lighthouses

Morlaix
Binic
St. Brieuc

Southampton

Portsmouth

Littlehampton

Shoreham
Kingston
Brighton

Newhaven

Solent
Isle of Wight

Nab Tower

Beachy Head

The Needles

St Catherine's

Greenwich
Light Vessel

ENGLISH CHANNEL

p de la
ague

Cherbourg

Cotentin
Peninsular

Le Havre

Honfleur

Carteret

Ouistreham

Caen

ausey

Granville

NORMANDY

Baie du
Mont St Michel

t Malo

CHAPTER ONE
The earliest services

'So rapid and certain has the communication between these islands and England become of late years, that many will smile when they are told, that scarcely a century has elapsed since a journey from Guernsey to London was a serious undertaking. Now, we may go there and return in three days, of which one day can be spent in London'.

[Guernsey & Jersey Magazine, June 1836]

Prior to the late 18th century shipping links between the Channel Islands and England were infrequent and slow, and mails could take weeks to reach their destination. Most letters from England were sent to Southampton, to be handed to the masters of cargo vessels heading for the Islands. They in turn gave them to agents in Guernsey and Jersey, who arranged delivery. With closer and easier links to the French coast, it was often quicker but more expensive to send English mail via France. There were no regular passenger sailings to English ports, and those wishing to travel had to approach a cargo vessel's master and barter a fare.

This informal approach remained the norm until 1778, when the strategic position of the Islands during the war with France prompted a more reliable service. The Postmaster General arranged for the armed sailing cutter *Express* to be transferred from the Dover-Calais route to operate 'as often as practicable' – in practice fortnightly - from Southampton to the Islands. The *Express* returned to Dover after peace was restored in 1783 and the mail service resumed in private hands.

In 1791 the British Post Office undertook a survey of mail being passed through

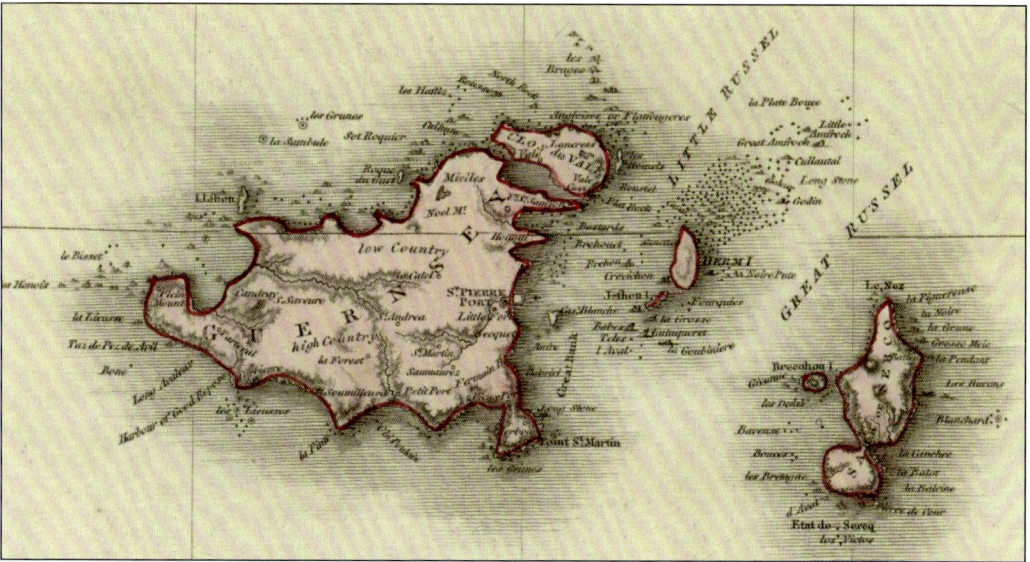

1814 plan of Guernsey from John Pinkerton's Modern Atlas. Hazards to shipping are already well identified and understood. St Pierre Port is the island's capital with a well defined harbour; Clos de Vale is still shown as an island on the north east coast, although the tidal channel was drained in 1806. *(Author's collection)*

Southampton, which suggested that the annual total to Guernsey and Jersey was under 30,000 letters. Whilst the States' Governments and Islanders seemed indifferent to the establishment of regular links, General Conway, the Governor of Jersey, pressed repeatedly for a regular packet service to support the military, observing that communications with England could on occasion be interrupted by up to five or six weeks at a time. The British Government determined that a packet service should be established, although the Post Office did not believe that it would be viable. Portsmouth and Southampton were considered as possible homeports for the service before Weymouth was selected on the

1814 plan of Jersey from John Pinkerton's Modern Atlas. The harbour is marked in St Helier and the rocky nature of the southern approaches is made plain. *(Author's collection)*

basis of the shorter sea crossing.

The timely wartime suspension of the Dover-Calais service allowed the transfer of two 80-ton packets to undertake the sixteen-hour passage to Jersey. The *Rover* (Capt. Bennett) and the *Royal Charlotte* (Capt. Wood) were both owned independently, and the Post Office paid a fee that partially covered costs, allowing masters to make up the difference by carrying passengers who bargained for their passage. Given the value of their cargo the vessels were armed, with instructions to throw the mail overboard if attacked.

A notice dated 3 February 1794 formally announced that a packet would sail from Weymouth with mail and letters for Guernsey and Jersey every Wednesday, with the first departure set for 6 February. An Act of Parliament formally established the new service on 28 March. The round trip was planned to take a week: -

'Notice is hereby given, that a Packet will sail every Thursday from Weymouth for the Islands of Guernsey and Jersey, and a Mail with the Letters for those Islands will be made up and sent from this Office every Wednesday night. The First Mail is to sail, if possible, on Thursday the 6th instant.

The Course the Packet will take, and the Times of her Stay and Return, will be in general, and, unless in Cases of particular and occasional Orders to the contrary, the same as in the last War, namely, to Guernsey and drop her Letters there, to proceed immediately to Jersey, there to deliver her Letters, and to stay Three Days for the Answers, then to return to Guernsey, deliver her Letters, stay there Two Days, and return to Weymouth.

By Command of the Postmaster-General

Anth. Todd, Sec.'

[*London Gazette, 5 February 1794*]

In the event the first sailing was delayed by a week, and the *Royal Charlotte* (Capt. Wood) eventually sailed from Weymouth with mails for Guernsey and Jersey at 5:00 p.m. on 13 February.

In an era when news travelled slowly, the arrival of the packet boats was an important source of intelligence of international events, which was transmitted by newspaper across the country: -

'The *Royal Charlotte* Packet left Guernsey on the 23rd, and arrived at Weymouth at 7 a.m. Monday - The Viscount Poiger, aid du camp to the Marquis de Dresnay, the French General who commands the Emigrants, came to Weymouth in the Packet, and we learn that the Royalists of the banks of the Loire are 80,000 strong, but that only half that number are properly armed, the rest having only flicks, clubs, or any weapon they can get.'

[*Cumberland Pacquet, and Ware's Whitehaven Advertiser, 1 April 1794*]

Royal Charlotte's next sailing was more problematic. She: -

'left Guernsey on Saturday morning last, but having got the length of the Caskets (sic), it blew such a gale of wind that she was obliged to bear away, and the same evening came to an anchor in the Guernsey Roads. She sailed again on Sunday, and arrived at Weymouth at seven a.m. on Monday... The packet brings advice, that on Saturday night seven large transports, with troops and stores from Jersey, under convoy of two frigates, a sloop of war, and an armed cutter, arrived in Guernsey.'

[*Hereford Journal, 2 April 1794*]

The departure day of the packet from England was switched to Saturday following pressure from the States of Jersey. The Bridport-built *Earl of Chesterfield* joined the fleet in June 1795 and the *Royal Charlotte* was withdrawn. However the weekly frequency of the packet boats was not sufficient to meet demand, and competition arose with the operation of the 'Bye Boat', a common term used to describe a Post Office stand-by vessel: -

'Guernsey Extra Packet, or Bye Boat
The Public is hereby informed, that the *Alert*, extra Packet or Bye Boat between Weymouth and Guernsey, most completely fitted for passengers which has hitherto given the greatest satisfaction, will in future sail from Weymouth every Thursday evening (wind and weather permitting) for Guernsey, and sail from thence on its return to Weymouth on the Monday following - Goods directed to the care of Mr Nicholas Robilliard, at Weymouth, will be taken the greatest care of. The Bye Boat entering the harbour immediately on its arrival in Guernsey, prevents the greatest inconvenience to passengers which those by the packets experience, in consequence of their sailing at once for Jersey, and thereby obliging them to get into boats from the roads, frequently at a considerable distance from the shore'.
[*Hampshire Telegraph*, 17 November 1806]

Nicholas Robilliard, a Guernsey businessman, carried letters in an unofficial capacity on the *Alert*, circumventing the regulations by arranging for mail to be sent to him at Weymouth, where he was already an established Agent. Post Office packets' passenger receipts fell from £700 to £400 in 1806 as business was lost to the *Alert*, which filled the gap in the schedule and was free to convey any cargo it chose.

Whilst the establishment of the packet boat service had been a wartime expedient, there was sufficient demand and pressure for this to become a more permanent arrangement. The *Earl of Chesterfield* was replaced by the *Chesterfield* in 1806, and a third packet boat, the *General Doyle*, was added to the Weymouth station in 1807, allowing the Post Office packets to offer a twice-weekly schedule on Wednesdays and Saturdays. This was sufficient to force the *Alert* out of business in 1809 and Nicholas Robilliard was declared bankrupt in October 1810. A new packet, the *Francis Freeling*, was ordered to replace the chartered *General Doyle*, which made its last voyage in November 1809, and the *Hinchinbrook* was added to the fleet in 1811. However other private packets continued to take a significant proportion of the passenger traffic to the Islands.

In the 1809 'Summer stroll through the islands of Jersey and Guernsey', it was noted that the journey from Weymouth could take anything between nine and twenty four hours, dependent upon weather conditions. The fare was £1 7s 6d, but passengers had to take their own provisions on board, requiring them to make an educated guess as to the possible length of the passage. There were no regular packets sailing from Southampton, but frequent trading boats offered a passage at £1 1s to make this the preferred route to London, with the shorter overland journey compensating for a longer sea crossing, which could take up to thirty hours. Capt. Nicolle of Jersey of the ship *Hero* received special mention for the superior accommodation offered on his vessel.

The passage in wartime conditions was a difficult one and vessels were subject to attack by French privateers. The *Chesterfield* saw off just such an attack on 12 July 1810, but was not so lucky on 29 October 1811 when she was captured by the French privateer *L'Epruvier* and taken to Cherbourg as a prize. The mails and dispatches were thrown overboard but a passenger died during the capture and the captain and two members of the crew later died of their wounds in Cherbourg. The Post Office paid compensation of £1,626 to her owner, Capt. Starr Wood; he laid down a new vessel, also to be called *Chesterfield*, chartering the

Rapid in the meantime.

In October 1812 as the *Chesterfield* neared completion, Capt. Starr Wood took several of the crew of the *Rapid* to speed work on the vessel. The *Rapid* sailed from Weymouth for the Islands without seven of her crew of fifteen; the mate took charge but was drunk throughout the two-day crossing, leaving navigation in the hands of two experienced captains who were travelling as passengers. The outcome was sufficiently frightening for passengers to complain to the Postmaster General, leading to the dismissal of Capt. Starr Wood and his mate. Starr Wood set up in opposition to the packets flying a flag similar to the Post Office pennant, and misled passengers into believing they were sailing on a packet boat. He was granted a licence to operate to Southampton and did significant damage to the Weymouth trade. Capt. Naylor took his place at Weymouth on 22 January 1814 with the *Countess of Liverpool*, but she proved too large for the run and her owner was soon in debt. The *Sir William Curtis* took over the service before her owner also found himself in financial trouble, and the *Countess of Liverpool* returned under Capt. White in June 1817.

In this period the Southampton service was maintained by three 80 ton sailing cutters, the *Aeolus, Brilliant* and *Diligent*, which sailed on an ad hoc basis whenever there was sufficient cargo and the weather allowed.

There was a more successful outcome to privateer action in January 1814 when the *Brilliant* was captured by the American privateer *Prince de Neufchatel* whilst on passage from Guernsey to Southampton. The privateer intended to take her as a prize to Cherbourg but mistook Alderney for the French coast and permitted the *Brilliant*'s helmsman to steer her into harbour, allowing the vessel to be recaptured.

The first cross-channel steamship sailing took place in 1816 and this new form of propulsion soon began to take traffic away from Post Office packets around the country, despite the initial unreliable nature of the vessels. The Post Office eventually began to invest in the new technology, but the Island services were a low priority.

The end of the Napoleonic Wars ended a period of prosperity for the Islands as the military presence was reduced and privateering opportunities were curtailed. Both Islands saw high levels of unemployment and depression in the agricultural and maritime trades in the immediate aftermath, but conditions improved from the 1820s as migrants boosted the population.

In 1821 a group of Jersey investors bought the *Royal Charlotte*, a sailing cutter of 90 tons, to operate a passenger and cargo service between Jersey and Southampton. She had capacity for forty passengers and could accommodate up to twenty in berths. *Royal Charlotte* made her first crossing on 15 November 1821 and maintained a service, blatantly advertising her mail connections, until she was transferred to Weymouth in September 1823 and lost in a gale off Cap de la Hague the following month.

The steamer *Triton* operated a summer service in 1823 between Southampton and Le Havre, demonstrating that the new technology could operate to a regular schedule. Meanwhile the Islands got their first glimpse of the future when the 1822-built *Medina* became the first steam-powered vessel to visit Guernsey and Jersey. *Medina* was chartered by Colonel Fitzgerald of the 72nd regiment and sailed with his family and effects from Southampton on 9 June 1823, anchoring overnight off Cowes before proceeding to Guernsey, where she arrived during the night and entered harbour the following morning. The novelty attracted a large crowd, and after the Colonel and his family had disembarked, the commander, Mr. Knight, invited 'those who were desirous of viewing the machinery' to board the vessel. Many accepted the invitation 'and expressed their astonishment at the mechanism, and admiration at the accommodation on board her'. On 11 June the *Medina* started for Jersey, with 130 Islanders on board and Mr. Knight again issued a general invitation to visitors from the thousands of spectators who gathered on her arrival. One trooper, seeing smoke issuing from the funnel, went for help to assist the 'packet on fire'. The *Medina* returned to Guernsey 'cheered by the numbers assembled in boats to witness his departure'. The *Medina* took 4hrs 5min to sail from Guernsey to Jersey and 15hrs 30min on her return crossing from Guernsey to Southampton.

Reaction to the visit was strongly positive and the Lieutenant Governor of Jersey wrote to the Postmaster General urging the use of steam-powered vessels for the Island mails, proposing a contract-operated service from Portsmouth or Southampton. The Post Office replied that if steamers were used they should be on the shorter Weymouth route, where smaller, more economical vessels could be employed. This stance created an opportunity, and an advertisement in the Gazette de l'Isle announced that: -

HIS MAJESTY'S POST OFFICE
STEAM PACKETS.

One of these Packets with the Mails and Passengers, leaves Weymouth for the Islands of GUERNSEY and JERSEY, every Wednesday and Saturday, at 9 o'clock, P. M. weather permitting, and leaves the Islands for Weymouth, every Tuesday and Saturday, the time being dependant on the tides.

RATES OF PASSAGE MONEY.

Cabin Passengers, each...............	£1	1	0
Female Servants, each	0	15	0
Male Servants, each	0	12	6
Children under Ten years of age, to be charged half the rates paid by their Parents.			
Carriages with Four Wheels, each	3	0	0
Ditto, Two Wheels, each	1	10	0
Horses, each........................	1	10	0
Dogs, with their Owners, each.........	0	2	6
Ditto, on Freight, each...............	0	5	0
Parcels of or under 30lbs. weight.......	0	2	6
Cash or Bullion, per Thousand Pounds ..	1	1	0

The above Rates to be paid in British Money, and the Freight of all Parcels must be paid for at the time they are received on board.

These Packets possess every accommodation for Passengers, are remarkably fine Vessels, and the Captains Gentlemen of great skill in their profession.

RESIDENT AGENT,
CAPT. J. AGNEW STEVENS, R. N.
COMMANDERS,
Capt. ROBERT WHITE, *Watersprite,*
Capt. LIVEING, *Flamer,*
Capt. COMBEN, *Ivanhoe.*

'A public meeting will be held in the British Hotel in St Helier of subscribers to a steam vessel. The subscription book is at Mr. Robert Collyers'.

[*Gazette de l'Isle*, 29 August 1823]

This led to a group of Jersey and Southampton merchants placing an order for a steamer, *Lord Beresford*, for a service from Portsmouth; the Gazette later reported that £3,000 had been subscribed in Guernsey. In response another group of Southampton merchants, led by William Chamberlayne MP, ordered the *Ariadne* 'to keep the advantages they had so long reaped by the trade to and from these islands'. The 197-ton *Ariadne* won the race to be the first to arrive. She was launched at William Evans of Rotherhithe on 1 May 1824; at 96ft long she was twice as large as other vessels commonly operating at the time. *Ariadne* arrived at Southampton on 6 June 1824 and sailed for the Islands the following day commanded by Capt. Bazin, arriving in Guernsey at 7:00 p.m. on 8 June, having been delayed by fog. *Ariadne* returned from Jersey to Guernsey on 11 June and sailed thence to Southampton. Thereafter *Ariadne* sailed every Tuesday under the General Steam Navigation Company banner.

William Scott & Co of Swansea built the 160-ton *Lord Beresford*, named after the governor of Jersey. Carvel-built of wood, she attained 10-12 knots on trial 'without producing any unpleasant sensation'. *Lord Beresford* measured 100ft in length, with two engines of 36 horsepower each. She went into service from Portsmouth in June shortly after the arrival of the *Ariadne*, sailing under Capt. Masterman directly to Jersey and returning via Guernsey. In October she became the first steamer to sail from Jersey to St Malo.

Large crowds frequently greeted arrivals of the *Ariadne* at Southampton. Both the *Ariadne* and the *Lord Beresford* called at Cowes as required during their passage, with a connection to Cowes also provided from the *Lord Beresford* at Southampton at the owners' expense. The *Lord Beresford* left Portsmouth on Saturday afternoons and returned on Wednesdays. In October 1824 she was fitted with a hold capable of carrying 30 tons of cargo, suggesting that her earlier sailings were for passengers only. The *Ariadne* was laid up for winter from December 1824, but the *Lord Beresford* replaced her from Southampton until January 1825, when sail replaced steam until April 1825. On her return to traffic *Lord Beresford* operated from Southampton, calling at Portsmouth in each direction. Fares were identical to each Island, with both services priced from Southampton at £1 1s 6d in the main cabin, 16s in the fore cabin, and 10s 6d on the fore deck; fares were 7s 6d and 5s between the Islands.

Passenger traffic began to migrate to Southampton with the arrival of *Ariadne* and *Lord Beresford,* increasing pressure on the Weymouth packets. The Treasury finally gave approval for the Post Office to operate its own vessels in December 1824. There were plans to transfer *Ivanhoe* and *Meteor* from Milford to Weymouth, but in March 1825 the Post Office ordered a new steamer.

Meanwhile the Plymouth & Portsmouth Steam Packet Company introduced the 175-ton *Sir Francis Drake* (Capt. Smith) for a weekly sailing to the Islands from June 1826. The *Sir Francis Drake* left Plymouth Stonehouse Pool on Thursday evenings and returned from the Islands on Friday afternoons, arriving back in Plymouth on Saturday mornings, before heading out on Mondays for a return trip to Falmouth. Her first arrival in St. Peter Port was on 9 June. The *Brunswick* was also employed on this seasonal passenger service, and the company had ambitions to serve St Malo from Jersey.

Vessels berthed in St. Helier around La Folie in the English and French harbours, and at low water there was a landing stage at La Collette that could be reached by small boat from the vessel.

The hazards of early cross-channel travel were emphasised by the loss of the *Hinchinbrook*, which was wrecked on a reef near Longy off north east Alderney during a passage from Weymouth to Guernsey on 2 February 1826: -

'It appears, that Thursday night, about eight o'clock, (the night being very dark, and blowing hard), Capt. Quirk hove to, for the purpose of shortening sail, when near Alderney; but whilst in the act of changing jibs, and taking two reefs in the main-sail, the current then running seven or eight knots an hour, the *Hinchinbrook* struck upon a reef of rocks east of Alderney, and not far from the spot where the *Cimone,* Greek brig, was totally wrecked. Fortunately the passengers, (15 in number) and the crew, were landed in safety in Alderney. Among the passengers was one Miss Maingy, from the Roquettes, (the only female passenger on board), and she conducted herself in a manner that would have done credit to any man, however brave. It is remarkable that among many persons. Miss Maingy's trunk and that of another passenger were the only two picked up in Alderney. The mail was fortunately saved, and taken to Guernsey by the *Experiment,* Capt. Simon, on

Saturday afternoon. The mail for Jersey was conveyed on one of the oyster smacks. Capt. Quirk and his crew arrived Weymouth by the *Francis Freeling* Packet on Wednesday, which packet returned the same afternoon with the mails for Guernsey and Jersey'.

[*Dorset County Chronicle, 6 February 1826*]

Whilst Capt. Quirk secured the use of the *Queen Charlotte* as a replacement vessel he was later deemed liable for the sinking of the *Hinchinbrook* and pensioned off at the age of 67.

In March 1826 the *Lord Beresford* was sold to Robert Collyer and her captaincy transferred from Capt. Masterman to his former mate Capt. Goodridge, thereby beginning a long family association with the services. The following month *Ariadne* started her seasonal programme on 4 April carrying forty passengers. The passage times of both *Ariadne* and *Lord Beresford* between Guernsey and Southampton were averaging fourteen hours. Potential competition was in the offing when the new Post Office steamer *Watersprite* was launched on 9 May, with a trial crossing on 26 June for a party of officials from Weymouth to Jersey taking eight hours. However the mail service remained in the hands of the sailing packets. In September *Lord Beresford* was noted putting into St Malo, but she 'disarranged some of her works' on her last trip of the season and was forced to put into Lymington for repair. She went to Neath to be fitted with new engines and upgraded passenger accommodation, returning in May 1827.

The *Francis Freeling*, which had sailed on the Weymouth station since 1811, was lost with all hands during a passage to the Islands on 6 September 1826. Initially the fate of the vessel was unclear, until wreckage was discovered: -

'A piece of board has been picked up off Portland and identified as part of the fittings of the *Francis Freeling* Packet, from thence to Guernsey and Jersey, which sailed 6th instant, and has not since been heard of.'

[*Lloyds List, 29 September 1826*]

It took time to establish the circumstances of the loss and eventually became apparent that the *Francis Freeling* had been hit by a Swedish brig: -

'The fears entertained for the safety of the *Francis Freeling* Weymouth packet, there is every reason to believe, were too well founded. A Swedish brig, in the course of the tempestuous night of the 6th inst. encountered a vessel of the size of the packet, off Portland, and did not see her in time to avoid running her down; every endeavour was made to preserve the persons on board, but whether she foundered too suddenly to allow any of them to throw themselves on the chance of escape offered by the waves or the darkness of the night and violence of the storm rendered it impossible for the Swedes to discover them must remain a matter of conjecture. The brig, in her passage up the British Channel, left a statement to this effect at Cowes, and comparing the time at which the packet left Weymouth with other circumstances, little doubt can be entertained that she was the ill fated vessel that was destroyed. Sixteen persons, including the crew of nine, were on board, and not less than a hundred children, it is stated are rendered fatherless. The fate of the commander, Mr Wilkinson, who had undertaken the temporary direction of the vessel in the absence of Capt. White, is peculiarly melancholy, in consequence of his recent appointment to one of the steam-vessels which is about to be established between Weymouth and the Islands - a lucrative situation for which he had been particularly anxious.'

[*Salisbury & Winchester Journal, 30 September 1826*]

Capt. White had, fortuitously for him, been in London on packet business. The loss of the *Francis Freeling* with so many lives was devastating to a small community like Weymouth. A disaster fund for dependents of the crew was established both in the town and in the Islands, and the Postmaster General granted them an annual allowance. The *Countess of Liverpool* maintained the mail packet service from Weymouth with support from the former Milford packet *Iris*, until the arrival of steam vessels. The steamer *Ivanhoe*, built in 1820 by J. & C. Wood of Greenock, was transferred from the Holyhead-Dublin service to bolster the Weymouth fleet. She was powered by two 30 horsepower Maudsley engines driving two 12ft 6in paddle wheels.

At Southampton the *Ariadne* added a monthly call at St Malo to her Islands schedule from April 1827.

The transition from sail to steam increased the capital investment requirements for new vessels and made it impractical for masters to continue the practice of owning and operating their own ships. The Post Office took over the running of the Weymouth station from 5 July 1827, utilising the *Watersprite* and *Ivanhoe*. The *Watersprite* (Capt. White) became the first mail carrying steam packet to sail from Weymouth with a delivery for St Helier on 7 July, over a year after her trial visit. She was seen as threat to the Southampton steamers, and on her inaugural arrival in St. Helier *Watersprite* found her allocated berth occupied by the *Ariadne, Lord Beresford* and *Sir Francis Drake*. The private vessels initially refused to move to allow *Watersprite* to berth, and her arrival was severely delayed.

The new service left Weymouth on Wednesdays and Saturdays at 9:00 p.m. and returned on Sunday and Wednesday mornings, and was deemed to be speedier and more reliable than the old sailing cutters, which were quickly withdrawn. The *Ivanhoe* and *Watersprite* opened up a new era of unprecedented rapid travel: -

'His Majesty's steam packets *Watersprite* and *Ivanhoe* are now regularly fixed to convey the mails from Weymouth to Guernsey and Jersey; and such is the expeditious regulation of these packets that on Wednesday last two gentlemen having taken breakfast in London, departed by the Magnet coach, arrived in Weymouth the same evening in time for the packet, and on the following morning were comfortable seated at their breakfast in Guernsey, thus accomplishing the journey from the metropolis to the island in 24 hours.'

[*The Globe, 16 July 1827*]

The success of the Weymouth packet service and the desire to continue to compete strongly with Southampton prompted the transfer of another paddle steamer from Milford from 5 April 1828; the *Meteor* made her first trip on 13 April. She was built by Evans of Rotherhithe in 1821 and had Boulton & Watt engines generating 60 horsepower. The packets were now dispatched on Tuesday, Thursday and Saturday evenings.

From 1828 the *Brunswick* sailed a Plymouth-Guernsey-Portsmouth-Plymouth circuit for the Plymouth & Portsmouth Steam Packet Co, whilst *Sir Francis Drake*, which had been re-boilered to increase her power in 1827, operated the schedule in reverse. Passengers transferred to a timetabled connection to the Post Office packets in Guernsey to travel on to Jersey. The *Brunswick* was then the largest steam vessel yet seen in the Islands.

The *Ariadne* was fitted with new boilers in 1828, and was observed flying the 'Great Standard of England' when acting as a guard ship at the Southampton Regatta in August. In October the Lords of the Treasury in Guernsey allowed the exportation of fruit and

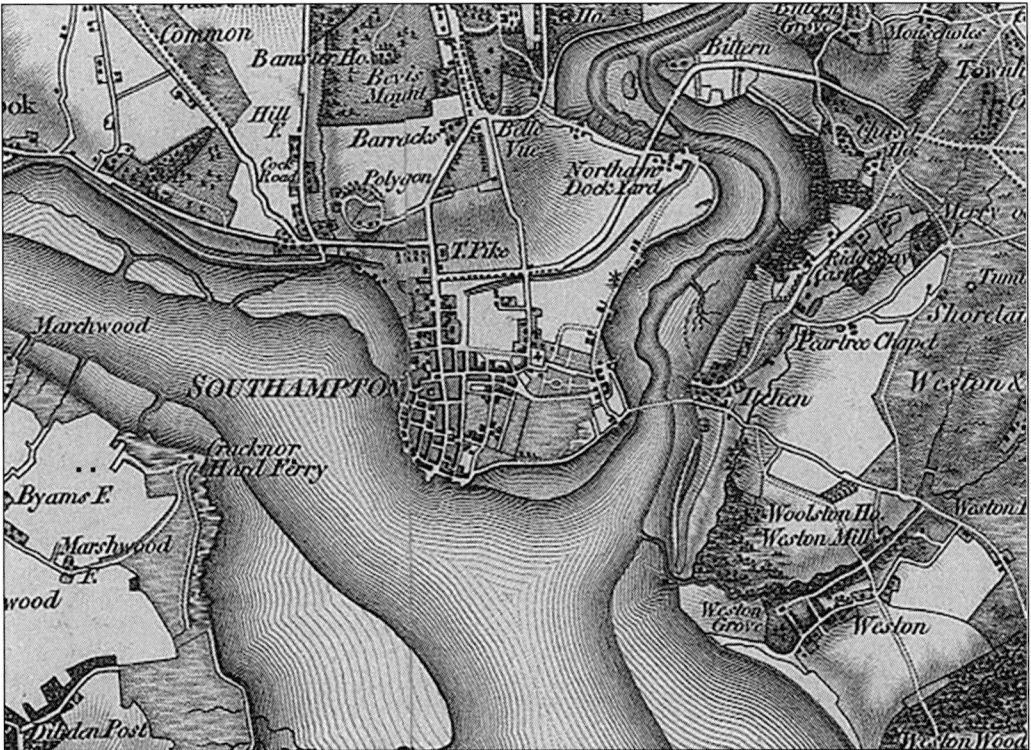

1810 Ordnance Survey map of Southampton. The areas of future dock development to the south east and west of the town are largely mud flats, whilst the shipbuilding dockyard at Northam is already active. *(Ordnance Survey 1st edition)*

vegetables on the *Ariadne* and *Lord Beresford* using the Agents' certificate rather than that of the master, saving a requirement to visit the Custom House and speeding up the transit of goods, which could now be loaded in the Roads at any state of the tide. The *Lord Beresford* was fitted with new boilers during the winter to increase her speed.

Summer 1829 saw a single-season operation of the *Bristol* (Capt. Hermann) from Southampton to Guernsey and Jersey, with some calls at Sark and St Malo. *Ariadne* sailed on Tuesday evenings from Southampton, returning on Fridays, except when, once a month, she sailed from Jersey to St Malo on Thursdays, returning on Saturdays from St Malo via Jersey and Guernsey to Southampton. Fares from Southampton to the Islands were £1 11s 6d in the main cabin, 18s in the fore cabin, and 10s 6d on the fore deck. In August the *Bristol* offered reduced fares of £1 1s and 12s. The *Bristol* struck the Scillette Rock near St. Helier whilst under control of a pilot during rough weather at the end of September, remaining fast for a short period. She sustained slight damage but was withdrawn after this incident and went on to operate a Bristol-Swansea service.

The thrice-weekly Weymouth sailing schedule proved too great a strain on the fleet, so from autumn 1829 it was reduced to twice weekly, with a two vessel operation and the third held in reserve as cover. *Ariadne* sank a fishing boat off Hurst Point in October 1829 and her owners were required to pay half the cost of a replacement vessel. Meanwhile the *Sophia Jane* temporarily relieved the *Sir Francis Drake* whilst she received new boilers; she later became the first steam vessel to visit Australia in 1831.

Winter gales at the start of 1830 claimed another casualty: -

'We regret we have to announce the wreck of HM Post Office Steam Packet, *Meteor*, Lieut. Connor, commander, on her homeward voyage from the islands of

Jersey and Guernsey. On the evening of the 23rd inst. the weather being so excessively thick as to prevent the Portland lights being visible at any great distance, the packet went on shore at Red Bricks, a spot a little to the eastward of Church Hope Cove, and just below Rufus Castle, in the island of Portland. At the moment she struck it was high water, about 6 o'clock. It is consoling to be enabled to add that the Captain, crew and passengers (who were, we believe, 14 in number) were all saved: as were the luggage and mails, which later reached the Post Office, Weymouth, about 2 o'clock, a.m. Every possible exertion is making to preserve the machinery, but as there is a very heavy ground swell, it is much feared that the hull will prove a total wreck.'

[*Dorset County Chronicle, 25 February 1830*]

The paper later reported that: -

'a great part of the machinery, anchors, cables, stores &c of HMPO steamer *Meteor*, have been saved from the wreck at Portland'.

[*Dorset County Chronicle, 4 March 1830*]

Early reports of a total wreck proved to be correct and the wooden hull was sold locally after the salvage operation was completed, but not before a group of a hundred people had engaged in plundering the remains, including looting passengers' baggage.

A replacement for the *Meteor* was ordered in August and the new packet *Flamer* was launched by Fletcher & Farnall at Limehouse, London on 29 April 1831. She was fitted with 60 horsepower engines and reached Weymouth in July having cost £7,190. *Flamer* (Capt. White) proved capable of handling the roughest of conditions, but had a tendency to roll, making her crossings uncomfortable.

Proposals to enhance facilities in St. Peter Port by constructing a breakwater from Havelet Rock to the Castle, with a second arm north-eastwards from the Castle to provide protection from southerly and south easterly winds, were hotly debated in Guernsey. The exposure of the existing harbour to gales was proving a deterrent to merchant vessels, with many captains arriving only under duress. The proposed cost of £35,000 was deemed excessive, and a committee was appointed to look further into the matter. This allowed a succession of plans to be considered but little progress was made until 1851.

The Post Office packets were still encumbered by bureaucratic commercial restrictions, which posed serious issue for their viability. Regulations determined that the only source of revenue other than delivery of mail was the carriage of passengers, which took second place to the mails. The packets had a poor service reputation compared to competitors at Southampton, with their Captains frequently berated in the press for their attitude towards customers. The packets were not able to take advantage of the expanding cargo traffic; Guernsey grew more produce under glass than anywhere on the continent at this time. These problems were not unique to Weymouth, and government reports on the state of Post Office packet operations were made in 1830, 1832, and in 1836, when it was noted that all five services were loss-making. Losses at Weymouth were small compared to other routes and the levels of incompetence and fraud prevalent elsewhere were notably absent there.

The opening and early success of the Liverpool and Manchester Railway in September 1830 provided an impetus to the promotion of a host of other railway investment projects. The first prospectus for the Southampton, London and branch Railway Company, published in October 1830, sought £1m of share subscriptions at £100 each. Part of the justification for the project lay in: -

'The extensive shipments to the Islands of Jersey and Guernsey will be transmitted by the proposed Railway, and the rapidity and cheapness with which the Merchants and Traders of those Islands will receive their commodities, must ensure their entire support'.

[*Hampshire Advertiser, 23 October 1830*]

This was the first of several proposals and it was to be another ten years before a railway linked London with Southampton. Weymouth was to wait much longer. Land transport was still primitive, difficult and slow, and there were distinct advantages in taking long sea crossings to reach London. The London Guernsey & Jersey Steam Packet Company was formed in 1831 with capital of £11,520 in 64 shares of £180, to operate a service from London to the Channel Islands via Brighton, and also from Brighton and Southampton to the Islands. The 'new and beautiful' Thames-built 345 ton *Lord of the Isles* had seventy-four sleeping berths and a 22ft long, 15ft wide dining saloon. Her first visit to Guernsey was on 24 June 1831 under Capt. Hide, and she sailed on to Jersey, returning the following day. The homeward trip reached Brighton in fourteen hours and London in thirty-three hours. Letters for London landed at Brighton were delivered two hours earlier than those despatched via Weymouth ten hours earlier. The *Lord of the Isles* left London on the 10th, 20th and 30th of each month. From August she sailed twice monthly from Southampton and claimed to be the fastest vessel on the route with a passage time of twelve hours. Fares were reduced to 10s in the main cabin, 5s in the fore cabin, and 2s 6d on the fore deck.

In November, strong winds forced the *Lord of the Isles* back to Southampton whilst approaching Alderney on a crossing from London, as she was running short of coal. On approaching Lymington she hit and sank the *Julie* from South America, which had anchored overnight without lights in the western Solent. The crew were rescued and signed a statement absolving the *Lord of the Isles* of any culpability but this marked the end of her sailings for the season. Notwithstanding this letter of exoneration, the owners of the *Julie* were awarded damages and costs of £12,000 in March 1833.

The ambitious sailing schedules of the *Brunswick* and *Sir Francis Drake* were placing significant strain on the vessels, the latter having been badly damaged on passage from Portsmouth in December 1830, and the Plymouth & Portsmouth Steam Packet Company abandoned the Guernsey leg in 1831.

Both *Ariadne* and *Lord Beresford* were lengthened in the winter of 1831-32, the former by 7ft and the latter by 27ft, perhaps to counter some of the positive publicity being garnered by the *Lord of the Isles*. The Plymouth & Portsmouth Steam Packet Company services were replaced for a single season in 1832 by a weekly sailing of the new vessel *Cornubia,* operated by the Plymouth, Falmouth and Penzance Steam Packet Company, which departed from Plymouth for Guernsey and Jersey on Monday evenings, returning from the Islands on Tuesday evenings.

In May 1832 the *Lord of the Isles* recommenced sailings from London Bridge to the Islands, calling at Brighton. This proved increasingly popular, as Brighton offered a faster stagecoach journey to London than Southampton and it was possible to get from Guernsey to the capital in twenty-one hours. Despite this, *Lord of the Isles* was withdrawn at the end of November and spent the next year operating to Portugal.

Competition between the operators continued in 1832, with prices held at 1831 levels, and racing between vessels was common. A passenger on the *Lord Beresford* described a race with the mail steam packet *Flamer* between Jersey and Guernsey thus: -

'We were neck and neck and every quarter of an hour we found the *Lord B* gradually drawing ahead and giving the crew of the *Flamer* an opportunity of looking into her cabin windows, and in 2hrs and 51mins we arrived in Guernsey Roads when the command was given to 'ease her'. At this time, the *Flamer* was nearly three quarters of a mile astern, and when she came alongside the Commander politely acknowledged that victory go the *Lord B* by touching his hat and saying 'Goodridge, I wish you much joy!'

The racing was not without its casualties. In September the *Ariadne,* under Capt. J Goodridge, collided with the *Lord Beresford,* suffering a damaged lifeboat, cookhouse, paddle box and bulwarks. The captains of both vessels blamed each other. In the winter of 1832-33 the *Sir Francis Drake* received technical improvements that accelerated her passage times significantly, allowing her to return to Island service and speeding her first trip of the season from Plymouth by between three and four hours.

The Harbour Board in Southampton arranged for a new pier to be designed and constructed for passenger services to the Isle of Wight and the Channel Islands. It was opened by HRH Princess Victoria on 8 July 1833 and was known as the Royal Victoria Pier, although this was later shortened to the Royal Pier. The pier was originally built of wood, but was later replaced by a cast iron structure.

The *Ariadne's* woes continued in August 1833 when she was damaged during a gale whilst on passage from Guernsey to Southampton, losing one paddle box and part of the captain's cabin. The *Flamer* suffered later that year, described graphically in a despatch from Weymouth: -

'The post office orders, which are so imperative with regard to the sailing of the mail packets hence to the Channel Islands, obliged the chief mate William Roberts, acting commander of the *Flamer* during the severe indisposition of Capt. Frederick White to put to sea on Thursday evening last, as this was impossible to be effected the evening before, the regular night for sailing. The wind was blowing heavy from west-south-west. The voyage was however deemed dangerous, if not impractical, and the *Flamer* was brought to in the roads until Friday evening, when the wind, still very fresh, having shifted to west-north-west, the resolute commander again dared to brave the raging elements and succeeded after a most tempestuous voyage in making the casket (sic) lights when a tremendous wave struck the starboard paddlebox and carried away bulkheads fore and aft, her quarter boat, and main cabin skylight, leaving her a complete wreck at the mercy of the storm. Three of the seamen, John Duke, William Beal and Thomas Hunter were washed overboard, but providentially they were saved by means of ropes and the prompt exertions of the commander, and thus rescued from a watery grave. Out of the crew not one escaped without being severely bruised and wounded, so much so that had it not been for the timely assistance of three or four seafaring individuals who were on board as passengers the *Flamer* must have been totally wrecked. By the aid off these the chimney shrouds were restored the wind having now again shifted to the southward the vessel was put before the gale, and left to find her way back to Weymouth, which port she made the greatest difficulty this morning, at half past three o'clock.... Five of the poor fellows, Duke, the two Beales, Hunter and Painter, together with the commander, Roberts, were carried on mattresses to their respective homes, where they all lie as the medical attendants are not yet prepared to say whether any bones are fractured or not, but the result is much feared... We hope the poor men will receive the charitable consideration of the Post Office, and that the commander, Roberts (should he recover) will reap a reward worthy of his steady and active services, which have proved him every way worthy of the trust reposed in him. The packet is rendered totally unfit for service for some weeks. One of the seamen has since died.'

[*Salisbury and Winchester Journal, 8 December 1833*]

The *Watersprite* left Weymouth with the mails on the following Monday, but sailed just twelve miles before a boiler burst and she was forced to return. The cutter *Ellen* took over the mails, but was forced to shelter off the Isle of Wight, eventually ending up in Portsmouth, whence the mails were returned overland to Weymouth to be taken to Guernsey, where they eventually arrived on the Friday on the pilot boat *Blessing*.

The *Ariadne* suffered three broken main shafts in three weeks in September 1834, and was fitted with new engines at the end of the season. This was a common issue. In 1832 the *Camilla* relieved the *Lord Beresford* for a short time, when the latter suffered a broken main shaft and was stranded in Guernsey.

In June the *Watersprite* left Weymouth to be lengthened by 20ft at White's of Cowes and had new engines fitted on the Thames. She returned to Weymouth following her refit on 25 December and was reported in the Jersey Times as being 'wonderfully improved in speed since her lengthening'.

The spring of 1835 brought more competition for *Ariadne* and *Lord Beresford*. Initially as the *Ariadne* bedded in her new engines and the *Lord Beresford* achieved a passage time of 11 hours 30 minutes from Guernsey to Southampton all appeared well. The London, Guernsey & Jersey Steam Packet Co introduced the *Isle of Guernsey* to a new Southampton-Channel Islands service from April, alongside the 500 ton London-route chartered vessel *Liverpool*. Built in 1830 for the Glasgow Steam Navigation Co, the *Liverpool* was 136ft in length, with a 180 horsepower engine. Her paddle boxes were indented into the sides of the vessel. She had a quarterdeck 68ft long and 26ft wide and a large state cabin, and could accommodate thirty-five passengers in cabins, some of which were two berth and incorporated collapsible bulkheads or screens as partitions. The saloon of the *Liverpool* was described in The Comet: -

'There are also as many elegant sofas, with mahogany chairs, and dining tables of peculiar construction which can be extended the whole length of the saloon. The berths in this place are parted off by the partitions so that persons in it are not incommoded by those who may be sick in their berths'.

Washing facilities were ground breaking...

'There is also a table of peculiar construction, containing several wash-hand basons (sic) which are supplied with water from pipes for that purpose, so that by the simple operation of turning a brass cock the required quantity of water is obtained, and by a similar process is let off without the least trouble or assistance from servants'.

[*The Comet April 1835*]

Capt. J. Goodridge Jnr was appointed to the *Liverpool* in competition with his father on the *Lord Beresford*. By early July the *Liverpool* had abandoned her London calls and operated solely from Southampton on the same nights as the *Lord Beresford*. On 3 July both vessels left Southampton around 6:00 p.m. and by 2:00 a.m. the *Liverpool* was some ten miles ahead, but she suffered a burst steam pipe and had to transfer her passengers to the *Lord Beresford*. The *Liverpool* resumed again two nights later alongside *Ariadne*, but agents of the latter went to great pains to promote the safety of their vessel to prospective passengers on the *Liverpool.*

Competition drove fares down further to 5s and 2s 6d by August; whilst this generated a significant increase in traffic - 2,000 passengers were landed in a single week in St. Helier - it did little to improve profitability, and the lower fares attracted a different social mix of passengers to the lounges. The *Liverpool* increased fares to try and gain some respectability but the papers reported in detail on raucous behaviour on board. There were insufficient berths for all passengers, and the usual method of overcoming this was to put mattresses and pillows along the floor of the main cabin. This brought conflict between those who wished to drink and gamble, and those trying to sleep.

Competition came to an abrupt end on 20 August 1835, when passengers arriving in Southampton were told the *Liverpool* had been sold to a 'company of gentlemen'. The *Liverpool* was sold to the London & Dublin Steam Packet Co for 12,000 guineas, sailing on a Falmouth-Lisbon route. There was immediate speculation about fares: -

'The fares on the channel island station will be raised to something like a remunerating rate, though considerably below the original scale'.

[*Hampshire Advertiser, 22 August 1835*]

With the *Liverpool* gone, fares were quickly restored to £1 5s, 16s and 10s 6d. But the legacy of high on board standards was one that the remaining operators could not ignore. It later transpired that the Glasgow Steam Packet Company had not been reimbursed for the hire of their ship and the charterers turned out to be 'dazzling speculators' who left many victims in the Islands.

Co-operation between the owners of the *Ariadne* and *Lord Beresford* to help see off the *Liverpool,* and the impending arrival of railway interests in Southampton, was a prelude to advertisements in September 1835 for a South of England Steam Packet Company. With a capital of £200,000 it aimed 'to secure the purchase of vessels plying between Southampton, the Isle of Wight, the Channel Islands and France, in view of the development of Southampton and the coming of the railway steam packets'. In the event it was the slightly differently titled South Of England Steam Navigation Company that took shape on 17 November, and purchased the Channel Islands stalwart *Ariadne* and the *Camilla,* which operated between Southampton and Le Havre.

The new company soon saw further competition. The British & Foreign Steam Navigation Company of London sought capital of £200,000 in £20 shares: -

'The great advantages of Steam Power to the purpose of navigation ... are now so fully proved and universally admitted, that It becomes unnecessary to enlarge or comment on the benefits ... Several large Ports are still without this expeditious and certain means of conveyance, while others are very inadequately provided, particularly in a Southerly direction... Southampton and Bristol will, with the completion of these Railroads, necessarily become most Important Packet Stations, and afford, with other Ports similarly situated, further profitable employment for the Capital of the Company... The Directors intend, as early possible, to establish, for the conveyance of passengers and merchandise, regular communication between Loudon and the Outports and the Channel Islands, France, Oporto, Cadiz, Gibraltar, the Mediterranean, &c., with New Powerful Vessels...'.

[*Salisbury & Winchester, Journal 2 November 1835*]

The offer was quickly subscribed and the British & Foreign Steam Navigation Company soon advertised the 'new and powerful' *Lord Byron* on a Southampton-Channel Islands service, sailing on Tuesdays and Fridays from 8 December. In the event the company decided to purchase a new vessel, and postponed the start of the service until the *Lady de Saumarez* could make her maiden voyage under Capt. J. Goodridge Snr. on 6 January 1836, taking 11 hrs and 35 mins from Southampton to Guernsey. The 172 ton vessel was two masted and schooner rigged with a female bust head of Minerva (after whom she was initially planned to be named), sham galleries and two Seaward engines delivering 90 horsepower, with twelve berths in the gentlemen's cabin, twelve in the ladies cabin and eighteen in the fore cabin, thereby offering much superior facilities to her rivals. Capt. Comber of the mail packet *Ivanhoe* challenged Capt. Goodridge of the *Lady de Saumarez* to a race between Jersey and Guernsey. Despite leaving forty minutes earlier the *Ivanhoe* was overtaken at Grosnez and the *Lady de Saumarez* arrived in Guernsey thirty-five minutes ahead of her rival.

The South of England Steam Navigation Company responded with an order for the *Atalanta* for Channel Islands services and the *Monarch* for the Le Havre services. But the company was at a disadvantage in the early part of the year when the *Ariadne* was pitched against *Lady de Saumarez*, operating on the same days; *Ariadne* took 7½ hours longer to reach Guernsey on her first trip of the season in March. Her master, Capt. Bazin, was transferred to supervise construction of the *Atalanta*.

The *Monarch* was launched for the Le Havre service at Northam on 1 May 1836, and the *Atalanta*, built by Thomas White of West Cowes, followed on 2 June for the Islands. A large crowd watched the ceremony, including 200 from Southampton who had travelled across on the *Camilla*. At 162 tons, the *Atalanta* was two masted with a woman bust head, mock galleries and two engines totalling 120 horsepower. She was 140ft long and 'splendidly fitted up with the cabins and saloons lined with mahogany, rose and satin woods - no suite of apartments in a home residence can excel her!' Sadly Capt. Bazin died of apoplexy whilst supervising construction of the *Atalanta*. The *Atalanta* was sent to London for installation of her machinery and arrived in the Islands on 24 August 1836 beating the *Lady de Saumarez* by ninety minutes on her inaugural sailing to Guernsey, and departing for Jersey before many who came to watch her had reached the port. She was met in Jersey by the *Ariadne*, which took passengers on to Granville. The *Lady de Saumarez* claimed to be suffering from pistons clogged with loose coal dust and cinders. The *Ariadne* had found herself relegated to the Jersey-France services before being relieved by the *Camilla* on 30 July 1837 and sent to cover the Southampton-Le Havre route.

A group of businessmen met at the George & Vulture tavern in London on 16 August 1836 to begin the planning of Southampton Docks. The Southampton Dock Company had acquired 216 acres of mudflats near the Town Quay for £5,000, and although there was some local opposition and scepticism at the scale of the proposals, the plans went ahead.

The *Lord Beresford* had been taken out of service in the winter of 1835-36, to be fitted with a new boiler and paddle wheels. She was restored to the Islands service, having been placed on the Le Havre route for a time, and made her first trip in 11 hr 20 min, 1 hr 45 min faster than the *Lady de Saumarez*. However she soon returned to the Le Havre service and was eventually put up for sale.

At Plymouth the *Sir Francis Drake* was lengthened by 20ft in 1836, and her schedule was extended to incorporate calls in Jersey. She was given a new boiler in 1837 and her engines were moved forward to match her extended length. This produced a notable increase in speed and capability, and she was able to achieve a twelve-hour passage time from Plymouth to Guernsey.

The Guernsey & Jersey Magazine noted in June 1836 that improvements in journeys subsequent to the introduction of steamers allowed the London evening papers to be delivered via Weymouth in thirty-six hours, with morning papers arriving within twenty-four hours via Southampton. Responses to a letter sent to London on the *Lady de Saumarez* could now be received in three days, compared to eight previously. Intense competition between Southampton operators led to another price war: -

> 'The British & Foreign Steam Navigation Company's favourite new river-built powerful and superior sea-going Steam Packet, *Lady de Saumarez*, Capt. J Goodridge (entirely free from that tremulous motion found in other Packets) leaves the Royal Pier, Southampton, for Guernsey and Jersey, every Tuesday and Saturday evening at six o'clock; also from St Malo direct, calling at Guernsey and Jersey every Tuesday evening, returning every Monday and Thursday. The extraordinary low fares of 5s and 3s have been decided on as long as the Managers of the *Atalanta* and *Ariadne* continue the unwise and unprofitable course of running these vessels on the days of the *Lady de Saumarez*'.
>
> [*The Comet, 13 October 1836*]

An 1836 Commissioners report into the management of the Post Office department highlighted the inability of the Post Office to manage a large fleet of steam vessels and proposed that management of the entire service be taken over by the Admiralty, with the Post Office retaining control over routes and sailing times. The report gave a detailed portrayal of the state of the Weymouth operation.

For the four years from January 1832 to January 1836, receipts at Weymouth totalled £15,725 1s 1d against expenditure of £22,443 14s 0d, producing a loss of £6,708 12s 11d. This was the smallest loss of the Post Office stations at Dover, Milford, Holyhead, Liverpool and Portpatrick. 7,866 passengers, nine carriages, fourteen horses, ninety-seven dogs and 528 parcels were carried in 1834. The running costs of the three ships in 1834 were noted as follows: -

	Flamer	Ivanhoe	Watersprite
Pay and provisions	£881 19s 0d	£870 4s 9d	£868 17s 9d
Wear and tear of ship	£746 19s 3d	£762 0s 3d	£555 19s 5d
Wear and tear of machinery	£65 0s 0d	£21 14s 7d	£55 11s 11d
Other repairs	£230 3s 10d	-	-
Total	£1,924 2s 1d	£1,653 18s 10d	£1,480 9s 0d

The 'other repairs' for the *Flamer* addressed the damage caused by the gale at the end of 1833, noted above.

The Weymouth Post Office agent, Capt. Stevens, was convinced that 'with larger and fast vessels a very considerable revenue would be returned from passengers alone, especially if a French mail was sent that way'. Stevens was held in high regard by the Commissioners, who expressed their satisfaction at his strong management. The report noted that private companies running steamers to Guernsey and Jersey constantly altered and improved their vessels 'as the science of steam navigation increases'. Serious losses were made at Weymouth because of the superior power and speed of the Portsmouth and Southampton vessels. The Post Office packets had remained without improvement, and were required to use Holyhead for repairs rather than a more local dockyard, adding ten days passage time to any work. The report considered the advantages of Southampton as a packet port, but concluded, despite strong lobbying from the British and Foreign Steam Navigation Company, that Weymouth benefitted from the shortest sea passage and the greatest certainty that any crossing would be made, and advised against any change.

The report included statistics on the relative performance of vessels in the Weymouth fleet on the Jersey run, which demonstrated the effectiveness of the work done to the *Watersprite* in 1834:

Packet	*Flamer*	*Ivanhoe*	*Watersprite*
Average passage time	14h 29m	14h 57m	11h 50m
Tons of coal carried	17	20	19
Consumption per hour	7 cwt	8 cwt	6.75 cwt

(Passage times between Weymouth and Jersey included time calling off Guernsey to land passengers).

The Weymouth mail packets were brought under Admiralty control from 16 January 1837. The Post Office retained an interest in the departure times and routes of vessels, but these were now naval ships commanded by naval officers and the packet captains began to wear cocked hats and swords. The *Ivanhoe* was sent to Woolwich Dockyard for repairs as she was 'leaky and exhibiting signs of age' but her condition precluded further remedial work, and she was transferred to minor naval duties and renamed *Boxer,* operating until around 1841. This left the Weymouth service in the hands of two vessels; the *Flamer* was renamed *Fearless,* and the *Watersprite* renamed *Wildfire* in May 1837. Since March 1837 fares to the islands had returned to £1, 5s and 10s.

Winter bad weather prompted a description of a journey from Guernsey to Weymouth in the *Flamer* to appear in the Jersey Argus: -

'When we left Guernsey the wind was favourable but in about two hours a sudden calm came on which was speedily followed by a white squall, the forerunner of a tremendous gale. About 4 pm we shipped a heavy sea which knocked in the larboard paddlebox and sent the ships bulwarks on that side and one of the boats adrift. The Mate, Mr. Roberts, had his collarbone put out. I do not know what we should have done without Captain Symonds who gave orders with great spirit. At 11 o'clock we shipped another heavy sea which filled the places forward as well as the boats on the booms in the bottom of which they had to make a hole to let the water out and we were thus left quite unprovided with boats. The captain found we could not reach Weymouth and took us to the Isle of Wight. Were very near landing at Lymington but finally reach this place (Weymouth) at 2 o'clock this day. Had we been a few hours longer we would have been out of coals'.

[*Jersey Argus, 9 February 1836*]

The Guernsey Star updated readers on development with the packet services:-

'It is pleasing to notice the efforts that have been continually making with a view to accelerate the speed of the steam-packets connected with this station, since first they were started in 1824. The *Ariadne,* which was then by far the swiftest boat, and has since had her speed considerably increased, is now one of the slowest boats on the station, so very rapidly do the others run. The voyage to and from Southampton, which ten years ago averaged from 13 to 15 hours, now averages only from 10 to 13, and the *Atalanta* a few weeks since made it in the unprecedentedly short space of 9 hours and 50 minutes; whist, on another occasion, she made the passage from this island to Southampton in ten hours, including a call and stoppage off Alderney to land several passengers. She is unquestionably one of the finest boats that ever ploughed the British Channel. A trial of speed between her and his Majesty's packet *Wildfire*, Capt. White, Commander, took place on Tuesday, which more than ever served to display the superiority of the *Atalanta*. The former vessel was some months since lengthened by Messrs. White, of Cowes, and new and powerful machinery put into her, by which her speed was so accelerated that Cap. White declared he would not fear to run her with the *Atalanta*. An opportunity offered last Tuesday, both vessels having to start from Jersey for this island at six o'clock in the morning. The weather was remarkably propitious for a trial of this nature, there being scarcely wind enough out to cause a ripple on the water. The *Wildfire* had six minutes start of the *Atalanta*, but the latter vessel overtook her a short distance off Corbière Point, and arrived here sixteen minutes before her, making a difference of twenty-two minutes on the passage.

The *Lady de Saumarez* appears to have rather fallen off in speed this season, as she now seldom arrives here within twelve hours from her leaving Southampton. This may be owing to her having had her patent paddles, which were apt to get out of order, replaced by others of the old construction, which, although they stand much better than the patent ones, cause a great loss of power by their lifting the water, instead of propelling it like the former in a horizontal direction. It should also be borne in mind that the engines of this fine vessel, though rated fifties, are but of forty horsepower each, whilst those of the Atalanta are sixties, making upon the two engines a difference of fifty horses in favour of the last-mentioned vessel.

The *Harlequin*, belonging to the General Steam Navigation Company, is about to be put on this station, in opposition to the *Lady de Saumarez* and *Atalanta*. She will leave Southampton on Monday evening.

[*Guernsey Star, 8 June 1837*]

The news that the *Harlequin* was to be added to the Southampton fleet, albeit as a retaliatory measure for incursion by the British & Foreign Steam Navigation Company into General Steam Navigation Company territory, prompted a supportive response in the letter pages: -

SIR, I read with much satisfaction a paragraph in your last paper intimating that a new steamer was about to be placed on this station in opposition to the *Lady de Saumarez*. Should such prove to be the case, the new competitor will doubtless meet with every encouragement; and it is sincerely to be hoped that public will at once show their aversion to the monopolising imposition practised by the *Atalanta* and *Saumarez*, by relinquishing the support of these vessels in favour of the newcomer, whose fares will certainly be at a lower and fairer rate. I can only say opposition is loudly called for, and I heartily wish the opponent success. JUSTITIA.

[*Guernsey Star, 9 June 1837*]

In the event the two companies resolved their differences and the *Harlequin* was withdrawn on the day of her inaugural sailing. In July 1837 the *Sir Francis Drake* caught fire with smoke issuing from her deck abaft the funnel whilst off Grosnez Point on passage between Guernsey and Jersey. Capt. Nicholls steered her into St Ouen's Bay with the intention of running her onto the beach, but the ship's carpenter opened up the deck with an axe and dowsed the flames. The vessel hit a rock, but passengers were put ashore in boats and Capt. Nicholls managed to kedge the vessel into deeper water and sail into St Helier for repair.

Laying the foundation stone for Southampton Docks on 12 October 1838. A large crowd is gathered as the stone is laid from a tripod to the right of the picture, whilst a salute is being fired from guns on the Battery. *(Southampton City Council Arts & Heritage Services)*

The British & Foreign Steam Navigation Company was taken over by the Commercial Steam Navigation Company on 29 July 1837. The latter, which had been active in the Spanish trade, had been gradually expanding its interests and acquired the fleet to help build channel traffic. When the Peninsular Steam Navigation Company won the Iberian mail contract, on 22 August 1837 the Commercial Steam Navigation Company retrenched to concentrate on its domestic interests.

Further vessel deployment changes followed. On 17 September 1837 *Fearless* went to Chatham for improvement works, being replaced by the *Pluto*, until she returned to the Weymouth station in January 1838. *Pluto* was a larger, more powerful vessel and was left to operate through the winter until the *Dasher* was ready. The latter was launched at Chatham on 27 December 1837, as replacement for the *Ivanhoe*.

The Commercial Steam Navigation Company extended the *Lady de Saumarez* schedule to include calls in St. Malo, outflanking the rival South of England Company's service that required a change of vessels from the *Atalanta* to the *Camilla* in St. Helier. Another price war developed, with fares falling from £1 1s and 14s to 10s and 4s.

The new *Dasher* replaced the *Ivanhoe* at Weymouth from April 1838. *Pluto* returned to Portsmouth, her higher manning requirement making her more expensive to operate than anticipated. It was now the turn of the *Wildfire* to undergo refit and re-boilering at Chatham. On 19 April 1838 the Guernsey Star reported 'The *Dasher* appears to be an excellent sea boat, and in good calm weather should be able to reach Weymouth in six hours'; later on 26 April it was noted that 'a newly invented and very elegant lifebuoy hangs over the stern in constant readiness'. Highlighting the speed of the new vessel, the Sherborne Mercury reported: -

'Rapid communication between Guernsey and England.
On Saturday seven night, Mr. Roberts, commander of Her Majesty's packet *Dasher*, left Guernsey at half past eight in the morning for Weymouth, went six miles into the country, and returned again to the island at half past four on Sunday morning by Her Majesty's packet *Fearless*, thus twice crossing the channel in twenty hours'.
[*Sherborne Mercury, 13 August 1838*]

The *Dasher* was fitted with cycloidal paddle wheels in November 1838, but her low boiler pressure of 8 pounds gave her a potential speed of 7½ knots in a cross sea and 9 knots in calm water. She was described as deficient in size and power in an Admiralty report as early as 1841.

In February 1839 the Commercial Steam Navigation Company introduced the *Transit* (Capt. J. Goodridge Jnr.) and *Grand Turk* to the Island routes alongside *Lady de Saumarez* (Capt. J. Goodridge Snr.) in competition with the *Atalanta*. They sailed from Southampton on Monday (through to St Malo), Thursday and Saturday, whereas the *Atalanta* sailed on Tuesdays and Fridays, with connections to St Malo being provided by *Camilla*. This intense competition led to fares dropping from £1 1s and 14s, to 5s and 2s 6d. A series of exchanges in advertisements compared the speed offered by rival companies. The South of England Company observed: -

'The public is respectfully informed that the *Atalanta* beat the *Grand Turk* from Southampton by 2.5 hours on the 15th, and by 2 hours on her passage to Southampton on the 14th, also beat the *Lady de Saumarez* by 6 hours on the passage to Guernsey on the 17th with a strong headwind and flood tide'. The public was also 'respectfully informed that the *Atalanta* would not be allowed to race'.
[*The Comet, 18 April 1839*]

The *Atalanta* proved a faster vessel than her rivals, but this did not deter the Commercial Steam Navigation Company from exploiting the *Ariadne*'s lack of speed in their advertisements: -

'passengers are also cautioned against the false statements in circulation as to the difference of speed between the *Atalanta* and the Commercial Company's vessels; for, taking the average passages there is little difference between the *Atalanta*, *Lady de Saumarez* or *Transit*; and it is well known that on a late occasion *Ariadne* was 10 hours going between Jersey and St Malo when the *Lady de Saumarez* did it in five hours making on the whole passage from Southampton a saving of time saving of expense and saving of fatigue to the passengers who proceeded by the Commercial Company's vessels'.
[*Salisbury & Winchester Journal, 13 May 1839*]

Intense competition was unsustainable. After three months of heavy losses the departure days from Southampton were shared, and the *Lady de Saumarez* dropped her St Malo call. The *Grand Turk* was withdrawn and the *Transit* placed on the London run, operating every ten days.

The foundation stone of the first dock at Southampton (later the Outer Dock) was laid at the confluence of the Test and Itchen rivers on 12 October 1838, at a point south east of the intended terminus of the London & Southampton Railway. Construction was slowed by a lack of capital, but labour was thrown at the project to allow the dock to open on 29 August 1842, and the railway company elected to provide a branch from the newly opened line.

At Weymouth the *Fearless* could only sustain a speed of 4 knots in any strong head sea, with such heavy coal consumption that supplies of coal had to be stored in bags on her deck. This could not continue so the 15-year-old *Cuckoo* was brought in to replace the *Fearless,* which went to Woolwich to perform naval duties as a survey vessel until being broken up in 1875. Formerly the *Cinderella*, the *Cuckoo* was the first steam vessel on the Milford-Ireland service in April 1824. Her first sailing from Weymouth was recorded in the Dorset County Chronicle: -

'The Post Office new steam packet *Cuckoo*, W Comben, master, made her first trip from the port to the Channel Islands last week. She proves to be a fine vessel, remarkably well fitted up, and said to be the largest government packet in this station.'

[*Dorset County Chronicle, 17 October 1839*]

Her cabin accommodation was described as 'replete with every comfort' and she was once recorded as beating the *Lady de Saumarez* between Guernsey and Jersey by 14 minutes.

From April 1839 the Commercial Steam Packet Company began operating a twice-weekly coastal service from London Bridge Wharf to Southampton and Weymouth, thence to Cherbourg, using the *Kent* and *City of Glasgow. Transit* joined the fleet and extended the sailings to Guernsey with her maiden run on 30 August taking fifty passengers to London in 27 hours. This service was short lived, being withdrawn on 1 November 1839.

As the decade neared its close the balance of power between Southampton and Weymouth was about to swing strongly to the east with the opening of the London & Southampton Railway.

CHAPTER TWO

Enter the London & South Western Railway 1840-1856

'At a public meeting held in Weymouth on Tuesday last, to receive the report of the deputation appointed to wait upon the Chancellor of the Exchequer relative to the contemplated removal of the Channel Islands' Mail Packet Establishment from that port, Mr. A. W. Horsford announced that they had been most courteously received by the Minister, who admitted all the facts set forth in the memorial as to the superior claims of Weymouth; but they were met by the startling information that the Southampton company had offered to convey the mails at one half the present cost, on which account the Government had determined to give up the port as a packet station, and contract for the conveyance of the mails. On this intimation, himself and Mr. Eliot urged upon the Chancellor the Exchequer the justice and fairness of affording the inhabitants of Weymouth time to consider they could not, with the aid of some steam company, or by their own resources, make the same offer had been made from Southampton. The Right Hon. Gentleman then consented to give three weeks for this purpose. (Hear, hear). The deputation then had an interview with the Directors of one of the principal Steam Companies on the subject, with the view of ascertaining whether they would be inclined to join in the undertaking; but they required to be furnished with details before they could give decisive answer. It was, therefore, now for the town of Weymouth to consider this point, without loss of time. After some discussion, it was resolved to form a committee to adopt such steps as may be deemed advisable for retaining a Channel Islands Mail Establishment at Weymouth, and open a communication with the Great Western Railway Company for establishing a branch line rail connexion with that port'.

[Salisbury & Winchester Journal, 15 June 1844]

The opening of the London & South Western Railway Company's (L&SWR) route from London to Southampton on 11 May 1840 brought the port within three hours of the capital and changed the dynamics of long distance travel. Southampton was transformed into an interchange hub, where passengers from London to southwest England changed from rail for onward sea connections to Weymouth, Torquay, Dartmouth and Plymouth. The Islands were still served by the Commercial Steam Packet Company's *Lady de Saumarez* and *Transit* in competition with the South of England Steam Navigation Company's *Atalanta;* both companies benefitted from the improved transport links.

The Post Office quickly gave their approval to the new railway service, permitting letters for the Islands to be sent via Southampton, subject to being marked 'to Southampton by private steamer'. The mails could now take around twenty four hours to reach London via Southampton, compared to three days via Weymouth.

The arrival of the railway prompted the Admiralty to appoint a committee on 30 May 1840 to look into the 'the best port of arrival and departure for Her Majesty's Packets employed in the conveyance of Mails between England and the Channel Islands, and the size and power of Steam-vessels best adopted for that service.' The committee spent several days in Weymouth accumulating evidence, inspected the harbour and took advantage of the *Dasher* being made available to them for a trip to Guernsey and Jersey. On the Islands they were furnished with resolutions expressing 'a concurrent and earnest desire that Weymouth might be continued the immediate point of communication with England'.

The committee's subsequent report considered the depth of water in Weymouth to be an issue, but the authorities pledged to achieve a depth of twelve feet at low-water spring tide within eight months. They noted that the journey time by rail from London to Southampton was now six and a half hours quicker than over land to Weymouth, but observed that the longer sea passage reduced this advantage to just two and a half hours, and a straight course of the Southampton passage 'would somewhat entangle a vessel with the Caskets'. Further, Weymouth was better placed for receiving the mails from the 'western world', as the ocean mails were still being landed at Falmouth, and 'their early arrival must be of vast importance to the mercantile community of the Channel Islands'. Lobbying by Weymouth route interests proved very effective and the committee understated the value of the railway link to Southampton. They concluded that 'Weymouth will be found to be the best port for Her Majesty's packets conveying the mails between England and the Channel Islands'.

Answering the second part of their brief, the committee noted that in the twelve months leading to their Inquiry, the average passage from Weymouth to Jersey, calling at Guernsey to land the mails, was 13hrs 12mins, with the return journey taking 12hrs 55mins. Failures of the service had been few, exhibiting 'strong testimonials to the zeal and abilities of the commanders of these vessels'. The committee recommended the construction of three new vessels of around 400 tons each to offer a thrice-weekly service.

Under the Railways Act the L&SWR was not permitted to operate services in its own right, but the company was still anxious to see cross-channel trade develop to support its fledgling railway operation. After a failed attempt to encourage the Commercial and South of England companies to amalgamate, the directors of the L&SWR appealed to shareholders to subscribe to a new 'independent' South Western Steam Packet Company, but the General Meeting in February 1842 reported that the response was poor; shipping companies were seen as even more risky investments than railway companies at that time. Nonetheless the parent company was supportive of the new venture, and eventually encouraged railway shareholders to subscribe £46,000, secured against debentures on the steamers, to add to the £30,000 raised by the South Western Steam Packet Company.

The new company acquired the Commercial Steam Navigation Company on 1 May 1842, leading to the formation of two new subsidiary companies. The New Commercial Steam Navigation Company was established to operate from London, and the South Western Steam Packet Company from Southampton. The new company's fleet comprised the *Calpe, Grand Turk, Lady de Saumarez, Robert Burns* and *Transit.* The *Lady de Saumarez* and *Transit* maintained the Southampton-Channel Islands service, the *Calpe* was moved to Plymouth and the *Grand Turk* and the *Robert Burns* were employed on the Le Havre route. The Hampshire Advertiser noted that 'Mr. Chaplin and other directors of the South Western Railway are on the board of the new company. No doubt, the South of England Company will be next!' The new company also acquired the *Edinburgh Castle* and the *Windsor Castle,* but these vessels did not form part of the Islands fleet. In May 1842 the South Western Steam Packet Company temporarily introduced the *Duchess of Kent* to Channel Islands service, making the passage in twelve hours. A loan from the L&SWR enabled the company to announce an order for two new vessels in September 1842.

The first ships used the new Southampton Docks on 29 August 1842, and business quickly outgrew the sixteen-acre facilities of the Outer Dock and plans were put in place for expansion and the provision of three dry docks.

The South Western Steam Packet Company's first iron steamer *South Western* (Capt. J. Goodridge Snr.), was launched on 15 May 1843 and arrived for the first time in the Islands on 1 August. Built by Ditchburn & Mare of Blackwall, she was a 204 ton, 143ft long vessel, powered by 80 horsepower Seaward engines. Although initially planned to operate on the Le Havre route to support the opening of the railway from Paris to Rouen, she spent most of her early career serving the Islands, as the railway did not reach Le Havre until March 1847. She became the third vessel on the route alongside the *Lady de Saumarez* and the *Transit,* offering a thrice-weekly schedule, reverting to twice-weekly in the shoulder season and weekly in winter. The *South Western* averaged 12 knots on passage to Guernsey and Jersey, and beat the South of England's *Atalanta* to Guernsey by some 2hrs 45mins. The fares of both companies remained at £1 5s and 18s to the Islands and £1 15s and £1 5s to St. Malo.

The *Lord Beresford* was sold to Joseph Price of Neath Abbey in May 1843 for a service from Swansea. The *Camilla* (Capt. Priaulx) now sailed for the South of England Steam Navigation Company from Plymouth each Tuesday for Guernsey and Jersey, sailing on from Jersey to St. Malo on Wednesday in competition with the Plymouth and Portsmouth Steam Packet Company. She remained on the route until sold in June 1847.

The *Wonder, a* twin to the *South Western,* became the second new vessel to be added to the South Western fleet on 4 October 1844. She was described as 'a beautiful model, she looks like a bird cleaving the air'. Also built by Ditchburn & Mare of London she was 251 tons, 158 ft in length, with three Seaward & Capel atmospheric engines delivering a trial speed of 14 knots, making her one of the fastest ships of her day. The South Western

Atalanta leaving St Peter Port for Southampton in 1840. *(from Paynes Privileged Islands (1840))*

The Post Office packet *Flamer* arrives at Weymouth *(National Maritime Museum)*

Steam Packet Company could still not achieve the full level of funding it required, so the L&SWR sought powers to operate steamships in its own right in a Bill of 1844, but this was rejected in Standing Orders.

When the Bristol & Exeter Railway reached Exeter in 1844, the *Ariadne* was used to start a service from Topsham via Torquay and Brixham to Guernsey and Jersey, although this operation encountered difficulties in maintaining a schedule due to the depth of tides at Topsham and the necessary canal transit. The service later operated solely from Torquay.

The arrival of two new vessels increased pressure on the South of England Steam Navigation Company and the two companies agreed to a closer working relationship from November 1844, and for the remainder of the year services were advertised under the South Western Steam Packet Company banner, and maintained by the *Atalanta* and the *Transit*. Co-operation proved to be short-lived, and the timetables of the South of England Steam Navigation Company were soon advertised separately.

One of the key advantages of Weymouth as a mail packet port was undermined when the landing port of most Ocean Mail services was switched from Falmouth to Southampton from September 1843. The Post Office responded by announcing the transfer of Island mail to the Southampton steamers the following spring: -

> 'It is finally determined that the Channel Islands Mail Packet Station shall be removed from Weymouth to this port (Southampton). The alteration has been long talked about, and now the post-office authorities are making the necessary arrangements for the removal, which will take effect in about six weeks. The advantages to the public of this alteration, will be a saving of time in the transmission of correspondence, and a considerable saving to the revenue in the expense of conveying the mails.'
>
> [*Salisbury and Winchester Journal, 1 June 1844*]

A fortnight later, the same paper reported on a public meeting in Weymouth that had been 'met with the startling information that the Southampton Company had offered to convey the mails at one half of the present cost, on which account the Government had determined to give up the port as a packet station'. Following an approach to the Chancellor of the Exchequer by a deputation from Weymouth the port was given three weeks to come up with a matching offer, but this proved unachievable.

On 31 December 1844 Capt. J Goodridge Jnr. brought the *Transit* into Southampton at speed in front of a crowd of sightseers, sailing across the dock and hitting the dock wall bow-first without slacking, severely damaging her bowsprit, figurehead and cutwater: -

> 'She had entered the dock and was taking up her berth when the Captain ordered the engineer to 'back her' in order to place her properly; when the paddles were put on forward, and in spite of the exclamations of the captain to stop her, she was worked against the North Quay wall, and her bowsprit, figure head and cut water all smashed. Upon enquiry being instituted it appeared that the second engineer did not know how to back the paddles. The first engineer was ill when the vessel left on her onward trip and hands in the engineers room arranged to say nothing about it (in order perhaps to prevent any stoppage of pay to the sick man); Capt. Goodridge, however, found it out soon after they have left, but could not then help himself. It is providential that the *Transit* did not come in direct proximity with any of the vessel, as from the want of skill on the part of the second engineer the most serious consequences might have arisen'.
>
> [*Hampshire Advertiser, 4 January 1845*]

The Weymouth fleet was gradually run down in anticipation of the transfer of the Mail contract to Southampton. The *Dasher* left for Woolwich with her stores on 5 April under Capt. R. White, leaving the *Wildfire* to make her final crossing on 19 April before transferring to fishery protection duties at Gorey, and the *Cuckoo* wound up the service on the 26th. The Sherborne Mercury took a keen interest in the changes, noting on 5 April that the mails 'will be conveyed by private steamers, and the trifling saving thus effected is the only reason for the removal' (from Weymouth).

The Earl of Lonsdale, Postmaster General, provided justification for the change: -

'The measure of changing the port... has not been determined without the mature consideration of the Government. There are, however, strong motives of economy in its favour, and therefore the decision has been come to of making the change to Southampton.' He went on 'This arrangement, however, does not rest with my department, but with the Admiralty, which has the Post Office packets under its direction... I am sure that all the circumstances were carefully weighed before the determination to make the change was arrived at.'

[*The Star, Guernsey, 5 April 1845*}

The South Western Steam Packet Company was awarded the £2,000 contract, which required them to operate thrice-weekly sailings on Tuesdays, Thursdays and Saturdays. The *South Western*, *Transit* and *Wonder* were initially employed, but the *Transit* was replaced by the *Calpe* from 14 May 1845.

There was more positive news for Weymouth on 30 June, when the Wilts., Somerset & Weymouth Railway Company (WS&WR) was authorised to construct a railway line from the Great Western Railway (GWR) near Chippenham through to the town. Construction proceeded very slowly, as the company suffered during successive financial crises with many shareholders unable to meet the calls on their shares. Later in the year the Southampton & Dorchester Railway was authorised to construct an extension from the existing L&SWR line to Dorchester, to connect with the new WS&WR and offer services through to Weymouth. On 3 August 1846, the Bill for the WS&WR was amended and subsequently authorised to incorporate a one-mile extension of the railway to Weymouth Harbour.

The Southampton Royal Pier Act compelled 'captains, masters and others in command of steam boats carrying passengers, immediately before their departure from the said port of Southampton, to come alongside the Royal Pier, for the purpose of enabling passengers and their baggage to embark from the said pier'. Normally the South of England Steam Navigation Co and the South Western Steam Packet Co made alternate use of Dock and Pier at four-monthly intervals to comply with the Act of Parliament. However on 5 July 1845 Capt. G. Babot of the *Atalanta* and Capt. R. White of the *Monarch* were fined £4 for violating this clause, by sailing to the Islands without calling at the Royal Pier. The Hampshire Chronicle reported that this was their second conviction under the Act.

On 14 February 1846 the L&SWR proprietors approved the formation of the New South Western Steam Packet Company, with a Board comprising fifteen railway shareholders, at least ten of whom were to be directors. The prospectus offered a five per cent dividend. Relationships with the South of England Steam Navigation Company had been sour for a while but in July 1846 talks began on a merger, which was formally announced on 1 August to take effect from 1 October.

The summer schedule saw the *Calpe*, *Grand Turk*, *Lady de Saumarez*, *Robert Burns*, *South Western* and the *Wonder* variously employed on services that left the Royal Pier, Southampton for Guernsey and Jersey on Tuesdays, Thursday and Saturdays at 7:00 p.m., returning on Tuesdays, Thursdays and Sundays. The South of England Steam Navigation

Company advertised for the last time on 30 September. The Hampshire Chronicle reported on 10 October 1846 that 'this new arrangement had caused all competition to cease between Southampton and the Channel Islands'. It also marked the end of the *Ariadne's* service from Torquay, and she sailed from the Islands for the last time on 25 September. The Portsmouth-Le Havre service was replaced with a sailing from Southampton, with an intermediate call in Portsmouth.

The New South Western Steam Packet Company purchased the assets of the South of England Steam Navigation Company, including the *Atalanta, Ariadne, Camilla* and *Monarch* plus their agencies in Guernsey and Jersey for £29,500, and the South Western Steam Packet Company vessels the *Wonder, South Western, Grand Turk, Lady de Saumarez, Transit, Calpe* and *Robert Burns* for £58,500. The *Transit, Calpe* and *Robert Burns* were gradually disposed of. The new company was loaned £50,000 by the L&SWR in November 1846 to order three new vessels and improve efficiency, and given five acres of operational land in Southampton, although it still elected to base three steamers in Portsmouth.

The autumn weather quickly caused difficulties: -

'The *Atalanta* will take the mails today. The new South Western Steam Packet Company have not a boat that can battle with the late weather, except the *Monarch* and *Atalanta*, late of the South of England Steam Navigation Company.'
[Hampshire Chronicle, 10 October 1846]

The bad weather continued. On Tuesday 20 October the *Wonder* left Southampton at 7:00 p.m. hitting a storm at around 11:00 p.m. that continued throughout the next day. Capt. Goodridge described it as the worst he had ever encountered; the seas swept across the decks and washed away part of the bulwarks, causing significant damage to the vessel. *Wonder* was brought into St. Peter Port at 1:00 p.m. on Wednesday before proceeding on to St. Helier, where she arrived at 4:30 p.m. Passengers were so relieved at their safe arrival that testimonials were presented to Capt. Goodridge and the ship's company at a ceremony in St. Helier on 1 January 1847. £5 was distributed amongst the crew, and the first and second mates and the principal engineer were promised silver medals. Capt. Goodridge entertained guests in the state cabin where his health and that of Mr. Matthews, who had arranged the presentation, 'were pledged in bumpers with all the honours'. Capt. Goodridge was presented with a silver speaking-trumpet richly chased and ornamented with pictures of the *Wonder*, bearing the following inscription: -

'Presented to Captain James Goodridge Jnr of the Mail Packet *Wonder* on the 1st January 1847 in token of the high admiration in which his character for nautical ability so eminently displayed throughout the fearful storm of Wednesday 21st October 1846 and his uniform devotion to the interest and comfort of the public is held by the inhabitants of Jersey'.

The new company inherited an aged fleet, with just the *South Western* and *Wonder* being of recent vintage. The 1836 paddle steamer *Monarch* was added to the fleet from 7 June and operated passenger services through the rest of the year, before taking up a cargo service. The loan from the L&SWR was used to order a new steamer from Ditchburn & Mare for completion in just six weeks. The *Express* was similar to the *Wonder* at 225 tons, 159ft long, two funneled and iron hulled, with a 'shield' head, powered by two Maudsley engines generating 180 horsepower. Her 19ft diameter paddle wheels and 5ft dip of floats helped her achieve a speed of 12-13 knots. She was allocated to work on the Le Havre station, releasing the *Grand Turk* to operate a Southampton-Penzance service.

Reduced fares were noted in an advertisement in the Railway Times on 20 March 1847, with the thrice-weekly departures sold at £1 1s in the main cabin, 14s in the second cabin, with carriages and horses shipped for £3 each and dogs for 5s. Horatio Miller was the General Manager, based in offices at 78 High Street, Southampton.

On 12 July 1847 the *Atalanta, Ariadne, Camilla, Monarch, Transit,* and *Wonder,* were assigned to the L&SWR as security for a loan of £25,000. Further investment in a second new steamer followed in October 1847. Ditchburn & Mare were again employed to build the *Courier,* at 314 tons, 167ft long, two funnelled, two masted and schooner rigged and iron hulled, she had a 'shield' head, quarter galleries, and two Maudsley engines generating 200 horsepower. Her 19ft diameter paddle wheels had a 5ft dip of floats at 42 revolutions per minute which generated a speed of 12-13 knots, although a top speed of 17 knots was once claimed. *Courier* was described as 'the handsomest and most speedy vessel that ever sailed out of Southampton'. The *Courier* was registered as the *Courrier* and bore the name on her hull, but was only described in the shorter spelling. Her maiden voyage to the Islands took place on 12 November 1847 and she later recorded a passage of 7hr 10min between Southampton and Guernsey, but proved very light in rough seas; on one occasion an elderly passenger was thrown out of seat and died from head injuries when the *Courier* rolled heavily.

Progress on railway construction to Weymouth was initially good. On 1 June 1847 the Southampton & Dorchester Railway opened their new line linking the L&SWR to Dorchester, including a branch railway to Hamworthy. But the operation of trains to Weymouth awaited completion of the WS&WR. This has started well, but a slump in the post-railway mania era saw work stopped when construction reached Westbury.

A Parliamentary Select Committee convened on 26 November 1847 considered a large number of railway bills, embracing applications from several railway companies to establish steamship operations. The Committee reviewed the position of the L&SWR and recommended that the company be granted steamship powers for a limited period subject to: -

1. the services being only to Havre, the Channel Islands, and the parts of France immediately adjacent thereto;
2. arbitration on fares;
3. the railway company not being empowered to lend money or subscribe to any other steam-vessel company; and
4. passengers who used the steamers only, without travelling by rail, should not be treated disadvantageously

From 1848 the value of the mail contract was raised to £4,000 per year. In early January a deputation from Poole approached the New South Western Steam Packet Comany to assess their interest in the operation of a service between Poole and the Islands. Reaction was positive and on 2 May the third new steamer *Dispatch* (Capt. J. Babot) made her maiden voyage from Poole, recording a passage time of 90 minutes between Guernsey and Jersey. The company had again used Ditchburn & Mare for construction of a sister to the *Courier,* the *Dispatch* was a 149 ton vessel, with two Maudsley engines delivering 200 horsepower which achieved 18 knots on trial. The *Dispatch* was replaced by the *South Western* on the route after two trips. The Poole service met with resistance from the Admiralty, local ship owners and Poole Council and lasted one season, the *South Western* ran aground on leaving Poole on 30 September, with her passengers transferred to the *Monarch.*

The *Courier* and the *Dispatch* were added to the list of vessels assigned to the L&SWR as loan security on 14 September 1848.

Passenger traffic on the steamers remained below expectations but the L&SWR finally secured powers to operate vessels in their own right on 14 August 1848 when the House of Lords approved the 'London and South Western Railway, amendment of Acts, Power to Purchase, and Extensions Bill'. This enabled the Company to adopt the boats and pay off the capital of the New South Western Steam Packet Company and operate for a period of fourteen years. Part of the justification for the Bill was that passengers might be carried from London to the Channel Islands at reduced fares and under one continuous management. The company stated that 'the Post Office are desirous that we should run a boat from Weymouth to the Channel Islands'.

The proposals to lease the vessels and assets of the New South Western Steam Packet Company proved difficult to sell to shareholders, as traffic levels were low, the fleet was in a poor condition and there were no guaranteed returns on the capital investment. The lease was eventually concluded on 16 March 1849, to last for 13½ years from 1 January 1849. A special committee was established on 21 September to manage the business. The New South Western Steam Packet Company brand was retained in advertising until May 1851.

The railway reached Plymouth in 1848 and the *Brunswick* and *Sir Francis Drake* severed their links with Portsmouth, and focused on Falmouth and the Islands instead, with a weekly sailing. The *Brunswick* had been lengthened by 20ft in 1839 and *Sir Francis Drake* grew by 11ft in 1848. Torquay was later added to these schedules.

The L&SWR began to dispose of the older vessels in their fleet. The *Monarch was* sold for £900, plus £180 for her machinery, 'to a gentleman connected with emigration to New Zealand'. Her engines were removed and she was converted to a 356 ton brig. The *Calpe* was sold and had her machinery removed and was converted to a sailing ship. Other vessels proved more difficult to sell, and the *Ariadne*, *Camilla* and *Robert Burns* were laid up. This left the *Courier* and the *Dispatch* on the Channel Islands mail service, the *Express* and the *Wonder* on the Le Havre service and the *South Western* as relief vessel, with the *Atalanta*, *Lady de Saumarez* and *Transit* held in reserve.

In the summer the company's vessels began to berth at Southampton Dock rather than at the Royal Pier, and the offices in Southampton were moved from the High Street to occupy what was once the gentlemen's waiting room at the Terminus railway station 'for economy's sake'.

An advertisement placed by Henry P. Maples on 15 January 1850 stated that the screw steamer *Collier* would commence a service between London and Jersey from 20 January, operating three times a month. On 2 February two steamers arrived in Jersey, the *Collier* and the *Director*. The former returned to operate a Maples-managed service from Shoreham for the London, Brighton & South Coast Railway Company (LB&SCR).

Meanwhile on 14 March the WS&WR was taken over by the GWR allowing construction work to bring Weymouth onto the railway map to recommence, but progress continued to be slow.

The *South Western* was initially based in Jersey for the 1850 season for services to France, Alderney and Sark, but demand from Weymouth was tested from 14 August when she began an auxiliary packet service to St. Malo via Guernsey, Jersey and Granville. Fares were set at 15s and 10s single, with a steward's fee of 1s 6d and 9d; horses and carriages were carried at £2 5s each, and dogs for 4s each. The response was poor in the absence of a railway link from Dorchester, and the *South Western* returned to Southampton at the end of December. The *Atalanta* went to Weymouth to initiate a seasonal cargo service to Jersey.

In August, Maples formally entered into an agreement with the LB&SCR to operate sailings between Shoreham and Jersey, in conjunction with their railway services. The *Collier* was joined by the *Ladybird*, an iron screw steamer of 353 gross tons capable of 11 knots, which was built by Denny of Dumbarton and launched on 10 March 1851. The iron paddle steamer *Paris* was added to the fleet from 1855. Maples had interests in other cargo vessels, notably the wooden schooner *Marco* and the iron steamship *Alar*, both from 1854. The operating arrangement was not a great success for Maples and in 1859 he found himself in financial difficulties and his vessels were transferred to the LB&SCR, who subsequently operated intermittent services from Littlehampton and Newhaven to Jersey and St Malo.

The *South Western's* trial service from Weymouth to St Malo proved beneficial in the rescue of passengers from the wreck of the *La Polka*. The *Superb* was due to sail from St. Helier on an excursion to St. Malo on 16 September, but as her machinery required repairs the tugboat *La Polka* was substituted. Capt. Priaulx sailed with between thirty and forty passengers, but the *La Polka* sprang a leak some six miles from the Minquiers rocks. The vessel had no pumps on board, so Capt. Priaulx headed for the reef with the ship slowly sinking. He was able to run her close to the easternmost rock, the Mâitre Ile, before he was forced to load his passengers and crew into two lifeboats and abandon ship. The *La Polka* foundered in deep water and sank. The passengers endured a dismal night on the rock, with two 4lb loaves and some biscuits and water furnished them by three fishermen who lived there. They lit a fire without attracting any assistance. The mate, John Fleming, rowed out to sea and was able to attract the attention of the *South Western*, bound from Weymouth for St. Malo under Capt. Goodrich. He steered for the rock and took the passengers and crew off. Passengers subscribed £10 for the fishermen and gave the crew 10s each and presented a lady passenger, who had the distribution of the rations, a handsome bracelet.

Back in service and commanded by Capt. Priaulx, the *Superb* left St. Malo for Jersey at 7:30 am on 24 September with sixty passengers and crew, including several who had been on the *La Polka*. On approaching the Minquiers some of the passengers asked Capt. Priaulx to show them where the *La Polka* sank. At around 9:30 a.m. the mate, John Fleming, steered the vessel through the eastern passage but struck La Pointue du Blanc Roc bow first; she immediately filled with water and heeled over throwing passengers to the starboard side of the vessel. Capt. Priaulx ordered the two boats to be lowered. Passengers found themselves adrift without oars in lifeboats without plugs, and they gradually sank in calm water. All were lost. The ship was left stranded on rocks as the tide fell but distress signals were successfully made to the cutter *Jupiter*, about five or six miles off. The *Courier*, which had just arrived in St. Helier from Shoreham with Mr. Maples on board, came to assist and took survivors to the cutter at about five in the afternoon, but on approaching St. Helier in the dark, she touched the Oyster Rock, further alarming surviving passengers.

The Jersey Times reported that seventeen were lost, with thirty-eight survivors and a further three or four unaccounted for. It noted that the *Superb* had been left high and dry on the rocks by the receding tide but afterwards disappeared, having sunk in deep water. Four persons who survived the wreck of the *La Polka* were lost in the sinking of the *Superb*. A coroner's Inquest returned the verdict that the wreck of the *Superb* was the result of culpable imprudence on the part of Capt. Priaulx in taking the *Superb* in a dangerous place without knowledge of its ordinary course and that Fleming was guilty of imprudence in attempting to take the said vessel on that course. Priaulx and Fleming were not permitted to sail again but the former engaged in a lengthy court battle to clear his name, although the issue remained unresolved when he died some sixteen years later.

The London, Jersey and Guernsey Screw Navigation Company made another attempt

Wreck of the **Superb** stranded on La Pointue du Blanc Roc on 24 September 1850. *(Illustrated London News)*

to improve services from London with the introduction in October and November 1850 of the new builds *Caesarea* and *Sarnia* to the Islands route, replacing the *Director*. They were owned by the London, Jersey & Guernsey Screw Navigation Company, but their service was short lived.

The first trip of the *Caesarea* was eventful: -

'Guernsey - Oct 9th.
The new screw steam-ship *Caesarea* built for the London and Jersey trade, left the Custom House Quay, Thames Street, on Friday night at 12 o'clock, on her first voyage from London for Guernsey and Jersey. Soon after she got under way she run foul of a barge and swamped her, and the lighterman navigating her was immersed in the stream. After a short detention the *Caesarea* proceeded on her voyage, and the pilot ran her on shore at Erith, about 2 o'clock in the morning, and she remained there for ten hours before she could be got off. On Saturday night there was a good deal of lightning, and on Sunday the ship encountered a violent hurricane, which continued until Monday. On Monday evening she took refuge in Cherbourg harbour, where she remained until next morning, when she got her steam up, and at 8 o'clock started for Guernsey, where she arrived yesterday at 4:00 pm.'

[*Shipping and Mercantile Gazette, 10 October 1850*]

The Illustrated London News gave a fuller description of the vessels: -

'Two beautiful new steam-vessels, on the screw principle, were lately launched from the building-yard of Messrs T and W Pim of Hull, the first practical engineers and iron ship-builders who adapted the screw as an auxiliary power to merchant vessels, the last being their twelfth steamer on this construction. The *Caesarea* and *Sarnia* (the ancient names of Jersey and Guernsey) have been built solely for the line between London and these islands, and everything requisite for the comfort of passengers, as well as convenience for stowage of cargo, has been well and carefully considered and adopted. The cabins are on the poop deck, and can accommodate up to 60 passengers with bed-berths. The burthen of each vessel (for they are sister ships, being in every respect built and fitted up in the same manner) is 265 tons; length aloft, 133½ ft; breast of beam, 20 ft; and depth of hold,

The new *Ladybird* soon dominated the Shoreham-Jersey route, setting new standards in on board accommodation that matched those experienced on transatlantic liners. *(Painting by Philip Ouless; original in Maritime Museum, St Helier)*

13 ft. Their engines are 40 horsepower, and the boilers upon the principle lately patented by the Messrs Pim, which at the same time saves both space and coals, an important desideratum in steaming.

In conclusion, we congratulate the London, Jersey and Guernsey Screw Steam Navigation Company on the spirit they have shown in providing the trade with a line of vessels so long required in it, and so well adapted to it; and we entertain no doubt but that the liberal plans they have formed will be productive of a handsome remuneration to themselves, and a great boon to all concerned in the trade'.

[*Illustrated London News, 30 November 1850*]

The cargo service from Southampton resumed from February 1851 using the *Transit*, and carried passengers as a cheap alternative to the main service. On 7 March the *Sir Francis Drake* ran aground on the north west Grunes with 100 passengers on board, but managed to get off under her own power. Meanwhile the *Grand Turk* returned under Capt. Goodridge to open a Southampton-Guernsey-Morlaix route from April, but this lasted a single season.

There were new developments at Shoreham: -

'The London and Brighton Railway Company, in conjunction with Mr Henry P Maples of 5 Arthur Street East, London Bridge, who has taken the contract, are now running packets between Newhaven and Dieppe, Shoreham and Guernsey and Shoreham and Jersey. The *Collier* iron screw steamer, F Gillett, commander, runs twice a week to Guernsey, and the *Ladybird* iron screw steamer, S R Doke, commander, twice a week to Jersey. The communication between Shoreham Harbour and Jersey was opened on the 15th of August, 1850, by the *Collier*, but as that vessel was not found large enough for the trade, the *Ladybird*, an entirely new iron screw steamer, was built for the purpose (by Messrs Denny Brothers, of Dumbarton) and has within the last fortnight taken the place of the *Collier*, which is transferred to the Guernsey station. The *Ladybird* is 160 ft in length; her quarter deck is 72 ft.

From a personal inspection we can state that this is decidedly the most trim-built vessel that was ever placed on this station. It is elegantly fitted up, especially in the first class department. Following up the arrangements of the Railway Company, it has first, second and third-class berths and is capable of sleeping 101 persons. Those acquainted with the manner in which the Cunard mail steamers from Liverpool to Halifax and from Liverpool to New York are fitted up, may judge what the *Ladybird* is. The deck saloon - that is above deck - is a beautiful apartment fifty ft long, most elegantly furnished. This is used for the first class dining room; but at night it is converted into sofa berths accommodating thirty persons. The ladies saloon below is beautifully furnished, with every convenience. There are six best cabin staterooms, containing from one to eight berths to suit families, which will be found exceedingly convenient. The fore cabin has four berths'.

[*Brighton Gazette, 5 June 1851*]

The L&SWR and the LB&SCR disputed working arrangements of the railway route to Portsmouth, and the LB&SCR undercut the L&SWR £1 fare to Jersey by offering through rates of 12s 6d from London to Jersey. Two weeks later the Brighton Gazette reported on a reception during which a newly married Mr. Maples gave 'elegant entertainment' to a group of railway managers and local press on board the *Ladybird* at Kingston Wharf, the visitors being conveyed there by special train. A sumptuous dinner was served during which a toast was drunk to Mr. Hawkins, the 'originator of the traffic between London and Jersey via Brighton and Kingston'.

The States of Guernsey approved plans for a floating dock with lock gates put forward by a Mr. Rendel, and awarded a construction contract to Hutchings, Brown and Co. of Grimsby at £44,221 was signed on 17 August 1851. The scheme did not incorporate any low water landing places for the steamers, leaving passengers at the mercy of landing by small boat. Construction was hindered by the insolvency of the original contractor.

September saw the *Atalanta* lengthened by 18ft at White's Yard, in Cowes. Her old bow was upended and used as a workmen's shelter in the yard.

At Southampton the new Inner Dock was extended to provided further ten acres and 2,575 ft. of additional capacity from 1851.

In March 1852 the steamer *William Miskin* was placed on the London station, and she arrived in the Islands for the first time on 13 April, visiting thereafter on an intermittent basis. By 1853 the *Caesarea* and the *Sarnia* were being managed by London shipping agents Cheesewright & Miskin. The pair had been active in handling Channel Island business in London for over a decade, but had no direct association with the London, Jersey and Guernsey Screw Navigation Company, which disappeared from the scene. They sought buyers for the *Caesarea* and the *Sarnia*, and these were disposed of later in 1853. The agents introduced the paddle steamer *Foyle* (Capt. Coker) to the London route in 1854 on a passenger and cargo service, which operated on a ten-day cycle. The *William Miskin* was also sold.

The L&SWR chartered their first screw steamer, the *Lady Seale*, to operate the low price cargo service between May and July 1852. The *Courier* had a major overhaul in the spring with new boilers and a ventilation system added; she returned to service on 6 July. *Dispatch* received similar treatment the following winter.

The foundation stone for the harbour works in St. Peter Port was laid on 24 August 1853 with a crowd of 20,000 in attendance. Mr. Rendel was asked to prepare plans for a breakwater to Castle Cornet and a low water landing place at Cow Bay.

The *Dasher* towed the mail steamer *Dispatch* to safety when her main shaft broke during a violent storm in October 1853 near Corbière: -

'The mail steam packet *Dispatch*, Capt. Babot, left the harbour of St. Helier at her usual hour on Monday the 17th inst. for Guernsey and Southampton, in a heavy gale

The dramatic rescue of the *Dispatch* by the *Dasher* after being disabled by a shaft failure near Corbière on 17 October 1853. Passengers were subsequently highly critical of maintenance standards on the vessel. *(Painting by Philip Ouless; original in Maritime Museum, St Helier)*

and high sea. Soon after nine o'clock she signalled at Fort Regent as in distress; and the following are the particulars of the accident which had befallen her.

When she arrived off Corbière her main shaft broke in two places and two eccentric rods also snapped, at once rendering her steam machinery unusable for further navigation. In this extremity Capt. Babot attempted to make sail to return, but in setting the mainsail the peak halyards block broke, and when it was replaced the placard broke. He then let go the anchors between the three rocks called the Oaks. HM Steamship *Dasher*, Cdr. Lefebvre, on perceiving the distress signal had immediately left the harbour to go to her assistance; and when the *Dispatch* saw her approaching within about 1½ miles she cut her cable leaving the anchor and about 30 fathom of line, and got under way. The *Dasher* met her near Corbière and going round her stern observed that she was drifting to leeward; she then took her in tow with two hawsers. These broke short one after another and were again replaced in the same manner. The wind being fair, the *Dasher* relied mainly on her canvas, working her engines now and then to keep the vessels clear of each other. The *Dasher* encountered some tremendous seas; one of them went high over her bridge, and carried away the stern boats from the davits, leaving the deck so encumbered with water as to render it necessary to knock out the ports for its escape. Shortly after twelve o'clock she arrived safely with her rescued companion in the outer roads of St Helier, and at twenty minutes to four o'clock the anxious crowds assembled on the pier heads and the delight of seeing the war steamer passing safely in Victoria Harbour, tugging after her the disabled *Dispatch*.

[*Illustrated London News, 29 October 1853*]

Whilst grateful for their rescue, one of the passengers called for an Inquiry into the near disaster, citing that the main shaft of the *Dispatch* was heavily rusted and there had been significant delays in exchanging distress signals.

Steamers now left Southampton on Mondays, Wednesdays and Fridays, with onward services to St. Malo and Granville supplied by the Jersey Steam Packet Company, whose fleet included the *Rose, Venus, Comète* and *Dumfries*. The combined rail/sea fare was £1 1s, 6d and 10s on the cargo boats.

Maples & Morris operated a service from Newhaven to the Islands from 1853 on behalf of the LB&SCR, with the paddle steamers *Collier, Ladybird* and *Paris*. This was far more capacity than the route could support, and by 1858 the summer service was being operated by the *Brighton*, with the *Alar* covering the winter months.

With their new steamers operating reliably but profits hard to sustain the New South Western elected to dispose of their more elderly assets. The *Camilla* had reached the end of her useful life and was broken up in 1853. The *Grand Turk* was sold in 1854 and replaced by the *Alliance;* she was a 168 ton vessel, two masted and schooner rigged with a shield head, sham galleries and two funnels built by Ditchburn & Mare for the Le Havre route at a cost of £19,460, entering service from 11 July 1855. The *Transit* was the next to go, following her last sailing on 31 October 1855, with the cheap boat service covered initially by the *South Western* and then *Atalanta*. The *Brunswick* was also withdrawn and sold by the Plymouth and Portsmouth Steam Packet Company in May 1855.

The market was still small. Between January and June 1855 passenger arrivals at Southampton from the Islands totalled 5,671, but these were twice the carryings of the Le Havre route.

The *South Western* carried an unusual load to Jersey on 12 November 1856, when she brought across the second of two cast iron six-sided lighthouses for the St. Catherine's breakwater. The *Atalanta* (Capt. Lewis), acting as the relief boat for Jersey was hit by the P&O steamer *Sultan* at the mouth of River Itchen on 21 November 1856, losing her port-quarter boat and bulwarks, extending from forward sponson to the taffrail, but no injuries were sustained.

In November 1856 South Western captains Goodridge and Cook visited Weymouth to review the opportunities presented by the imminent opening of the WS&WR, which would give the L&SWR the ability to operate through trains to the town via Dorchester. Whilst the harbour and quayside were generally in a poor state of repair after having been largely unused for six years, the captains were generally satisfied with what they saw. There were, however, wider concerns particularly from merchants and other interested parties in Jersey about the South Western's ambitions for the port, given their strong competing interest in Southampton. Capt. Stevens, who had retired to Jersey, put proposals to William Eliot, a Weymouth alderman, for a two-steamer service from Weymouth, claiming that the South Western would employ the *South Western* and the *Atalanta* - their slowest and worst boats - on the route.

The imminent connection of Weymouth to the railway network presented the opportunity for shipping services from the port to enjoy railway connections from two companies. The L&SWR monopoly of rail-sea business could now be broken.

The *Victoria* harbour in St Helier with three paddle steamers outnumbered by a forest of sailing ship masts. Print published on 3 April 1855. (*Author's collection*)

CHAPTER THREE

Competition from Weymouth 1857-1889

'Communication between England and the Channel Islands is now rendered both agreeable and economical by the railways and steam-vessels in connection with the ports of London, Southampton, Weymouth, and Plymouth. In connection with Jersey only, there is also a line of direct communication via the Brighton and South Coast Railway and Kingston near Shoreham. As changes are always liable to occur in such matters, it is advisable to consult the current timetables issued by Bradshaw and the various offices. With the following information there will be no difficulty in selecting a route and making the further inquiries that may be necessary.

The South Western Railway Company issues through tickets from the Waterloo Station, London, via Southampton or Weymouth, the sea passage being made during the night. The fares are 31s. first-class, and 21s. second-class. Through tickets can be obtained, on Tuesdays, for 25s. 6d., 17s., and 11s. 6d.

The GWR Company issues through tickets from Paddington Station, via Weymouth, the sea passage being made by day. The fares are 31s. first-class, and 21s. second-class.

The Metropolis steam-vessel also plies between London and the Channel Islands, leaving Custom-House Quay, Thames Street, once in ten days during the summer, and fortnightly in winter. Fares, 12s. 6d. or 10s.

The Atalanta steam vessel sails from Southampton every Tuesday, and returns every Thursday. Fares, 18s. or 12s.

The Sir Francis Drake steamer runs between Falmouth, Plymouth, Guernsey, and Jersey, from April to October inclusive ; leaving Plymouth every Thursday at 5-30 p.m., and returning the following Friday. Fares, main-cabin, 18s. ; fore-cabin, 12s. ; deck, 7s'.

[*The Channel Islands, a guide; Frank Fether Dally 1858*]

GWR and L&SWR railway services began to operate to Weymouth Town station on 20 January 1857, but by then powers to extend the railway through to the Harbour had lapsed. The line was of mixed gauge northwards as far as Dorchester, with the GWR running on broad gauge tracks and the L&SWR on the narrower standard gauge. This restricted GWR services to running through to the west, the Midlands, South Wales and London, whilst the L&SWR could offer services eastwards on the Southampton & Dorchester section before connecting to the national standard gauge network.

Two GWR directors, F N Micklethwait and D Ogilvy, visited Weymouth and the Islands to evaluate support for a new shipping company. A prospectus for a 'Weymouth and Channel Islands Steam Packet Company Ltd' was issued, proposing an optimistic twelve hour journey from London to Jersey; five hours by rail and seven for the transfer from the station and passage, including a call in Guernsey, explained later as being a 'miscalculation of distances'. Response in Jersey was positive, but lukewarm in Weymouth. Nonetheless the promoters proceeded with their plans using two paddle steamers that were lying idle in Victoria Dock, London. The *Aquila* and the *Cygnus,* had been built in 1854 for an abortive Harwich-Antwerp service by the North of England Steam Navigation Co., and were offered for £9,000 each. They were 182ft in length with two funnels and a clipper bow and allegedly could achieve 14 knots. The Weymouth and Channel Islands Steam Packet Company took them on an 18-month charter at £50/week each, with a purchase option after 6 months at the asking price less charter fees, despite the company having no legal status. In the event the target start date for the service of 11 April had to be postponed.

As rumours of the plans of the Weymouth and Channel Islands Steam Packet Company spread, the L&SWR informed the GWR Company Secretary, Charles Saunders, of their intention to start services from Weymouth on 13 April 1857 at fares of £1 15s First Class and £1 5s Second Class, being higher than the Southampton fare of £1 11s First Class and £1 1s Second Class. Believing that these rates would disadvantage the Weymouth trade, Saunders responded that the Weymouth Company would charge the equivalent of the Southampton fares, and the L&SWR was forced to reduce fares to match the lower rate. The spat dashed any hopes of ticket inter-availability between the two companies.

News of an impending competitor forced the Weymouth and Channel Islands Steam Packet Company to accelerate progress at Lowestoft in preparing the *Aquila* and the *Cygnus* for service. Company director Capt. Prowse RN oversaw the work, and trials began on 11 April; *Aquila* reached 12½ knots, and *Cygnus* was slightly slower at 11¼ knots. Meanwhile the South Western's *Express* arrived in Weymouth on 8 April and held an open day for inspection. Her first sailing to the Islands was undertaken on 13 April as scheduled, with seven passengers on the ten-hour outward crossing and eight on the return: -

'On Monday the South Western Railway Company's steamer the *Express,* Capt Harvey, opened the campaign of steam communication from Weymouth to Guernsey and Jersey... the extreme coldness and severity of the weather would have rendered a sea voyage anything but delightful, therefore only those impelled by necessity accompanied the *Express* on her first trip from our harbour... The manner in which the noble vessel steamed through the bay showed her to be admirably calculated for her work, and even in much more boisterous weather her very great steadiness of motion will tend to obviate many of the disagreeables attendant on salt water travelling... the *Express* will doubtless secure a good share of public support'

[*Dorset County Chronicle, 17 April 1857*]

The same bad weather that discouraged passengers from this maiden voyage also hit

The *Aquila* enjoyed a long career on the Weymouth route, sailing from 1857 to 1889 for the Weymouth & Channel Islands Steam Packet Company, before serving from Plymouth for a further five years. The open nature of the bridge is clearly evident in this painting. *(Painting by A Meaden; original in Maritime Museum, St Helier)*

the *Aquila* and the *Cygnus* on their delivery voyages from Lowestoft, and the crew of the *Cygnus* were forced to bale out with buckets off Beachy Head when the pumps failed. Capt. Prowse brought the *Cygnus* safely into Weymouth Bay on 14 April and she was shown off to the public alongside the Custom House. Meanwhile the *Aquila* headed straight across the channel for a similar public exhibition in Jersey, where she was well received.

On 14 April the Weymouth and Channel Islands Steam Packet Company was formally incorporated with authorised capital of £40,000 in £10 shares, with provision to increase this to £100,000 by special resolution. 2,000 shares were allocated to Jersey, 1,000 to Guernsey and 500 each to Weymouth and the GWR. GWR shareholders included Isambard Brunel and Daniel Gooch, but the Weymouth portion was undersubscribed. Of the twelve appointed directors, Micklethwait and Ogilvy represented the GWR, Henry Tupper and Thomas Priaulx represented Guernsey, with four each from Weymouth and Jersey, including Elias Neel as Chairman. The first sailing was advertised in the County Chronicle on 16 April to start the following day, but it went largely unremarked as it was taking place a month earlier than previously advertised and the *Express* had gained most of the publicity. However the *Cygnus* earned salvage when she rescued and towed in the *John Dixon* off West Bay on her maiden voyage. The schedule allowed London-bound passengers to leave Jersey at 6:30 a.m. and Guernsey at 9:30 a.m., to catch the 5:20 p.m. service from Weymouth and reach London Paddington shortly after 11:00 p.m.

The heroic effort to get the Weymouth Company operational resulted in a number of shortcomings; crewing of the vessels proved difficult, Capt. Falle was not appointed to the *Aquila* until July, and the vessel charter relied on the guarantee of a single shareholder, a Mr. Mills. The relationship with the GWR was also weak, resting on a gentlemen's agreement. This led to the resignation of the Guernsey directors, although Thomas Priaulx later relented. An 18-month Working Agreement with the GWR was signed at the Victoria Hotel, Weymouth on 14 May. This required the Weymouth and Channel Islands Steam Packet Company to operate a minimum of two double crossings a week to connect with train services; through fare rates and apportionment of revenue remained to be agreed upon but at the end on twelve months any loss on the steamers would be made good by the GWR from their share of the receipts, after deductions for cartage and terminals.

The agreed fare apportionment for second class fares was as follows: -

From	Through fare	Steamer Guernsey	Steamer Jersey
London	21s	7s	8s 9d
Bristol	21s	10s 2d	12s

Four return crossings were provided each week, with the *Express* offering three, but initial carryings averaged twenty passengers per crossing and cargo business was slow to develop. 847 passengers were carried in the first five weeks, about one-third of the level of the Southampton business, generating receipts of £678 from passengers and £300 from cargo. Traffic picked up as the summer progressed, with special 'Aquatic excursions' offering a one week stay for a single fare, with company revenue supplemented by shilling-a-head excursions round the Bay. At the first general meeting held on 1 July 1857 the directors were sufficiently encouraged by the growth of business to agree to purchase the vessels, but offered just £13,000 for the pair, as their condition was worse than expected and both needed new boilers. To prove the point, the *Cygnus* experienced a collapsed furnace crown in one boiler on an outward crossing to Guernsey, and saw the other boiler fail similarly on the crossing. Despite this, the owners rejected the company's offer and refused to meet repair costs, so the Weymouth and Channel Islands Steam Packet Company advertised a tender for a new 18 knot iron paddle steamer to be ready for 1 March 1858.

Sensing opportunity, the L&SWR replaced the *Express* with the superior *Wonder,* whilst the former was in dock. The *Cygnus* could not be replaced whilst she was being repaired, and the Weymouth and Channel Islands Steam Packet Company soldiered on with the *Aquila*, which reliably maintained the thrice-weekly service pattern until the *Cygnus* could return at the end of August. The fourth sailing of the week was abandoned; this had replicated the L&SWR's outward Friday departure, returning on Saturday. The Weymouth and Channel Islands Steam Packet Company purchased the *Aquila* and the *Cygnus* for £14,000 after independent valuation, and ownership was transferred on 21 November; any idea of new vessels was abandoned.

It was the turn of the L&SWR to suffer on 28 April 1858 when the *Wonder* (Capt. Clements) on an outbound sailing for the Islands hit the *Havre* (Capt. W. Smith), inbound from Le Havre, in the Solent. The *Wonder* lost her port lifeboat and most of her bulwarks on the port side, but damage to both vessels remained above the waterline. The second mate of the *Wonder* was held accountable for the incident.

The new sailings from Weymouth allowed the Post Office contract of three weekly sailings from Southampton to be supplemented on alternate days by 'auxiliary mail' via Weymouth. In their first year of operation the Weymouth and Channel Islands Steam Packet Company carried 9,000 passengers, generating £6,632 revenue; added to £5,179 cargo receipts to give a total income of £11,811. But expenditure was £19,575 and the losses far exceeded the railway mileage proportion. The Company sought to expand its way out of the problem and launched a Weymouth-Cherbourg service in conjunction with the Ouest Railway of France. Some £9,500 was spent to introduce the *Brighton* - the former Maples & Morris vessel that had been operating on the Shoreham-Jersey service. The *Brighton* left Shoreham for Weymouth on 26 July under Capt. Prowse and was initially allocated to operate to the Islands with satisfactory results. On her maiden trip *Brighton* undertook the journey from Jersey to Guernsey in two hours, with a 5hrs 20min passage from Guernsey to Weymouth. The thrice-weekly operation to Cherbourg started in

The *Express* lies wrecked on Grunes Houillieres after her Captain sustained a sudden illness on 20 September 1859. The cause of the accident was never ascertained. *(Illustrated London News)*

September 1858, with an Alderney call offered weekly.

The North Quay of the floating dock in St. Peter Port was extended by 158ft and adapted to become the mailboat landing place by the addition of a sloped end against which a wooden landing stage was built, with buildings for luggage storage on the north side. Discharge of passengers could thus be competed in a few minutes. The *Aquila*, *Dispatch* and *Express* were the first mailboats to use it on 11 October 1858.

On the London route Cheeswright & Miskin replaced the *Foyle* in 1858 with the new *Metropolis*, which was purpose-built on the Thames. By 1861 the *Metropolis* was sailing regularly from Fenning's Wharf, London Bridge to the Islands with fares of 15s in the saloon (steward's fee 1s 6d), 10s in the fore-cabin (steward's fee 1s), with children carried at half price fares. Return fares were available at £1 2s in the saloon and 15s in the fore-cabin.

1858 marked the end for the Plymouth link and the *Sir Francis Drake* was sold in November. The *Atalanta* sailed the Monday/Wednesday rotation from Southampton to Jersey, then Guernsey but she was withdrawn the following month and sailed thereafter as an intermittent freight vessel.

The Alderney link offered by the Weymouth and Channel Islands Steam Packet Company carried mail from March 1859, giving the island a direct postal service for the first time. But the venture was still loss making, forcing the company to seek a loan from Elias Neel and three of the Jersey shareholders, which was secured against mortgages on the three vessels. The Cherbourg service closed in June 1859 after 111 round-trips had been made and losses of £6,000 accured. The *Brighton* was put up for sale, and the Weymouth and Channel Islands Steam Packet Company neared bankruptcy. Elias Neel resigned as Chairman, to be replaced by Abraham Bishop, a Guernsey linen draper. Just as it seemed the service would close, fate took a hand.

The New South Western Steam Packet Company's *Express* left St. Helier at 6:45 a.m. on

20 September 1859 bound for St. Peter Port and Weymouth under Capt. Mabb, loaded with 160 passengers many of whom were heading for the Guernsey races. The *Express* passed close to Corbière then struck submerged rocks at Grunes Houillieres, badly holing the vessel. Capt. Mabb, who was absent from the bridge through sudden illness at the time of the incident, attempted to return to St. Helier, but the vessel was down by the bow and flooded forward, so he was forced to run her aground on rocks 100 yards from the shore. 157 passengers and three racehorses were saved, but three passengers panicked and fell into the sea before the boats could be launched. The *South Western* was dispatched to assist, but the *Express* was a total loss and within a fortnight was beyond salvage. A Court of Inquiry was unable to reach any conclusion, as witnesses offered conflicting evidence.

The New South Western Steam Packet Company service from Weymouth continued through the autumn using the *Wonder* and the *South Western*, but the service was 'temporarily' suspended from around 15 December 1859 and the Southampton service increased to four sailings per week to compensate. Weymouth traffic had been a small proportion of their business and, whilst there was nuisance value in irritating the GWR, it did not justify the expense.

The Weymouth and Channel Islands Steam Packet Company providentially found itself with a monopoly of Weymouth services, but the company's financial troubles were far from over. In August the GWR had offered annual support of £2,000 in return for greater control, and the Company had little choice other than to sign a new agreement. Chairman Bishop wanted the service to be fully taken over by the GWR and operate with a three-vessel fleet. The GWR offered to guarantee a six per cent return for five years on additional capital of £9,000 subject to this being raised; it was, thereby diluting the interest of the original shareholders. The *Brighton* was withdrawn from sale; the shorter crossing to the Islands was still attractive and Jersey interests were campaigning for the return of a Weymouth mail service.

From 1860 the L&SWR supported the floundering Jersey Steam Packet Company with a £225 payment in excess of their proportion of the freight rates, to discourage transfer of the St. Malo traffic to Weymouth. This proved insufficient to sustain the company's finances, and from November 1860 the Jersey Company asked to be taken over. The L&SWR refused, but upped its support to a weekly payment of £50. This sum was reduced to £40 from 1 April 1862.

The L&SWR went back to parliament to secure permanent powers to operate vessels from the end of the lease agreement with the New South Western Steam Packet Company in 1862. These powers were granted in August allowing negotiations to begin between the two companies, but agreement could not immediately be reached and arbitration was used to broker a solution.

On 12 October, the paddle steamer *Southampton*, built by Palmer Bros & Co of Jarrow, and now the largest of the New South Western Company's vessels at 215½ft, made her inaugural sailing from Southampton to the Islands under Capt. J. Goodridge, as replacement for the *Express*. The *Southampton* was the final clipper-bowed paddle steamer to be built for the company. She had two funnels, two masts, was schooner rigged with a shield head, and had two oscillating engines generating 200 horsepower, but could only achieve a service speed of 13½ knots and she was destined to spend most of career on the Southampton-Le Havre route.

In January 1861 the New South Western Steam Packet Company gave notice to the Post Office of their intention to revert to the contractual number of mail sailings from Southampton. The Post Office responded by re-introducing mail to Weymouth sailings, weekly in winter and thrice-weekly between May and October, adding £80 each month to route revenue. But the Southampton route still dominated; the journey to London was significantly slower via Weymouth, and if the vessel was late into port the GWR had no obligation to operate a connecting train, forcing passengers to stay overnight in Weymouth. At Southampton the integration of services meant that the L&SWR would operate an additional service if the inbound sailing was delayed. The daytime crossing from Weymouth left too early in the morning to allow for any connecting rail services, so this departure also necessitated an overnight stay for most passengers. Further, the GWR had built their network to the broad gauge, which meant that cargo for the north required trans-shipment to standard gauge wagons at the break of gauge in the Midlands, and it was often quicker to send traffic from Weymouth northwards on the standard gauge route via Southampton and Reading. Nevertheless the GWR ran two special trains a week from Weymouth during the Jersey potato season. This traffic helped the Weymouth and Channel Islands Steam Packet Company report a surplus in 1862.

With the Islands' traditional maritime trades in decline, the Chambers of Commerce in Guernsey and Jersey cooperated in a joint advertising campaign to promote the Islands as a tourist destination, paying WH Smith £150 in 1862 to display an advertisement extolling the virtues of the Islands and the passages from Southampton and Weymouth at 100 railway station bookstalls.

The L&SWR formally took over the New South Western Steam Packet Company from 1 July 1862 on expiry of the lease. The company had a cash value of £114,679 8s 7d. The L&SWR added the Jersey Steam Packet Company to its portfolio from 11 July 1863, acquiring the company's goodwill and the steamer *Dumfries* for £3,100, and a direct link between Jersey and St. Malo. The *Wonder* was allocated to this service, and the *Dumfries*, ended up in Southampton on cargo duties. The directors of the Weymouth and Channel Islands Steam Packet Company hoped for a similar takeover of their services by the GWR but their approaches were rebuffed.

With all assets now under their direct control, the L&SWR embarked on a substantial fleet investment programme; the *Atalanta* was overhauled to allow her to continue to operate the cargo service and the *Southampton* was refitted in an attempt to improve her speed capability. A new paddle steamer, the *Normandy* (Capt. Babot) made her maiden voyage to the Islands on 18 September 1863, allowing the *Southampton* to transfer to the Le Havre service. The *South Western* was sold to a Japanese company, who removed her paddles and rigged her as a sailing vessel in 1863.

Meanwhile the Cheeswright & Miskin *Metropolis* was wrecked near Jersey in February 1861. The *Metropolis*, built in 1857 by Messrs. Joyce and Company of London, had just undergone a thorough overhaul and been fitted with new boilers, and was insured for £9,000: -

The new light tower at 'St Pierre Port' as seen in the Illustrated London News on 30 March 1867. *(Illustrated London News)*

'The *Metropolis* Capt. Coir, left London on Sunday afternoon (10 February), at 2 o'clock, anchored all night at Southend, and resumed her voyage at day-break on Tuesday morning. She made a fine run and when in St. Brelade's Bay, took on board, as bound by law, a pilot, John Battam by name, who was then of course in charge of the vessel. On arriving near the port she was kept in motion whilst waiting for the tide to enter; when suddenly she struck upon the Rouandiere rock. The weather was boisterous, and the sea rushed into her fore-cabin so rapidly that the crew had only time to lower the life-boat and the gig (leaving a third boat behind) in which they all succeeded in effecting their escape to land, losing every thing, as we stated yesterday. The crew were 14 in number, the Captain, first mate, second mate, able seamen, engineers, 3 stokers, cook, and cabin-boy. Besides these, there were 2 or 3 sailors on board who were working their passage to Jersey, and who also lost everything but what they stood upright in. The *Metropolis* had on board a very valuable cargo partly for Jersey but the greater portion was for Guernsey. There were altogether about 300 tons of goods on board, including about 60 pipes of wine, 50 hogsheads of gin, 100 cases of sugar, £800 worth of copper, a quantity of merchandise for Newfoundland, and numerous other shipments of value, the property of merchants and tradesmen in the Islands... Tuesday night was tempestuous, and the state of the weather of course hastened the breaking up of the vessel. The *Metropolis* is now an utter wreck; she appears to have slipped off the rock, and to be now embedded in the adjoining sand; only the tops of her masts are visible from the Pier heads... The pilot, Battam, was yesterday suspended, and his license taken from him preparatory to an enquiry. We learn that immediately before the vessel struck Captain Corr asked the pilot if he was sure all was right, to which Battam answered, he was quite sure.

[*Jersey Independent and Daily Telegraph, 14 February 1861*]

The *Metropolis* was replaced by the Clyde-built iron steamer *Esk*. She was the first to use the St. Julien's Pier in St. Peter Port, which was allocated to the London boats until 1947. Facilities included a ten-ton crane and a weighbridge. The following year the London berth was moved to Fenning's Wharf, London Bridge.

On 12 November 1863 a steam packet cargo service was initiated between Littlehampton and the Islands with vessels owned by Mr. Maples. The West Sussex Gazette reported:

... A continental steam packet service was inaugurated by the arrival of the first cargo boat, the *Vibourg*, from Jersey and St. Malo, on Wednesday of last week, with a cargo of wine, brandy, eggs, fruit, etc. By great despatch, the cargo was discharged in time for the *Vibourg* to sail on her return voyage in the evening, and on the Saturday at three o'clock in the afternoon, the first passenger and cargo boat (*Rouen*) sailed for St. Malo and Guernsey.

[*West Sussex Gazette, 20 November 1863*]

L&SWR directors went to meet with their counterparts at the LB&SCR on 1 December 1863 as they deemed the expansion to Littlehampton to be in breach of their territorial agreement on traffic.

The *Normandy* was badly damaged in a collision with the Holland America Line liner *Bavaria* in Southampton Water on 21 April 1864.

In May 1864 H. P. Maples' operation was acquired by the Channel Island Steam Ship Company, which continued to operate through to May 1968. The Maples contract with the

View over St Peter Port, with crowds waiting to board a steamer berthed alongside the South Pier – dated 17 August 1861. *(Illustrated London News)*

LB&SCR ended in 1867, and the railway company gradually withdrew their Island services.

Channel Island vessels stopped calling at the Royal Pier in Southampton from May 1864, as the old arrangement, whereby cargo was loaded in the docks before the vessel sailed to the Royal Pier to collect rail passengers, had caused much delay and inconvenience. In St. Peter Port the Weymouth boats began to use the new No.1 berth at White Rock from July, following extension of the pier works. The L&SWR vessels began using the berth at low water.

The L&SWR's next new vessel the *Brittany*, made her maiden voyage to the Islands on 17 November 1864. Built by J. Ash & Company of Cubitt Town, the 525 ton steamer had J. Stewart engines delivering 250 horsepower and a speed of 14 knots. She could carry 250 tons of cargo. In 1865 the *Wonder* was re-boilered and the *Griffin* purchased from Mr. Beard, a Scottish ironmaster, for the Jersey-France routes.

The directors of the Weymouth and Channel Islands Steam Packet Company reported an £8,000 reduction in their original mortgage debt in 1865, but the company's other liabilities precluded the declaration of any dividend. The annual dividend subsidy was increased by £900 when the preference shares expired, giving a two per cent return for all shareholders. £2,000 was set aside annually for mortgage repayment, which was reluctantly accepted by the GWR as an alternative to closure of the company. The company advertised its 6:00 a.m. departure by the 'well known, fast, iron paddle steam ships' as giving 'day passages and the shortest sea route by several hours' avoiding 'the unpleasantness and dangers of Night Travelling'.

Weymouth Harbour was finally connected to the railway network by a tramway opened on 16 October 1865, which eliminated the double handling of cargo at the Town station. The route was built to the GWR's broad gauge, thereby limiting access to that company's trains, and included a sharp 223ft radius curve that restricted the range of vehicles able to access the Harbour until it was eased in 1938; special long loose couplings had to be used for bogie stock.

On 24 April 1866 a cargo of undeclared explosives on the *Havre* blew up whilst being craned ashore at the Inner Basin, Southampton, killing one person and injuring two others. Capt. Wright of the *Atalanta* was aboard at the time and was so shocked by the explosion that he died on return to his ship.

The Weymouth and Channel Islands Steam Packet Company again considered the sale of the *Brighton* in 1867. Meanwhile the L&SWR ordered construction of the screw steamer *Caesarea* for the Southampton-St. Malo service, which had opened in 1864 following completion of the railway from Paris. Her inaugural sailing was on 22 March, and she was to make intermittent calls in Jersey. The Jersey-Granville route was purchased in December; with it came the steamer *Comète*, which was retained on the route, and renamed the *Granville* after refit at Southampton. The second hand paddle steamer *Waverley* was added to the fleet for the Islands service on 23 December 1868, having been acquired from the North British Railway in August and refitted at Northam. She boasted a lounge fitted out with glass images from Walter Scott novels.

The States of Jersey considered the issue of better harbour accommodation in 1867, and advertised a competition for harbour designs in England and France. The harbour was still tidal, forcing passengers to embark and disembark into small boats at anything outside the highest state of the tide. The Chamber of Commerce lamented that no facilities were available for low water landing of passengers, and noted that 'numbers of visitors will be deterred from coming to Jersey at a moment when trade languishes'. Some forty-two proposals were received, and the Harbour Committee was given the task of evaluating the designs. Eventually the submission of Sir John Coode was selected, and works began in 1872. His proposal embraced two separate arms, extending either side of the small entrance roads. The western 'Hermitage' arm, some 2,665 ft in length and 86ft wide at the top, was to run from Elizabeth Castle over the Crow Rock to the Hermitage Rock then across to the Platte Rock. The eastern arm, which was to form the landing point for vessels, extended 3,690 ft from Pointe de Pas, heading south west for around 1,700ft before turning west north west with a cant of 300 ft at the end. This would create a berthing area protected from the sea, providing protection in rough weather. Three landing stages, accessible by stairs to match different levels of the tide, were to be provided. The original estimate of £282,500 was raised to £379,000 following amendments to the plans.

By 1868 the Weymouth and Channel Islands Steam Packet Company losses had been reduced sufficiently to avoid drawing down on the whole GWR contribution to meet the deficit. The GWR paid an additional £1,600 to help meet heavy vessel repairs in both 1867 and 1868, but this was appropriated to running expenses. John Wimble was appointed as manager of the Company having been the Jersey agent from 1862 to 1868.

A new L&SWR route from Southampton to Cherbourg was opened by the *Dispatch* on 10 May 1869. The L&SWR also purchased the 1859-built two-funnelled clipper stemmed sister paddle steamers *Fanny* and *Alice* 'on very advantageous terms' to meet growing trade with France precipitated by the Franco-Prussian War. The two vessels had been blockade-runners during the American Civil War. They were only occasional visitors to the Islands. Their arrival allowed the *Atalanta* to be withdrawn, and she was towed to Jersey by the *Fannie* in September to be stripped down for use as a coal hulk to service local vessels.

In January 1870 the Weymouth mail service was withdrawn by the Post Office and the Southampton service expanded to operate from Monday to Friday in summer, with an extra sailing to Jersey on Saturdays. This additional frequency provided employment for smaller vessels and the new schedule began to stretch resources. More strain was added with the loss of the *Normandy* in a collision in foggy conditions on 17 March 1870.

The *Normandy* left Southampton for the Islands shortly before midnight on 16 March under the command of Capt. Harvey, with twenty-eight crew and thirty-one passengers. At about 3:30 a.m. when some twenty miles from the Needles, the *Normandy* collided with the screw steamer *Mary* under Capt. Stranack en route from the Danube to London with a cargo of maize. There was a dense fog and the two vessels sighted each other at a very short distance. The *Mary* had been coming up Channel dead slow, with little or no headway, when a steamer's green lights were observed within a quarter of a mile on the port bow. Capt. Stranack ordered the engines to be stopped, the whistles blown, and turned the engines astern, but the *Normandy* was continuing at speed and turned to starboard directly in front of the *Mary*. The *Mary* struck the *Normandy* with her stem, cutting her down shortly abaft the paddlebox, carrying away her lifeboat and davits. The cabins began to fill with water and Capt. Harvey called to the *Mary* for assistance. A boat was launched in support and two of the *Normandy*'s boats loaded with passengers. As the lifeboats pulled away they hailed the *Mary*'s boat to pull across quickly but the second mate replied he had no such orders from his captain, and pulled back to the *Mary*. It was believed that thirty-four lives were lost and thirty-one saved. Capt. Harvey was last seen on the bridge, giving orders to keep the *Normandy*'s head to sea, as she was sinking by the stern.

Capt. Stranack waited for two hours around the collision site before heading for the Needles as his own vessel was in a dangerous condition. The *Mary* came into Southampton at the West India jetty around 8:00 p.m. and discharged her cargo, a considerable quantity of which had been thrown overboard during the day to lighten the vessel. She was inspected by thousands of sightseers; her escape seemed miraculous, with her bow lying open to below the watermark, and her bowsprit and figurehead torn away. Only her iron bulkhead had kept her afloat. Surviving passengers from the *Normandy* signed an address to Capt. Stranack, 'thanking him for his kindness to them, and for the manly manner in which he remained on the spot till all hope was over of being able to render any further aid'.

The Inquiry concluded that the *Normandy* was solely to blame for the collision. The master of the *Mary* did all that lay in his power to avoid a collision and save life, and the Court returned Capt. Stranack's certificate to him. The Court noted the 'irresolute conduct' of the second-mate of the *Mary* feeling there to be 'no valid reason for his return to his own ship without carrying out the orders he had received from his master. Had he obeyed these orders, and proceeded in the first instance, as requested by the crew of the *Normandy*'s boats, more lives might possibly have been saved.'

The directors of the L&SWR formally recorded 'their sense of the bravery and devotion of the late Capt. Harvey and all his officers and crew, many of whom, by sticking to the ill-fated ship, perished in endeavouring to save the lives of the passengers.'

Victor Hugo praised the heroism of Capt. Harvey and wrote 'it is important to remind the rich companies, such as that of the South Western, that human life is precious, that seafarers deserve special solicitude, and that, if the *Normandy* had been provided, first of all, with tight containments, which would have located the waterway; secondly, lifebelts available to shipwrecked persons; third, devices, which illuminate the sea, whatever the night and the storm, and which allow to see clearly in the sinister; if these three conditions of solidity for the ship, of safety for men, and of lighting of the sea, had been fulfilled, no one would have probably perished in the sinking of the *Normandy*'. [*Ce que c'est que l'exil IX, in Actes et Paroles: Pendant l'exil, 1875*]

A monument to the crew of *Normandy* was erected at Mount Bingham, St. Helier. The inscription reads: -

Harvey

To noble heroism
Normandy
Lost by collision in Channel in a fog

H. B. Harvey Commander
J. Ockleford Chief Mate
R. Cocks C. Marsham Engineers
P. Richardson Carpenter
J. Coleman H. Hoskins
J. Wadmore Seamen
A. Clement Boy
J. Allen G. Cadick J. Head
W. Stairs H. Waller Firemen
G. Rolp W. Rolp Trimmers

Giving up boats to passengers
stood by their sinking ship and
sank with her at early morn
March 17.1870

Harvey memorial, St Helier *(author)*

The *Normandy* was replaced by the *Wolf*, purchased from G. & J. Burns of Glasgow and quickly refitted before entering service to St. Malo on 24 May 1870. The *Wolf* was the final paddle steamer to be added to the cross-channel fleet. Meantime the *Brittany* was re-boilered and fitted with a forecastle in 1871.

In 1871 the GWR sought powers to operate their own steamers. The move was precipitated by dissatisfaction with arrangements for the Irish traffic at Milford, where the company had inherited a relationship with Ford & Jackson when it amalgamated with the South Wales Railway. The GWR (Steam Vessels) Act of 13 July 1871 authorised the company to own and work steamers between Weymouth and/or Portland and the Channel Islands, Cherbourg and St. Malo, as well as between Milford Haven, Cork and Waterford. The GWR envisaged building new vessels for the Milford route and transferring the displaced vessels to Weymouth. Notwithstanding this development, the agreement between the GWR and the Weymouth and Channel Islands Steam Packet Company was renewed. Meanwhile negotiations began for the possible use of the new breakwater at Portland as an alternative to Weymouth, opening up the possibility of services to St. Malo and Cherbourg. The L&SWR was party to these discussions.

By now the London route operated by the Cheeswright family had stopped carrying passengers and was concentrating the *Esk* on cargo, with a focus on Guernsey granite. Cheeswright & Miskin were very active in the stone business and had four of their own sailing ships engaged in this trade.

Work on the Hermitage breakwater scheme at St. Helier began in April 1872 with an official party watching the first blasting at Crow Rock. The £360,175 contract was awarded to John Coode, the most expensive of the three tenderers. Construction was to be of concrete blocks, with cement imported from England, and granite and gravel brought by barge from St Brelade's Bay and from South Hill respectively. Dignitaries were taken from Albert Pier to a point south of the Castle Harbour for the foundation stone ceremony on 29 August. The first concrete blocks of the La Collette arm were laid on 17 December 1873.

In February 1873 the Jersey directors of the Weymouth and Channel Islands Steam

Packet Company gave notice of foreclosure of their mortgages, following suspension of trading by the Jersey Mercantile Bank, and in April the GWR gave notice of their intention to terminate their agreement with the company. A report to the GWR Board two months later concluded that the Channel Island trade had been of no value to them. Meanwhile on 3 July the Jersey Joint Stock Bank (chaired by Elias Neel), bankers to the Weymouth and Channel Islands Steam Packet Company, suspended payment, as they owed the Jersey Mercantile bank the sum of £36,000 - many shareholders now faced ruin. The agreement between the GWR and the Weymouth and Channel Islands Steam Packet Company was now being extended on a month-by-month basis. Fresh pleas to be taken over were rejected, but the GWR entered into new mortgages to the value of £15,000 in the names of F G Saunders (Secretary) and T Merriman (Registrar).

The L&SWR continued to be beset by accidents. On 5 June 1873 the *Waverley* struck the Platte Boue rock off Guernsey fortunately without loss of life: -

'The *Waverley* left Southampton for Guernsey and Jersey at a quarter before midnight on Wednesday, under the command of Capt. Mabb, an able and experienced seaman, thoroughly acquainted with the passage, and an efficient crew of thirty men; having also on board between 80 and 90 passengers, and a miscellaneous cargo. The weather at the time was calm and fine, and everything promised a prosperous voyage. And, indeed, all went well till shortly after 7 o'clock on Thursday morning, when the vessel was between the Caskets lighthouse and Guernsey. At this time there began to arise a fog which continued to thicken till past 8, by which time all the leading marks were completely hidden. The speed of the vessel was then greatly decreased, and every precaution was taken to secure her safety, by placing two men at the wheel and two on the look out. Notwithstanding these measures the ship, as it proved, had deviated to the north-westward of her proper course, and thereby got into a dangerous position. The result was that at about half past 8 o'clock, she went bodily on to the rock named the Platte Boue, situate at about three and a quarter miles N.E., of Fort Doyle, and about six miles from her destination — the town harbour. She struck three times, although, owing to her reduced speed, not with any extraordinary violence, and hence no great alarm was felt by the passengers at the first moment. The blows, nevertheless, were fatal. The ship was hard and fast on the rock, some part of the bow was pierced, and in less time than it takes to describe the occurrence, the sea poured into the fore-cabin with such rapidity as to render it necessary for the passengers who were in the compartments to flee with the utmost haste... Captain Mabb, who saw at once the danger in which he was placed, did not remain a moment in indecision. He immediately ordered the boats to be lowered, and this order was so well obeyed, and the tackle worked so smoothly - without any of the hitches which so frequently attend these operations in the moment of peril - that in little more than five minutes the boats, three in number, were in the water with their crews and oars, and the whole of the passengers, the females being first cared for, were embarked, most of them taking with them their lighter articles of luggage... At this moment the fog began to lift, and it was then seen that there was a large rock standing well out of the water at about a mile to the south eastward. This rock was found to be the Grande Amfroque the upper portion of which is at all times uncovered, and clothed with a stunted vegetation. Thither the boats were pulled, and there the passengers, with their effects, were safely landed. The mail packet *Brittany*, heading from Jersey for Southampton... was on the point of resuming her voyage, and Mr. Spencer, the agent of the company, ordered her to go to the distressed vessel, himself embarking in her with seven or eight assistants. The *Brittany* was in a short time near the *Waverley*, but owing to her draught of water and having a heavy cargo and a large number of passengers, she could not approach her within half a mile. Here, therefore, she dropped anchor, and sent her boats off to the *Waverley*... The whole of the passengers, with the articles they had saved, were then taken into the boats, and, being conveyed to the *Brittany*, were brought by that vessel to Guernsey, where they were landed in safety, none of them having sustained any accident, although many, it is understood, had lost part of their luggage'.

[*The Star, 7 June 1873*]

The mails were carried on to Jersey on the *Dasher*. The *Waverley* quickly broke up and her remains were sold to W. W. Bird for scrap, although the remnants only amounted to six davits and two ladders. At the subsequent Inquiry Capt. Mabb was exonerated of any blame for the incident.

The steamers accelerated the decline in local Island shipping, taking an increasing proportion of the produce trade through offering much faster transit times to the main UK markets. The improved service enabled growers to expand their business, and from 1873 this began to justify the chartering of cargo vessels to meet seasonal demand. The mail service from Southampton was reduced to a thrice-weekly frequency in the winter from November 1873, but supplemented by the reintroduction of the cheaper passenger-carrying 'cargo' service on a twice-weekly basis, using the *Caesarea* and the *Honfleur*.

The L&SWR took advantage of technological improvements in ship engine design, and rapidly introduced five new screw steamers. These offered considerable efficiency improvements over paddle steamers, as the propeller was not affected by the state of the sea, being substantially below the water line, and was well suited to the shallow depths of the Island harbours. The *Cherbourg* was launched in December 1873, but was destined to spend most of her life on the French routes. The smaller cargo and passenger vessel *Honfleur* followed in February 1874, entering service for the winter cheap cargo operation to the Islands and sailing on to Granville for the rest of the decade. The *Guernsey* was completed in May 1854; she largely operated on the St. Malo route, but was also employed as a cargo vessel during the Jersey potato season. In December 1854 the *South Western* joined the fleet for the St. Malo route, but operated trial services to the Islands to evaluate the potential for screw steamer operation. This proved a success and led to an order for the *Diana*. Finally the *Alderney*, incorporating improvements learned from her sisters, ran trials in May 1875, before joining the French fleet. Four different yards were used to deliver the five new vessels.

The Weymouth Harbour tramway had been temporarily closed from June 1873 when a portion of the quay wall collapsed, allegedly due to the heavy wagons being employed by the GWR. The Corporation and the GWR undertook protracted legal wrangling over responsibility for repairs and the tramway did not reopen until March 1874. Meanwhile the connecting WS&WR, together with the Portland branch and the Harbour Tramway closed between 18 and 22 June 1874 to be converted from the GWR's broad gauge to the narrower national standard. This overcame the problems of trans-shipment of cargo between the gauges in the Midlands, and Jersey potatoes could now go directly to market in the Midlands and North. The response was immediate. Special potato boats were run from the following year with a temporary siding built at Weymouth to accommodate rail wagons. Some 3,500 tons of potatoes were manhandled from ship to wagon during the five-week season of 1876. However the use of the tramway was still restricted to freight services.

The December gales caused damage to the works on the Elizabeth Castle breakwater;

creating a significant repair bill. The Hermitage works were less affected as they were anchored in rocks at both ends.

The London cargo service was now operated by Cheesewright & Cheesewright, and the company replaced the *Esk* with the *Steperayder*, which was later joined by the steamer *Stannington*.

The L&SWR's operational misfortunes continued on 15 February 1875 when the *Havre* was wrecked in the Little Russel Channel whilst on passage from Southampton to Guernsey: -

'Since 9 o'clock this morning our island has been greatly excited, first, by learning that a steamer was on the rock at the entrance of the Russel, and next, that that vessel was the *Havre* coming from Southampton with mails and passengers. Fortunately, at the very time the disaster was discovered, the steamship *Honfleur* also belonging to the London and South Western Company, arrived here from Jersey on her way to Southampton. Mr. Spencer, the Company's agent, immediately ordered her to proceed to the assistance of the *Havre* to aid any work that might be necessary, while several sailing boats hastened to the spot. The steam-tug *Rescue*, Captain Lihou, also, without loss of time, proceeded to the scene of the disaster, and George Hughes, licensed pilot (there being no other pilots on the pier), was hailed by Captain Martin, Harbourmaster, as the vessel passed, who requested him to take charge of the *Honfleur*. The answer was that he preferred remaining where he was. We consider the conduct of this pilot highly reprehensible. On arriving at the stranded steamer it was learned that she had struck on the Platte Boue Bock exactly on the same spot where the *Waverley* foundered on the 3rd of June, 1873. All had gone well throughout the night, the weather had been calm and fine, and the *Havre* was proceeding at her usual speed, passing through the Swinge and entering the Little Russel at the head of which is the Platte Boue Rock, where she suddenly, and without any previous warning, struck on this ill-omened spot. A scene of confusion ensued for a short time, but the conduct of both Captain and crew was admirable. The boats were immediately lowered and, by the stern order maintained by the officers of the ship, the women passengers first placed in them, a matter of no small difficulty, on account of the surf which was running, and conducted to the Amfroque Rock, a distance of a mile and a half, being afterwards followed by the male passengers. Arrived at the Platte Boue, where she anchored some hundred yards away, the *Honfleur* immediately despatched her boats to the Amfroque Rock for the purpose of transhipping the passengers, of whom there were more then fifty. The *Rescue* and the pilot boats in the vicinity were occupied in the meantime in securing the cargo and luggage which, on account of the rising tide and the gradual settling down of the ship, were washed out of the *Havre*. The passengers having been received on board, with what few effects they still possessed, the *Honfleur* steamed without delay to our harbour, where she arrived about half-past 2, proceeding shortly afterwards to Southampton.

[*The Star 16 February 1875*]

The *Havre* lay broken in three parts lying directly across the much-flattened wreck of the *Waverley*. She was not considered to be a great loss to the company as her fuel consumption had been prodigious, consuming up to five times as much coal as a modern screw ship on the Le Havre crossing. However the company received much criticism in the Island press, with questions asked as to the professionalism of their operation given the succession of accidents that had been incurred. At the subsequent Inquiry Capt. Long was deemed culpable for the loss of the *Havre* and his certificate was suspended for twelve months.

The L&SWR ordered a replacement steamer in 1876; the *Diana* was the first screw passenger vessel specifically built for the Island mail services. This was a pioneering investment as paddle steamers were still being ordered for the short sea routes at this time. Breaking the tradition of working with London shipyards, the L&SWR turned to Aitken & Mansel of Whiteinch for the new vessel. She had a raised forecastle and single funnel, and her two-cylinder compound engine delivered speeds of 14 knots on trial. The *Diana* was launched on 30 November 1876 and entered service to St. Malo on 14 February 1877, before her maiden visit to the Islands on 7 April 1877, and was to remain on the route for thriteen years. The combination of passenger vessels with cargo carrying capacity proved a success and led to further orders for the *Ella* and *Hilda* in 1881 and 1882.

Expanding shipments of produce via Weymouth prompted the Weymouth and Channel Islands Steam Packet Company to operate three extra boats during the growing season, which the GWR supported by running extra trains. John Wimble was instrumental in expanding this traffic for the Company, as he was familiar with the trade from his time in Jersey. The GWR imposed a 'terminal charge' of 8s a ton at Bristol, 15s at Birmingham and 20s north of Wolverhampton; this enabled the company to cover costs without these being offset through mileage charges against the shipping losses being incurred by the Weymouth and Channel Islands Steam Packet Company. The shipping company had little choice but to agree.

The GWR approached the L&SWR to consider a joint operation from Portland to the Islands and France, but this proposal was rejected. A tripartite agreement between the GWR, the Weymouth and Channel Islands Steam Packet Company and the Ouest Railway of France was also considered; the GWR would transfer the *Great Western* and *South of Ireland* from Milford to the Weymouth and Channel Islands Steam Packet Company and take shares to represent their value. But the Weymouth and Channel Islands Steam Packet Company, whilst happy to strengthen their service to the Islands, was reluctant to re-enter the Cherbourg market and plans proceeded without them.

In September the Weymouth and Channel Islands Steam Packet Company approached Weymouth Corporation to provide a wooden landing stage or platform to support cargo discharge, pointing out that cargo that necessitated a twelve-hour discharge at Weymouth could be handled in five hours at Littlehampton, where there was suitable equipment. The Corporation did not have the resources but the GWR advanced £1,000 for the works, which included a steam crane built by the Corporation. Facilities were further enhanced when an agreement was signed in 1877 for a new 200ft x 20ft landing stage at Weymouth, which was completed for the potato season. The port was soon handling up to five boats and 400 tons in a day.

The GWR was left with £13 after paying off the Weymouth and Channel Islands Steam Packet Company deficit in 1876. The *Brighton* was found to require hull and mechanical renewal at an estimated cost of £7,000. The GWR offered to charter the *Great Western* or *South of Ireland* from Milford and advance money against a further mortgage, but the offer was declined.

The December gales again damaged the Elizabeth Castle breakwater works, this time beyond repair. More gales followed in 1876 and in June the States decided to abandon the project but continue with the Hermitage breakwater, and accepted the resignation of Cooke. There was still a need to expand the facilities as traffic continued to grow, but the States halted work on the Hermitage breakwater project on 27 January 1877, when the foundations had been extended to 1,580ft in length, with the top superstructure 1,493ft long.

Caesarea I made her maiden trip to the Islands on 16 April 1867 and was a regular visitor from 1875 to 1881. (*Ambrose Greenway collection*)

On 1 August 1878 the GWR inaugurated their Weymouth-Cherbourg service, operated by the *Great Western* and *South of Ireland*. Pleas from Philip Mesny, magistrate of the court of Alderney, for this to be extended to Alderney were rejected.

Onesimus Dorey purchased the Guernsey-built wooden screw steamer *Commerce* in 1878 and revived the Plymouth link, with an onward service to St Brieuc.

The *Hogarth* was chartered by the L&SWR from the Aberdeen Steam Navigation Co and after a successful season on the St. Malo service was purchased and renamed the *Caledonia*. Her use on Island services was limited to a period when the *Fannie* was being repaired and her time with company was to prove short.

In January 1879 the GWR appointed three directors to report on the Channel Islands service; they concluded in favour of continuing to support the route but against perpetuating the £2,000 annual support. Weymouth still offered poor rail connections with the steamers, and many Jersey shareholders continued to use the L&SWR service for their cargo needs. The £2,000 subsidy was withdrawn, replaced by an annual payment of £700 for depreciation and a £900 dividend payment. The GWR waived further mortgage interest - the debt had been reduced from £15,000 to £9,000 despite all the challenges - but required closer control, particularly over heavy expenditure. A clause added to the Weymouth and Channel Islands Steam Packet Company articles permitted the charter of vessels to the GWR or Ouest Railway of France. This was invoked when the *Brighton* operated three Cherbourg sailings and the *Great Western* one to the Islands, and the *Aquila* made three trips to Cherbourg at the end of the year. The *Cygnus* was used as a joint stand-by boat until May, but she broke down in mid Channel and was replaced by the *Vulture*, transferred from Milford.

The L&SWR withdrew the *Southampton* in December 1879, lengthened her by 20ft and employed Day and Summers of Southampton to fit new engines and boilers. She returned to Island service in June 1880 and was transferred to the Le Havre route in summer 1883. From May 1880 the Southampton service was expanded to operate from Monday to Saturday throughout the year.

Traffic grew sufficiently strongly through Weymouth to allow the Corporation to clear their debt on the Landing Stage including the five per cent interest payment. The GWR was left with £7,000 in 1880 after paying the Weymouth and Channel Islands Steam Packet Company deficit. In June an extension to the 380ft Weymouth cargo stage was completed, followed by the installation of additional cranes.

1881 began with the loss of the *Caledonia* on 19 February: -

'This morning at an early hour the news was circulated in the town that the London and South Western Railway Company's fine steamer *Caledonia* had been lost on the Oyster Rock in eye-range of the Victoria and Albert Piers. Immediately large numbers of persons rushed to the post office and the harbour to learn the particulars and extent of the disaster to which at first credence could hardly be given. The report however speedily proved to be correct at which the excitement increased as many were naturally anxious for the safety of friends expected by the

Alice had a short career on the Island services between 1879 and 1882, ending her operational life as a coal hulk in Jersey. (*Ambrose Greenway collection*)

The *Southampton* encounters a choppy sea approaching Le Havre. (*Ambrose Greenway collection*)

boat. For the past six years the company have been singularly fortunate in avoiding casualties to their vessels, the last steamer lost being the *Havre*, Capt. Long, which foundered on 16 February 1875 on the Platte Boue Rocks, off Guernsey.'

[*British Press, 19 February 1881*]

The *Caledonia* left Southampton at 12:30 a.m. on 18 February under Capt. Lainson with twenty-three passengers, a crew of twenty-six, and about thirteen tons of cargo. The weather became very thick on leaving Southampton Water and the *Caledonia* was brought up off the Calshot Lightship until 10:00 a.m. when the weather cleared sufficiently for her to proceed. After calling at Sark, she reached Guernsey, then left at about 4:25 a.m. for Jersey, with moderately clear weather and light winds. The *Caledonia* passed Corbière and ran along the coast until she reaching Noirmont Point at 6:10 a.m. At this time Capt. Lainson was on the upper bridge, the chief officer and an able seaman were forward on the top-gallant forecastle on the look-out, and the second mate and another able seaman were at the wheel.

Capt. Lainson determined to enter St. Helier Harbour by the western channel on a half flood tide. On nearing the harbour the white light at the end of the Victoria Pier was visible and the breakwater came into view, but Capt. Lainson thought it was too far upon his port bow, so ordered the helm to starboard, then hard-a-starboard, and then steadied, with the vessel still going at full speed. The forward look-out reported a beacon on the starboard bow, but had to repeat his message, whereupon the master saw the beacon and signalled 'stand by' and 'half speed' to the engine-room. The engineer had no time to obey the order and had only got the engines to about three-quarters speed when the vessel struck. The fore part of the vessel was quickly under water, but passengers were promptly put into the boats, to be joined by the crew, Capt. Lainson being the last to leave. The vessel sank within thirty minutes, and became a total wreck. The *Caledonia* had grounded on the Oyster Rock, on the western entrance to St. Helier Harbour: -

'The *Caledonia*, which all this time had been gradually settling down, then slipped off the rock into deep water, and sank leaving nothing visible but the tops of her masts and funnel. Some of the parcels and newspapers, and a quantity of luggage, which were seen to be floating, were brought ashore by means of boats, as were also the Guernsey mailbags. The loss will be that of the company's as they are their own underwriters. The ss *Alliance* left between 11 and 12 o'clock this morning with the mails for Guernsey and England, which in the ordinary course of events would have been taken by the *Caledonia*. The mailroom on-board the sunken vessel is situate under the forecastle deck. This is an exception to the general rule, the mailrooms being invariably below. The ss *Dispatch* having Mr. R Spurrier, the Company's agent on board, proceeded to the *Caledonia*, in order, it possible to render assistance, but her services not being required she proceeded on her voyage to Granville'.

[*Jersey Weekly Press & Independent, 20 February 1881*]

The Inquiry concluded that fault lay with Capt. Lainson in attempting the entrance to the harbour without having sighted the upper red light, and brought the two lights in one; so that when he starboarded his helm he had no certainty that his course passed safely between the Oyster Rock and the end of the breakwater. However the Court felt Capt. Lainson had shown great care in a twelve-hour voyage that had lasted thirty hours, and the evacuation was completed with admirable discipline. Taking all these circumstances into consideration, his certificate was suspended for three months, with the recommendation that he be allowed a first mate's certificate during the period of suspension.

The wreck was sold to Mr. Gautier de Ste. Croix for £140 and he was successful in recovering the boiler and engine in July.

The *Ella* was launched on 28 May 1881, with her maiden voyage to the Channel Islands on 30 July. She incorporated improvements to the design of the *Diana* and had an iron hull, a single deck and two masts located fore and aft close to her single funnel. The *Ella* could carry 450 passengers and her twin-cylinder compound engines delivered a service speed of 13½ knots. The *Hilda* followed, being launched in July 1882, but was then delayed by a shipyard strike and did not enter service until 19 January 1883. The *Ella* was primarily employed on the Le Havre service, with *Hilda* covering the Islands and St. Malo. A boat deck was added to the *Diana* in October 1881.

Work began on widening the North Pier in St. Helier in May 1882, proceeding slowly and utilising the concrete blocks from the aborted 1872 scheme at La Collette. The Jersey Chamber of Commerce noted that 'the potato traffic has increased during the past few years, as also in the tonnage of steamers passengers to the Island, and ... it is highly important that there should be sufficient room for steamers taking in cargo, more especially during the potato season'. By February 1884 the work had progressed sufficiently to reclaim land on which to hold the materials and equipment needed for the job.

Repair costs to vessels of the Weymouth and Channel Islands Steam Packet Company again absorbed most of the GWR mileage contribution in 1882, causing yet more concern to the railway company. The GWR insisted that any future expenditure must be limited to meeting mandatory Board of Trade requirements. The company reviewed the future of the service, including the possibility of termination of the arrangements, but left any decision until the future of accommodation at Weymouth and Portland was resolved. The year ended with the *Transit,* which by now had become a coal and stores hulk, being rammed and sunk in Southampton Water on 16 November.

In 1883 the *Brittany* was lengthened by 21ft and had new compound oscillating engines installed, returning to service on 12 October 1883 which allowed the *Fannie* to transfer to the Le Havre route, displacing the *Alliance* back to the Jersey station and permit the *Dispatch* to be withdrawn and converted to a coal hulk.

The *South of Ireland* under Capt. Pearn ran aground at Worbarrow Bay, east of Lulworth when approaching Weymouth from Cherbourg in dark foggy conditions on 25 December. The *Aquila,* a launch and two barges were sent to the rescue and managed to recover the passengers, crew and portable gear. Eventually two-thirds of the cargo was saved but the vessel broke free and sank on 3 January 1884. Capt. Pearn was deemed culpable and was dismissed from the company. The GWR's intention had been to construct a new vessel for the Cherbourg service to partner the *South of Ireland,* allowing the *Great Western* to act as relief; now the plans needed review. The *Brighton* was chartered from the Weymouth and Channel Islands Steam Packet Company to cover this service between January and May 1884.

Plans for Portland had by now been abandoned. Senior directors Gooch and Saunders visited Weymouth to see what could be made of the existing facilities, and proposed a programme of further dredging and widening, doubling the length of the cargo stage, equipping the Quay with three railway tracks and extending it eastwards, plus the doubling of the tramway route to take passenger stock - all in anticipation of enabling new tonnage for the port.

The GWR purchased the 1867 paddle steamer *Gael* from the Campbeltown & Glasgow Steam Packet Joint Stock Company for £3,000 on 8 April 1884, and she was sent to Laird Bros of Birkenhead for alterations that included the addition of cargo space. She was to prove too small for the Cherbourg route, and by July was employed on Portishead-Ilfracombe excursions, prior to returning to Weymouth for the winter Islands service.

The L&SWR fleet was reduced again by the loss of the *Caesarea* in a collision with the *Strathesk* off Cap de la Hague on 27 June 1884. The *Caesarea* left Southampton for St. Malo at 7:20 p.m. on 26 June, with eleven passengers, a crew of nineteen and about twenty tons of general merchandise. The weather was clear and fine and the sea smooth, and *Caesarea* proceeded at full speed, making about 12 knots. At 12:40 a.m. she entered a thick bank of fog, and her engines were put first at half speed, then slow and she proceeded at around 4 knots until 2:00 a.m., when the whistle of the *Strathesk* was heard three times at two minute intervals ahead or to the starboard bow. The master ordered the helm to be put hard a-starboard, but the masthead light of the *Strathesk* was seen close at hand. The engines were ordered to be stopped and reversed full speed, but the stem of the *Strathesk* struck the *Caesarea* on the starboard side, abaft the bridge, at an angle of about 6 degrees, stoving-in the lifeboat. The vessel filled fast, and the master ordered the two remaining boats to be got out; all hands boarded them and pushed off. Realising that a French sailor had been left behind, the master ordered the jolly boat to return but the *Caesarea* sank stern foremost before they could reach her. The crew were taken on board the *Strathesk,* and landed the same afternoon in Southampton.

The *Strathesk,* an iron screw steam ship of 217 tons gross built at Bowling, Dumbarton, in 1881 was the property of Mr. Alexander Marshall Hay of Glasgow, and several others. She left St. Helier at about 8:30 p.m. on the 26 June for Littlehampton, with a crew of eleven hands, three or four passengers, and about 140 tons of potatoes, with a Jersey pilot to navigate her through the Race of Alderney. Having cleared Jersey, she proceeded at full speed, making about 9 knots, in clear fine weather and smooth sea conditions. By midnight there was a thick fog, and by 1:30 a.m. the weather was so dense that the engines were put at half speed, and the vessel proceeded at 5 knots until a little before 2:00 a.m., when the whistle of the *Caesarea* was heard. The whistle was heard again, and then the masthead light of the *Caesarea* was observed a little on the port bow, and the chief officer ordered the helm to be put hard a-port; but the green light of the *Caesarea* was seen, upon which the chief officer telegraphed to the engine-room to stop and reverse full speed; shortly afterwards the two vessels collided.

The mate of the *Strathesk* told the Court that the master was intoxicated when he came on board at St. Helier; other crew both supported and opposed this view and the Court was unable to draw a conclusion. However the *Strathesk* was steering a course 'incomprehensible to a master in perfect possession of his faculties', and the Court concluded the charge 'not proven'. The Court felt that the accident occurred due to errors of judgement but declined to punish the officers involved. The master of the *Strathesk* was deemed guilty of very grave misconduct in leaving the bridge but there was no proof that the accident was his error.

The Court observed a marked contrast in management styles between the two vessels. On the *Caesarea* the master and second officer were on the bridge, there was a man forward on the look-out, another at the midship wheel steering, and a third attending to the whistle; and all were actively engaged attending to their duties. On the *Strathesk*, although it was the master's watch, he spent the half hour before the collision smoking in his cabin. The chief officer was on the bridge at the time of collision, but it was not his watch, and the third in command was unfit for the post and actually steering the vessel. Nobody was attending to the ship's whistle. The *Caesarea* was well equipped, manned, and well kept up; and both officers and men were 'intelligent respectable men, who gave clear evidence'. For the *Strathesk* all from the Captain downwards appeared to be 'an indifferent lot', and the manager, Mr. Gow refused to say what the vessel had cost, what her value was, and for what amount she was insured, and the Court was left in doubt whether she was or was not over-insured. Counsel for the owners, Mr. Baden Powell, stated that they had given full information to the Board of Trade, but Counsel for the Board of Trade disputed this.

The crew of the *Caesarea* were awarded £75 from the Steam Packet Insurance Fund for lost clothes, but the company determined that 'for the future the officers and crews must insure their effects on board the company's steamboats'. The *Laura* was quickly ordered to replace the *Caesarea*; she was launched on 20 March 1885, the first in the company fleet to be built of steel but the last to be built by Aitken & Mansell. She cost £23,500 and was initially allocated to the Southampton-St. Malo route, entering service on 18 May 1885.

The *Gael* broke down In January 1885 and was replaced by the *Vulture* for a round trip before the *Aquila* was brought in to cover the service until March, when the *St Andrew* was chartered.

The *Guernsey* sank the French pilot boat in St. Malo on 24 May, costing the company £360 in compensation. Later in the year the L&SWR Board approved the installation of steam steering gear across the passenger fleet, together with enclosed wheelhouses following an experiment on the *Hilda* and *Laura*. Officers and crew were no doubt very grateful...

The French partners gave the GWR notice of termination of the Weymouth-Cherbourg agreement at the end of the season in September because of poor results. When they asked for this date to be brought forward the GWR agreed to terminate the arrangements at the end of June.

On 13 January 1886 the *Brittany* struck a pier whilst entering the harbour at St. Helier during a strong squall. On the same day and in similar weather conditions, the *Hilda* lost her fore topmast and sails whilst on passage from Guernsey to Southampton.

A large crowd congregates at the Pier Heads in St Helier to watch the departure of *Diana*, the first iron screw passenger ship for the L&SWR. (*Ambrose Greenway collection*)

The Weymouth and Channel Islands Steam Packet Company continued to struggle on with three ancient vessels contrasting with the continued investment and development of the L&SWR fleet. In December 1886, Daniel Gooch of the GWR met with the company Chairman and indicated that either the GWR would run the service alone, or it would have to close. There could be no financial support for a new build. This stark position for the company worsened on 29 January 1887 when the *Brighton* was sunk off Guernsey, the first loss of a Weymouth route steamer.

The *Brighton* left Weymouth at 12:10 a.m. on 29 January, under Capt. Painter with a crew of twenty four, twenty three passengers, and from thirty to forty tons of general cargo, bound for Guernsey and Jersey. Capt Painter, had sixteen years service for the company, and had made the voyage 816 times. The weather was thick and foggy, but there was a smooth sea with no wind and orders were given to go full speed as the fog cleared. Shortly after 1:00 a.m. the weather thickened, and Capt. Painter telegraphed for the engines to go half-speed. At 6.30 a.m. the Walker's patent taffrail log showed a distance of forty-eight miles travelled, indicating that they were about a mile south of the Casquets, and the *Brighton* continued on its course. No attempt was made to ascertain the depth of water using a lead. About twelve or fourteen minutes later the chief officer went to the log, and found that it registered fifty miles. Rocks were then observed on all sides, and orders given to stop and reverse full speed, but almost immediately the *Brighton* struck rocks.

The *Brighton* filled rapidly with water, and Capt. Painter ordered the boats to be got out; all hands got into them and pulled clear as the vessel foundered in deep water within twenty minutes of striking. The boats drifted with the tide, but in about an hour the fog cleared, and the crew found themselves in the entrance to the Little Russel Channel, and were able to identify that they had struck the Braye Rocks. They pulled for Guernsey, and at about 9.30 a.m. landed in Bordeaux Harbour, north of St. Sampson's. A coffin containing a body intended for burial in the Islands was later washed up in Alderney.

The Court of Inquiry concluded that the *Brighton* was lost due to excessive speed, having been kept on her course without ascertaining her true position or the distance run. Running at 10 knots, almost full speed, through thick fog without taking a cast of the lead, was 'neither proper nor seamanlike conduct'. The Court concluded this was a case of reckless navigation, arising from over-confidence and suspended Capt. Painter's certificate for six months but agreed to recommend that during the suspension he should be allowed to act as chief mate.

Reduced to a two-ship fleet by the loss of the *Brighton*, it was increasingly clear that the fragile Weymouth and Channel Islands Steam Packet Company could not continue without external help. The *Great Western* was chartered for the remainder of the season to replace the *Brighton*, but the GWR was being forced to make a long overdue decision on whether it wished the service to continue. The *Great Western* was again chartered for the 1888 season.

Meanwhile the States of Jersey decided on 2 January 1887 to complete the Hermitage breakwater works as one of a number of projects to commemorate the Golden Jubilee of Queen Victoria. In March 1887 Robert Kinipple accepted the contract to extend the North Quay in St. Helier by 500 ft and work began the following month. The works comprised the extension to the breakwater, completion of the New North Quay, the building of a wooden landing stage on the Victoria Pier, and dredging of the Harbour. He elected to use granite from the quarries at La Mole, rather than the concrete of the earlier scheme, pointing out that many of the concrete blocks from this project had begun to corrode. The projects to extend the Elizabeth Castle breakwater, dredge the harbour and complete the landing stage at Victoria Pier were all supposed to be completed in time for celebrations on 20 June 1887. A meeting was called in the Town Hall in St. Helier to protest at the state of the Harbour improvements on 29 September.

The formation of the Plymouth, Channel Islands and Brittany Steam Ship Company in 1887 brought the operation of a single ship service using the *Commerce*. Onesimus Dorey of Guernsey was one of the founders and also part owner of the vessel. The *Plymouth* was later purchased to join the fleet.

The future intentions of the GWR became clear in July 1887 when they contracted with Laird Bros of Birkenhead to construct three twin-screw steamers at £25,000 each. The identical 672 ton vessels would each be capable of 17 knots and carry over 400 passengers, with a 6hr 15min passage time to Jersey compared to the ten hour journey time of previous vessels. They were to be the first twin-screw triple expansion vessels on the English Channel and the first in the GWR fleet to have electric light. Whilst it had been evident for some time that the Weymouth operation was facing takeover or closure, the boldness of the GWR plan was surprising, and the L&SWR services faced serious competition for the first time.

In May 1888 the L&SWR sought tenders from six yards for the construction of a 16 knot steamer for the Channel Islands services. This time the contract went to Robert Napier & Sons of Glasgow with the lowest bid of £32,800.

Improvements were needed at Weymouth to accommodate the new vessels, and on 15 August 1888 agreement was reached for Weymouth Corporation to dredge the harbour to maintain a minimum depth of 12ft, purchase and demolish properties opposite the Custom House on the south side of the harbour to permit the swinging of vessels, and erect a landing stage with all necessary passenger accommodation including a rail platform and direct rail access, with work to be completed by 30 June 1889. The GWR agreed to establish an improved steamer service on or before 1 July 1889, and to maintain it at least

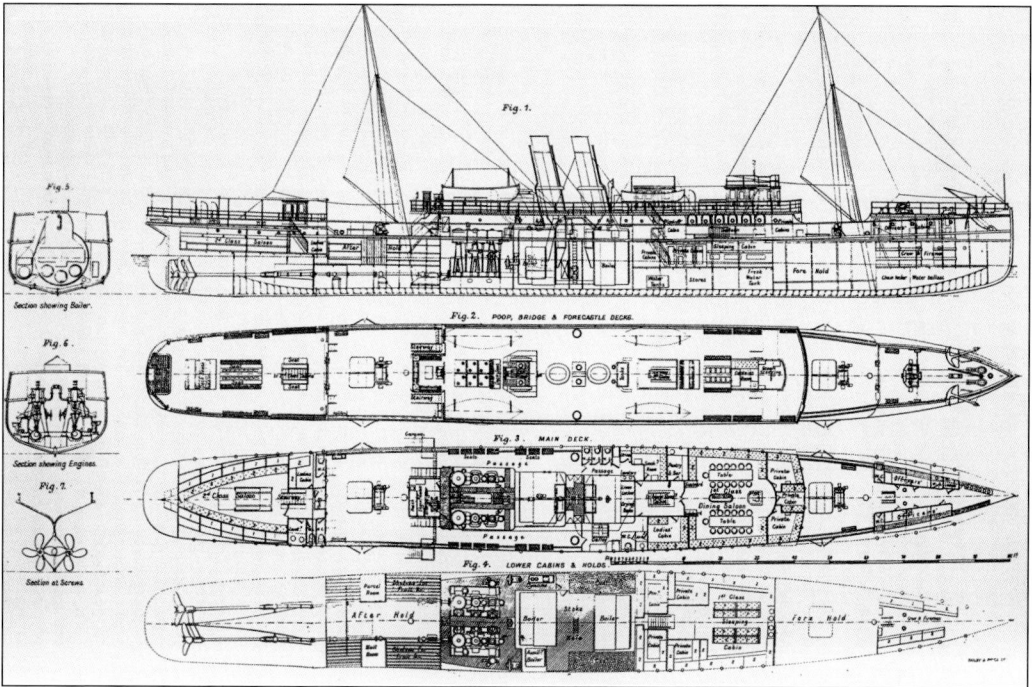

Laird Bros drawings of the Lynx class vessels built for the Great Western Railway in 1889. *(Engineering)*

twice-weekly with steamers of a specified minimum tonnage, and to pay the cost of the works in proportion to the unexpired term of the agreement in the event of choosing to transfer the services to Portland or otherwise ceasing to carry traffic at any time before 1 July 1896. The GWR were also empowered to increase the clearance under the Town Bridge arch to permit the passage of passenger carriage stock over the tramway, and to extend the tramway at their own expense, estimated at £2,600.

Works on the North Quay at St. Helier nearing completion in December 1888, but the Harbours and Piers Committee were unhappy with progress, and forced the resignation of Kinipple. With new ships now on order, and the GWR ready to take over the Weymouth service, the need for better facilities was becoming paramount. The work was completed by the States' Engineer Thomas Berteau.

The GWR's plans were still incomplete when Laird Bros enquired as to the name to be applied to the first vessel under construction on 23 January 1889. This was launched without ceremony at Birkenhead on 29 January and named the *Lynx*. Driven by two triple-expansion engines with steam from two single-ended boilers, the *Lynx* could achieve a service speed of 16 knots. Her bronze propellers overlapped slightly with the starboard screw mounted forward of the port screw; during the winter months iron propellers were substituted. The design included capacity for 430 passengers, a turtle back forecastle and a long bridge deck with two raked masts and twin closely set funnels. The imminent arrival of the new vessels finally encouraged the GWR to give the Weymouth and Channel Islands Steam Packet Company notice of termination of their agreement from 30 June 1889.

Meanwhile the L&SWR's *Dora* was launched by Robert Napier & Sons on 2 March 1889, incorporating improvements from experience with the *Hilda*. The *Dora* was the first triple expansion vessel to operate on the English Channel, and the first to have electricity throughout the ship. She undertook trials on 30 April and her maiden voyage from Southampton to Guernsey and Jersey took place on 26 May. A single screw vessel, she

The 1889-built *Gazelle* going astern into Weymouth Harbour; she was converted to cargo use and is seen carrying a removal wagon amongst other tarpaulined goods on the deck. (*Ambrose Greenway collection*)

was almost immediately outclassed by the arrival of the GWR's twin-screw competition.

The second new GWR vessel, the *Antelope,* was launched at Birkenhead on 4 May, although neither the GWR nor Weymouth Corporation were coming close to fulfilling their contractual obligations for the start of services. The GWR contemplated using the *Pembroke* to open up the Island service, with the *Gael* or the *Great Western* as standby vessels.

Work was completed on the new shore facilities at Weymouth in spring 1889; these comprised a landing stage and wooden baggage examination shed, a 173ft baggage hall, including sundry offices and a refreshment room. The tramway was extended by 475ft, the last 220ft being on the pier, giving accommodation alongside the landing stage for a train of four bogie carriages. A siding at the west end of the cargo stage was set aside for the transfer of steam coal from rail wagons to barges from which coaling could be done with a minimum of dirt and inconvenience. No cargo was dealt with at the new stage; after disembarking passengers the steamers moved up the harbour to the old cargo berths to discharge cargo, with outward sailings operating this procedure in reverse. John Wimble was appointed district traffic superintendent for the Islands and the GWR offered jobs to other Weymouth and Channel Islands Steam Packet Company staff. The existing offices in Weymouth, Guernsey and Jersey were taken over by the GWR.

Delivery of the *Lynx* was further delayed by faults in the draughting and ventilation systems and full implementation of the GWR service was postponed until 1 August; for July it was to be advertised as being delivered by one of the 'well known fast iron paddle steamers'. The *Gazelle,* the last of the new trilogy, was launched at Birkenhead on 13 June.

The *Aquila* and the *Cygnus* were sold for what the Star called a 'nominal sum' to a

The *Alliance* was allocated to the Jersey station to operate services to France between 1880 and 1896, and is seen berthing at St Malo. *(Ferry Publications Library)*

Gravesend tug owner, Alfred Tolhurst. He in turn sold *Cygnus* for service between Liverpool and Douglas, and *Aquila* to Onesimus Dorey to operate for the Plymouth, Channel Islands & Brittany Steam Ship Company, the *Plymouth* being sold to make way for her. The *Cygnus* left the Islands for the final time on 28 June, sailing empty to Southampton. The *Aquila* arrived in the Islands on 29 June and returned that evening to Weymouth, whilst the chartered *Great Western* brought the Weymouth and Channel Islands Steam Packet Company sailing into the Islands on 30 June, in readiness to return as a GWR operation on 1 July.

The Weymouth & Channel Island Steam Packet Co ceased operations on 30 June. The surplus assets were valued at £25,193 less expenses, but shareholders failed to agree how these should be distributed. The question was later settled by a decision in Chancery in accordance with which holders of the 2,917 paid-up original shares received £7 a share. Ten years previously shares had been bought at auction for as little as 17s. The Weymouth & Channel Island Steam Packet Company was eventually wound up on 19 February 1891 with a final dividend payment of 19s a share.

CHAPTER FOUR

The Great Western Railway takes control 1889-1899

'Amongst the many resorts that are open to the choice of the tourist, in which to spend his summer holiday, the Channel Islands take a deservedly high rank, containing, as they do, so many and varied attractions. The sea voyage alone is an inducement to some, although it must be confessed that it is a deterrent to others; but whether mal de mer be an accompaniment of the voyage or no, the visitor cannot fail to congratulate himself on his improved hygienic condition, and to realise the good effect of a little knocking about in the Channel'.

[Tourist's Guide to the Channel Islands, G Phillips Bevan 1889]

GWR sailings commenced from the Islands to Weymouth on 1 July 1889 with the *Great Western* taking the first departure from Jersey and the *Gael* sailing the following day, but operating with two twenty-year-old paddle steamers was not quite the launch that had been intended. The *Lynx* was delivered from Birkenhead to the GWR at New Milford on 6 July, but further delays were incurred whilst she was made ready for public service and the *Lynx* did not arrive in Weymouth until 21 July, when she went on public display. The *Antelope* arrived in Milford on 25 July and sailed directly from there to Jersey. The *Gazelle* was not ready to join the fleet until September. The full GWR service with the new fleet finally commenced on 3 August operating to the following schedule: -

London Paddington	dep	9:15 p.m.	Jersey	dep	8:00 a.m.
Weymouth Town	arr	1:48 a.m.	Guernsey	dep	10:20 a.m.
Weymouth Quay	dep	2:10 a.m.	Weymouth Quay	arr	3:15 p.m.
Guernsey	arr	7:05 a.m.	Weymouth Town	dep	4:10 p.m.
Jersey	arr	9:25 a.m.	London Paddington	arr	8:40 p.m.

Weymouth carriages were added to the 9:15 p.m. train from London Paddington to New Milford and detached from the train at Swindon. The 4:10 p.m. departure from Weymouth Town was a new service dedicated to steamer passengers, although in practice through carriages to Weymouth Quay operated from the introduction of the new vessels but did not appear in the timetable until October. The platforms at Weymouth Quay could only accommodate the first four coaches of a train, which remained in the station from early morning until meeting the 3:15 p.m. arrival from the Islands.

There was still competition from Plymouth (Sutton Pool), whence the *Commerce* departed on Fridays at 8:00 p.m. for Guernsey, Jersey and St. Brieuc, returning on Mondays. The London steamer service was still active, departing from London on Saturdays and returning 'as soon as ever she is loaded in Jersey – and if this happens to be in the potato season, the tourist will find on the return voyage his comfort somewhat interfered with from the piles of potato baskets' [Bevan 1889]

The GWR was quick to capture a dominant share of the Island traffic, with a large rise in business from August leading to Weymouth becoming the leading route after the *Gazelle* was added to the fleet from 8 September. The impact of three fast new steamers coupled with a dedicated train service began to reap dividends for the Company.

	Southampton			Weymouth		
Passengers	1888	1898	%	1888	1889	%
May-July	6,735	6,807	+ 1	2,408	2,359	- 2
August	4,063	3,653	- 10	1,984	3,103	+ 56
September	2,867	2,136	- 25	1,163	2,314	+ 99

From October the timings of the Weymouth service were tightened to give an outward journey to Jersey of less than twelve hours: -

London Paddington	dep	9:15 p.m.	Jersey	dep	8:00 a.m.
Weymouth Quay	arr	2:05 a.m.	Guernsey	dep	10:00 a.m.
	dep	2:15 a.m.	Weymouth Quay	arr	2:30 p.m.
Guernsey	arr	6:45 a.m.		dep	3:45 p.m.
Jersey	arr	9:00 a.m.	London Paddington	arr	8:40 p.m.

Even these times could be improved upon, with *Gazelle* quickly recording a four-hour passage from Weymouth to Guernsey, and an overall 11hr 5min journey from London Paddington to Jersey. By the winter the GWR was carrying fifty per cent more passengers to the Islands than the L&SWR, despite the new fleet suffering teething problems; the *Antelope* burst a feed pipe, the *Lynx* damaged a propeller, and both vessels ran aground in Weymouth. All three new vessels suffered from issues with steering gear and over-hot stokeholds.

Having been dominant for so long, the L&SWR found itself with declining passenger figures and its newest vessel embarrassingly outclassed by her GWR counterparts. The Company responded quickly by offering a new fast direct connecting train service from Southampton Docks to London Waterloo to meet arriving boats from November, matching the offer of the outward service. In the same month the company ordered three new twin-screw 712-passenger vessels from J&G Thompson, Clydebank at a cost of £185,000. A premium was offered if the ships could achieve above 19 knots. The vessels were needed quickly and it was intended that the first should be available for the 1890 summer season. In the meantime the company experienced a twenty two per cent year-on-year fall in passengers from the start of the new GWR service to the end of 1889, losing £8,500 in revenue. The GWR advertised the 'Shortest Sea Passage. Quickest and Best route' whilst the L&SWR responded with 'The short and direct route to the Channel Islands' using 'Swift and Powerful Mail Steam Ships'.

The rivalry extended to passengers travelling on the respective company's vessels. The GWR Magazine reported in 'On Board a Jersey Boat': -

'there was a great hurry and bustle to get the cargo for Guernsey unloaded and take on cargo for Jersey, on account of the SS *Dora*, from Southampton, preparing to leave for Jersey. This boat gained 10 minutes start of us and it was questionable whether we would catch her and reach Jersey first... Our competitor had got a long way in front but we were going fast and the distance became less and less between the respective boats. Excitement ran high as to which would reach their destination first. As we came off the Corbière, the *Lynx* was running parallel with the *Dora* and a great cheer went up from the passengers on each vessel. We enter into St. Helier amid great enthusiasm'.

The performance of the GWR vessels compared to the new build *Dora* was proving intolerable to the L&SWR. In January 1890 the *Dora* received a new manganese bronze propeller and was fitted with a Lee Anderson induced draught system to increase her power at a cost of £860. In mid February she found her performance being compared with the *Antelope*:-

'The arrival of the steamers belonging to the Great Western and South Western companies at Jersey, every morning, is watched from the pierhead with great interest, more especially when the *Dora* is known to be the mail boat from Southampton. Although it cannot, perhaps, be termed racing, there is no doubt that by a tacit understanding, the run from Guernsey to Jersey is generally made by the fast steamers smartly. The Jersey Times of Saturday last speaking on the subject says 'notwithstanding a stormy weather experienced during the night, both of today's mail steamers arrived here at about 10 o'clock this morning. The *Dora* had about five minutes start of the *Antelope* from Guernsey, but the latter gradually overhauled her on the passage and reached St. Helier some five minutes ahead. After entering the harbour, however, she grounded in attempting to get alongside the slip, causing considerable delay before her passengers could be landed'.

[*The Star, 18 February 1890*]

The *Antelope* also ran aground in Weymouth in February 1890 during an exceptionally low tide, some 2ft below the ordinary low water spring tide and said to have been the lowest experienced in fifty years. She remained aground for about an hour; passengers were transferred with their baggage to a Cosens' tug, and were still able to catch the boat train. All three GWR vessels had certificates for 431 passengers, but the upturn in business and the impending higher capacity of the L&SWR's new ships prompted the addition of new ladies' cabins aft of the bridge on each ship in 1890.

The volume of agricultural exports dramatically expanded in the 1890s as the shipping

GREAT WESTERN RAILWAY.

Shortest Sea Passage.
Best Route.

GUERNSEY & JERSEY

via

WEYMOUTH

Express Royal Mail
Twin Screw Steamers.
Most Comfortable Boats.
In Channel Service.

JULY, AUGUST & SEPTEMBER

DAILY Mondays Excepted

Weymouth (Direct Boat)	depart	2.15. 2.30.
Guernsey	arrive	7. 0.
Jersey	arrive	8. 0.

DAILY Sundays Excepted

Jersey	depart	9. 0.
Guernsey	depart	10.45.
Weymouth	arrive about	3. 15.

SPECIAL ADDITIONAL DAYLIGHT SERVICE

SATURDAYS.

Weymouth	depart	1. 30.
Guernsey	arrive	6. 0.
Jersey	arrive	7. 30.

MONDAYS.

Jersey (Direct Boat)	depart		10. 30.
Guernsey	depart	10.45.	
Weymouth	arrive about	3. 15.	4. 30.

For train service to & from Weymouth & particulars of
Excursions to CHANNEL ISLANDS See bills & pamphlets

services improved. The number of packages of fruits, flowers and vegetables exported from Guernsey grew from 391,906 in 1889 to 493,398 in 1890. The GWR chartered the *Gypsy* for Guernsey fruit traffic and introduced a fleet of specialised ventilated fruit vans for the onward rail transit. It was reported that 'Guernsey feeds its own population and sends 400,000 packets of garden produce to Covent Garden annually'. This was significant business.

The L&SWR's *Frederica* was launched at J&G Thompson, Clydebank on 5 June 1890. She was powered by two sets of triple expansion engines of 5,700 indicated horsepower, with compound direct acting inverted cylinders. Her two steel boilers were made by her builders, with 160 lbs. pressure, giving a speed of 19½ knots under forced draught. *Frederica* cost £62,980, and was insured for £30,000, the owners taking the remainder of the risk. The L&SWR paid an additional £1,125 for each of their three new vessels as they exceeded the design speed specification of the contract.

On 10 June the *Antelope* was holed when striking the Cavale Rock off Guernsey: -

'The *Antelope* started punctually, in calm weather, from Weymouth and made a most prosperous passage across the channel... at 6:20 the fog had suddenly enveloped us, and the command was given 'All hands on the lookout'. The Captain and another officer was standing on the bridge, and several sailors on the forecastle strained their eyes through the fog to catch any landmark from which to shape the vessel's course, steam being 'half speed' and then 'slow ahead' as I read it on the pass register in looking up at the Captain's bridge as we moved on. Suddenly one of the sailors in the forecastle shouted 'Land on the right side' and then almost immediately afterwards 'square topped rock on the right, sir'. This was the Rousse and no doubt the Captain recognised it, for he immediately gave the order to 'back her' and tried to slew round in order to get out of the trap in which, through no fault of his own, he found himself. Whilst this was being done, and we were standing watching the order being carried into effect, suddenly we experienced a severe shock and the vessel heeled over so on to one side, we all had to run quickly and to hold on to something. She immediately righted however, and remained fast. We heard the Captain being asked by another office on the bridge some questions, but part of his answer given 'no, lower the boats'. We then realised how serious an accident had happened. I must say that I never could have imagined people would be so calm and quiet. There were white faces and quivering lips, with tears from some few ladies, but there was no panic as the sailors began to cut away the roped and lower the boats. Gradually the boats were filled and the passengers landed on the Rousse, a wet seaweed covered outlying rock near Herm. There were many surmises as to the fate of the *Antelope* as we watched her from our place of refuge, having her baggage transferred to the Rescue. By the bye we saw the small boats again approaching, those present took us off to the *St. Malo*, London & South Western steamer, and we were safely landed at the Guernsey Quay. I am sure I shall only express the feeling of my fellow passengers, for the admirable way in which, after the steamer struck, everything was done to ensure our safety...'

[*The Star, 12 June 1890*]

Capt. Painter was acquitted from all blame at the Inquiry, and resumed his command a few days later. The *Antelope* was returned to Laird Bros for repair and returned to service on 5 July under Capt. Le Feuvre. The GWR took the opportunity to shorten her funnels to stop her being blown off course when entering harbour at slow speeds in crosswinds, and a Ladies Saloon was added below the bridge. The *Gael* was recalled to act as relief vessel in the interim. The same funnel alteration was subsequently made to the *Lynx* and *Gazelle*.

The States of Jersey embarked on a programme of dredging to lengthen the time available to vessels entering or leaving St. Helier, and built new waiting and storage sheds on the quay. The GWR Traffic Committee undertook a tour of inspection in July, with the objective of securing more favourable facilities for their vessels. L&SWR boats used the Victoria Pier where multiple staging levels allowed them to operate at all states of the tide, but GWR boats were restricted to the tidal Albert Pier. The States agreed to invest £4,691 to widen the North Pier and provide a new landing stage at the end. These works were difficult, as they required the removal of large quantities of rock before the quay could be constructed.

On 31 July the new *Frederica* made her maiden trip for the L&SWR. The Railway Magazine described her accommodation: -

'On lower deck aft is a magnificent first class dining hall 50ft long with table accommodation for 46 and sleeping berth room for 48 passengers. This apartment is handsomely furnished in mahogany and satinwood. Immediately forward of this are two apartments, with berthing accommodation for 48 male passengers; whilst on the quarter deck aft is a deck house, with sleeping accommodation for 44 ladies, and four special state rooms. The bridge deck extends for 150ft. Second Class sleeping space for thirty nine gentlemen and thirty ladies is provided on the lower deck forward. These vessels are fitted throughout with electric light.'

[*Railway Magazine, January 1903*]

Not to be outdone and mindful of the potential impact of the *Frederica* class vessels, the GWR placed a £57,000 order with Laird Bros for a new vessel 'embodying all the points found deficient in the present vessels' intended for a new daylight service. Later named the *Ibex*, she was twin screwed with two sets of powerful triple expansion engines delivering a service speed approaching 19 knots; her passenger capacity was increased to 600 passengers, and she had 210 berths.

The *Lynx* was hit by the German tanker *Oevelgonne* on passage from New York to Hamburg, whilst she was inbound to Weymouth from the Islands on 5 September. The *Oevelgonne* did not stop but was later arrested when she put into Plymouth for repair. The Inquiry concluded that the collision was the result of false manoeuvres on the part of both ships, and found each to blame. The *Gazelle* was also under repair at the time, so the paddle steamer *Snaefell* was chartered from the Isle of Man Steam Packet Company for two weeks whilst the *Lynx* was repaired at Day Summers & Co in Southampton.

The *Lydia* entered service for the L&SWR on 7 October, followed by her sister the *Stella* on 6 November. The new fleet was advertised as the 'Largest, Fastest and most Comfortable in the Channel Service'. Faster train services were introduced In the autumn between London Waterloo and Southampton Docks to give an overall journey time of 10hr 15min to Jersey and 11hr 30min for the return trip to London.

The *Stella* burst a cylinder when leaving St. Helier during a storm on 24 November: -

'The gale predicted on Saturday was not long in reaching Jersey and making full its effects... the *Lydia* encountered some heavy seas in her passage cross-channel yesterday and sustain some slight damage; she was some considerable time behind the Weymouth steamer, the *Gazelle*.... The *Gazelle* left Jersey this morning at about her usual hour, reaching Guernsey is due course at 10:40 and leaving for Weymouth at 11:33. A rumour that was widely current this morning that she had been compelled to anchor in Portelet Bay, but this was, very apparently, unfounded. The

Stella, however, was singularly unfortunate. In going out of the pier heads some mishap occurred to the cover of the high pressure cylinder which disabled the port engine, the result being that she was unable to proceed further than the outer roadstead. Here she therefore remained with those passengers who had ventured on board. It is said that no one was injured by the mishap in the engine room - a fortunate circumstance. Owing to the state of wind and tide, it was practically impossible for the *Stella* to return to St. Helier harbour, though one of the mates and some of the crew managed to come ashore in one of her boats; they were however unable to go back to the steamer. The latter made her way to St. Aubin's Fort this afternoon. The *Lydia* left the harbour at 4 o'clock to wait by her sister steamship, when the two Capt. s will decide what course to follow, whether to steam to Guernsey together or remain at anchor during the night. We might add the *Lydia* on her arrival yesterday after landing her passengers steamed into the roads again, it being impractical, due to the state of the weather and tide, for her to get alongside her berth; she came into harbour in the afternoon. We are informed that the *Frederica* is to leave Southampton for the Channel Islands at 8 o'clock tonight, leaving Jersey at the usual time tomorrow morning'.

[*The Jersey Times, 24 November 1890*]

In the event the *Stella* returned to St. Helier at around 6:30 p.m., having transferred passengers to the *Lydia*, which took them on to Southampton. She remained at the Albert Pier whilst the damage was assessed before a week of repairs was undertaken.

The numbers of visitors to Jersey between May and September 1890 grew by twenty per cent year-on-year to 42,803, having languished around 30,000 for much of the 1880s. It was the last full year in which landing by boat was a feature for many GWR passengers in St. Helier; of the 312 GWR arrivals from Weymouth that year, 150 (47.5 per cent) were landed in small boats; 132 (42.5 per cent) of the corresponding departures were loaded from small boats. Dredging of St. Helier Harbour from 1891 began to solve this problem.

The GWR considered how best to utilise the forthcoming arrival of the *Ibex* to counter the strong competition being offered by the L&SWR service, and decided to employ the vessel on a thrice-weekly daytime service from Weymouth at 1:30 p.m. returning from St. Helier at 10.30 a.m. the following morning.

A comparison of ship running costs was presented to the L&SWR Board in February 1891, based on each undertaking twice-weekly sailings from Southampton to the Islands: illustrating the high fuel costs of the Frederica class vessels-

	Hilda	Dora	Frederica
Coals	£73	£80	£113
Stores	£4	£5	£10
Wages	£36	£41	£56
Harbour dues	£60	£27	£28
Total	£173	£153	£207

The Jersey Harbours Committee secured £700 to construct a landing stage on the Albert Pier slipway on 26 March 1891. Works had begun by May and preparatory works were well advanced by the middle of the month. The project was completed on 3 August.

The GWR now offered a sufficiently reliable service to allow mails for the north and west of England and Wales to be transferred to the Weymouth route from 1 April 1891, attracting a subsidy of £200 per year compared to the £6,500 for the Southampton mails; the *Gazelle* was soon noted flying the Royal Mail pennant. The *Lady of the Isles* was chartered by the GWR for the 1891 fruit traffic season, another year of dramatic growth with a thirty-five per cent rise in Guernsey agricultural exports.

In further efforts to improve the GWR service, trial runs of corridor coaches were undertaken in June to see if they could be used on the Quay Tramway. The summer timetable featured a retiming of the 'Channel Islands Boat Express' from Weymouth Quay to leave at 4:30 p.m. and head directly for Swindon, where the Weymouth Town portion of the service joined it. The sheer volume of produce being shipped from Guernsey frequently delayed this train.

The launch of the *Ibex* was delayed until 6 June by a shortage of steel plate caused by a strike. She was delivered to Milford in August, and on 4 September left directly for Jersey and Guernsey for public shows to 'respectable people', before reaching Weymouth on 7 September after a record 3hr 35min crossing with invited guests. She discharged rockets on arrival in Weymouth and was again open to guests by ticket. However it was too late in the season to inaugurate the daylight service, so *Ibex* took her place on the roster with the other vessels, making her maiden passenger voyage from Weymouth on 9 September. In the event, no corridor-train connections were provided. The vessel was well equipped: -

'She possesses five decks, the first class saloons being placed on the main deck amidships, with cabins and state-rooms on main and lower decks. The main dining saloon extends right across the ship, and measures 30ft by 20ft, with table accommodation for forty passengers at one sitting. The saloon is tastefully decorated in green velvet, and is brilliantly lighted by means of electricity. Second class accommodation is provided on main deck aft, with sleeping space on deck below. It is fitted in hardwood, and upholstered in haircloth. The sleeping cabin of this class is a room with berths placed round the sides. Space for promenade is provided on bridge deck for first-class, and on poop deck for second class passengers. The propelling machinery of the *Ibex* consists of two independent sets of direct acting inverted three cylinder triple expansion engines, the cylinders being 22in, 34in, and 51in in diameter respectively, with a stroke each of 33in. The screw propellers are of bronze, and are 10ft in diameter. Steam is supplied to the cylinders by two double and Scotch boilers, and the indicated horsepower of the vessel is 4,000, giving a mean speed of 19kts. The *Ibex* is certified to carry 600 passengers, full sleeping accommodation being provided for 140 first class passengers and 70 second class passengers'.

[*The Railway Magazine, June 1903*]

The Star contained a fulsome description of a departure from Weymouth in September 1891: -

'we stepped from our comfortably equipped smoking carriage onto the quayside, where was deposited a huge collection of 'empties' and fruit baskets, besides quite a substantial cargo of merchandise which was being lowered into the spacious hold of the good ship. That railway system works in beautifully with the steamers, and older travellers did not need to be told of the convenience and comfort of such an excellent line as this, where the passenger may step from his railway compartment onto the quay ladder, which conducts him to the steamer's side. When we boarded the *Antelope* she was lying with steam up by the spacious landing stage along which the railway runs, and in the company of a large number of passengers from London, the Midlands and the Western counties, we made our way into the brilliantly lighted saloon, where one of the most courteous stewards we ever had the good fortune

Disembarking passengers are flanked by a large crowd as the *Laura* arrives in Granville. *(Author's collection)*

to meet attended to our creature wants. The numerous cosy berths around the saloon were already filled, and but for our precautions in securing a 'number' beforehand we might have had our accommodation below, which I'm sure on such a summer like night would have been far less preferable than the delightful and airy comfort which we found on the middle deck. The boat train was disgorged of its living and dead cargo with all possible speed, and punctually at the register time Capt. Painter, a grey headed gentlemanly old sailor who has been on the line and a good many years and knows the road to Jersey and Guernsey as few men do, was at his place, with the most businesslike precision the quaymen obeyed the orders to 'let go' and at about 2:40 we were speeding out of Weymouth Harbour'.

The return journey on the *Ibex* was equally enjoyable: -

'When we left Jersey for our return voyage the weather had undergone a complete change, the tide was low and we had to be rowed out in small boats to the *Ibex*, which lay outside the harbour, and the whole prospect presented a striking contrast to the brilliant appearance of the island when we landed. It was raining hard and a stiff breeze was blowing, so we were not sorry to make our first acquaintance with the steward's quarters. The saloon of the *Ibex* surpasses in elegance and comfort that of the *Antelope*, which is saying a good deal. Every detail is of the most luxurious description, and the passengers were loud in their praises of the new ship. Of the seagoing qualities of the *Ibex* everybody had nothing but high commendation. Between Jersey and Guernsey we encountered quite a strong breeze, and though the weather was not sufficiently severe to afford a real test of the merits of the ship, she behaved so well on the occasion that everybody was delighted with her. In the opinion of competent judges she is by far the best ship online, and Capt. Renouf is a happy man to be master of such a craft. We made a remarkably quick passage; we reached to Guernsey quite up to time, and steamed alongside Weymouth Landing Stage only ten minutes behind the time table'.

[*The Star, 13 October 1891*]

With both companies now offering services with new fleets it was time for a clear out of the older vessels. For the L&SWR the *Dora* was retained as the relief vessel for Island services, and the *Brittany* displaced to the Southampton-Le Havre route, which allowed the *Fannie* to be withdrawn and scrapped. The *Hilda* also went to the Le Havre route and *Diana* and *Ella* were transferred to operate from Southampton to St. Malo. The GWR sold the *Gael* to David MacBrayne in 1891 and she remained in the Scottish fleet until 1924. The *Great Western* operated a service from Preston to Douglas in 1890, before also joining the MacBrayne fleet in 1891.

The L&SWR purchased the Southampton Docks Company in 1892, and began a programme of investment that would make the port the home of transatlantic liners. This added to the volumes of traffic for the Le Havre route. *Frederica* was transferred to offer an additional weekly sailing from 6 September 1893, and the transfer was made permanent in December. It was evident that the standards experienced by transatlantic passengers were not matched on the cross-channel services, and the L&SWR ordered the *Columbia* and *Alma* from J&G Thompson Ltd for the Le Havre route, for delivery in December 1894.

For the 1892 season the GWR's *Lynx* carried fruit from Guernsey, allowing the Jersey service to run direct to Weymouth and offer a 10hr 45min journey from Jersey to London. The outward journey via Weymouth was reduced to 10hr 15min. Midweek tickets were offered at £1 5s saloon return and 17s 6d after cabin return - a reduction of twenty-five per cent. The Jersey vessel also made a round trip to Guernsey to support inter-island traffic, sailing from St. Helier at 11:00 a.m. and returning at 5:00 p.m. From June the GWR established a dedicated boat train from Weymouth Quay to Trowbridge and Swindon to depart immediately on discharge of the boat. This gave an 8:25 p.m. arrival at London Paddington from a connection at Swindon with the 2:15 p.m. service from Plymouth. The boat train could, on occasions, run direct through to Paddington. On 2 June the *Ibex* recorded a 3hr 45min crossing from Guernsey and passengers from Jersey were in London just 10hrs 30mins after leaving St. Helier.

The *Dora* struck the Tasse Rock off Guernsey on 17 September 1892, sustaining hull damage that cost £779 to repair. Capt. Dyer, who had been reprimanded for being in command when *Diana* ran aground in the Solent in 1889, was reduced to serve as mate. The following year the *Dora* was again in trouble when she grounded in thick fog on 16 May, being towed into St. Peter Port by the Great Western's *Lynx*, which claimed £100 salvage. This time the repairs cost £487 and Capt. Nutbeam was adjudged to have miscalculated the tide and failed to use the lead, and was reduced to serve as mate.

The volumes of fruit, flowers and vegetables exported from Guernsey reached 1,048,171 packages in 1893, more than triple the volume handled just five years earlier.

The *Columbia* and the *Alma* were delivered to Southampton in October and December 1894, releasing the *Frederica* back for the Island services. The new vessels were powered by two four-cylinder triple-expansion engines with steam generated by two vertical tubular boilers delivering a service speed of 19 knots. Each had two masts and two widely spaced funnels. Designed to attract French Line transatlantic passengers from Le Havre to Southampton, the *Columbia* and the *Alma* were fitted with private twin-berth cabins in First Class.

The L&SWR response to the GWR train service improvements came in July 1894 with the introduction of a direct overnight 11:30 p.m. service from Southampton to Guernsey, returning at 11:00 a.m. each weekday. This enabled the advertising of a one hour reduction in the passage time from Jersey to Southampton, with the departure put back to 9:00 a.m. and arrival times unchanged. A summer relief boat train from London Waterloo left at 9:35 p.m. supplementing the scheduled 9:45 p.m. departure. The L&SWR advertised an 'Accelerated Improved Daily Steam Packet Service' with an exaggerated three hour reduction in journey time.

The following year the GWR introduced a daytime service on summer Saturdays leaving London Paddington at 9:18 a.m. and giving arrivals in Guernsey at 6:30 p.m. and Jersey at 8:30 p.m. The return service on Mondays left Jersey at 4:00 p.m., Guernsey at 6:00 p.m. and arrived back in Weymouth at 10:30 p.m., but there was no train connection to take passengers onward from the port. Despite this, the service proved popular.

After completion of dredging, sheet piling and the erection of the Albert Pier landing stage in St. Helier in 1895, the proportion of GWR and L&SWR arrivals being landed by small boats was reduced to 16.5 per cent, and 15.5 per cent respectively; departure figures by small boat were 11.75 per cent and 8.5 per cent, representing a good return on the £14,000 investment. This was a welcome overall reduction from 45 per cent to 13 per cent between 1890 and 1895. The States of Jersey voted to complete further dredging activities to create sufficient water to enable steamers to discharge and embark passengers between 7:00 a.m. and 10:00 a.m., and between 7:00 p.m. and 10:00 p.m. daily, thereby eliminating any requirement for small boats between these hours. Visitor numbers to Jersey between May and September had continued to grow through the first half of the decade and now stood at 55,867.

The veteran *Aquila* was sold by Onesimus Dorey in 1895 with the proceeds used to finance the *Channel Queen*, a new twin-screw vessel for the Plymouth, Channel Islands and Brittany Steam Ship Company to run alongside the *Commerce*. The pair operated a Plymouth-Guernsey-Jersey-St. Brieuc (or Treguier) schedule for the next three years. The *Scott Harley* was advertised in The Star on 26 October loading at the British and Foreign Steam Wharf, Lower East Smithfield, London and sailing weekly to Guernsey. Her agents were Fred Cheeswright in London, C W Le Blancq in Jersey and G J Coles in Guernsey.

The *Diana* struck a rock in thick fog off Cap de la Hague whilst sailing from St. Malo to Southampton on 21 June 1895.

'Saturday afternoon it was rumoured that the *Diana* belonging to the South-western Company had been lost off Cape La Hague. The first intimation we had of the disaster was by receiving a telegram from one of the Jersey papers asking for particulars of the affair. Notwithstanding enquiries we were unable to glean anything concerning the vessel. As the *Stella* coming up from Jersey on Saturday morning had passed the *Hilda* shortly after 9 o clock, it was said here that it was the *Diana*, and many consequently did not believe the rumour of the loss of the latter. However telegrams came later confirming the loss of the *Diana*, an account of which we take from our contemporary the Evening Post: - "The steamer *Laura*, commissioned to proceed to the scene of the recent disaster off Cape La Hague, arrived at Southampton at 5 a.m. on Sunday, having embarked the passengers and crew of the ill-fated screw steamer *Diana* at Cherbourg. Immediately on the return of the *Laura* she was boarded by our Southampton representative who, in the course of an interview with two male passengers, adduced some additional facts with respect to the catastrophe. He was informed that the *Diana* left St. Malo early on Friday evening. On clearing the harbour hazy weather was experienced. Intermittent, heavy fogs prevailing, all went well until midnight, French time, when the vessel crashed with great violence on the rocks off Cape La Hague, the force of the impact

A collection of bonnets gathers to watch the departure of *Frederica* from St Peter Port. *(Author's collection)*

knocking a great hole in her hull. At the time of the accident the lighthouse lights could not be discovered, though the ship struck within two miles of the same. It was pitch dark, and strong currents were running in shore. The *Diana*, on stranding, immediately settled down. With commendable promptitude the passengers were summoned on deck by the stewards. The members of the crew worked pluckily in the manipulation of the lifeboats, and though there were evidences of suppressed excitement, there was no approach to a panic, Captain Kemp, assuring the passengers of a speedy rescue. The ladies, eleven in number, were placed in the boat on the starboard quarter, whilst the five male passengers were accommodated in a boat on the port quarter. At this stage the boat from the French Custom House arrived upon the scene, and the passengers were transferred to her and skillfully landed at Auderville, a small village on the French coast, where they were most hospitably received by the inhabitants. The crew, numbering twenty-six, landed in the ship's boats, and together with the passengers were conveyed to Cherbourg, where they were housed until the arrival of the *Laura*. The mails were saved. The captain of the *Diana* remains at La Hague with a view to the removing of a portion of the vessel's fittings. The *Diana* lies in an upright position on the rocks, a few feet of her bulwarks and deck gear being visible. Captain T. Roberts (pilot) informs our representative that, whilst on the passage to Jersey, the *Opal* came within 1¼ miles of the *Diana* on Sunday, about midday. He states that the *Diana* is lying between Cape La Hague Lighthouse and a rock, named La Foraine, and that her bulwarks, funnel, and two masts were visible at low water. Her head is in a N.E. direction. Captain Roberts says it is only a question of rough or calm weather as to the time that may elapse before she breaks up. Captain Kemp is much respected by the residents of the towns round St. Malo, and about five years ago the inhabitants of

St. Servan presented him with a gold watch and chain as testimony of their regard for him'.

[*The Star, 25 June 1895*]

The Court of Inquiry noted that Capt. Kemp had left the bridge before the passage through the Race of Alderney had been completed, leaving the vessel in the control of the mate, who had not previously been in charge of a vessel passing through those waters. The *Diana* was set on a course further to the east than was appropriate in the conditions, and the mate did not summon the master back to the bridge. Capt. Kemp was deemed solely culpable for the loss. Notwithstanding the esteem in which he was held, Capt. Kemp was dismissed and his mate reduced in rank.

In 1896 the L&SWR introduced a Saturday daytime service leaving London Waterloo at 8.55 a.m., reaching Guernsey at 5:30 p.m. and Jersey at 7:30 p.m., thirty-seven minutes quicker than the GWR service. Acceleration of GWR services produced near identical timings, but made the Monday service direct from Jersey to Weymouth at 10.30 a.m., giving a London Paddington arrival at 9:30 p.m. via a connection from Weymouth Town. The London Paddington departure for the Weymouth night service was put back to 9:45 p.m. Both routes now offered a 10hr 15min journey to Jersey and a 10hr 30min return - although GWR services were slower in winter at 11hr 45min and 12hr 30min respectively. In practice service delays meant that the advertised timings were rarely achieved.

Competition between the two companies was intense, encouraged by passengers. The Star reported on a race in May 1896 between the *Ibex*, which was undertaking an excursion from Jersey to Alderney with Capt. Hemmings, the GWR Deputy Marine Superintendent on board, and the *Stella* leaving Jersey for Guernsey and Southampton. Both vessels let go in St. Helier at the same time, but as the *Stella* left the Victoria Pier she cut across the bows of the *Ibex*, forcing her astern. A steel hawser became entangled in the *Ibex*'s propeller, but it snapped allowing the vessel to proceed. The correspondent picked up the story from on board the *Ibex*: -

'This little manoeuvre had give the *Stella* a decided start of several minutes, an

The *Ibex* in Weymouth. (*Dave Hocquard collection*)

Mooring ropes are made ready as the **Antelope** arrives in Weymouth. *(Ambrose Greenway collection)*

interval which it was thought by several on-board could never be made up, but it is proved otherwise. Many were the remarks made respecting the action of the SWR Capt., and excitement run high on the *Ibex*, when the word was passed round that the Capt. and engineers had decided to do their best to make up for lost time. Slowly but surely the *Ibex* gained upon the *Stella* - until, before the halfway mark between Jersey and Guernsey was reached, the *Stella* was fairly left behind. A small subscription was started and in a very short space of time about 25s was collected, which in due course was presented to the firemen who had been so instrumental in giving the palm of victory to the GWR'.

[*The Star, 28 May 1896*]

The GWR ordered two new vessels, both larger and faster than the *Ibex*, in anticipation of introducing a daytime schedule. The £110,000 contract went to Naval Construction & Armaments Co. at Barrow in Furness. In readiness for their arrival, the landing stage at Weymouth was extended westwards by some 40ft, the GWR berths in St. Peter Port were dredged, and the company was allocated two berths at the newly completed New North Quay in St. Helier.

The L&SWR introduced the *Victoria*, a smaller version of the *Columbia*, for the Jersey-France services, on 1 August 1896. She displaced the *Alliance*, the last paddle steamer in service. The *Guernsey* ran aground in fog off Calshot on 14 November 1896, cracking her high-pressure cylinder.

The progress made by the GWR since taking over the services was summarised in a

The *Reindeer* alongside in St Helier. Railway management of the facilities is made very clear. *(Author's collection)*

letter by Capt. Hemmings, the Deputy Marine Superintendent, quoted in The Star on 4 February 1897. He noted that the speed of vessels had increased from the 17 knots of 1889 to achieve 22 knots from 1897, with the passage time from Weymouth to Guernsey reduced from the 8-10 hours of the old regime to a claimed 3¼ hours. Frequencies had improved from one sailing per day to three, with between five and six boats maintaining the passenger and cargo services during June and July. The GWR investment was paying off, with passenger carryings rising from 39,000 to 55,000 between 1890 and 1896, and freight business trebling in the same period to almost 33,000 tons. The arrival of the *Roebuck* and *Reindeer* would prove that the Weymouth route 'was by far the most expeditious and comfortable'.

The *Roebuck* was launched at Barrow in Furness on 6 March 1897. Of 1,280 gross tons she was powered by two three-cylinder reciprocating engines with steam delivered by two double-ended Scotch boilers, capable of delivering a speed of 21 knots. With capacity for 842 passengers and berths for 150 First Class and 76 Second Class passengers, the *Roebuck* was both larger and faster than other vessels; competition was taking services to a different level.

Much of the desire for faster timings was achieved by acceleration and retiming of the connecting train services, as the overall journey time from London was a key feature of advertising. There is no doubt that the concept of racing was also manifest in the operation of the respective fleets, but there was also pressure to improve passage times on the outward sailings if connecting rail services to the port were delayed. The tides at St. Helier remained an operating constraint, and with similar arrival times advertised by both companies there was a practical desire to get there ahead of the competition to avoid being stranded in the Roads and forced to land passengers by boat. This came to a head on Good Friday, 16 April 1897.

The *Ibex* was timed to leave Weymouth at 2:10 a.m. after the arrival of the connecting

Luggage being carried ashore after the *Ibex* is beached in Portelet Bay on 16 April 1897. *(Dave Hocquard collection)*

The **Ella** was a stalwart of the Channel Islands route during the 1880s, before being displaced by the Frederica class vessels and relegated to relief work. *(Ferry Publications Library)*

train from London Paddington. This was late arriving, so the *Ibex* left for Guernsey 52 minutes late at 3:02 a.m., commanded by Capt. Le Feuvre, with 309 passengers and a small amount of general cargo on board. The weather was fine and clear, with a light southwest wind. Before leaving Weymouth, Capt. Le Feuvre instructed the chief engineer to keep the engines at full speed, so as to save the tide at St. Helier. The *Ibex* arrived at St. Peter Port at 7:32 a.m., when 109 passengers landed and a small quantity of cargo was discharged. Having embarked sixty-one passengers, she left for St. Helier, passing the pier head at 8:05 a.m., whence a course was steered to pass Corbière at a distance of half a mile. The engines were at full speed, with the vessel making about 18 to 19 knots.

Meanwhile the *Frederica* had left Southampton at 1:04 a.m. for Guernsey with 456 passengers, mails and some general cargo, some 64 minutes behind schedule after her connecting train also arrived late. Capt. Allix also instructed his engineer to work the engines at full speed to save the high tide at St. Helier, which restricted the arrival of both vessels to before 9:45 a.m. The *Frederica* arrived at St. Peter Port at 7:47 a.m., where passengers were landed and cargo discharged, and she left smartly at 8.10 a.m. for St. Helier with 260 passengers on board. Her engines were at full speed, making over 19 knots, with *Ibex* ahead on the starboard bow. The master went below to his breakfast, and on returning to the bridge at 8:50 a.m. observed *Ibex* about half a mile distant on the starboard bow, *Frederica* having gained considerably on her since leaving St. Peter Port. When off Les Boiteaux the course was altered slightly to port to give *Ibex* a wider berth.

Passing Green Rock off Corbière at a few yards distance with *Frederica* about two vessels' lengths away on the port quarter, the master of the *Ibex* determined on passing inside the Noirmontaise Rock, with the view of 'cheating the tide', which ran with less force near the shore, to arrive first in St. Helier and prevent the *Frederica* from entering the harbour during his manoeuvre, miss the tide and force her to anchor in the bay. The *Ibex*'s course was altered to pass inside the Noirmontaise, and two short blasts of her steam-whistle intimated the move to port to the *Frederica*. However the *Frederica's* course was not changed, and the master of the *Ibex*, fearing there would be a collision, ported his helm, the *Frederica* passed within a few yards, and at 9.19 a.m. *Ibex* struck the Noirmontaise and passed over. As her engines raced, the engineer shut off the supply of steam, perceiving that damage had occurred to the propellers, reducing the revolutions to the normal number, and the vessel continued her course.

The watertight doors were closed, and a 'stand by' signal made to the *Frederica*, which was then half a mile to a mile distant. Water was observed entering the stokehold and another compartment within ten minutes, and the chief engineer reported that steam would not last long, whereon the master decided to beach her in Portelet Bay, with the *Frederica* accompanying her. The *Ibex* was beached, the *Frederica* anchored in close vicinity, and the passengers and mails were landed by the boats of both vessels. Some of the fires were drowned out before the vessel was beached, but there was about five feet of water in the stokehold. Having assisted with the ship's boats in landing the mails and passengers from the *Ibex*, the *Frederica* proceeded to St. Helier, arriving at 11:20 a.m.

At low water the *Ibex* was found to be seriously damaged, with water in three compartments and a 30ft tear in her hull. All the blades of the port propeller and three from the starboard propeller were broken off. The *Ibex* was floated on the following tide, and towed by the tug *Assistance* out of the bay, but the tug was not powerful enough and the cables broke, with the *Ibex* driven by the tide as far as Corbière, where she anchored at 7:10 p.m. with 90 fathoms of cable. She remained at anchor until Easter Sunday, when the *Gazelle* towed her to St. Helier to receive temporary repairs.

Remarkably the Court concluded that the *Ibex* and *Frederica* were not racing against one another, but were both pressing on with a view to saving the tide at St. Helier. Counsel for both railway companies and officers were adamant in their evidence that no racing was

The *Antelope* in St Helier with the alterations made to her in 1896 clearly evident. *(Ambrose Greenway collection)*

The *Gazelle* berthed in St Helier. *(Author's collection)*

taking place, even though it was obvious in questioning that there was considerable animosity between the respective Captains. The Court considered that the master of the *Ibex* was not justified in making the alteration in the course when so near the Noirmontaise Rocks, with *Frederica* within two ship's lengths of the vessel on the port quarter with her stem being abreast of the bridge of the *Ibex*, and both vessels steering the same course. The *Frederica's* course was being altered to port at the time the signal was given, and her speed was not reduced. The Court did not attach blame to her master for not having reduced speed, there being room for both vessels to pass inside the Noirmontaise Rocks. The Court suspended Capt. Le Feuvre's certificate for six months.

Despite the desire of both Captains to reach St. Helier first, the Court suggested that occasions when the first vessel arriving at St. Helier prevented the later one from being berthed were so rare, that the semblance of racing is 'practically inappreciable'. The 'difficulties and inconvenience for delivery of the Government mails and conveyance of passengers, if the times of starting the vessels from Southampton to Weymouth were made dependent on the tide at St. Helier', appeared to the Court to be so great that it did not think that it advisable to make any alteration, especially as the depth of water in the harbour of St. Helier was being increased by dredging.

The *Ibex* was sent to Barrow in Furness to effect permanent repairs alongside the new additions to the fleet then under construction, with the *Pembroke* transferred from Milford to cover.

The GWR was able to make the first use of the new berth on the North Pier at St. Helier on 15 June 1897, but it was 25 October before the new waiting rooms were ready for public use. There were still a number of unsightly sheds on the Quay and the Harbours Committee looked to replace them with more modern structures, seeking offers from anyone who might wish to rent space in May 1898. Facilities were also improved for the L&SWR after the States agreed to build new waiting facilities and a luggage shed on the

Victoria Pier in September 1898, then a shelter for the use of Bristol, Plymouth and St. Brieuc services on the Albert Pier was approved in January 1899.

Ibex returned to the Weymouth fleet in late June ready to launch the new daytime service with *Roebuck*. *Roebuck* crossed to Guernsey on a press trip in under 3hr 30min - a new record; she then set a record of 5hr 7min on her inaugural scheduled run to Jersey on 1 July. Her facilities were described in the Illustrated London News: -

'The first class accommodation is fitted amidships, forward of the boilers, and provides berths for 150 passengers. On the promenade deck in a large steel house, are the ladies' sitting room, smoke-room, and first class entrance, with broad staircase descending to the dining-saloon and ladies retiring-room on the main deck, and to the state-rooms, gentlemen's and ladies' sleeping-cabins on the lower deck. The dining-saloon is a large and spacious compartment, capable of dining about fifty persons comfortably'.

[*Illustrated London News 17 July 1897*]

The new daylight service operated from Monday to Saturday, with cargo carried only for Jersey, to minimise the length of the call in Guernsey.

London Paddington	dep	8:50 a.m.	Jersey	dep 8:30 a.m.
Weymouth Quay	arr	1:10 p.m.	Guernsey	arr 10:15 a.m.
	dep	1:30 p.m.		dep 10:30 a.m.
Guernsey	arr	5:00 p.m.	Weymouth Quay	arr 2:30 p.m.
	dep	5:15 p.m.		dep 2:50pm
Jersey	arr	7:00 p.m.	London Paddington	arr 7:15 p.m.

The night boat offered a morning service from Guernsey to Jersey, with a new sailing from Jersey to Guernsey departing at 5:00 p.m. and arriving at 6:45 p.m.; the vessel remained in Guernsey overnight before offering a morning cargo and fruit sailing to Weymouth, arriving at 4:00 p.m. The L&SWR increased their daytime sailings to operate on Tuesdays, Thursdays and Saturdays, but the return passenger crossing sailed only from Jersey to Guernsey, returning to Southampton with cargo. In 1898 the Great Western arrival time in Jersey was put back to 7:30 p.m.

The *Channel Queen* of the Plymouth, Channel Islands, and Brittany Steam Ship Company struck on the Roque Noire, to the north of Guernsey on 1 February 1898. She left Sutton's Wharf, Plymouth, bound for Guernsey, Jersey and St. Brieux, at about 10:50 p.m. on 31 January, with fifty passengers, a crew of eighteen and general cargo, under the command of Capt. Collings. He had been her master since she joined the route in 1895 and Captain of the *Commerce* and the *Aquila* before; a Plymouth man, he had crossed the Channel more than 3,000 times and been in the service since 1863. Forty-four of the passengers were Breton onion-sellers from Roscoff and St. Pol, who were returning home with the proceeds of six months hard work.

At about 11:10 p.m. *Channel Queen* passed the Mewstone and the patent log was put over, and the main trysail and fore staysail set; the weather was fine with a fresh westerly breeze and the ship proceeded at full speed of 12 knots. At 4:45 a.m. the weather thickened and the first mate called the master to report he had not seen any lights. The master went to the bridge and, on seeing the log showing seventy-six miles, reduced speed and gave instructions to have the deep sea lead ready for casting. The ship continued on her course until about 5:00 a.m., when the engines were slowed, the port engine stopped, and the helm put to starboard. Breakers were observed close to the

The ill fated *Stella*. *(Ambrose Greenway collection)*

starboard bow, upon which the helm was put 'hard-a-starboard'; the vessel struck and passed over a submerged rock, and then struck between two rocks on the Roque Noire, remaining fast and bumping heavily on her starboard bilge, which caused her to fall over on to her port beam ends.

Passengers were called and supplied with lifebelts. The crew attempted to fire rockets as signals of distress, but they were wet and failed to ignite. The lanyard of the steam whistle was made fast, keeping the valve open and the whistle blowing as long as steam remained in the boilers. Attempts to get out the port lifeboat were dashed when it was washed away by the sea, with several crew carried overboard. The lifeboat capsized, and some passengers clung to her and got on to her keel, and were subsequently rescued.

On the *Channel Queen* the starboard boat was dashed against a ventilator by the lurching of the ship, and broke in two. The master advised everybody to take shelter on the bridge; all those who acted on his advice were saved, whilst those who neglected it were nearly all lost. The jolly boat floated out of the chocks and subsequently picked up several people, but could not return to the vessel as it was nearly full of water; it drifted clear to land in a small sandy bay where it was rescued. Fishermen manned the jolly boat, and returned with other boats to the wreck but the heavy sea prevented them getting alongside. A line was eventually landed on the ship and those left on the bridge were hauled to safety in the boat, with Capt. Collings being the last to come ashore at 10:35 a.m. Of the sixty-eight people on board, five crew and fifteen passengers were killed.

News of the disaster spread quickly, causing consternation in the islands. The day after the tragedy the Jersey survivors arrived in the Island on board the GWR's *Antelope*. The ordeal for the thirty surviving Frenchmen was not yet over. The *Alert* was chartered to take them to St. Brieuc but had to return to Guernsey during another gale. Eventually they arrived home a week late without their clothes or money.

The Inquiry considered that the *Channel Queen* was navigated correctly up to 4:30 a.m. of 1 February, but not afterwards. The master was deemed in default for not stopping the ship and taking soundings when he found seventy-six miles recorded on the log; the chief mate for not calling the master earlier, given the weather. The Court, in consideration of the past career and his conduct after the vessel struck, suspended the certificate of Capt. Collings for three months and censured P. W. Keagan, the first mate.

In a rider to the judgment two members of the Inquiry Board felt strongly that, in view of previous correspondence between the GWR and the Trinity Board concerning the erection of a lighthouse and fog signalling apparatus on the Brayes Rock, it was regretted that the Trinity Board, instead of putting the responsibility upon the Guernsey Authority, had not erected a light and fog signal. If this had been done the *Channel Queen* would not have been lost. The GWR had written to the Trinity Board on 28 March 1892: -

'It will therefore easily be understood how the Captains, anxious to make a quick passage befitting such vessels, are tempted, notwithstanding instructions to the contrary, to advance further in thick weather than prudence would dictate, until some day a terrible accident may happen.'

In the opinion of the Court, including that of the assessors, this was precisely the explanation of the present disaster. They concluded: -

'In as much as the number of passengers proceeding from this country to the Channel Islands each year is known to be very considerable, we are of opinion that the erection of a light and fog signal on the Brayes is imperative, and the Trinity Board should, if necessary, obtain power by an Order in Council for the purpose'.

The Hanois was subsequently equipped with a new warning system. In March the Guernsey Star reported: -

'The steamer lies in pieces. The funnels lie 30ft away from the hull, after portions of the ship have been carried further away. At low tide some of the wreck is visible above the water and piles of wreckage have been washed up along the shores'.

Following the loss of the *Channel Queen* the Plymouth, Channel Islands, and Brittany Steam Ship Company was wound up and the *Commerce* sold. Dorey was not deterred and established the Anglo-French Steamship Company to re-open the Plymouth route using the *Rossgull*, but this vessel was also to have a short life on the route.

The L&SWR's new relief vessel *Vera* was launched at the Clydebank Yard on 4 July 1898. She could reach 19½ knots powered by two sets of quadruple expansion engines with steam from four single ended return tube boilers. Intended to act as relief vessel for the Channel

Capt. William Reeks of the *Stella*. Aged 49, he had been with the L&SWR for 25 years, working his way through the ranks from able seaman to master. He had considerable experience on the Channel Islands run. *(Author's collection)*

Contemporary postcard graphic of the sinking *Stella*, with Capt. Reeks raising his arms on the bridge. *(Author's collection)*

Island and Le Havre routes, she replaced the unsuccessful *Dora*, which was sold to the Isle of Man Steam Packet Company as the *Douglas* in 1901.

On 12 August the GWR (New Works) Bill received the Royal Assent. This incorporated plans for a new harbour at Newton's Cove, Portland, outside the Admiralty breakwater with a connecting 4½-mile branch railway to Upwey at a total cost of £375,000. Two 800ft jetties were planned, with approach roads and two breakwaters to enclose 56 acres of land. Meanwhile discussions began on a truce between the GWR and L&SWR on the timings of their services. These were brought into sharp relief on 30 March 1899 with the loss of the *Stella*.

The Easter period marked the start of daylight services to the Islands, and both the GWR and L&SWR chose to operate the first such crossings of the season on Maundy Thursday 30 March. This was a busy period for the L&SWR. The *Vera*, commanded by Capt. Winter, left Southampton with mails for Guernsey about midnight on 29 March. The *Stella* was scheduled to leave Southampton at 11:15 a.m. and due to arrive at Guernsey at 5:30 p.m., Jersey at 7:30 p.m. and remain in Jersey until Saturday 1 April. The *Frederica*, commanded by Capt. Allix, was to leave Jersey on Good Friday morning, 31 March. An overflow boat, the *Dora*, commanded by Capt. Vanderplank, was ready to sail from Southampton for the Islands on Thursday, 30 March, but in the event was not required.

The L&SWR boat train left London Waterloo with 110 passengers and arrived in Southampton just after 11:00 a.m. on 30 March. The *Stella* commanded by Capt. Reeks left Southampton some ten minutes late at 11:25 a.m., with about 147 passengers on board, there being no surviving exact count. Capt. Reeks held Pilotage Certificates for Jersey, Guernsey and Southampton, and had joined the L&SWR in 1874, being promoted to acting master in 1886, and master in 1891, and chiefly employed on the Channel Islands service.

Passenger Mrs. Aylett dined in the captain's saloon with Dr. Davis, Capt. Reeks, and the first officer. Capt. Reeks was noted as being very pleasant. The fog became very thick, and Dr. Davis asked Capt. Reeks if this would delay the boat; he replied "We'll be there on time. I'll get there at five o'clock, if I break my neck for it". Shortly after the conclusion of dinner the captain and the first officer went up on deck. [reported in *Western Gazette, 7 April 1899*]

The weather became thick soon after 2:00 p.m. as the *Vera* passed to starboard on her return crossing to Southampton, and again about 3:00 p.m. forcing a reduction in speed. The weather cleared, but continued hazy, and thickening weather was again encountered at about 3:30 p.m. but the speed was not reduced. The fog-signal of the *Stella* was blown regularly from 3:30 p.m.

The Casquets' fog-signal had been regularly sounding from 12.45 p.m. The chief lighthouse keeper stated that the mouth of the siren was turned to the west, facing the wind, in accordance with usual practice. Thick fog is known to deaden sound, and provide uncertainty as to its direction, and the sound of the siren was only heard once by the *Stella;* it is possible that her steam-whistle may have been blown almost simultaneously with the siren. The sound should have been audible within fifteen minutes range of the Casquets at the speed of the *Stella*.

Capt. Reeks was on the bridge when the weather became thick, and remained there after 3.30 p.m. It was the practice before leaving Southampton to give orders to the chief engineer to ring up to the bridge on two occasions when a certain number of revolutions had been made, so that the master might judge the distance from the Casquets. The first bell rang at 3:42 p.m. as the fog was increasing considerably. At 3:55 p.m. the engine-room bell was again rung up to the bridge.

The *Ibex* (Capt. Baudains), on the afternoon sailing from Weymouth, also found navigation difficult in the fog and lost her bearings near the Casquets. When rocks were sighted the mate took soundings, reversed the engines and remained stationary for some considerable time until the fog lifted. The siren of another steamer was heard around 4:00 p.m.

At 4:00 p.m. Hartop, the lookout man on the *Stella*, heard a siren blast, and reported 'Land right ahead' then 'Stop her'. The second officer stated he heard only one blast, and Capt. Reeks immediately gave orders, 'Port' 'Hard-a-port', while the second officer put the telegraph for the starboard engine to 'Stop,' and 'full speed astern'. The foot of the Casquet rock was suddenly clearly visible about 100 yards ahead, but the upper part could not be seen in the fog. The *Stella* paid off rapidly to starboard but scraped along the rock and swung to port, whereupon she hit a second large rock and drove hard into a partially submerged granite reef, coming to an immediate stop with sufficient force to shake her

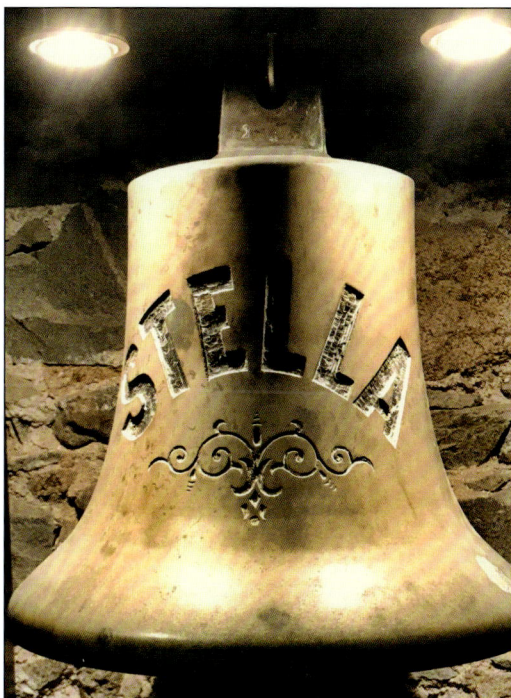

Ship's bell recovered from the *Stella* by Richard Keen in 1973 and on display in the Maritime Museum in Castle Cornet, St Peter Port. *(Author)*

95

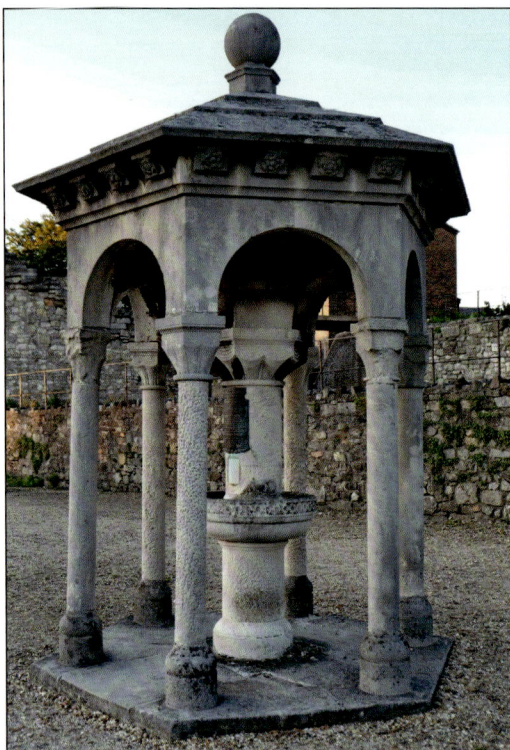

Memorial to Mary Rogers commemorating the **Stella** disaster in Southampton. *(Author)*

engines from their bed plates. The engines were stopped and two of the seven watertight doors closed, but the hull had sustained significant damage and water levels rose rapidly. *Stella* was lying near the foot of Noire Rocque held amidships by a submerged ledge, but with her stern above a thirteen fathom drop. Her bow was raised causing water to rush in and flood towards her stern.

Capt. Reeks called the crew to 'Stations', and to 'Hurry up and get the boats out', and gave instructions for the carpenter to sound the bell. The chief officer advised passengers to 'keep cool, there is plenty of time; all will be saved' and the crew assisted them with lifebelts. The starboard lifeboat was lowered and brought to the gangway. The chief officer called out, 'Ladies and children first' upon which some of the passengers gave a cheer. About thirty-seven persons, including four members of the crew got into her, and she shoved off from the vessel. The starboard cutter got away with about twenty six persons, including one lady, and the dinghy with two crew and eleven passengers, including nine ladies and a boy. No more ladies were seen on the starboard side of the vessel. When the starboard cutter was about twenty yards away from the vessel three ladies appeared on the main deck and appealed for help. The chief officer approached them and said, 'Ladies, your boat is on the other side', and they went with him. At this time the ship was rapidly sinking by the stern.

In the meantime the port cutter was lowered, and about four crew and eighteen passengers, including five ladies, left the ship in her. The port lifeboat had been lowered to the rail when the ship suddenly began to slip off the rocks into deep water. The lifeboat turned turtle stranding those women who had been reluctant to enter the boats. The angle of the *Stella* steepened until she stood vertically in the water before slipping under. Capt. Reeks was last observed gripping the handrail to maintain balance with a hand raised above his head.

Second mate George Reynolds, who initially went down with the vessel, resurfaced and swam to board the starboard lifeboat, where he took charge. A passenger swam to the same boat and was picked up, bringing the total number aboard to about thirty-nine. Soon after the starboard cutter fell in with the dinghy and took her in tow, the dinghy having previously picked up another passenger. The boats were lying very low in the water, with just 12 to 16 inches freeboard. Reynolds instructed the survivors to pull away from the rocks, and their lifeboat was dragged by the Alderney Race as far as Cherbourg, before the tide turned and they found themselves heading back towards Alderney, forcing them to row hard to avoid being dragged back onto the rocks. Around 7:00 a.m. they saw the *Vera* in the distance and tied handkerchiefs to an oar and a boat hook and waved them to attract attention. They were seen and picked up shortly afterwards. The *Lynx*, which was on the night crossing from Weymouth, picked up the starboard cutter and dinghy after 6:30

a.m. from a position about ten miles west of the Casquets. Neither vessel was aware of the sinking of the *Stella*.

The port lifeboat capsized when the *Stella* foundered, but some fourteen persons managed to reach her bottom. She was later righted by a wave, and all but two occupants managed to get into her, but they were unable find a plug to free the boat from water, although there were two properly attached. Two crew members and two passengers subsequently died from exhaustion and exposure. The lifeboat was eventually observed by a French coastguard, and the French tug *Marsouin* was sent to rescue them some seven miles north of Cherbourg at about 2:00 p.m. on Good Friday.

A furniture van stowed on the deck of the *Stella* floated off, and was clung to for a time by some passengers and crew, but was soon lost to view. One of the small deck rafts supported four persons, who subsequently transferred to the bottom of the port lifeboat. Two passengers clung to a grating; one was later picked up by the starboard lifeboat, whilst the other drowned. The steamer sank eight minutes after striking, so there was insufficient time to open out and lower the two Berthon collapsible boats, which were capable of containing seventy-four persons.

The non-arrival of the *Stella* in St. Peter Port at the scheduled time was initially not a cause for concern as the island was shrouded in fog and it was assumed that she had stopped at anchor or was proceeding slowly. The *Ibex* arrived at 7:00 p.m. running about two hours late, and concerns grew when the *Stella* still failed to arrive. The scale of the disaster did not become apparent until the *Vera* arrived towing an empty lifeboat at 8:00 a.m. on Good Friday, some 16 hours after the sinking. The L&SWR office was unable to provide passenger lists, as these had been held on board the ship, so it was not until bodies began to be recovered that the full death toll could be calculated.

The *Honfleur* was sent from St. Peter Port to look for survivors around the Casquets, but she only observed wreckage and two empty

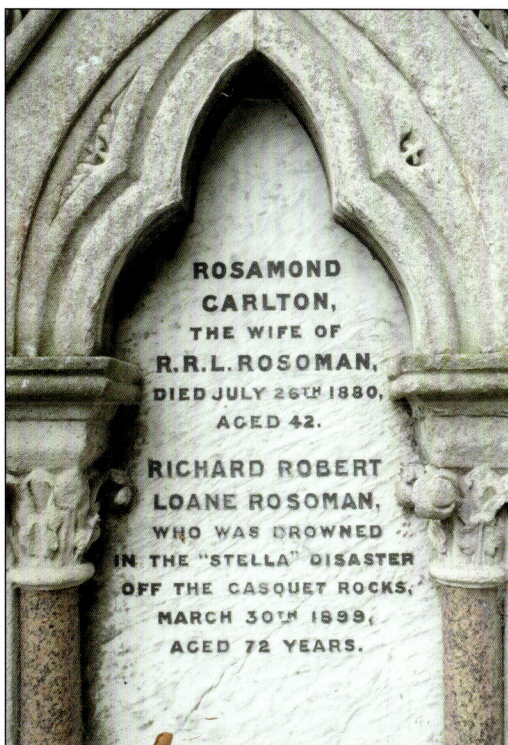

Memorial to Richard Rosoman, a passenger on the *Stella*, in Peartree Church, Southampton. *(Author)*

Mary Rogers, heroic stewardess on the *Stella*. A widower, her husband had been swept overboard and drowned on L&SWR service in 1883. She left two children and had been caring for her elderly father. *(Author's collection)*

lifeboats. The crew signaled the lighthouse crew to see if they had heard or seen a vessel wrecked, but although they had heard a steamer the previous afternoon, they were oblivious of the drama being played out around them. The *South Western* and *Frederica* also sailed from Southampton to look for survivors but found only wreckage. The *South Western* became lost in the fog whilst searching for bodies, which it was believed would drift towards the French coast, and briefly ran aground at St. Germain des Vaux near Cap de la Hague, but was not seriously damaged.

Both Islands were in official mourning from Easter Saturday, and relief funds were set up in Guernsey, Jersey and Southampton. Lily Langtry offered to donate the proceeds of a special stage performance to the widows of the drowned crew. Queen Victoria sent a telegram of sympathy to the General Manager of the L&SWR on 6 April.

The disaster received widespread media coverage. Attention quickly turned to why Capt. Reeks had maintained speed in such difficult conditions. The Jersey Times reported 'a grave suspicion on our part that the desire to enter harbour at a given hour to show what the *Stella* could do tempted the Captain to depart from ordinary prudence'. The Guernsey Evening Press observed on 6 April that 'evidence is accumulating to show that the terrible accident must be attributed in part to reckless navigation'. The Times commented on 11 April that 'many persons in the Islands attribute Capt. Reeks' anxiety to bring the *Stella* in on time to complaints which have appeared recently in the local press regarding the unpunctuality in the arrival of the South Western Company's boat'.

The Court of Inquiry noted that two circulars as to the navigation of the L&SWR's vessels, dated 2 September 1889, and 20 October 1892, respectively, were issued by the Company to their masters. The latter was sent to Capt. Reeks, but not the first, as he was not then a Captain. The first circular stated that proper care and sound prudence must be exercised during fog, and a sharp lookout kept, and the lead used in good time and freely. The second circular urged on captains the absolute necessity to be careful, and navigate their ships by careful and proper courses, and by the various marks when visible, and also not to run any risks or attempt any short cuts.

Counsel probed Capt. George Lewis, the L&SWR Assistant Marine Superintendent, about the question of racing, but he denied that it took place and stated that he knew that the GWR said it did not exist, and no instructions on the matter had been issued by either company.

The Court concluded that the cause of the stranding and consequent loss of the vessel was that she had not made good the course set, and that the master continued at full speed in thick weather when he must have known his vessel was in the immediate neighbourhood of the Casquets, without taking any steps to verify his position. George Reynolds, the second mate, who took charge of the starboard lifeboat, was given great credit for his courage and conduct. The Court drew no conclusion on the question of racing, despite five members of counsel claiming that is was 'self evident'. They recommended that the GWR and L&SWR arrange their schedules to arrive at different times in St. Peter Port and that lifeboats and cutters should be carried swung out in foggy weather during calm seas.

The Inquiry concluded that eighty-six passengers and nineteen crew were lost, but the accuracy of these figures remains in doubt. Among those lost was Capt. Reeks and stewardess Mrs. Mary Rogers, who in an act of heroism gave up her lifejacket for a passenger and refused to join a lifeboat to leave space for another passenger. Miss Frances Power Cobbe wrote to the Jersey Independent praising the heroism of Mary Rogers and offered to administer a fund to collect money for a monument to her heroism, pledging

Opposite page: Memorial window to Mary Rogers in the Lady Chapel at Liverpool Cathedral. *(Author)*

Stella

Stewardess of the

faithf[ul]

Rogers

serv[ant]

£25 of her own money.

> 'This poor stewardess, pursuing her family duties, courageously to the very last, aiding the lady passengers to secure their lifebelts and take their places in the boat, and then refusing to overcrowd that boat by entering it herself, and going down to death with the prayer 'God have me!' seems to be one of the most sublime figures in our island story'.
>
> [*Jersey Independent, 22 April 1899*]

This heroism struck a chord and Mary Rogers was commemorated in memorials in Southampton, and Postman's Park in London. As the Lady Chapel of Liverpool's Anglican Cathedral neared completion in 1908, the committee chose twenty-one 'noble women' to feature in a stained glass window, including Mary Rogers. She is depicted against a background of the Casquets rock and lighthouse.

The L&SWR made a grant of £3,000 to dependents of the crew who had been lost, and the company's staff contributed to a relief fund. The Board used the courts to limit their liability for damages to the statutory maximum of £15 per ton (totalling £15,885), but a provision of £25,000 was made in the accounts to meet compensation claims of £112,021; claims from railway free pass holders were not accepted, so the dependents of Joshua Le Mare, a chief officer of the London & North Western Railway (L&NWR) received no compensation.

With growing recognition that safety was far more important than speed, the L&SWR issued a strongly worded letter to masters on 12 June, 1899: -

> "I am instructed by the directors to send you a copy of the decision of the Board of Trade assessors in the case of the recent sad wreck of the *Stella*, involving the unfortunate loss of so many lives. I must particularly draw your attention to the answers given by the Court on questions Nos. 10, 13, 16, 17, 18, and 20. Several orders have been given from this office to the Captains at various times, and I am again to impress upon you that the first consideration under all and every circumstance is to be the safety of the passengers carried in the company's steamers. Comment has been made in the Press as to the company's vessels racing with the steamers of other companies to the Channel Islands. If any case of racing is proved, I am instructed to inform you that the Captains responsible will be subject to immediate dismissal. It is impossible to lay down any strict rules as to what Captains should do under varying circumstances, but in case of fog, soundings must be taken, and the speed so regulated that all possible risk may be avoided. Under no circumstance whatever are any unnecessary risks to be run, either by excessive speed or by attempting to take short cuts, but the vessels are to be navigated by the correct and proper courses, and by the various marks when visible. Officers and men must always be at their posts, and a good and efficient look-out kept both by the mates and men throughout the voyage; and whenever leaving or coming into port all hands must be at their posts for a sufficient and proper time after leaving or before approaching the port. It is the duty of the Captains to maintain strict discipline on the part of the crew, and not to allow any unnecessary attention to passengers on his own part or the officers or crew to interfere with the due and careful navigation of the ship. Boat drill should be frequent, and every man must know his post. The boats must be frequently and regularly inspected in order that it may be seen that they are fitted for every emergency and are so placed as to be ready for use on the shortest notice. The lifebelts must also be regularly overhauled at short

intervals. Be good enough to make this communication known to all chief and other officers on board your ship, and acknowledge receipt by signing and returning to me the annexed slip."

The *Stella* lay in such deep water that recovery was not an option. It was not until June 1973 that two divers found her 49m down on the sandy seabed, well to the south of the rocks where she foundered. In 1994 John Ovenden produced a BBC documentary 'The Wreck of the Stella', later working with David Shayer to write the definitive book on the disaster.

The L&SWR was able to fill the gap in the fleet with the newly arrived *Vera*, which had intended to be the back up vessel for Channel Island and Le Havre routes, but now found herself in a more prominent role. The L&SWR accepted a tender from Clydebank Engineering & Shipbuilding Co (later John Brown & Co) for a permanent replacement vessel for the *Stella* on 2 August.

Relationships between the GWR and L&SWR began to thaw and discussions began on a new co-operative arrangements between the two companies.

Encouraged by this development, and backed by the Pile family, attempts were made to revitalise the London service. The London & Channel Islands Steamship Co. Ltd. was incorporated on 2 April, with 405 shares being taken by Stanley Cheeswright and 485 by Matthew Wharton Ford, henceforth the managers were shown as Cheeswright & Ford; Stanley Cheeswright was appointed Chairman. The service, which had operated from the British & Foreign Steam Company Wharf, was moved to a berth at the East Dock, London Docks from 4 May. On 8 November an advert for the London & Channel Islands Steamship Co. Ltd. stated that 'the new and fast *Saxon* is to leave London Dock on Saturday 11th. Signed Cheeswright & Ford'. The following day the Board noted that the *Scott Harley* had been sold for £7,500 to foreign buyers being too small for the service, and that the *Saxon* had been fixed to run for six months at £450 per month.

Sir Charles Owens, general manager of the L&SWR, updated directors in June on the discussions with his counterparts at the GWR to 'curtail the steamboat service to the Channel Islands by both companies, and pool the receipts'. Agreement was reached between the two companies in August such that, for a period of fifteen years from the start of the winter timetable on 1 October 1899: -

1. For the winter service from 1 October to 30 April, each company would operate three sailings weekly on alternate nights from England, returning on alternate days.
2. For the summer service from 1 May to 30 September, each company would operate six times weekly, by night from Southampton and by day from Weymouth, both returning by day.
3. Gross receipts, less agreed deductions, would be pooled and divided in the ratio of the companies' corresponding receipts for 1897 and 1898.
4. Tickets would be inter-available between the operators.

The century ended with the signing of a formal pooling agreement between the GWR and L&SWR on 20 December 1899. Competition between the two companies had dramatically raised the speed and quality of the Channel Island fleets but had also heralded a decade of intense rivalry, with tragic consequences. The new century provided an opportunity for a fresh start.

CHAPTER FIVE

Co-operation and war 1900-1922

'There are two routes, viz that of the London and South Western Railway, via Southampton, and that of the Great Western Railway via Weymouth. For a long time these were worked independently, but by an arrangement made some years back the service is regarded as a joint one. During June, July and August there is a boat every night except Sunday from Southampton, and every afternoon except Sunday from Weymouth. Passengers are allowed to go on board the night steamers ant time after 8:30 p.m. For details as to times, etc., readers should consult the current timetables of the two Companies concerned. Return tickets are available by either Company's route, either via Southampton or via Weymouth'.

[Ward Lock Guide to the Channel Islands and parts of Brittany and Normandy, 1919]

The start of the new century heralded the end of intense competition between the two principal shipping operators to the Channel Islands and the practice of racing between the fleets was all but eliminated by the advent of non-conflicting timetables. From Weymouth the GWR employed the new *Roebuck* and *Reindeer*, backed up by the *Ibex*. At Southampton the L&SWR operated the *Frederica* and *Lydia*, with the *Vera* temporarily covering the relief vessel position whilst the *Alberta* was made ready for her first summer as replacement for the *Stella*; the *Victoria* could be found on the Jersey-St. Malo run. Although the outward appearance of the railway fleets differed, the services provided were very similar. Both routes could offer passage at around 19 knots, with first and cabin classes of travel available, with the latter in the poop on GWR vessels and forward on the L&SWR.

Tickets entitled passengers to travel to Weymouth by any train on the date of ticket issue and they could board from 8:30 p.m. for the following morning's 2:15 a.m. departure, or on the morning of departure for summer daylight sailings. Cold luncheon baskets were supplied on trains between London Paddington and Weymouth Quay, and private cabins for up to four persons could be reserved on the steamers.

The GWR used a homogeneous cargo fleet with the three sisters *Antelope, Gazelle* and *Lynx* each just over a decade old. The L&SWR in contrast employed a range of craft for their cargo services, including the veteran mail boats *Dora* and *Laura* and the *Cherbourg, Guernsey, Honfleur, St. Malo* and *South Western* which dated back up to three decades.

The cargo business was substantial; exports of vegetables from Guernsey in 1899 had totaled 1,265,023 packages, with over 1,000,000 packages of tomatoes and 117,934 of grapes. Huge congestion and tailbacks were caused around the harbours as individual growers took their horse drawn vehicles and queued to offload their packages. Flowers were packed in wooden boxes, tomatoes in heavy wickerwork baskets, vegetables in barrels, and grapes in secured wooden boxes lifted aboard by crane. The tomato baskets were trans-shipped by sliding them down a series of planks into the ship's hold, with the state of the tide dictating the speed with which they descended. The baskets returned empty and were stored behind the berths ready for collection. The lack of a schedule led to cargo being shipped on the mail boats, which left passengers sharing their trip with mountains of produce on the decks and frequently led to heavy delays. The railway companies did not begin to formally schedule their cargo services until 23 July 1900, when they bowed to pressure from the Chamber of Commerce, and timed departures from Guernsey each evening, except Sundays.

There was a significant inbound trade in cattle to Guernsey, which were landed at White Rock before being taken to the abattoir by the Albert Pier. The GWR discharged their cattle from the ships by a belly band, contrasting with the more humane use of horse boxes by the L&SWR.

In St. Peter Port, berths at the White Rock were dredged to be available at all states of the tide. No. 1 berth was used by the GWR and No. 2 by the L&SWR, with both companies using No. 3 as necessary. Cargo boats were breasted off the berths to the buoys if they blocked access for mail boats. The main offices and storage were between No. 1 and No. 2 berth, so No. 3 was unpopular as it soon became heavily congested. There were two

The **Caesarea** at speed. She was an uneconomic vessel to operate and spent many of her winters laid up in Southampton water. *(Ferry Publications Library)*

The *Ibex* was successfully raised after striking the reef off Platte Fougère on 5 January 1900, and was to return to service in almost new condition.*(Ambrose Greenway collection)*

steam cranes on each berth. Access to vessels was only available on the main deck, so as the tide fell it was necessary to use the lower landings to board the ships.

In St. Helier the GWR vessels were now berthing at the widened North Pier. The sheds had been replaced by new offices and stores, with five freshly built sheds numbered 'A' to 'E' dominating the Quayside. The L&SWR still occupied the Victoria Pier.

Services to the Islands were also provided by the London & Channel Islands Steamship Company from London East Dock on Tuesdays and Saturdays, by the Anglo-French Steamship Company from Plymouth Millbay on Mondays, and there were occasional sailings by the St. Malo & Binic Steamship Co. from Poole to Alderney and Guernsey, with the 59 passenger *Fawn*, which also served Jersey and St. Malo.

Any hopes that the new millennium might bring a safer era of travel were quickly dashed. The *Ibex* was once again the centre of attention. She left Weymouth for Guernsey and Jersey at 2:30 a.m. on 5 January 1900 under the command of Capt. Baudains, with thirty-three or thirty-four passengers, a crew of thirty-five, mails and about sixty tons of general cargo. The *Ibex's* engines were soon delivering her full winter speed of about 17½ knots in fine, clear conditions, with a smooth sea. At 5:39 a.m. the Casquets were passed about 3½ miles distant bearing east south east, the wind being light from the west. The ship continued on her course, and Capt. Baudains came on deck to take charge.

By 6.15 a.m. the leading lights for the Little Russel Channel were visible, and Capt. Baudains sought to take a bearing from the Casquets Light, now some fifteen miles behind him, as was normal practice. The Light was hidden from the position of the compass by the wheelhouse, so he ordered the helm to be starboarded in order to bring it into view. Having obtained a bearing, Capt. Baudains ordered the helmsman to bring her back on course, but the *Ibex* swung beyond it to south west by west and an irritated captain sent for another experienced helmsman.

The *Ibex* continued at full speed just half a mile from the Platte Fougère, a mile west of the line of lights leading through the channel. Sensing danger, Capt. Baudains ordered the helm to be put hard-a-starboard, and ran towards the telegraph with a view to stopping and reversing the engines, but almost immediately he observed the beacon on the Platte Fougère, and within a few seconds the vessel struck a rock on the reef to her starboard side before proceeding clear, still going at between 17 and 18 knots.

The engines were initially stopped and the boats put in readiness for evacuation, but Capt. Baudains then ordered full speed, hoping to be able to save the *Ibex* by beaching her at Herm or elsewhere. The *Ibex* began to go down by her head, and the inrush of water flooded the boiler room, dropping the steam pressure. The boats were lowered to the rail, allowing passengers to board them. With the ship filling fast the boats were put into the water and the remaining crew boarded. Capt. Baudains, believing that no one remained on board, was the last to leave the vessel at about 6:42 a.m.

As the boats shoved off, the voice of crewman Francis Randall was heard from the ship. Capt. Baudains called to him to run up the mast, but he went aft to the flagstaff. Several attempts were made to rescue him but he was dazed and said he could not swim. George St. Croix, a naval seaman from *HMS Excellent*, was still asleep in the second-class saloon, and did not wake when the other occupants abandoned ship. The cabin steward failed to spot him when making his final inspection, but the Court did not subsequently attach any blame to him. The *Ibex* went down head foremost in about 40ft of water, about 2¾ miles northeast of St. Peter Port near the Gant Rock.

Of the three boats that left the vessel, the starboard lifeboat was towed by a steam launch to St. Peter Port soon after 8:00 a.m., and two reached St. Sampson's at about 8:30 a.m. The officers and crew were praised by the survivors and Miss Lowman, one of the stewardesses, was presented with a gold watch; there were however complaints in the Guernsey Evening Press about the speed with which the lifeboats were launched. Newspapers reported the experience of a Mr. James of Guernsey, for whom it was his third shipwreck in a year, having also survived the *Stella* and the *Paris*.

Faced with the loss of their back-up vessel, the GWR dispatched the tug *Sir Francis Drake* from Plymouth and she arrived on site at 8:45 a.m. on 6 January with company officials and two divers to assist with salvage. The *Alert* had been able to salvage detritus from the *Ibex* on the falling tide, but her two funnels were washed away during a storm

A coach leaves for the Pomme D'Or hotel with passengers arriving off the Granville boat in St Helier, as a queue of horse and traps awaits business. The *Frederica* lies in the background. *(Author's collection)*

and heavy seas. The Marine Superintendent was said to be sanguine of success in the salvage operation. A diver was sent down on 8 January to try and recover the mails but he found the door to the mailroom obstructed. Two days later divers from the German salvage vessel *Neva* inspected the vessel, but decided against making a recovery proposal. Divers from the *Sir Francis Drake* eventually raised forty-two mailbags whose contents were delivered after being dried out and stamped to show they were from the *Ibex*. Divers recovered St. Croix's body on 23 January, a rug still wrapped around his legs. The *Sir Francis Drake* returned to Plymouth on 25 January.

The Court of Inquiry concluded that the loss of the *Ibex* was caused by the default of Capt. Baudains, and suspended his certificate for six months. He resigned from the GWR. The Court suggested to the GWR that, given the practice of taking a bearing from the Casquets Light when approaching the Little Russel Channel, arrangements should be made whereby this could be ascertained without altering the vessel's course. Both railway companies had previously lobbied for a lighthouse to support the use of the Little Russel Channel, but to no avail. The Court also recommended that lifebelts should be placed in the saloons and cabins and be visible to passengers, with advisory notices placed in the cabins, and other conspicuous places.

The *Ibex* was lying on a rock 230ft long, supported amidships, and was deemed to be in a salvageable condition. The GWR accepted a £15,000 tender from the Northern Salvage Company of Hamburg to raise her on a 'no cure, no pay' basis, as no British firm would contemplate the task. In the meantime the *Antelope* was drafted in by the GWR to support *Roebuck* and *Reindeer* on a daytime service pattern.

In February the L&SWR disposed of the forty-five year old paddle steamer *Alliance* to ship breakers in the Netherlands for £1,550. Meanwhile the *Alberta* was launched on 3 April as a permanent replacement for the *Stella*. The company had returned to the *Stella's* builders, now known as John Brown & Co Ltd, for the 710 passenger ship, specifying the same hull form and similar layout as the *Vera* with the addition of a bridge deck. *Alberta* was delivered to Southampton on 28 May in good time for the summer season and undertook her maiden sailing to the Islands on 1 June.

The Railway Magazine described her passenger accommodation thus: -

'The first class cabin is arranged amidships instead of aft, to lessen the risk of 'mal de mer', and provides accommodation for 136 passengers. The afterdeck has two and four-berth staterooms sufficient for forty passengers. The dining saloon, which is really magnificently fitted and furnished, is 11 ft high and 14 ft under dome, and has folding berths on the Pullman Car system. The second-class accommodation comprises three rooms, with space for fifty passengers'.

[*Railway Magazine January 1903*]

Work began to raise the *Ibex* on 30 May using cables passed underneath her hull, deriving buoyancy from two pontoons and hulks with a combined lifting capacity of 700 tons, and relying on the tide to raise her. The tug *Sea Addler* arrived from Cuxhaven to support local tugs in the first attempt to raise her on 9 July; this raised the bow by some fifteen feet, but the stern barely moved and the attempt was abandoned. A second attempt on 20 July also failed, but the *Ibex* was finally raised on the 21st by the efforts of seven vessels, and slowly brought to St. Peter Port, resting on the seabed at the harbour entrance, prior to being beached in the harbour the following morning. The vessel was in a sorry state after five months under water, with two indentations to starboard, one 40ft by 8ft, the other 6ft by 4ft, the bilge keel missing and with substantial damage to plating and frames.

'The appearance of the *Ibex* herself is most weird. Everywhere is seaweed of various kinds, sand and water. The cabins are, of course, filled with water, even at low tide, but the interior may be seen through such of the ports as were open at the moment the vessel struck the rocks... On the deck the scene is also strange. All doors and windows have been washed away by the strong tide of the Russel, leaving ugly gaping holes. Rails on the deck have been bent and broken, and the force of the water has bent even the strong wheels and blocks over which the rudder chains pass. A rapid transformation is however being effected. Work was first commenced on the bows of the vessel, and here all the seaweed has been scraped away, and the deck washed clear of sand'.

[*Guernsey Evening Press, 24 July 1900*]

On 29 July the *Ibex* had been sufficiently patched to allow her to be removed to St. Sampson's for further work to make her seaworthy for the passage to Cammell Laird, Birkenhead. *Ibex* was fitted with a temporary funnel and four vertical boilers to power steam pumps in the event that they were needed for the journey. She left St. Sampson's at 6:00 p.m. on 9 September, towed by the salvage tugs *Sea Addler* and *Albatross*, and arrived in the Yard on 12 September where work started to bring her back to serviceable condition.

The opening to passengers of the GWR's new 'cut-off' railway route between Westbury and Patney & Chirton on 1 October 1900 reduced the distance from London Paddington to Weymouth by 14 miles to 155¼ miles, allowing an acceleration of the service by 15 minutes.

In October 1900 the L&SWR sold their 1864 paddle steamer *Brittany* to Thos. W Ward for £2,500 and she was scrapped at Preston. She had been a favourite vessel of the company's directors, often used for their annual trip from Southampton round the Isle of Wight. The 1889 *Dora* had proved an unwise investment for the L&SWR, quickly outclassed by the GWR competition and with a reputation for rolling badly. With the arrival of the *Alberta* she was also deemed surplus to requirements and was sold to the Isle of Man Steam Packet Company in June for £12,000; she was renamed the *Douglas*.

The year's second major accident brought the loss of the Anglo-French Steamship Company's *Rossgull* on 4 December. She had arrived in Guernsey from Plymouth under the command of Capt. Blampied at 12:30 p.m. and, after discharging cargo, left for Jersey at 8:07 p.m. with eight passengers, seven of whom were bound for Brittany, and a crew of eleven or twelve, mostly from Plymouth. Capt. Blampied, who had been mate and then master of the *Commerce* for many years, had commanded the *Rossgull* since she had joined the Plymouth station in 1898. The weather was stormy and wet, with a near full moon. At 9:30 p.m. the mate reported that he had seen the Corbière light, but the weather was 'very dirty'. Sometime around 10:45 p.m. the *Rossgull* struck rocks at what was initially believed to be Grande Grune or Petite Grune off St Brelade's Bay, but turned out to be Hubaut Rocks. The engines were reversed and two rockets fired whilst attempts were made to get the ship off the rocks. One boat was lowered and filled with the eight passengers and three crew; initially attached to the stern, it drifted when the painter parted and the crew rowed to the Albert Pier where they arrived at 1:45 a.m. They were helped ashore and taken to the Temperance Hotel. Meanwhile the rest of the crew took to the vessel's second boat. The St. Helier lifeboat was launched shortly before 5:00 a.m., and a pilot boat went out under sail soon after, but despite an extensive search no trace of the second lifeboat could be found. The surviving passengers spoke highly of the professionalism of the crew and the perfect order maintained during the abandonment of the *Rossgull*.

The St. Helier lifeboat returned at 10:00 a.m. having gone as far as La Moye without seeing any trace of either the *Rossgull* or the missing boat. Capt. Breach, on the out-going GWR steamer, was asked to report if he saw anything on the way to Guernsey. He sent a brief telegram to the Harbour Master from Guernsey: 'Seen nothing'. The Captain of the incoming L&SWR steamer also stated he had seen nothing of the wreck or boat in crossing from Guernsey. Later, a paraffin or petroleum cask was washed ashore in the big roads and wreckage was reported in St Brelade's Bay and St. Clement's Bay, which included an oar, two deckchairs, several articles of clothing and a bag of onions.

At 8:19 a.m. Onesimus Dorey, the Guernsey Agent and managing director of the Anglo-French Steamship Company, received a telegram from Jersey stating 'Rossgull wrecked eleven last night near St Brelade's Bay. Boat and eight passengers and three crew reached the Albert Quay at one this morning. Believe crew land elsewhere in other boat.' By 11:45 a.m. the message had been updated to 'Pilot boat and lifeboat returned. Nothing seen but oil cask. Fear loss of other boat with remainder of crew. All passengers saved ... Surmised ship struck on Grunes off Noirmont Point'.

In a remarkable postscript to the incident, the lighthouse keepers at Carteret rescued fireman F. Whiting from the *Rossgull* some 43 hours after the vessel went down. He had lashed himself to a raft of spars as the ship sank and was alone in getting clear from the sinking vessel. He was able to return to Plymouth. A disaster fund was established in Jersey and had reached £162 by Christmas.

The *Ibex* finally returned to the Weymouth fleet on 21 April 1901, after completion of salvage and repairs totalling £47,250, which represented some eighty per cent of her original cost, but this was significantly less than the cost of a replacement vessel. The GWR took the opportunity to extend her promenade deck aft and she was to return to Weymouth an almost new ship.

The L&SWR's summer service was maintained by the *Alberta*, *Frederica* and *Lydia* from 1 July. *Ella* and *Hilda* had maintained the Southampton-St. Malo service since the loss of the *Diana* in 1895, but these ships were not up to the required modern standards, and the *Vera* operated experimentally on the route for the summer 1902 season, subsequently being

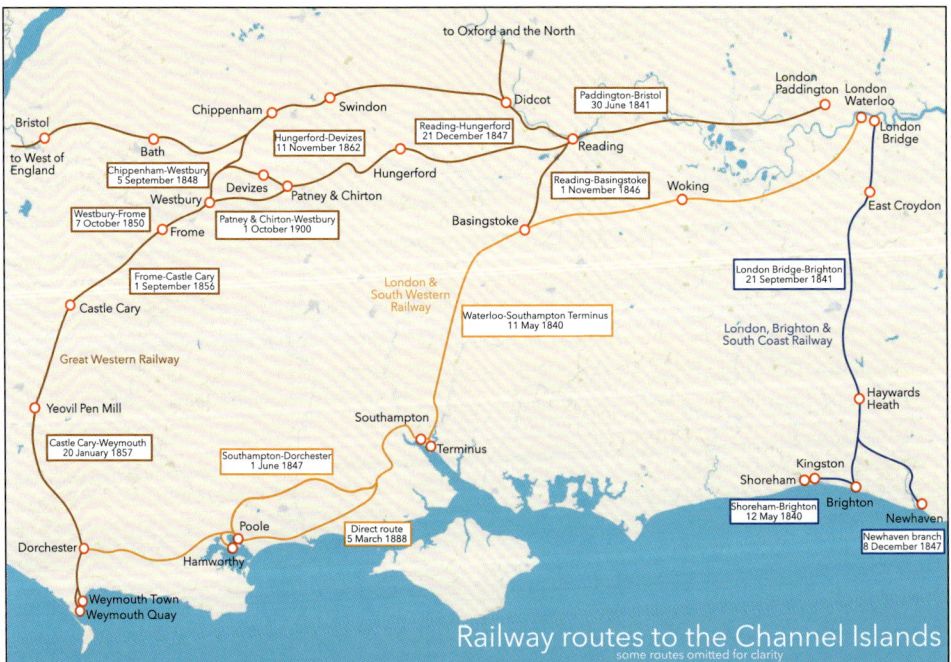

Railway routes to the Channel Islands
some routes omitted for clarity

altered to give her better facilities for the 1903 season.

The ever-growing number of liners using the expanding port of Southampton also created opportunities at Plymouth, where many liners called on their inbound journeys to discharge urgent mail and passengers who wished to reach London as quickly as possible. The reverse applied on the outward voyage and the GWR operated tenders to service this trade. The Lynx-class vessels were under-employed at Weymouth under the pooling agreement, so the *Lynx* and *Antelope* were dispatched to take up tender duties at Plymouth in January 1903. They also operated a range of excursions from the port. Even with this programme the Lynx-class vessels were under-utilised and the GWR looked at the possibilities of operating a service between Weymouth and Nantes in the autumn of 1903, but this idea was not progressed.

The new pattern of winter services was established as follows: -

Great Western
Tuesday, Thursday and Saturday

London Paddington*	dep	9:15 p.m.	Jersey		dep	8:00 a.m.
Weymouth Quay	arr	2:00 a.m.	Guernsey		dep	10:00 a.m.
	dep	2:15 a.m.	Weymouth Quay		arr	3:00 p.m.
Guernsey	arr	7:00 a.m.			dep	4:10 p.m.
Jersey	arr	9:00 a.m.	London Paddington	arr		8:20 p.m.

* calling at Reading, Swindon, Trowbridge and Yeovil

L&SWR
Monday, Wednesday and Friday, daily in summer

London Waterloo*	dep	9:50 p.m.	Jersey		dep	8:00 a.m.
Southampton Dock	arr	11:55 p.m.	Guernsey		dep	10:00 a.m.
	dep	12.30 a.m.	Southampton Dock		arr	4:00 p.m.
Guernsey	arr	7:00 a.m.			dep	4.30 p.m.
Jersey	arr	9:30 a.m.	London Waterloo	arr		6.30 p.m.

* calling at Basingstoke, Winchester and Eastleigh

The L&SWR watched the Plymouth trade developing, and in late 1903 withdrew the *Victoria* from Jersey, altered her facilities to allow passengers to make full use of the boat deck, and sent her to Plymouth from 25 March 1904. The *Laura* replaced the *Victoria* on the Jersey station and increased the frequency of sailings from Jersey to St. Malo to six per week. *Honfleur* maintained the weekly winter sailing.

St. Malo was served thrice-weekly from Southampton by the *Ella* and *Hilda*, with the faster *Vera* added in summer 1903 after the successful experiment of the previous year. The start of the summer service on 1 June brought daytime L&SWR sailings with *Alberta*, *Frederica* and *Lydia* in June, July and August, reverting to night crossings during September. The cargo services were operated by *Cherbourg*, *Maria* and *St. Malo*.

In 1904 the *Lynx*, *Antelope* and *Gazelle* were used primarily for GWR cargo traffic and as relief vessels, but they continued to spend time as tender vessels for the Ocean Liners at Plymouth.

With increasing numbers of ships offering private cabins, the L&SWR withdrew older vessel from their fleet to allow their accommodation to be modernised. *Lydia* returned to service on 16 June 1904 after a complete rebuild of her first-class accommodation, which was placed aft in the vessel. There were more improvements across the rest of the ship, with the mainmast removed and a new large cabin built on the aft promenade deck to accommodate the ladies' lounges. Private cabins and larger dining saloons were also added to the *Frederica* and *Lydia* during their winter 1904-05 refits. *Frederica* had a new boiler installed by Day, Summers & Co capable of burning cheaper and smokier fuel; this necessitated the fitment of an extension to her funnel. She already had a 9ft extension fitted to her old funnel in 1903 in an unsuccessful effort to improve performance under natural draught and reduce her coal consumption.

In October 1904 the L&SWR placed a £13,200 order with Gourlay Bros of Dundee for a new cargo steamer, to be known as the *Ada*. She made first trial trip on 20 April 1905 and sailed from Southampton to Jersey with cargo of Scottish coal on the 29th. She was to be primarily employed on the Southampton-Honfleur route, but made intermittent visits to the Islands.

On 26 January 1905 the *Roebuck* suffered a fire in faulty asbestos lagging on her saloon-stove pipe, whilst wintering at Neyland. The GWR fire brigade was quickly on the scene, but applied water to extinguish the fire so enthusiastically that the *Roebuck* sank; she was raised nine days later. The *Roebuck* was estimated to be worth £30,000 and the company felt it a good investment to have her saved. She returned to service at Weymouth on 1 June after undergoing £11,000 of repairs at Barrow in Furness. The GWR purchased the *Melmore,* a second hand cargo steamer, from the Earl of Leitrim on 13 May, to augment the Weymouth fleet and support the Jersey potato traffic. She arrived in Jersey the following day. This reduced the company's reliance on chartered James Fisher boats during the main produce season.

The performance of the *Ada* encouraged the L&SWR to place another cargo steamer order with Gourlay Bros of Dundee in May for the *Bertha,* to be deployed on the Southampton-Honfleur route. The *Bertha* was launched on 9 November and arrived for the first time at Southampton on 2 December loaded with coal.

The L&SWR suffered another blow when the *Hilda* struck the Pierres des Portes rocks approaching St. Malo during a heavily delayed crossing in snow squalls on 18 November. There were only six survivors from a total of 138 on board. Such evidence as could be

The **South Western II** arrives in Granville from Jersey. *(Author's collection)*

The wreckage of the *Hilda* after striking the Pierre des Portes rocks off St Malo on 18 November 1905. James Grinter survived by clinging to the mast throughout the night. *(Ambrose Greenway collection)*

gleaned about the tragedy came from James Grinter, the sole surviving crewmember.

The *Hilda* left Southampton at 10:00 p.m. on 17 November 1905, bound for St. Malo with around 109 passengers and ten tons of general cargo, manned by a crew of twenty-eight (including the pilot), under the command of Capt. Gregory. He was an experienced master and had sailed into St. Malo on about 1,000 occasions, and was described by several witnesses as a man 'proverbial for his caution', and one whom passengers specially selected to travel with.

Capt. Gregory had delayed the departure for an hour and three-quarters owing to the presence of fog, and did not leave until it lifted. Yarmouth was reached shortly after 11:00 p.m. and Capt. Gregory chose to anchor after encountering further fog, resuming the voyage at about 6.00 a.m. on 18 November. The Grand Jardin light was seen about 6.30 p.m. around half a mile distant, bearing a little on the port bow. A heavy snow squall shut in all the lights, and Capt. Gregory ordered the engines to be slowed and the ship's head was brought to seaward. Grinter remained on the bridge until 8.30 p.m. as the *Hilda* manoeuvered off the land, the weather being squally with heavy snow falling. The master, pilot, and chief mate were all on the bridge when Grinter went below, his watch on deck being over.

Grinter slept in his bunk, but woke to the sound of the ship striking rocks at about 11:00 p.m.; he and the remainder of the watch rushed to their stations on the bridge and at the boats. At this time, it was snowing hard, a strong easterly wind was blowing, and there was a heavy sea. Capt. Gregory ordered the boats to be got ready, and the starboard lifeboat was lifted out of the chocks but it could not be lowered into the water on account of the nearness of the rocks. The port lifeboat and cutter were also unavailable. The master ordered the starboard cutter to be lowered, but a heavy sea smashed it against the ship's side rendering it useless and turning it upside down. About this time, the foremast, which had previously been seen swaying, went over the side. While all this was going on, Capt. Gregory had been alternately firing distress rockets and sounding the whistle.

The saloon passengers congregated round the after hatch, the most sheltered place on the vessel, and were assisted with lifebelts by the crew, while a group of Breton onion-sellers gathered along the starboard side under the bridge, assisting one another in a similar manner. As an attempt was made to launch the port quarter boat, the after part of the ship sank in the water, then a heavy sea swept over her stern, and everybody was washed off the deck. Grinter was washed alongside the private cabin under the port main rigging, which he managed to seize and climb up into, accompanied by the chief mate and the cook; the starboard main rigging was also full of people. The *Hilda* broke in two some twelve minutes after she struck the rocks, heeling over to such an extent that those who were clinging to the rigging found themselves in the water, and causing the loss of most of the others. *Hilda* righted again to an angle of about forty-five degrees, although subsequently rolled throughout the night. The chief mate and cook were lost during the night.

The vessel had struck on one of the Pierres des Portes rocks about six cables from the Grand Jardin light, and about two cables west of the Chenal de la Petite Porte. As it was high water at St. Malo at 9.53 p.m. on 18 November the vessel must have stranded when the tide had been falling for about an hour.

The *Ada* left St. Malo at 8.30 a.m. on 19 November, after being delayed overnight by the snowstorm; her crew spotted the men on the mast of the *Hilda* around 9:30 a.m., and sent out a rescue boat, a feat accomplished with great difficulty. A French pilot cutter also sent her boat, and managed to save one of the Breton onion sellers who had spent the night on the forecastle of the *Hilda*. The sole survivors consisted of James Grinter, A.B., and five Bretons, who were conveyed to hospital at St. Malo.

The first intelligence of the catastrophe was conveyed to St. Malo by the *Ada*, as the distress signals had not been seen from the shore, even though L&SWR employees were on the pier most of the night. Mrs. Eveleen Grindle, now the widow of one of the passengers on the *Hilda*, who was staying at St. Malo, later claimed she had seen the rockets but assumed they were signalling the vessels arrival.

The Court of Inquiry was unable to determine how the *Hilda* came to hit the rocks as 'all those who could have thrown light upon the matter were drowned'. It was not inclined to attribute the disaster to either rashness or negligence and concluded that every possible effort was made by the master, officers, and crew to save life. It did however suggest that although masters of steamers belonging to the L&SWR were required to provide their own charts - and in this instance, there was no reason to believe that the charts relied upon were not up to date - it was better that owners should supply all charts and sailing directions.

The L&SWR donated £3,000 to a relief fund and were quick to place an order for a replacement vessel with Gourlay Bros, who were tasked with building the *Princess Ena*, on a similar specification to the *Vera*, but to an accelerated timescale at a cost of £345,041.

On 23 January 1906 the Anglo-French Steamship Company advertised that the *Devonia* had been withdrawn from the Islands service replaced by the *Ferrum* on a cargo-only basis from the following Monday. The company was soon hit by the loss of the *Ocean Queen*.

The *Ocean Queen* left London at 3:00 a.m. on 28 February 1906, bound for Jersey and Guernsey under the command of Capt. Jones with a crew of twelve, and about 200 tons of general cargo. The vessel proceeded down the English Channel, and at about 1:30 p.m. on 1 March, Cap de la Hague bore south east about three miles distant; the weather at this time was hazy, with sleet and rain, a strong westerly wind and a rough sea. Sark was seen nearly abeam at 5:00 p.m. but was soon lost in the hazy weather; the wind veered to west-north-west with a heavy sea, and the ship was only making a speed of five or six knots. As the vessel proceeded southward the weather became worse, and nothing was seen of Corbière light or Jersey.

The *Ocean Queen* continued on her southerly course hoping for clearer weather south of the high land of Jersey; this proved to be correct, for at about 7:30 p.m. a light was seen

A crowd gathers as the *Roebuck* arrives in St Helier. The steam crane is made ready on the Quay. *(Author's collection)*

ahead from the north west gas buoy off the Minquiers. At 8:00 p.m. the course was set north, and the engines were put at full speed to counteract a perceived adverse current and take the ship within range of the Corbière light. At 10:00 p.m. with the rain and sleet continuing and no land being visible, the vessel's head was put at west northwest and the speed reduced to slow, to await daylight or clearer weather. The vessel was going head to wind and sea, and was making little headway, being carried northward by the tide.

The weather continued to be very poor, with the vessel rolling and pitching heavily and shipping much water. At about 1:55 a.m. on 2 March, Capt. Jones estimated that he was some seven or eight miles to the south of St. Martin's Point, Guernsey, and altered the course to north; hearing the cry of a gull, he became alarmed, and ordered the helm hard-a-starboard and put the engines at full speed ahead. Before she could turn westward the *Ocean Queen* struck on Les Kaines d' Aval rock, drove over it, stranded, and finally became a total wreck in Les Tielles Bay on the south coast of Guernsey. One of the lifeboats and the working boat were immediately got out and the vessel abandoned. The crew remained in the boats by the wreck until about 8:00 a.m. when they were picked up and landed by a pilot cutter.

The Inquiry concluded that the loss of the *Ocean Queen* was not caused by any wrongful act of the master and chief officer, but by an error of judgment on the part of Capt. Jones in not making use of the lead, and in underestimating the distance run and the northerly set of the tide. Capt. Jones had made about 200 voyages to the Channel Islands under all conditions of wind and weather and possessed pilotage certificates for both Jersey and Guernsey. Whilst holding that the master committed an error in judgment, the Court was 'fully sensible of the very difficult position in which he was placed, and desires to place on record its appreciation of his vigilant and constant attention to the navigation of his vessel'.

The *Ocean Queen* was replaced by the 300 ton *Wave Queen*. This proved a good move for the company, as the *Wave Queen* was better suited to the bi-weekly service. There were thoughts of further expansion to a four-ship fleet, but poor trading conditions constrained this idea.

In May the L&SWR sold the 1865 *St. Malo* to James Power & Co. of the Power

The *Alberta* at low tide in St Helier. *(Author's collection)*

Steamship Company of London for £300. She did not sail for her new owners, but was broken up in the Netherlands.

Construction of the *Princess Ena* was rapid; she was launched on 25 May and underwent sea trials on 22 June before being delivered to Southampton on 15 July. She entered service on the Southampton-St. Malo route on 18 July. The *Princess Ena* was the last channel steamer to be fitted with two three cylinder triple expansion reciprocating engines driving twin screws, which gave her a top speed of 19 knots and a service speed of 16 knots, allowing her to make the passage to St. Malo in nine and a half hours. The L&SWR next decided that a purpose-built tender was required to meet the growing Ocean Liner trade at Plymouth, and ordered another new ship from Gourlay Bros to be named the *Atalanta*. She was to be one of the last ships to be built at the Gourlay Yard, as the company was wound up in 1908 following financial difficulties.

During the summer months the *Lynx* was chartered to a Jersey syndicate to operate cruises round the island as well as day trips to Sark and France.

In November the *Ella* and the *Princess Ena* collided in fog off Cap de la Hague. The *Ella* was heading for St. Malo and the *Princess Ena* inbound for Southampton. The *Ella* struck the *Princess Ena* a slanting blow on her starboard bow, damaging several plates and beams, fortunately well above the water line. The *Princess Ena's* bulwarks were stove in for a distance of 25ft, but she was able to proceed to Southampton. The Board of Trade Inquiry blamed the master of the *Ella* for excessive speed; he was demoted to cargo service at a loss of £26 in salary.

In April 1907 the L&SWR sold the 1871 *Maria* to Robert J Campbell of Southampton under the trading address of the Anatolian Steamship Company of Galata, Constantinople for £700. The tender *Atalanta* was launched on 25 April and undertook sea trials on 9 May, taking up her duties at Plymouth on 27 May. On her arrival, the *Victoria* was converted back from a tender vessel, had her mainmast restored, and returned to the Jersey-France route.

The GWR's Plymouth-based vessels undertook other work as required in addition to their normal tender duties; in March 1907 the *Antelope* worked on the White Star liner *Suevic*, which had gone ashore at the Lizard. The following year, the GWR had two new tenders built for service at Plymouth and the Lynx-class ships were again displaced.

On 19 May the *Princess Ena* made her first visit to Jersey with a party of musicians from St. Malo for the Concours Musical. The vessel was received positively by the Jersey Evening Post on 23 May when her master described her as "the best sea boat that has ever been in these waters, and even in a rough sea, keeps an even keel and rides like a duck".

GWR cargo traffic through Weymouth had become synonymous with the transport of the Guernsey tomato and grape crops. There was commercial sense in converting under-utilised vessels to handle the cargo business and in February 1908 the *Gazelle* was sent to Cammell Laird, Birkenhead for conversion to a cargo boat, removing her saloon and other passenger accommodation and clearing deck space to make her fit for cargo handling at cost of £4,900. She returned to service in May for the main produce season. Not to be outdone, the L&SWR sent the *Guernsey* for conversion to a cargo steamer through removal of her passenger accommodation in the same month.

The night of 19-20 May 1908 proved eventful for the L&SWR, with a heavy fog contributing to the *Alma* being grounded off Bembridge on the Isle of Wight, *Laura* striking the shingles bank off the Needles and, more seriously, *Princess Ena* hitting the Paternoster Rocks to the north west of Jersey.

The *Princess Ena* left Southampton at 7:15 p.m., on the 18 May in clear weather, bound for St. Malo under Capt. Holt, in his first year on the St. Malo service. She carried a crew of thirty-six with forty-eight passengers, and five tons of general cargo. The *Princess Ena* passed the Needles at 9:36 p.m. going full speed, about 14 or 15 knots. At 11:00 p.m. fog set in, speed was reduced appropriately and the whistle kept going with Capt. Holt taking charge on the bridge.

At 2.30 a.m. on 19 May, Capt. Holt stopped the ship to take soundings, and after proceeding again, continued to sound at intervals without satisfactory result up to 7.56 a.m., when a good cast was made in thirty fathoms to a gravel bottom, and the master decided to anchor. The ship remained at anchor for almost twenty-one hours until 4:40 a.m. on 20 May, surrounded by fog the whole time. The weather then cleared and Capt. Holt found the ship to be four miles north east of Cap de la Hague. The anchor was hove up at 5:00 a.m. and the *Princess Ena* rounded the cape, and headed for a position east of Sark. Capt. Holt saw Sark at 6:50 a.m. and maintained full speed up to 7:20 a.m., when the weather set in hazy, and speed was reduced to half speed, about seven knots. The whistle was kept going, and a lookout maintained on the forecastle.

At 7:44 a.m. the lookout reported "breakers broad on the starboard bow." The master saw them and immediately had the helm put hard to port, and the engines full speed astern. Thirty seconds afterwards *Princess Ena* struck something under the bridge. The engines were stopped, but the ship listed to port, and floated clear. The anchor was let go, watertight doors closed, and the boats got out in about six minutes. A cast of the lead showed fourteen fathoms. The carpenter sounded the wells, and although she was found to be making water in the main hold, the leak was not extensive, and passengers were instructed to remain aboard. Capt. Holt was satisfied that he had struck the westerly edge of the Paternoster rocks, and he marked on the chart a rock which stands 12ft out of the water at low water a quarter mile within the north-west reef of the Paternosters.

At 8:10 a.m. the anchor was hove up, and the *Princess Ena* headed for St. Helier, where she arrived at 10:47 a.m. to take the ground at the Albert Pier: -

'An examination of the vessel's hull at low water this afternoon disclosed the fact that the plates beneath the main hold, just forward of amidships, have been dented in for a length of several feet, while number of rivets have been driven in by the force of the blow. It is principally through these rivet holes that the leakage took place, but the plates have not been penetrated. With the exception of a drawn rivet or two further aft, the damage is confined to the main hold, the water being kept from spreading to the other compartments by the watertight bulkheads. The vessel had but a few tons of cargo on board, and this was discharged this afternoon. It is intended to plug the rivet-holes and interstices between the plates, and the *Ena* will probably sail for Southampton tomorrow morning. The quay alongside the *Princess Ena* was the centre of attraction this afternoon, and was visited by a large number of curious sightseers, who watched with interest the process unloading the quantity of empty baskets and barrels of which the vessel's cargo principally consisted. Many of the baskets were soaked with the water, which had found its way into the hold. A few enthusiasts ventured down into the mud of the harbour and inspected what could be seen of the damage done'.

(*Jersey Times, 20 May 1908*)

On return to Southampton the damage was found to be slight and the *Princess Ena* was satisfactorily repaired in four days. The Court of Inquiry found that the striking of the *Princess Ena* was caused by her having been set by an abnormal tide to the eastward of her proper course, and by Capt. Holt misjudging his distance off Sark.

The GWR Magazine portrayed a typical scene at Weymouth Quay on 14 April 1908. The *Lynx* and *Roebuck* brought in 20,000 boxes of produce, largely from Guernsey, and these were forwarded in a special train comprising thirty railway vans heading primarily for London and Manchester, but with significant quantities for Edinburgh, Glasgow and the north of England.

The arrival of the mail boats was still a newsworthy item in the Islands: -

'Fairly good passages were made mail boats this morning, the *Ibex* arriving from Weymouth at 8.52 and the *Frederica* from Southampton, 9.28. The *Victoria*, from St. Malo, came in just ahead of the Ibex at 8.41'.

[*Jersey Times, 25 September 1908*]

'Good times were made by both the incoming mail boats this morning, the *Alberta* arriving at 8.53 and the *Roebuck* at 9.05. The two steamers were in close company all the way from the sister island, the *Alberta* leaving St. Peter Port three minutes ahead of the *Roebuck*, and rounding Noirmont Point five minutes before her. The outgoing Great Western steamer was passed between the Breakwater and Noirmont. Much interest was taken in the times made by the two vessels. The *Laura* arrived from Southampton with cargo at six o'clock this morning, and after discharging, took the place of the *Victoria* on the steamer service to St. Malo and Granville, leaving for the latter port this afternoon. The *Victoria* left for Southampton at 9.20 this morning, to undergo overhaul after her busy season's running'.

[*Jersey Times, 26 September 1908*]

'An excellent run from Southampton made by the *Lydia* this morning, in spite of the strong breeze and far from smooth sea. She left Guernsey at 7.05, but was somewhat retarded between the Islands by foul tide, and entered the harbour at 8.47. The *Ibex*, which left Guernsey at 7.45, arrived at 9.40. The *Laura* arrived from Granville at 8.55, she, the *Lydia*, and the French torpedo boat *293* being signalled at Fort Regent at the same time'.

[*Jersey Times, 27 September 1908*]

Fire broke out in the engine room of the *Roebuck* midway between Guernsey and Weymouth on 3 October 1908. The crew was able to contain the blaze through use of the fire hoses, with passengers assembled forward of the fire. The blaze was extinguished within twenty minutes and little damage was done, although the paintwork of the funnel casing was scorched and peeled by the heat. The *Roebuck's* passage was not delayed, and she arrived at Weymouth at 3.10 p.m. The *Ibex* took the return sailing to the Islands, as it proved impossible to discharge the *Roebuck's* large cargo in time.

The start of the winter schedule posed problems for growers: -

'The change of service, by which only one mail steamer sails from St. Helier each morning, commencing, as it has, at the busiest part of the tomato export season, is proving of no little inconvenience to shippers, who have to get their produce down to the quay in time to be put aboard a boat leaving at the early hour of 8 a.m. In consequence of this, there was record shipment on the *Roebuck* this morning, of over 20,000 packages, and at one time there was a long line of vans extending nearly the whole length the North Quay, awaiting their turn. It was found impossible to ship the whole quantity of tomatoes by 8 o'clock, and the steamer was unable to leave until over half an hour after her advertised time'.

[*Jersey Times, 10 October 1908*]

In 1907, Onesimus Dorey set up the family company Onesimus Dorey & Sons, registered at North Quay, St. Peter Port. By this time he had three sons, although it was only his oldest, Cecil, who was to succeed him in the business. With the establishment of the company the need for a separate Anglo-French Steamship Company Ltd was limited and the company was wound up in voluntary liquidation in November 1918. Trade recovered sufficiently for the London & Channel Islands Company to replace the *Wave Queen* with the larger *Foam Queen* in 1909.

In 1909, the *Melmore* was transferred to the GWR Weymouth-Nantes service, but also operated occasionally from the Islands to Plymouth. She reverted to Islands' service in 1910. The GWR Magazine again reported on freight traffic through Weymouth in June 1909, noting that there had been substantial outbound traffic of racing pigeons from Lancashire, Yorkshire and Cheshire, with up to 25,000 birds being released on arrival in the Islands. The Jersey potato traffic was particularly heavy, and one of the chartered vessels had brought in 400 tons. Guernsey flower traffic had peaked that season at 22,000 boxes received on 15 April 1909.

The shorter cross-channel routes had pioneered the use of turbine steamers following the successful introduction of *The Queen* in 1902, and the L&SWR evaluated the potential of the new technology before ordering the *Princess Ena*. With more replacement ships being required for the Island services, the matter was again considered in 1909. In October the L&SWR placed an order with Cammell Laird for two 20-knot triple-screw steamers for delivery by 30 June 1910, to be powered by three direct-drive turbines. Turbine steamers offered a considerable reduction in noise and vibration compared to reciprocating engines. The vessels had a three-shaft arrangement, with a central shaft linked to the high pressure turbine, and two wing shafts driven by low pressure turbines. The design incorporated a port propeller that rotated in the opposite direction to the other two to overcome a tendency to yaw to starboard at speed. The new vessels were built to accommodate 980 passengers in two-class accommodation with facilities for both long day and night crossings The company's initial choice of names for the vessels - *Anglia* and *Gallia* - was rejected by the Board of Trade, so the old Roman names *Caesarea* and *Sarnia* were substituted.

With the acceleration of the GWR services, the pooling arrangements between the companies required renegotiation, and on 13 May 1910 a new agreement was put in place. The growing GWR share of Island business resulted in pooling payments commuted to a fixed sum of £5,000, payable for the remaining five years of the agreement. L&SWR traffic was restricted to routes east of St. Malo, with the GWR restricted to routes west of Brest. Whilst this marked the end of L&SWR's ambitions for a Southampton-Roscoff route, the agreement permitted the GWR to maintain existing services to Cherbourg. All Ocean Liner tender duties at Plymouth were transferred to the GWR and the L&SWR Plymouth-based tender *Atalanta* was sold to the GWR for £24,500, sailing from Southampton on 10 June for delivery at Fishguard three days later. In June the GWR bought the *Chelmsford* from the Great Eastern Railway to replace the *Melmore* for their Brest service, which operated from Plymouth during the summer and Weymouth in winter. The *Lynx* class vessels had maintained the service, but the *Ibex* and *Reindeer* also featured at peak periods. The *Chelmsford* was renamed the *Bretonne* but was to be sold in October 1911 after the route closed on 30 September.

The year was another success for the L&SWR, with 154,766 passengers and 180,000 tons of cargo passing through Southampton. A further 40,693 passengers were carried between Jersey and France, and 14,519 sailed between the Islands.

During 1910 the London & Channel Island Steamship Company started a service from London to St Brieuc, later extended to Morlaix, with the intention that this would justify a third vessel to back up two on the Channel Islands run. The company moved into the Channel Island passenger business in November when the twenty-passenger capacity *London Queen* was delivered. She had triple expansion engines capable of generating a speed of 10 to 10.5 knots, with her Saturday departure from the Eastern Basin at London Docks to Jersey taking twenty-seven/twenty-eight hours for the passage. The return fare of £1 was valid for a month; the single fare was 12s 6d, with meals served at an inclusive 4s 6d per day. Passengers could do a round trip with meals for £1 18s., staying on board the vessel without extra charge whilst she lay in port. *London Queen* offered berths for twenty-two passengers compared to the twelve on the *Island Queen* and *Foam Queen*. The Railway & Travel Monthly reported: -

> 'She has proved to be an excellent sea boat, the boisterous weather experienced at the end of March and during April, making a severe, but satisfactory test of the vessel's powers'.

The London & Channel Island Steamship Co. placed an order for the *Channel Queen*, based on the success of the *London Queen*. She offered berths for forty to fifty passengers 'in first class style' and took up the Saturday departures on her arrival in July under Capt. Wetherall, transferred from the *Island Queen*, displacing the *London Queen* to the Tuesday rotation. The *Island Queen*, *Norman Queen* and *Saxon Queen* were now used only as required.

Delivery of both the *Caesarea* and the *Sarnia* for the L&SWR was delayed by a boilermakers strike at the Cammell Laird shipyard, with the *Caesarea* not launched until 26 May 1910 and the *Sarnia* following on 9 July. The company started a daylight service on the Southampton-Le Havre route from 22 July to meet growing demand using the *Lydia*, which had been due to be replaced on the Islands' services by the two new vessels; the *Frederica* was therefore retained on the Islands route.

The 980-passenger capacity *Caesarea* was finally delivered to Southampton on 17 September, too late for the summer season. A contemporary description stated: -

'She features accommodation for 186 First Class passengers, 114 in double cabins, and accommodation for 114 second class passengers. In the deck house on the promenade deck are the ladies saloon at the after end, a gentlemen's saloon forward, and 26 cabins each of two berths. First class state rooms on the promenade deck contained an upper berth that could be folded back to create a sofa for daytime passages. This deck house has double door entrances at both the fore and aft ends, the forward entrance being the main reception entrance for saloon passengers, and communicating by two stairways to the smoke room, general lounge and writing room, which are at the fore end of the boat deck. The ladies' saloon - a good example of the Sheraton style - is the piece de resistance, being framed in beautifully figured mahogany with inlaid decorations, the furniture including a large divan seat and basket chairs, being in keeping with the general scheme, and upholstered in silk tapestry of Rose de Barri shade. The floor is covered by a rich Axminster carpet. At the forward end of the main deck is the dining saloon, extending across the ship, framed in light oak, and seating 64 persons. Small tables for four are placed along the side of the ship - a most comfortable arrangement for families and small parties.

For second class passengers the gentlemen are located in the poop, with ladies being housed at the fore end of the after well in a large saloon, which is entered on a staircase leading from the after end of the promenade deck house. A spacious boat deck promenade extended over the poop deck house to the sides of the ship'.

[*Railway Magazine, May 1911*]

The article went on to state that the: -

'greater outstanding advantage which turbine-driven steamers possess over one driven by reciprocating engines and twin screws is the absolute freedom from noise and vibration. The thud of the engine and the noise caused by the exertion of enormous horse-power do not exist, and a wakeful passenger might well imagine that the ship stopped, so little oral evidence is there of propulsion'.

[*Railway Magazine, May 1911*]

The L&SWR summer schedule from 1 June to 30 September 1910 was: -

London Waterloo	dep	9:45 p.m.	Jersey	dep	8:00 a.m.
Southampton Docks	dep	12:30 a.m.	Guernsey	dep	10:00 a.m.
Guernsey	arr	6:45 a.m.	Southampton Docks	arr	4:30 p.m.
Jersey	arr	9:15 a.m.	London Waterloo	arr	6:30 p.m.

The *Sarnia* undertook trials on 23 December 1910 but required further modification and was not finally delivered to Southampton until 4 April 1911. Her maiden voyage left Southampton on 13 April and the L&SWR enforced nominal late delivery penalties of £500 on Cammell Laird. The two vessels were the L&SWR's only direct drive turbine ships and did not prove successful, as the high revolution speed of the engines proved too fast to be economical, and made the ships difficult to manoeuvre at slow speeds. They soon found themselves employed only in the summer, being laid up in Southampton Water during the winter months. The *Frederica* was surplus to requirements after the arrival of the *Caesarea* and the *Sarnia* and after her final sailing on 26 June she was sold to H. E. Moss for £9,000. Moss re-sold her to the Turkish government. The *Honfleur* was sold to S. Galbraith of Glasgow for £900, again for overseas re-sale this time in Cephalonia.

The *Roebuck* lies stranded on the Kaines Rocks shortly after leaving St Helier on 19 July 1911. It took almost four weeks to move her to the safety of St Helier and she was out of service for the rest of the year. *(Ambrose Greenway collection)*

Engine design was evolving rapidly, and the marine turbine was enhanced by the development by Sir Charles Parsons of the single reduction gear, improving the efficiency of transmission between turbine and propeller. This halved the propeller speed of the direct drive ships and the increased turbine speed delivered fuel efficiency, overcoming the problems experienced with the *Caesarea* and *Sarnia*. The next order from the L&SWR went to Fairfield Shipbuilding & Engineering Co Ltd of Glasgow for two further turbine ships to replace the *Alma* and *Columbia* on the Le Havre route. These were to be the first Parsons single reduction geared turbines on cross-channel services and were powered by one double-ended boiler and one single-ended boiler. After a succession of ships with single funnels the company reverted to a twin funnel design. Having trialled morse radio on the *South Western* on the Cherbourg service in late 1910, the L&SWR placed an order for the fitment of Marconi wireless equipment on four vessels in April, including the *Caesarea* and the *Sarnia,* but war intervened before they could be fitted.

As the summer 1911 season neared its peak, the *Roebuck* went aground in spectacular fashion. She left St. Helier for Guernsey at 8:30 a.m. on 19 July in calm conditions but with a thick sea mist making navigation difficult. Capt. Le Feuvre maintained a speed of 17 knots despite the poor visibility, and miscalculated his position until alerted by a lookout to the presence of swirling water, an indicator of submerged rocks. As he turned to port towards the open sea the *Roebuck* struck the Kaines rocks off Fiquet Bay, between St. Brelade's Bay and Corbière, and remained fast with some 200ft of her 280ft hull stuck firmly to the reef, and a 100ft gash in her side. Although the shore was some 300 yards away, it was invisible in the dense sea mist. Distress flares were let off and the ship's lifeboats launched, but the St. Helier lifeboat and the States' tug *Duke of Normandy* soon found the *Roebuck*. All passengers were safely landed ashore within an hour and the *Duke of Normandy* went alongside the *Roebuck* to load passengers' luggage. Some twenty tons of cargo were taken off the ship, which was wedged high on the rocks. The vessel soon became a popular local attraction but there were concerns about the impact on the holiday trade: -

'It is to feared that the wrecking of the *Roebuck* will also incidentally cause the wreck of the Jersey season, for it will scare nervous people from risking the crossing. One is almost always sure of shaking on the voyage to the Channel Isles, the boats to and from them catch the weight of the Atlantic broadside on, as well as the force of the innumerable and undependable currents which rush around that neighbourhood. A navigating chart of the Islands is a fearsome thing, and those who have gazed upon the torn waters around the Casquets, the euphemistically named Bank of Violets at Gorey, and the projecting rocks of Corbière, to mention only a few danger spots, can judge of the difficulties of navigation. But it is necessary to cross the Styx to reach the Blessed Isles, and when you get to Jersey you have your reward'.

[*Gloucestershire Citizen, 22 July 1911*]

Attempts were made to pull the *Roebuck* clear at successive high tides between 21 and 23 July with four salvage vessels in attendance, but the hull was stuck fast to a pinnacle of rock and she would not move. Engineers made temporary repairs to the hull using wood and cement in an attempt to make the *Roebuck* float higher. Finally on 28 July she was moved to a position on the sands of St. Brelade's Bay by *Em. Z. Svitzer* of Svitzer Salvage Co, in front of hundreds of spectators, becoming even more accessible to curious locals. Further repairs were made in situ and the *Roebuck* was towed towards St. Helier; however she took on so much water that she had to be beached in Belcroute Bay, and it was not until the mid-August that she finally reached St. Helier, before being towed to the Southampton yard of Harland and Wolff for permanent repairs costing £20,000. She did not return to Weymouth until 10 January 1912.

Capt. Le Feuvre was familiar with the workings of a Board of Trade Inquiry, as he had been master of the *Ibex* when she went aground off Corbière in 1897. This time his master's ticket was suspended for three months.

In December the *Lynx* was sent to Grayson of Liverpool for conversion to cargo service at a cost of £13,112 plus £2,000 for two new boilers supplied by Rollo and Sons. The refit was described as making her 'good for another twelve years'. She returned to traffic in March 1912 with her deck space now totally dedicated to cargo handling. This made the *Melmore* surplus to requirements, and she was offered for sale for £5,000 in February 1912. There were no takers at this price, but a sum of £4,200 was agreed with Charles Forbes on 10 June for her to support a treasure-seeking venture to the Cocos Islands. She was, however, quickly sold on to H Whitworth of Glasgow.

The *Normannia*, first of the new geared-turbine steamers for the Le Havre service, arrived in Southampton on 26 February 1912, and entered service on 2 April after the fitting of a radio. The new engine mechanism comprised high and low pressure expansion turbines and a reversing turbine, coupled to two independent screw shafts by single reduction gearing. A fully enclosed superstructure optimised the use of deck space for public rooms. *Normannia* encountered delays due to a coal strike, which had a big impact on Southampton services with many ships standing idle and seamen put on half pay.

Her sister was launched as the *Louvima*, but this was changed to the *Hantonia* before she entered service on 7 May. Both vessels immediately proved successful, and a further vessel was to be ordered in 1914. In the same month the L&SWR purchased the goodwill of the LB&SCR service between Newhaven and Caen, and the *Normandy* (for £15,200) and the *Brittany* (for £15,261), as part of a wider non-competition agreement. The two ships were delivered to Southampton on 31 May and 3 June respectively. On 18 June the *Ella* hit and sank the hopper *Rosina* off Netley, resulting in the drowning of two of her crew. At the end of the season, the *Caesarea* and the *Sarnia* were laid up in Southampton Water, with

A well loaded *Samia* leaving St Peter Port at low tide. *(Author's collection)*

the winter services operated by smaller vessels.

Meanwhile the Islands were reeling from news of the sinking of the *Titanic* on her inaugural sailing. The first hints of the disaster appeared in local papers on 15 April and it emerged that twenty-nine Islanders were amongst the passengers and crew on board.

The pre-war period was a peak time for the islands' growing industries and the shipping business was shared amongst a large number of cargo steamers. The list of occupants of stores on the New North Quay in St. Helier, gives an indication of the wide variety of companies involved: -

No 1	Great Central Railway
No 2	Bailhache Ltd
No 3	Goole & Jersey Steamship Co
No 4	Holyhead Steamship Co
No 5	Midland Railway
No 6	Great Northern Railway
No 7	Wilson & Co, Bristol
No 8	London & North Western Railway
No 9	Lancashire & Yorkshire Railway, Le Rossignol & Roissier Ltd, J G Hamel London, Jersey & Newhaven Steamship Co, Holyhead, Fleetwood & Liverpool Steamship Co

For the 1912 produce season the London, Jersey and Newhaven Steamship Company employed the *Essonite, Jargoon, Pearl* and *Nephrite* on a daily service to Newhaven; *The Duchess, Emden* and *The Marchioness* ran a bi-weekly service to Holyhead, Fleetwood and Liverpool, the *Thistle* ran to Bristol, the *Mersey* and *Theory* ran to Hull, and the *Alice M Craig, Helen Craig* and *Altona* to Goole and Holyhead. The GWR chartered vessels from James Fisher of Barrow in Furness to supplement the outgoing *Melmore*, and the L&SWR used the *Kelpie* and *St. Mirren.*

The L&SWR shipping division posted a loss of £26,253 for the year 1912. Over the course of the winter of 1912-13 lifesaving equipment was improved across the fleets following the *Titanic* disaster. Most vessels had their cutters replaced by large lifeboats, and a new type of life raft was introduced.

On 24 June 1913 the L&SWR sold the *Ella* for £4,500 to the shipowners' trade association the Shipping Federation, for use as an accommodation vessel for strike-breaking seamen on the Mersey. The GWR *Antelope,* which was also surplus following the closure of the Brest route, was sold in August to Navigation a Vapeur Ionienne in Greece for £4,500. She continued operating until scrapped in 1933. The GWR Act (1913) saw the abandonment of any ambitions to build a new harbour at Newton's Cove, Portland.

Since 1900, the volume of GWR cargo tonnage had risen from 33,000 tons to 44,000 tons in 1913; passengers rose from 42,000 to 63,589. The L&SWR saw passenger numbers rise from 54,811 to 81,434 in the same period. 1913 proved to very successful across all L&SWR routes, with even the Jersey-France routes seeing day excursion passengers turned away from the *Victoria.* Nonetheless the L&SWR shipping division posted a loss of £13,471. With further increases in traffic anticipated in 1914, the L&SWR approached Wm. Denny & Bros of Dumbarton with a specification for a large vessel to replace the *Lydia* and displace the *Victoria* on the Jersey station, and a small vessel to replace the *South Western* on the Cherbourg route. After a month of discussion, Wm. Denny & Bros tendered for the larger vessel, to be delivered in June 1915 at a cost of £107,640. In the event work was started but almost immediately stopped due to steel rib shortages, eventually coming to a halt as a casualty of the outbreak of war; work was suspended in August 1915 in favour of naval construction work, and the vessel was not finally delivered to the L&SWR, after Admiralty service, until 31 March 1920. The name *Lorina* was chosen for the vessel, after the wife of Lord Herbert Walker, a director of the L&SWR.

Legislation to enable the government to utilise ships from the railways' shipping fleets for military use had been in place since 1871, the height of the Franco-Prussian war. On 22 July 1914 a letter from the Admiralty to railway companies headed 'Navy War Order System' made them the first ship owners to 'volunteer' their vessels for active service in the event of hostilities.

War was declared on 4 August. Southampton became the main embarkation port for the British Expeditionary Force and some 120,000 officers and men, 38,000 horses, 314 artillery pieces, 5,000 tons of stores and 1,807 bicycles were shipped to France in August 1914. The *Caesarea* and the *Sarnia* were quickly requisitioned for war service as armed boarding vessels and on 6 August the *Reindeer* made her last mail crossing from the Islands. She was transferred to Fishguard on 18 August to replace requisitioned steamers on the Rosslare service. The *Roebuck, Reindeer* and the *Ibex* made special runs with troops between Weymouth and the Islands, including Alderney, and between Jersey and Le Havre.

There was an immediate decline in passenger numbers following the outbreak of hostilities, and this led to the introduction of the winter timetable from 24 August. The daylight service from Weymouth was withdrawn from 1 September, and henceforth thrice-weekly sailings alternated nightly with Southampton. After the initial flurry of activity the Railway Executive wrote to railway companies to express their concern that the outbreak of war had not allowed some 'to get away for their summer holidays' and they sanctioned the extension of excursion fares beyond 30 September.

The Admiralty initially employed trawlers to lay mines around Scapa Flow, but found them to be too slow for the purpose, so requisitioned the *Reindeer, Roebuck, Lynx* and *Gazelle* for the purpose. The *Roebuck* was requisitioned on 1 October, renamed HMS *Roedean* and equipped as a minesweeper. The *Reindeer* was similarly requisitioned and based at Mudros, followed by the *Gazelle* and the *Lynx* on 23 October. *Lynx* was renamed HMS *Lynn* and spent much of the war in the Mediterranean. The wartime Railway Executive Committee was responsible for finding alternative vessels for those withdrawn for active service. The L&SWR's *Bertha* was transferred to Weymouth on 26 October to handle Guernsey cargo. The *Ibex* carried Jersey cargo, with a succession of vessels drafted in to support her during refits and periods of boiler cleaning. In November 1914 for example, the L&SWR's *Vera* operated four sailings from Weymouth in her place.

In October the *Caesarea* was converted into an Armed Boarding Vessel, and the *Sarnia* sailed from the Islands on 20 November to be commissioned as the Armed Boarding Steamer HMS *Sarnia* on 1 December. The *Caesarea* and the *Sarnia* were fitted with light armaments and used to patrol domestic waters to intercept any vessel that might be attempting to beat the blockade of Germany. On 28 November the *Victoria* sailed from Jersey bound for Portsmouth, reportedly for use as a pilots' accommodation vessel, but she was employed as a 'Q' decoy ship before returning to Jersey on 11 January 1915.

Earlier in the year the London & Channel Islands company had replaced the *Island Queen* with a larger vessel of the same name. With the outbreak of war the company decided to sell their new ship to improve their financial position. The company continued with *Channel Queen* and *London Queen* for the early years of the war.

Pressure on port facilities at Southampton was intense as the Expeditionary Force continued to head for France. Congestion became a big issue, forcing the L&SWR to transfer cargo sailings for the Jersey potato and tomato traffic to Hamworthy Quay at Poole in 1915. The rail sidings here were far from ideal, being situated at right angles to the berth, with two tracks capable of accommodating twenty wagons each, and a third utilised for coaling the steamers. Two ships were chartered for the twelve hour passage from Jersey, some three hours quicker than Southampton. The vessels normally arrived at around 6:00 a.m. and took up to six hours to discharge a cargo of around 200 tons or 4,500-5,000 packages, each of which had to be manhandled. The ships returned in the afternoon, usually laden with empty barrels, baskets and other receptacles.

HMS *Roedean* (the *Roebuck*) parted her moorings and dragged her anchor at Scapa Flow, driving broadside into the ram bow of the depot ship HMS *Imperieuse* during a gale on 13 January 1915. Her crew climbed on to the *Imperieuse* as the *Roedean's* bow was stove in and she began to sink in thirty feet of water. This time she stayed down; it was not possible to raise her for a third time. She was the first railway steamer to be lost in the war, and set the standard for future loss compensation levels from the Admiralty.

In February the L&SWR *Vera* again operated four sailings from Weymouth in place of the *Ibex*, and on 21 February the Lancashire & Yorkshire Railway's (L&YR's) *Mersey* was transferred to Weymouth to support the cargo service.

The English Channel became a significantly more dangerous place for civilian shipping from 15 February 1915 when the German government adopted a policy of unrestricted submarine warfare in British waters, making civilian vessels legitimate targets for surprise attack. Previously vessels were required to identify themselves, before the crew was taken off and the ship sunk. The *Lydia* witnessed the new approach at first hand when attacked by U boat *U20* off the Isle of Wight on 5 March, but the torpedo missed her. Her final scheduled sailing from the Islands was on 12 March; she returned to Jersey a week later bringing POW's for detention but was then engaged as the government *Transport Vessel*

280 on the Southampton-Le Havre route. She was to survive a further attack by gunfire from *UC65* on passage from Le Havre on 27 February 1917.

The *Guernsey* struck a rock off Cap de la Hague during storm conditions and in the absence of any navigation aids due to the blackout, at around 10:00 p.m. on 8 April. The impact was so severe that her Captain was thrown overboard and lost. A boat was launched as the *Guernsey* sank with the loss of seven crew; twelve crewmen were rescued by the *Cherbourg*, to be taken to Southampton. The ship's papers were later washed up in a satchel at Rozel on 26 April. Three weeks later on 29 April, the *South Western* struck rocks in the same place, but managed to refloat herself and limped to Cherbourg with 5ft of water in her forward hold. She received temporary repairs before returning to Southampton. The *Guernsey* was replaced by the 1895 cargo vessel *Granuaile,* which was leased and then purchased from REV James Ltd for £10,430 on 29 July and renamed *Ulrica.* Her first sailing to Jersey was on 13 September.

The *Princess Ena* was taken over on 27 April to operate as a 'Q' ship in the southwest approaches under the command of Jerseyman Commander F.M. Simon RN. She proved unsuitable for the work and was converted into a troopship and sent from Southampton to the Mediterranean on 18 October, to maintain a service between Mudros and Salonica.

The *Reindeer, Lynx* and *Gazelle* all participated in the Dardanelles landings in May, with the diminutive *Gazelle* employed to lay fifty mines at a time. *Reindeer* operated as a minesweeper and saved the crew of battleship *HMS Majestic* when she was torpedoed. On 6 June *Reindeer* was acting as transport vessel for the 4th Battalion Royal Scots between Mudros and Imbos when she collided at 17 knots with the Great Central Railway's *Immingham*, sinking her, but saving the crew. Neither vessel was displaying lights due the wartime conditions. *Reindeer* sustained a 30ft gash above the waterline and was forced to return to Mudros.

Whilst passenger traffic to the Islands had declined since the start of the war there was still considerable cargo traffic. In 1915 the L&NWR's *Galtee More*, the L&YR's *Mellifont,* the L&SWR *Vera* and the GWR's *Great Southern* were brought in to cover at times for the *Ibex* at Weymouth. On 19 August the L&YR's *River Crake* was transferred to Weymouth to support the cargo service. The schedule comprised thrice weekly sailings alternating between Plymouth and Weymouth. The Anglo-French Steamship Company crews demanded 'risk money' for the duration of hostilities and this led to a rise in rates from June. This was the first of several rises as costs climbed, balanced against the competition from railway steamers and the London route. Dorey went to great lengths to retain the Anglo-American oil business from Plymouth, adding extra services to prevent it being shipped via London.

When the *Caesarea* and the *Sarnia* completed their domestic blockade service as armed boarding vessels. the *Caesarea* was transferred to the Southampton-Le Havre military route, whilst the *Sarnia* was sent to the Mediterranean. On 29 October, as the South Eastern & Chatham Railway's (SE&CR's) cargo vessel *Hythe* approached Cape Helles after the fifty-mile journey from Mudros she collided with the *Sarnia,* despite both ships attempting to change course. The *Hythe* was hit some 25ft from her bow on the port side, leaving a gaping hole. The impact caused her to stop dead, and the foremast collapsed, resulting in many casualties. The *Hythe* was sunk, and the *Sarnia* holed but able to limp back to port, steaming stern-first to avoid taking on water. The force of the accident was compounded by the lack of life jackets and emergency lifeboats, and 155 servicemen and crew were killed. The Inquiry found that there were no set navigation routes in and out of Cape Helles, and recommended that no soldier should travel on a ship without having a lifejacket. The *Sarnia* continued to carry out duties between Mudros and the Peninsular, and her Commander H.G. Muir was mentioned in dispatches for his efforts.

The L&SWR still retained four large passenger ships in the operational fleet, with the *Normannia* and *Hantonia* operating the Le Havre service, the *Alberta* on the Islands route and the *Vera* acting as relief for both routes. The *Vera* covered for the *Alberta* when she was off service in November 1915, but on the 19th she hit the quay wall whilst entering the dock at Southampton and sustained bow damage. The *South Western* was transferred to the mail service to cover for a month.

By early 1916 the GWR was still encountering great difficulties in obtaining ships to provide the necessary cover for the *Ibex*, and the *Pembroke*, a tender converted to a cargo vessel, was transferred from Fishguard for the cargo and mail service to the Islands, where she arrived for the first time on 30 March. On the same day the L&YR's *River Crake* was released from the Weymouth cargo service. The *Great Southern* spent a brief time covering for the *Ibex* after she broke down and was out of service for a week from 30 July.

The increasing need to focus short-sea shipping routes on transferring resources for the western front forced the Government to close cross-Channel routes for civilian use in May, except for the Southampton-Le Havre service, which henceforth attracted significant extra traffic requiring an increase in the number of sailings.

The unarmed *Pembroke* was attacked by gunfire from *U37* on 24 September, some twenty-two miles north of the Casquets. Daylight sailings were stopped as a precaution and the Admiralty suggested that both the *Pembroke* and the *Ibex* should be armed. At the end of October *Ibex* was sent to Plymouth for refit work, returning with a twelve-pounder gun at her stern, and on 30 November she managed to escape being chased by a U boat. *Pembroke* was fitted with armaments at Portland in January 1917. Towards the end of 1916 the L&SWR Island mail service was without its regular vessels and both *South Western* and *Laura* spent brief spells on the route.

The Anglo-French Steamship Company operation to Plymouth and the London services prospered as railway resources were stretched, but they did not receive government financial support as costs rose. In 1916 the company added another purpose built *Island Queen* to their two-ship fleet, with a view to chartering out one of the other vessels. The government chartered *Island Queen* from November 1916 and the two-ship fleet continued the Channel Island service. The *Island Queen* was sold to the government for £40,000 in September 1917. Although Channel Island traffic declined towards the end of the war, the company was able to make a profit from vessel charters.

Connecting trains to Weymouth Quay were withdrawn from 1 January 1917 as part of a general wartime cutback in services, and the departure time of the service from London Paddington to Weymouth Town was brought forward to 5:00 p.m. extending the journey time to Jersey to 16 hours 30 minutes.

The *Ibex* narrowly missed being torpedoed by *U20* whilst sailing from Weymouth to Swansea on 15 May. The Admiralty extended the provision of defensive armour to the L&SWR fleet in June with six pounder guns for the fast vessels, and twelve or thirteen pounders for the older, slower ships. This was accompanied by a requirement for all ships to be painted grey, contrary to L&SWR wishes. On 12 July the *Normandy* was fired on by Portsmouth naval defences and hit in twenty-six places. In a further wartime cutback, the Island services were reduced to twice weekly from Southampton and Weymouth from November 1917. The following month the Admiralty ordered resumption of construction work on the *Lorina* at Wm. Denny & Bros, but for completion as a transport ship for wartime service.

The government requisitioned the Anglo-French Steamship Company vessel *Devonia* as a Q ship in 1917, forcing the company into liquidation. The Dorey name was finished with shipping until it re-surfaced with the establishment of Condor in the 1960s.

The *Normandy* was torpedoed and sunk by *U90* eight miles from the Cherbourg

The 1912-built *Caesarea* in pre-war condition. She served as an armed boarding cruiser, and later as a troop carrier. *(Ambrose Greenway collection)*

breakwater, whilst on passage from Southampton to Cherbourg on 25 January 1918. Of the forty-five on board, thirteen passengers and fourteen crew were lost. This tragedy was followed on 16 March by the torpedoing and sinking of the *South Western* by *U59*, eleven miles south west of the Isle of Wight on a cargo sailing from Southampton to St. Malo; twenty-nine of the thirty-five on board were lost. The service to Cherbourg was suspended, with only the *Laura* of the smaller passenger and cargo vessels still available. On 18 March the *Ibex* came under gunfire from a U boat, but she put her armament to good use scoring a direct retaliatory hit on the submarine, which was accepted as being sunk. The Admiralty awarded the sum of £500 for distribution amongst officers and crew.

The Government chartered the *Alberta*, *Hantonia*, *Normannia* and *Vera* to carry troops across the channel after the German breakthrough on the Somme, forcing the suspension of L&SWR sailings to the Islands and Le Havre from 28 March to 9 April 1918. However, the *Alberta* broke her starboard crankshaft whilst leaving Southampton on 29 March, and was thus unavailable. From 1 May services from Southampton to Cherbourg and St. Malo were suspended and the Southampton-Channel Islands sailings reduced to twice weekly. Meanwhile the *Ibex* was transferred at short notice in May to operate troop services between Dover and Calais, with the *Pembroke* given a forty-passenger certificate in the interim.

The *Lorina* was finally launched for the Admiralty on 12 August. She was powered by two sets of Parsons geared turbines fed from one double-ended and one single-ended boiler and could exceed her contract speed of 19½ knots. She was fitted out as an Admiralty transport and arrived at Southampton on 30 December 1918, to take up duties on the military service to Le Havre from 4 January 1919. As one vessel arrived another departed; *HMS Sarnia* was torpedoed and sunk by *U65* in the Mediterranean soon after leaving her base in Alexandria on 12 September. In September, civilian ships were painted in the camouflage dazzle paint system required by the Government. The Admiralty requisitioned the *Victoria* on 18 September 1918, forcing suspension of the Jersey-St. Malo service. The last merchant vessel to be taken over for military service, she was given the name *Surf II*, but in the event peace was declared on 11 November before she could start work.

The return of peacetime conditions initiated a major transport exercise to repatriate troops and equipment, and it was some time before normality could be restored to civilian services.

The *Lorina* worked alongside the *Lydia* and the *Caesarea* to bring homebound troops from Le Havre. Meanwhile the *Reindeer* was being utilised to bring troops back from Cherbourg to Weymouth. The *Ibex* was transferred at short notice to operate troop services for twelve days between Le Havre and Weymouth, before she sailed to Plymouth for overhaul. *Ibex* had a commemorative plaque fitted stating: -

'During the Great War 1914-1919, this vessel maintained the Great Western Railway Company's Passenger and Mail Service between Weymouth and the Channel Islands, and on three occasions was attacked by enemy submarines, one of which she sank by gunfire. The Government requisitioned the steamer at various times for the conveyance of troops to France'.

The L&SWR made the strategic decision to discontinue the Jersey-St. Malo service from 27 March 1919, having suffered heavy fleet losses during the war. Occasional sailings continued with the *Laura* until mid-May, despite the decision to close the route. The *Victoria* returned from wartime service on 5 December but with the end of the Jersey-France routes she was surplus to requirements. In April 1919 the L&SWR attempted to sell her at a Baltic Exchange auction, but she failed to reach the reserve price. She was sold the following month to James Dredging Towage & Transport Co Ltd for £16,500.

The L&SWR considered that the wartime cargo service from the Islands to Poole was worthy of continuing, as an average of around 4,500 packages was handled on each sailing, and chartered the *Shotton* and *Trader* to maintain the operation.

The task of returning men and equipment from France continued throughout summer 1919, with the military shipping service between Southampton and Le Havre placed under the control of the L&SWR from 8 June. The service finished in the last week in October when the last two ships in Government service, the *Caesarea* and the *Lydia,* were handed back to the L&SWR. The *Lydia* visited Guernsey on 21 September, when she took returning troops to the island, and the *Caesarea* arrived in Jersey on 16 October with the King's Regiment. Their return allowed the resumption of thrice-weekly sailings from Southampton and Weymouth, with through carriages to London Paddington operating again from Weymouth Quay.

The L&SWR received £275,000 compensation from the government for their wartime losses, but faced a significant workload to return the fleet to its pre-war condition. The Wm. Denny Bros. yard was already busy with post-war repairs and rebuilding, and could not accept further work, so in October the *Lorina* was sent to the Caledon Shipyard in Dundee for conversion back to passenger service. The *Lydia* was not considered worthy of repair and, in a deal brokered by James Dredging Towage & Transport Co Ltd, was sold to Thomas Sales for £20,000, who in return sold a naval escort vessel to the L&SWR for £4,000. This was the former HMS *Peony,* one of seventy-two twin funneled escort ships built for wartime service, which had served in the Dardanelles and was now in Malta. The deal was agreed on 18 December 1919 and by mid-January 1920 the *Peony* had arrived at Southampton, to be accepted by the L&SWR and sent to the Caledon Yard for conversion alongside the *Caesarea* and the *Lorina*.

1920 saw a succession of vessels return to the post-war service. The *Reindeer* was overhauled in the Thorneycroft yard at Southampton, and returned to the Islands service on 8 February. The smaller *Lynx* made her first return call in Jersey on 12 March after refitting at Plymouth Devonport; one of the first to board her on arrival was Jerseyman Capt. H. Bond who had commanded the ship in the Mediterranean. On 31 March the *Lorina* undertook her first sailing from Southampton as a passenger vessel, disembarking 250 passengers and 200 naval and military personnel in Jersey before being opened to the public. She made a handful of trips to the islands, moving to the Le Havre route for a short time before taking up a more permanent role on the Southampton-St. Malo service. The arrival of the *Lorina* allowed the *Vera* to be released for a complete overhaul at Cammell Laird, Birkenhead, which included new boilers and a nearly completely new hull bottom at a cost of £75,844.

At Weymouth the *Gazelle* returned in April after refitting at Plymouth Devonport, following wartime service that included the ramming of a submarine. In May, the GWR transferred the Fishguard vessel *Waterford* to Weymouth for the seasonal cargo traffic, but on 22 May, whilst waiting to load potatoes in Jersey, she was sent back to Fishguard. In her place came the *Great Southern,* which was capable of carrying cargo and acting as relief passenger ship when required; this transfer became a regular feature of the spring and summer traffic for over a decade with the *Great Southern,* or more frequently her sister the *Great Western,* transferring to Weymouth to assist. The *Caesarea* returned to Southampton on 7 June and a month later *Princess Ena* arrived back after being refitted by the Admiralty at Devonport and took up the St. Malo service, where she was joined by the *Lorina* on 31 July. The two railway fleets had been returned to peacetime condition, and services restored to near pre-war levels in a remarkably short period of time.

The public responded to the return of peace with a summer rush to take holidays through the French ports and in the Channel Islands. The L&SWR was reported to be finding its capabilities 'taxed to the utmost' to cope with the flood of passengers. This wasn't made easier by an accident to the *Alberta* when she struck rocks north of Guernsey approaching St. Peter Port from Southampton in fog at low water on 21 July with over 300 passengers on board. The *Ibex* provided assistance in response to distress signals, as the *Alberta* was down by the head and her No. 2 hold was filled with water, but she managed to berth in the Inner Harbour at 8:30 a.m. Passengers were sent forward to Jersey

1920 map of St Helier harbour from the Ward Lock Red Guide

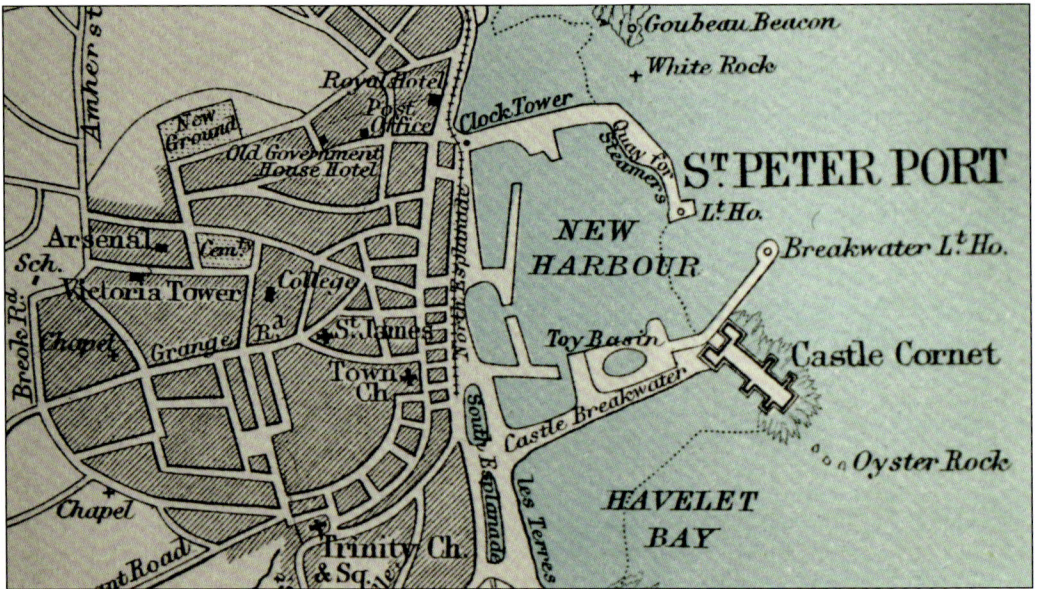

1920 map of St Peter Port harbour from the Ward Lock Red Guide

aboard the GWR's *Ibex* at 10:00 a.m. The *Alberta* received significant damage to six plates that took three weeks to repair in the Harbour. In the interim the L&NWR steamers *Rathmore* and *Galtee More* were chartered in to provide cover. Meanwhile *Laura* was converted to a cargo vessel by dockyard staff for £5,000.

As railway companies and coalmines returned to peacetime private ownership, there were worker protests at the effective denationalisation of the assets. Coal strikes in October 1920 caused restrictions to the mail service and the suspension of cargo sailings.

The winter schedule remained at the pre-war level of twice-weekly sailings from Southampton and Weymouth. The *Vera* arrived back at Southampton in early November to be permanently allocated to the Channel Islands station. Her arrival released the *Alberta*, which proceeded back to Dundee for refit. The crew of the *Alberta* returned with the *Peony*, which had been renamed the *Ardena*, arriving back in Southampton on 29 November. As a cargo and passenger vessel, the *Ardena* was limited to 15 knots, which placed her at a disadvantage relative to the dedicated passenger fleet. She made her maiden voyage to St. Malo on 6 December, spending most of her winters on this service switching in the summer to her intended Southampton-Cherbourg route, which she re-opened on 6 July 1921.

In the immediate post-war period both new and second-hand tonnage was scarce and expensive as there was a backlog of wartime losses to be made up, so the L&SWR decided to implement a life-extension programme. The forty-eight year-old *Cherbourg* was given an extensive refit at the Marine workshops in Southampton at cost of £12,000, with her compound engine replaced by an elderly triple expansion engine built in 1897 by J. P. Rennoldson at South Shields. This was intended to give her an additional ten years life.

Weymouth passenger volumes grew to 67,000 in 1920, slightly up on the 1913 figure. However cargo traffic had risen by nineteen per cent on the average of the previous seven years. 18,000 tons of tomatoes and fruit was shipped via Weymouth in 1920, more than double that carried at the turn of the century. The 2,000 growers in Guernsey were consuming in the region of 150,000 tons of South Wales anthracite each year to heat their greenhouses to service the demand for increasing volumes of produce.

The post-war economic boom was short lived, and by 1921 two million workers in the UK were without jobs. In spring 1921 services were again hit by coal strikes that caused restrictions to the mail service and the suspension of cargo sailings; L&SWR sailings from Southampton were suspended.

The *Great Western was* transferred from Fishguard to Weymouth between May and September 1921 to handle the Guernsey fruit traffic and act as the relief Mail steamer. The year saw a record tomato crop in Jersey with the *Pembroke* taking off 45,861 packages on one trip in September 1921, the largest cargo of fruit then exported on a single vessel. Connecting daytime passenger services were re-introduced by the GWR in July, with restaurant cars added to the services from Weymouth. Fares were now seventy-five per cent higher than pre-war levels, but vessel-running costs had doubled in the same period. Wartime conditions had brought a four-fold increase in docker's wages from the pre-war 5½d per hour to 1s 9d per hour.

The Islands received a visit from the King and Queen in July 1921 to inspect the local militia and garrisoned troops. It was customary for a mailboat master to act as pilot on the royal yacht and Capt. Mulhall of the GWR performed the duty.

The *Alberta* had been due back from her refit in time for the 1921 summer season but work was delayed due to industrial action at the yard, and she did not return until 31 October. A charter of the L&NWR's *Galtee More* filled in for her absence for two months at the height of the summer period from 11 July, although the charter was subsequently extended following an accident to the *Hantonia*.

In September the 9:15 p.m. service from London Paddington to Weymouth Quay was restored, but the winter schedule still comprised just two sailings from each port.

The L&SWR increased its cargo fleet in early 1922 when the *Laura* was converted into a cargo-only vessel and the *Algethi* (renamed the *Rina*) and the *Algeiba* (renamed the *Vena*), were purchased for potato traffic from R. Penny of Shoreham on 26 June for £9,083 each to avoid the charter costs of the *Steermans*. The *Great Western* was again the Weymouth seasonal steamer.

The two companies summer schedule was as follows: -

	GWR	L&SWR			GWR	L&SWR
London Paddington	dep 9:30 a.m.			Jersey	dep 7:30 a.m.	7:15 a.m.
London Waterloo	dep	9:30 p.m.		Guernsey	dep 10:00 a.m.	10:00 a.m.
Weymouth Quay	arr 1:05 p.m.			Weymouth Quay	arr 3:00 p.m.	
	dep 1:15 p.m.				dep 3:45 p.m.	
Southampton	dep	11:50 p.m.		Southampton	arr	5:00 p.m.
Guernsey	arr 6:00 p.m.	6:30 a.m.		London Waterloo	arr	7:20 p.m.
Jersey	arr 8:45 p.m.	9:15 a.m.		London Paddington	arr 7:35 p.m.	

By the middle of 1922 all the ships had been overhauled and most war losses made good, with the exception of the *Roebuck,* and the full pre-war winter sailing schedule was reintroduced in November. But almost all the ships were over ten years old and the railway companies were virtually bankrupted by the war. The network was worn out, and government compensation insufficient to cover the investment required across all aspects of the railway companies' businesses. The Railways Bill of 1921 sought to consolidate Britain's independent railway companies into four large regional groupings and give them the corporate muscle to address their financial weaknesses. The Bill came into effect on 1 January 1923.

CHAPTER SIX

Grouping to occupatio 1923-1940

"The s.s. Isle of Sark - the latest addition to the Southern Railway Company's Southampton-Channel Islands Service - is another instance of the policy of this Company to bring their steamer routes to the highest modern luxury. Nothing has been spared to give the passengers the comfort that makes so much difference even to the short sea voyage to and from the Channel Islands. The passenger accommodation represents a considerable advance on the earlier vessels for this service, for the Isle of Sark is fitted with beautiful upholstery, concealed lighting, soft carpets, and floorings. The Cabin and Saloon accommodation for first-class passengers comprises a general lounge and fixed seating for fifty-six persons, ladies' and gentlemen's lounges, dining saloon, smoke-room (panelled in a shade of dull polished mahogany) and entrance lounge. The private cabins are tastefully decorated in modern style, and include a couple of two-berth cabines de luxe (which can be made inter-communicable), nineteen two-berth private cabins on the promenade deck (which can be used as three-berth cabins), sixteen one-berth private cabins on the main deck, and thirteen two-berth and two three-berth and two four-berth private cabins on the lower deck. All the cabins are fitted with running hot and cold water, and, in addition, there are bathrooms and shower-baths. The ladies' and gentlemen's first-class lounges have sleeping accommodation for twenty-eight persons. Sleeping accommodation for second-class passengers is provided in open saloons aft, two for ladies and two for gentlemen. The first-class dining-room, situated on the main deck, attractively decorated on modern lines, has a seating accommodation for fifty-six persons at tables each for four persons, and is also fitted with a central display table.

[The Bystander, 13 April 1932]

The railway grouping of 1 January 1923 brought little immediate change to Island services. Weymouth services were transferred from the GWR into an identically titled Great Western Railway (Great Western), which acquired all the old company's shipping interests. L&SWR services from Southampton became part of the new Southern Railway (Southern), alongside the former LB&SCR and the SE&CR operations, thereby bringing the short-sea, western channel and Channel Islands shipping services together into one company. Southampton, with its extensive workshop and dry-dock facilities, became the new headquarters of the marine section under the Docks & Marine Manager.

Both companies were faced with significant investment requirements to replace their ageing and missing pre-war fleets. The Great Western opted initially for a programme of vessel refurbishment with the *Reindeer* sent to Liverpool early in 1923 for a major overhaul, including fitting a new shelter deck aft of the bridge. She returned to service on 11 March, but this was only postponing the inevitable; the directors toured their shipping operations during the summer and concluded that full fleet replacement was needed for the Channel Islands service, subsequently inviting tenders for two new mail steamers. Between May and September 1923 the *Waterford* and the *Great Western* were transferred from Fishguard to Weymouth to handle the Guernsey fruit traffic, with the latter also acting as the relief Mail steamer for the route.

The Southern faced more extensive fleet issues, and embarked on a substantial investment programme, which between 1924 and 1932 delivered twenty-nine new vessels - fifteen passenger, ten cargo and four car ferries. Plans to convert the *Caesarea* to burn oil fuel were considered in detail, but before any conclusion could be reached the vessel became a major casualty. The *Caesarea* struck a rock in thick fog off Noirmont Point on her outward passage from Jersey on 7 July with 373 passengers on board, sustaining severe hull damage and the loss of her port propeller and shaft. She returned to St. Helier, but water began to enter the stokehold and engine room and, with her stern now lying deep in the water, she sank on the approach to the harbour with lifeboats in her wake: -

> 'The *Caesarea* left Jersey at 7:00 a.m. and, owing to mist, touched the rocks off St. Aubin's. Very little damage was done, and the vessel got off again within about an hour and returned to port under her own steam. There was a large number of passengers, but there was little or no excitement among them'.

Later issues told more of the tale.

> 'It appears that Captain Smith of the *Caesarea* was making way for an incoming steamer, and the weather being hazy at the time his vessel struck the Pigonnet Rock inside Noirmont Point. The vessel made water rapidly, and the skipper, realising that she must be badly holed, turned his vessel round and made for St. Helier. He reached the inner roadstead with the vessel's bows practically submerged. He had no alternative but to beach her, and this he did just outside the harbour wall. Meanwhile the *Caesarea*'s boats were lowered and the passengers were got ashore. The *Alberta*'s boats were also soon on the spot, and in a comparatively short space of time the 300 odd passengers were landed. The vessel continued to make water rapidly, and it is feared she will be totally submerged at high water'.
>
> [*Portsmouth Evening News, 7 July 1923*]

A Press Association report from Mr. W. H. Smith, the Guernsey Agent for Lloyd's, who was travelling on the *Reindeer*, said that as they approached Noirmont Point 'siren blasts were heard, followed by a wireless message from the *Caesarea*, saying she had struck the

The *Caesarea* lies on rocks and covered in water at high tide just outside the harbour in St Helier after beaching on 7 July 1923. She was later recovered. *(Dave Hocquard collection)*

rocks. The *Reindeer* asked if any assistance was required, to which the *Caesarea* replied with a request to stand by. Capt. Mulhall of the *Reindeer*, at considerable risk owing to the dense fog and the narrowness of the fairway, the distance between the shore and the reefs being only 300 yards, turned his vessel and followed the damaged steamer by the sound of her siren. Occasionally there were glimpses of the *Caesarea* overtaking the steamer *Gazelle'*. There was no loss of life or injury and passengers were transferred to the *Alberta*, which left Jersey for Southampton at 9:30 a.m.

The *Caesarea* was stuck fast on the rocks and covered at each high tide, but a spring tide allowed her to be refloated on 20 July with the aid of hundreds of barrels and assistance from the pumping steamer *Gundreda*, and later towed to Southampton. She was sold to the Isle of Man Steam Packet Company, who converted her to oil firing and renamed her *Manx Maid* before entering service in 1924. The *Hantonia* was transferred from the Southampton-Le Havre route to cover the peak season, with the *St. Patrick* chartered from the Great Western to take her place. In 1971 a team of divers discovered the bronze propeller from the *Caesarea* lying off Noirmont and were able to recover it with help from a tug. The propeller is now on display outside the Maritime Museum in St. Helier.

In August the *Princess Era* struck rocks on the Minquiers in thick fog. Two lifeboats were lowered as a precaution and were loaded with fifty passengers, but at 7:00 a.m. *Princess Era* began to lift clear with the tide, and was able to continue to St. Malo. However the two missing lifeboats could not initially be found, but were picked up ninty minutes later by the *Bertha*, which headed to the area to answer the *Princess Ena*'s distress call.

Following sale of the *Caesarea* the Southern placed an order for two new ships with Wm. Denny & Bros. of Dumbarton, intended for the services from Southampton to the Islands. Later in the year it was made clear that the ships would be allocated to other routes if there was not a commensurate improvement in harbour facilities in St. Peter Port and St. Helier. This masked a change of heart by the company as there was insufficient time for the required work to be carried out, and whilst the new vessels *Dinard* and *St. Briac* were allocated to the Southampton station, they were to serve continental routes. During winter 1923-24 the facilities at the Outer Dock in Southampton were re-modelled

The badly damaged propeller from *Caesarea* recovered in 1971 and now on display outside the Maritime Museum in St Helier. (*Author*)

to cater for the expanding cross-channel traffic with berths 7 and 8 rebuilt and a new Marine Station constructed alongside them.

The Great Western placed their order with John Brown & Co Ltd. of Clydebank for two new geared-turbine steamers at a cost of £248,000 in March 1924. The seasonal vessel for the 1924 Guernsey fruit traffic and relief mail steamer was the *Great Southern,* transferred from Fishguard between May and September. In June the Southern unveiled their new fleet colour scheme. The former L&SWR vessels at Southampton had black tops added to their yellow funnels, but the rest of the fleet required more substantial repainting. The new colours and house flag were first on show for the visit of the Prince of Wales when he opened the new floating dock in Southampton on 27 June.

The *Dinard*, the first of the new Southern ships, made her maiden voyage to St. Malo on 22 July and her sister, the *St. Briac*, followed on the Le Havre route on 3 October. The pair cost £265,000. Each had twin sets of single reduction geared turbines and could be powered by coal or oil, the first cross-channel ships to have this capability. The *Dinard* was dedicated to the tidal St. Malo route, while the *St. Briac* operated seasonally, spending much of her time as relief ship on the Le Havre route, and later on excursion traffic. With the arrival of the *Dinard,* the *Lorina* was transferred to the Channel Islands service as replacement for the *Caesarea.*

The Great Western completed their ship investment programme with a £90,000 order for two new cargo steamers from Swan Hunter & Wigham Richardson of Tyneside in October. The pair were to be oil burners capable of carrying over 600 tons of freight spread across three decks to prevent crushing of fruit baskets. However the impending arrival of the new fleet was not matched by any improvement to facilities or capacity at Weymouth, although some dredging took place in early 1925.

The Great Western's new *St. Julien* was launched at John Brown & Co on 23 February

Passengers crowd the decks as the *Reindeer* approaches Weymouth. *(Ambrose Greenway collection)*

1925, followed shortly afterwards by the *St. Helier* on 26 March. Built to cater for 1,000 passengers in two classes of accommodation, they were designed with fore and aft holds capable of carrying 370 tons of cargo and mails and even crane-loaded cars. Both vessels were designed with two funnels, but the aft funnel was largely cosmetic. The vessels were fitted with two sets of double Parsons single reduction turbines, powered by four single ended fuel oil boilers to drive twin screws to deliver speeds of 18 knots. The vessels had a short raised forecastle, a large deckhouse and a further docking bridge aft. Their arrival allowed the company to rationalise the old fleet. The *Lynx* made her final cargo departure from Weymouth to Jersey on 16 March, sailing thence to Plymouth for disposal. The *Gazelle* was laid up at Weymouth from 31 March and sent to Plymouth for disposal on 17 April, just after the *Ibex* returned to Weymouth for the last time on 14 April. She followed her sisters to Plymouth on 7 May prior to withdrawal in November and sale for scrap at Sheerness in 1926. Of the older ships, only the *Reindeer* remained to act as relief cover and carry out a programme of day excursions. The *Great Western* was transferred from Fishguard for the seasonal Guernsey fruit traffic role and to act as relief Mail steamer. She remained as the seasonal vessel for the rest of the decade.

A hectic spring saw a succession of new vessels arrive in Weymouth. The cargo vessel *Roebuck* arrived on 29 April in readiness for her first crossing to Jersey on 18 May. She was joined on 4 May by the *St. Julien* under the command Capt. Langdon, which arrived in Weymouth Bay with the Great Western directors and principal officers on board. Ten days later the second cargo vessel *Sambur* arrived. On 23 May *Sambur* made her first crossing to Guernsey and *St. Julien* took up the overnight mail service. Finally on 7 June the *St. Helier* arrived in Weymouth, relieving the *St. Julien* on the night mail service from 17 June. Four new ships had transformed the fleet in just over four weeks. The Great Western changes were completed on 4 July when the *Pembroke* was laid up at Weymouth.

Everything was now in place for a step change in the service. On 29 June the St. *Helier* and the *St. Julien* inaugurated an accelerated daytime service to the Islands utilising new boat train rolling stock, the first set of the 1925-built articulated carriages to enter public service for the Great Western. The service featured rapid transfer between train and ship to

GREAT WESTERN RAILWAY

New Fast Turbine Steamers "St Julien" and "St Helier" now running between Weymouth and the CHANNEL ISLANDS Accelerated Services

GWR poster heralding the arrival of *St Julien* and *St Helier* in 1925.

reduce the overall journey times.

The Southern was forced to play catch up with the extensive investment at Weymouth. The company ordered a standard design of cargo ship, capable of deployment across the Dover and Southampton stations. The first of the Southampton-allocated vessels was the *Haslemere,* capable of carrying 500 tons of cargo, which was launched by D&W Henderson Ltd, Meadowside, Glasgow (a subsidiary of Harland & Wolff) on 22 May and ran trials on the Clyde on 3 July; the second was the *Fratton,* delivered at Southampton on 27 September.

Both companies continued to apply pressure on the Island authorities to improve their harbour facilities to match the growing passenger volumes and the fleet investment programme. In St. Peter Port a new jetty was constructed parallel to the No.1 berth at a cost of £110,743 following railway approval, and the harbour dredged between 1926 and 1929. The *St Helier* was the first vessel to use the new berth on 22 March 1929. Major works were carried out in St. Helier between 1928 and 1931, with Weymouth following between 1931 and 1933. Meanwhile at St. Malo the new lock that the Southern had expected to be in use for the 1925 season was not completed until 1931.

1926 started badly for the Great Western services. On 10 March the *St. Helier* struck the Pier Head in St. Helier whilst arriving from Weymouth, requiring her to be sent to Clydebank for repairs and keeping her out of service until May. *Reindeer* was readied at Weymouth to substitute and on the following day sailed to St. Helier but also struck the Pier Head on arrival, forcing her out of service for the rest of the month. The Southern's *Vera* was loaned from Southampton for three days, pending the return of the *St. Julien* from her refit in Plymouth.

A further Southern freighter, the *Ringwood*, was launched by D&W Henderson Ltd on 13 April.

The *St Julien* on the drying out berth at St Peter Port. A party of engineers has descended to small boats to inspect her propellers. *(Dave Hocquard collection)*

The Trades Union Congress called a General Strike in the UK on 3 May 1926 with the aim of forcing the government to act on the plight of locked-out coal workers. Mine owners had responded to foreign competition and declining profits by demanding wage cuts and longer working hours. A negotiated compromise was agreed with the government and the strike ended on 12 May. However the miners remained on strike for a further six months, severely hitting coal supplies. Although Weymouth services were able to continue with the oil fired *St. Helier* and *St. Julien,* scheduled Southampton sailings were suspended for almost five weeks, forcing all passenger services and most cargo to be sent via Weymouth.

On 25 August 1926 the *Reindeer* offered a day excursion from Weymouth to Guernsey, which attracted almost 700 passengers. However the Great Western decided that the cost of maintaining her to Board of Trade standards could no longer be justified and a new steamer was needed. The *Reindeer* was eventually withdrawn from the Weymouth fleet after her final mail sailing on 23 February 1928 and sent to Briton Ferry to be broken up on 30 November 1928.

1926 also saw the installation of a 'wireless listening in' station at the White Rock in St. Peter Port to enable communication with mail boats. The Guernsey States Telephone Department – which was then one of the most advanced in the world – set up a system whereby subscribers could be rung with vessel arrival times.

During the winter refit programme of 1927-28 the aft funnel and docking bridge on the *St. Julien* and the *St. Helier* were removed, thereby improving the appearance and handling of the vessels by reducing windage. The passenger certificate of the *Roebuck* was altered to permit the carrying of twelve passengers.

The Southern finally ordered two new passenger ships for their Channel Island services from Wm. Denny & Bros., of Dumbarton on 31 January 1929. The specification was unusual by cross-channel standards as they required the vessels to cater for up to 1,400 passengers on lengthy day and night crossings, with two classes of accommodation and be flat bottomed with the capability of sitting on the harbour bottom at low tide in St. Helier. Fore and aft cargo holds were specified to carry passengers' luggage, 235 tons of

Construction under way on the new jetty at St Peter Port in July 1926. The *Roebuck* and *Princess Ena* are visible in the distance. *(Author's collection)*

Chips of tomatoes being loaded in the traditional way by sliding down boxes down a plank onto the deck of the *Pembroke* in St Peter Port. The crane demonstrates a more efficient method of loading. *(Author's collection)*

cargo and craned cars. With twin pairs of single reduction geared turbines and three single-ended oil fired boilers, the vessels could achieve over 19 knots. The pair cost £340,000.

In April the Fishguard steamer *St. Patrick* was destroyed in a fire, prompting the Great Western to order a replacement vessel. From September the *St. Julien* was transferred to Fishguard as relief vessel, requiring the *St. Helier* to maintain the Channel Island service for a twenty-nine week period without break through the winter.

A petition to the Jersey authorities was raised by Great Western masters to complain about difficulties in hearing the fog signal at Corbière lighthouse.

The Southern's *Isle of Jersey* was launched at Wm. Denny & Bros on 22 October, followed by *Isle of Guernsey* on 17 December. Built at a cost of £170,271, *Isle of Jersey* replaced the *Alberta*. Powered by Parson's turbines connected to twin shafts through single reduction gears with steam from three single-ended return-tube Scotch boilers, she achieved 19 knots on trials. With accommodation for 800 first class and 600 second class passengers on day and night crossings, her facilities included cabins with hot and cold water and private lavatories, segregated sleeping areas for second class passengers and a fifty-six seat dining saloon. The Southern commended Denny's for building a steamer suitable for passengers who demanded 'the luxury of the Savoy Hotel, the accommodation of a New York skyscraper, the steadiness of a transatlantic liner, and the speed of a torpedo-boat destroyer – all for the price of a ride in a London taxi cab'. The *Isle of Jersey* entered Southern service from Southampton on 13 March 1930, with *Isle of Guernsey* following on 4 April.

The Great Western's replacement *St. Patrick* was launched on 15 January 1930 at Alexander Stephens & Co, Linthouse, Glasgow. She was the property of the Fishguard and Rosslare Railways and Harbours Company (F&RR&HCo), a joint company owned by the Great Western and the Great Southern Railway of Ireland, and was designed to operate to the Channel Islands in the summer months and from Fishguard to Rosslare in the winter. *St. Patrick* could accommodate 913 passengers in two classes and was capable of 22 knots. She had two sets of single-reduction geared steam turbines with steam supplied from four single-ended boilers. On arrival in Weymouth in March she damaged her rudder and had to be sent to Southampton for repair, incurring a three-week delay.

The *St. Patrick* made her inaugural crossing on 18 April, the first F&RR&HCo ship to operate to the Islands. Following her introduction, the Great Western altered the departure time from Jersey from 7:30 a.m. to 8:30 a.m., withdrawing the facility for passengers to sleep on board overnight. In July the Great Western provided a connecting rail service to Weymouth Town station from Shrewsbury, Wolverhampton and Birmingham, but this proved to be a bad timekeeper.

At the end of the year agreement was reached between the Great Western and Weymouth Corporation to rebuild the pier with two full-length tracks, cranes and quayside accommodation. Structural work, dredging and pier construction would be done by the Corporation with the remainder by the Great Western. In return the Great Western provided a twenty-year guarantee on loan charges for Weymouth Corporation. The works started in February 1931 when Bolton & Lakin commenced work.

The *Isle of Jersey* and the *Isle of Guernsey* proved an immediate success for the Southern, and encouraged them to order a further new vessel from Wm. Denny & Bros. in February 1931, as the *Isle of Sark*. After the keel had been laid the hull shape and machinery were changed and the *Isle of Sark* was fitted with an early semi-Meierform hull with a rounded bow intended to increase stability and reduce fuel consumption. She was the first cross-channel vessel to receive this design, and was launched on 12 November 1931.

In 1932 the Great Western and Southern took steps to collaborate over their freight

The *St Helier* alongside at Weymouth, with her name pennant and the GWR house flag clearly visible. *(Ambrose Greenway collection)*

businesses by amalgamating staff resources, with the Great Western running the Guernsey operation and the Southern running Jersey.

The *Isle of Sark* entered service on 19 March 1932. This created the opportunity to dispose of the *Vera*, but instead the completion of the new lock project in St. Malo allowed the Jersey-St. Malo service to re-open with a larger vessel. French companies had maintained a service with slow small vessels in the interim, and they were compensated by the Southern when the *Vera* took up the service on 1 June 1932. It was proposed that the *Ardena* would take over for the winter period to release the *Vera* for disposal, with a Newhaven steamer transferred to operate for the 1933 season, but in the event the new *Brittany* was ordered, and the *Vera* continued until her delivery.

In the summer of 1932 the Southern employed the *St. Briac* on a series of cruises embracing Rouen, Le Havre, Cherbourg and St. Malo, and calls were also made to the Channel Islands, taking advantage of harbour improvements that enabled larger vessels to call. The *Isle of Guernsey*, the *Isle of Jersey* and the *Isle of Sark* also undertook a programme of shoulder season excursions from the Islands to Dartmouth, Newhaven, Cherbourg, Le Havre and Rouen. Not to be outdone, the Great Western used their fleet for trips calling at Dartmouth, Plymouth, Alderney and Cherbourg, plus one special trip each autumn when the *St. Patrick* returned from Weymouth to Fishguard calling at the Scilly Islands on the way. Day excursion traffic from Weymouth and Torquay to Guernsey became significant, with calls also being made in Cherbourg and Alderney.

After a prolonged period without any major accidents, the *St. Patrick* ran aground on 5 August. She left Weymouth for Jersey at 1:40 p.m. under Capt. Sanderson with 295 passengers and a crew of fifty, plus baggage and mails. The weather was fine and clear, the sea smooth and the wind slight, but foggy conditions later prevailed. About 5:00 p.m. *St.*

Patrick passed the Trinity House vessel *Patricia* at a distance of two to three ships' lengths. The *Patricia* had left the Casquets at 4:00 p.m. but the fog was too thick for her to make Guernsey so she ran to a safe point six miles south-southeast of the Casquets and was anchoring when *St. Patrick* passed along her port side.

About 6:00 p.m. the fog came on thick and continued in this state. At 6.09 p.m. the explosive fog signal at Corbière was heard and the engines put to half speed, 14 to 15 knots, then at 6.10 p.m. to slow, about 10 knots. The records of La Corbière Lighthouse showed four 'extra shots for the *St. Patrick*, 6.5, 6.9, 6.11 and 6.14,' but Capt. Sanderson heard only the signal at 6.09 p.m. and two repetitions, and says that all three were very diffused and hard to take. After the third shot was heard, eddies were observed on the port bow about half a ship's length away. Capt. Sanderson immediately gave the order "Hard a port", and the engines were stopped. The vessel grazed a submerged rock with her port bilge abreast the bridge, and as she swung three more grazings were felt aft. The starboard engine was not reversed; this would have eased the vessel's way and canted her head more quickly.

Capt. Sanderson ordered the watertight doors to be closed and lifeboats and lifebelts to be got ready, but as there was no immediate danger the chief officer and chief steward were sent to reassure passengers. At 6:27 p.m. the vessel was anchored with 60 fathoms on the port cable. However a film of oil was coming onto the water surface, and water levels were rising in the boiler room. The fires were shut off and an S.O.S. message sent to Jersey. Between 8:30 p.m. and 9:00 p.m. the Jersey States tug *Duke of Normandy* and the *Isle of Sark* arrived to offer support. All passengers were safely transferred to the *Isle of Sark* and landed in Jersey the following morning. On Saturday morning *St. Julien* towed *St. Patrick* to St. Aubin's Bay, whence she was towed by *Princess Ena* to St. Helier for makeshift

A busy scene at Weymouth as passengers head from the Channel Islands Boat Express to the waiting **St Julien**. Steps have been placed to allow passengers to leave the carriages, as the train is too long for the platform. A fine collection of taxis is in attendance in this August 1929 view. *(Author's collection)*

The *Ringwood* lies idle alongside in Southampton. *(Author's collection)*

repair. *St. Patrick* was then towed to Plymouth for docking and ultimately went to Cammell Laird at Birkenhead for £6,283 of repairs.

The subsequent Inquiry found that the rock struck by the *St. Patrick* was in the neighbourhood of La Boue and Les Boiteaux, with the vessel lying about half a mile eastward of the course Capt. Sanderson believed himself to have set. In the opinion of the Inquiry this was deemed too fine a course and the accident was attributed to the wrongful acts and default of Capt. Sanderson. The 1929 complaints about the fog signal at Corbière lighthouse were upheld and the Court suggested that additional protection for mariners be provided by the installation of an efficient lighthouse and fog signal at Grosnez Point.

This was the last season in which the *Great Western* was transferred from Fishguard to assist with the Guernsey flower traffic. She was the last Great Western coal fired vessel to operate from Weymouth and at the end of the season was taken away to be broken up.

The *Brighton* was launched on 20 November 1932 at Denny's Yard for the Newhaven-Dieppe route at a cost of £169,950 under joint funding by the French and Southern Railways. A modified version of the *Worthing*, she was slightly larger, but had a shallower draught to allow her to offer relief services to the Islands.

The Southern's third new single funneled turbine passenger vessel the *Brittany* was launched by Wm. Denny & Bros., Dumbarton on 12 April 1933. She was smaller and slower than her sisters, but like them she was capable of sitting on the harbour bottom at low tide. The *Brittany was* designed to replace the *Vera* for the local excursion services around the Islands, the inter-island services and the Jersey-St. Malo route, but she could still accommodate 850 passengers, 500 in first class and 350 in second class. She cost £81,500. The official party travelled to Jersey for her inaugural run on 18 June and returned on the displaced *Vera,* which remained at Southampton until 28 October before being towed by the tug *Seaman* to Pembroke for breaking up. The *Brittany* hit a gale on her initial sailing from Southampton, which amply demonstrated that her light draught and buoyancy, whilst appropriate for her intended use, were unsuited to operating longer

The *St Patrick* was specifically designed to service the needs of the GWR's Channel Islands and Irish routes. *(Ambrose Greenway collection)*

crossings.

On 18 May the *Roebuck* discharged the first cargo of Jersey potatoes on the new quay at Weymouth. This was formally opened on 13 July by the Prince of Wales, with the *St. Helier* bringing an invited party from the Islands for 'Weymouth's Grand Civic Ceremonies'. The Prince elected to fly to Weymouth, but was forced by bad weather to land near Swanage and arrived two hours late for the ceremony. He was reported as saying "I am glad to learn that the new pier, the new berths for cargo boats and the electric crane track will bring your harbour up to date".

The rebuilt facilities comprised a 440 yard quay, 100ft wide with three berths, electric cranes with capacity from 30 cwt to 5 tons, two railway tracks capable of holding passenger trains or fifty wagons, electric capstans, refreshment rooms, offices and stores. The final cost was £150,000 against an estimate of £102,000. The expanded rail capacity allowed Birmingham trains to be transferred to Weymouth Quay, increasing the attractiveness of the port.

New competition appeared in December when Jersey Airways Ltd. established an air service between Jersey and Portsmouth using an eight-seater De Havilland Dragon. A trial flight on 15 December crossed in 54 minutes before the regular service was established from St. Aubyn's Bay on 18 December. A bus connection was provided from Portsmouth & Southsea railway station to the aerodrome. The single fare between Portsmouth and Jersey was £1 12s 6d with a return fare of £2 15s and the advance bookings encouraged the company to borrow two more Dragons and double frequency to twice-daily. The services operated from the beach at West Park near St. Helier and could only operate at low tide, but nonetheless expansion was rapid. On 28 January 1934 a daily two-hour flight was inaugurated from Heston (London) to Jersey, with a connecting bus to central London. The fares were £2 19s 6d single and £4 19s 3d return. Flights from Southampton began in March, with a service to Paris operating during the summer. In its first full year,

Heavy crowds are already aboard *St Helier* but there are still queues on the Quay as she prepares to leave Weymouth. *(Author's collection)*

Jersey Airways carried 20,000 passengers, using a fleet of eight De Havilland 84 Dragons, each capable of carrying eight passengers.

In February 1934 the rebuilt passenger berth was brought into use at Weymouth, and for the summer timetable the direct Bristol service was able to connect at the Quay. The London Paddington service was retimed to depart at 8:30 a.m., with the arrival time in Jersey becoming 6:15 p.m. The route of the winter rail service from London Paddington was diverted to run via Lavington, with the Channel Islands Boat Express departure put back from 9:25 p.m. to 10:15 p.m., whilst maintaining a 2:00 a.m. arrival at Weymouth Quay, giving the route the faster year-round timings. These were the quickest Jersey schedules since the races of 1896, and the fastest ever winter timings to Guernsey.

The London & Channel Islands Company replaced the *Island Queen* and *Channel Queen* in 1934 with a larger 1,100 ton *Island Queen* and 1,156 ton *London Queen*. With greater capacity the company began to expand its potato and tomato business.

Channel Islands Airways was registered on 1 December 1934 as the holding company for Jersey Airways and its new subsidiary Guernsey Airways, which had been formed a week earlier. Whilst the volumes of passengers carried by the airline were small in relation to sea carryings, the railway companies recognised the importance of their new competitor. After protracted negotiations one-third of the shares in Channel Islands Airways were bought jointly by the Great Western and the Southern. This allowed expansion, and Jersey Airlines placed a £50,000 order with De Havilland for six four-engined DH86 aircraft, which carried fourteen passengers and reduced the flight time from Heston to less than ninety minutes. Two further DH89 Dragon Rapides were introduced in 1935 to replace the Dragons. A service to Rennes operated from 8 January 1935 to 29 March. A Plymouth service began in April 1936, and Exeter, Dinard and Shoreham followed in 1938.

The Southern relief vessel *Princess Ena*, took a party of 500 Scouts from Southampton

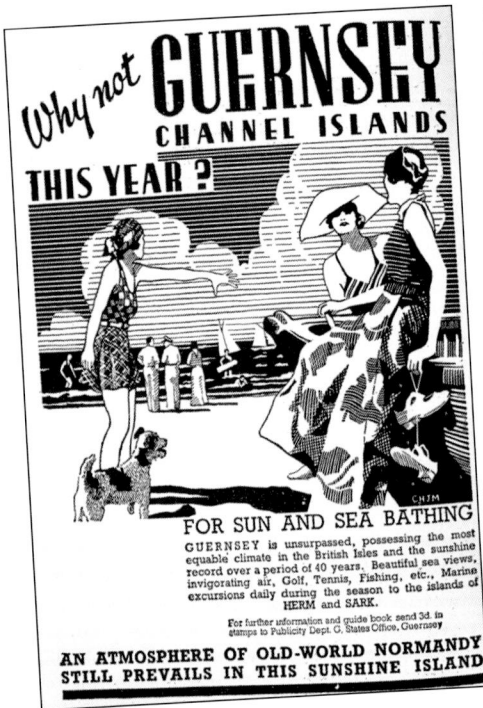

Why not **GUERNSEY** CHANNEL ISLANDS THIS YEAR?

FOR SUN AND SEA BATHING

GUERNSEY is unsurpassed, possessing the most equable climate in the British Isles and the sunshine record over a period of 40 years. Beautiful sea views, invigorating air, Golf, Tennis, Fishing, etc., Marine excursions daily during the season to the islands of HERM and SARK.

For further information and guide book send 3d. in stamps to Publicity Dept. G. States Office, Guernsey

AN ATMOSPHERE OF OLD-WORLD NORMANDY STILL PREVAILS IN THIS SUNSHINE ISLAND

to Jersey on 3 August 1935, arriving at 10:40 a.m. After discharging her passengers, *Princess Ena* left empty for St. Malo at 12:00 p.m. to reposition for the evening service to Southampton. She caught fire about six miles south of Corbière, and the blaze quickly got out of control. *Princess Ena* dropped anchor some nine miles south of Corbière and was abandoned by her forty-two crew, who were rescued by the Jersey States tug *Duke de Normandie* and the *St. Brieuc*. The fire continued to burn over the next twenty-four hours until at around 1:26 p.m. on 4 August *Princess Ena* sank stern-first. Capt. Lewis and his officers stayed alongside throughout the blaze and watched their vessel sink from the *Ringwood*. *Princess Ena* was the last railway steamer to be lost while on service from Southampton or Weymouth.

'Tributes were paid to the courage of the officers of the *Princess Ena*, the cross-Channel steamer which sank on Sunday after being on fire off Jersey on Saturday, when they arrived at Southampton last night. E. J. Missenden, the docks and marine manager of the Southern Railway Company, appealed to the crew to give all the information they could at the inquiry, which opens today. He said the company would, if possible, avoid dismissing any men. All their losses of kit would be restored, and they would each have a week's holiday with full pay'.

[Western Daily Press, 6 August 1935]

In December 1934 Denny Bros approached the Southern to propose the fitment of a trial stabiliser system to one of their fleet, at a cost of £4,400 for equipment and £2,800 for fitment. The two companies shared the risk of the venture. The *Isle of Sark* was selected and fitted with the experimental Denny-Brown stabiliser in March 1936, the first such fitment in the world. The device was put into reverse during a demonstration cruise, causing the vessel to roll by 9° despite being in a smooth Southampton Water, and the stabiliser reduced a 10° roll by half during a rough crossing in April. The prototype was a success and quickly appreciated by passengers.

Work commenced on a new Southern passenger shed in St. Helier on 6 January 1936 and passengers used it for the first time on 23 May.

Coast Lines Ltd. were expanding its shipping interests through a number of takeovers, and in 1936 made advances to the London & Channel Islands Shipping Company. The latter had been contemplating expansion but accepted the bid.

The *Brittany* sailed from Guernsey to view the maiden call of the *Queen Mary* in Cherbourg on 27 May 1936, and the *St. Helier* offered a similar excursion from Weymouth. At the end of the season the Southern considered withdrawing the *Brittany* as commercial results from the Jersey-St. Malo were still proving unacceptable.

The winter railway service to Weymouth had restaurant cars provided in both directions, with the service from Weymouth Quay to London Paddington operating directly over the Berks & Hants route, thereby accelerating the schedule by 55 minutes. *St. Julien* and *St. Helier* underwent extensive reconditioning during the winter refits to provide more

The *Isle of Sark* leaves St Peter Port. *(Dave Hocquard collection)*

covered passenger accommodation and increased dining capability; the number of berths was increased from 353 to 375 on each vessel.

In January 1937 the London & Channel Islands Shipping Company considered changing its name, as its activities were not solely confined to the Islands. At an Extraordinary General Meeting held on 31 May it was changed to the British & Channel Islands Shipping Co. Ltd. but this was further amended on 18 June to the British Channel Islands Shipping Co. Ltd., following representations from the Jersey authorities. The fleet gradually grew with the acquisition of seven vessels leading to 1939, and the company became active in distribution in the Islands. Coast Lines continued their takeovers of smaller companies, and made an approach to the Plymouth, Channel Islands & Brittany Steam Ship Co. to which the company agreed and the change took place at the AGM held on 2 March. Whilst the company was now managed by the London & Channel Islands Steam Ship Co., it continued to trade under its own name and acquired the goodwill of the Bristol route from the Bristol City Lines of Steamships Ltd. on 31 May 1937. The *New Verdun* and *Coombe Dingle* were acquired and soon replaced with new tonnage. *Coombe Dingle* was sold on 28 October and *New Verdun* on 13 December. In March Coast Lines Ltd. purchased the Dutch *Mimaja*, which was building alongside the *Denbigh Coast* and *Hampshire Coast*. She was launched as *Welsh Coast* but was transferred in May to the Plymouth, Channel Islands & Brittany Steam Ship Co. Ltd and renamed *Emerald Queen*.

Jersey airport at St. Peter was opened in March 1937, and the first regular airmail was carried to the island on 1 June. Henceforth all urgent mail was carried by air, and the arrival of the morning mailboat was reduced in significance for islanders. Jersey Airways carried 33,300 passengers and approaching one million pounds weight of mail and freight, mainly between Southampton and Jersey with a cumulative volume of 110,000 passengers in the first four years of operation. The railway interest ensured that air passengers enjoyed rail-air packages akin to those offered by sea. The railway companies saw themselves as multi-modal conglomerates, with air, sea and road interests as well as rail, profiting from

The *Normannia* lies alongside in Le Havre. *(Author's collection)*

passengers and cargo irrespective of how they travelled to the Islands.

The Great Western introduced a fleet of 200 specially built ventilated covered vans in 1938 for express goods services designed to get produce to market as quickly as possible. Up to four cargo boats were being operated each day between Weymouth and Guernsey. The Great Western cargo fleet made 212 special trips during the season, to be trans-shipped to 15,024 vans on 415 special trains, with up to five trains daily from Weymouth Quay to Westbury, then on variously to Birmingham Bordesley, Cardiff, Wolverhampton Oxley, London Paddington and Southall. To ease the requirement for special couplings on passenger trains, the Great Western embarked on an extensive realignment of the Weymouth tramway in March 1938, including a major deviation to relax the curve at Ferry's Corner and an improved alignment under a reconstructed Town Bridge. The works were completed in July 1939.

In March the *Saxon Queen* was delivered, registered to the Plymouth, Channel Islands & Brittany Steam Ship Co. The sale of the company and *Emerald Queen* and *Saxon Queen* to the British Channel Islands Shipping Co. Ltd. was approved at an Extraordinary General Meeting on 15 June.

There was a general increase in Southampton passenger carryings for the 1938 season, with the most marked being a seventy-seven per cent rise in the figures on the St. Malo route. It was a record year at Weymouth, with 133,000 passengers travelling on the Island services, and 22,379 on the excursion programme. 4,624,612 chips of tomatoes and 307,604 boxes of flowers were also carried.

1939 began positively for the Great Western and Southern companies, with spring passenger carryings surpassing the records of the previous year. The new Guernsey airport at Forest officially opened on 5 May and Guernsey Airways and Jersey Airways began operating passenger flights to Heston (London) and Southampton and weekend trips to Shoreham. These services carried 5,000 passengers, before being reduced at the outbreak of war.

Services to the Islands from Southampton were operated by the *Isle of Guernsey, Isle of Jersey, Isle of Sark* and *Lorina,* which sailed daily except Sundays, with additional steamers at weekends. The Jersey-St. Malo service was operated by the *Brittany,* with four trips weekly and special day excursions to Sark, Guernsey and Granville. The Southern also offered a nightly service from Southampton to St. Malo in both directions using the *Hantonia* and *Normannia*, with a twice weekly daytime service using the *Isle of Thanet*. At Weymouth the *St. Helier, St. Julien* and *St. Patrick* maintained the passenger services, backed by the *Roebuck* and *Sambur* for cargo sailings.

Passenger carryings to the Islands began to fall as the international political situation deteriorated during the peak holiday season. Many holidaymakers curtailed their stay and headed home as soon as they could be accommodated on the steamers. The British government requisitioned *Isle of Jersey* on 25 August. Two days later, all merchant shipping was brought under Admiralty control, but the majority of vessels remained on their existing schedules.

The daytime Southampton-St. Malo service was suspended from 27 August and overnight sailings withdrawn from 7 September. On both 28 and 29 August the *Brittany's* sailings between St. Malo and Jersey were cancelled, and on the 30th she left Jersey with 300 French reservists on board, returning from St. Malo on the following day. Provisional arrangements were made for a reduced service to be operated from Jersey at 11:00 a.m. on Tuesdays, returning from St. Malo at 11:00 a.m. on Thursdays. A weekly transfer of mails from the Island mailboat to the *Brittany* in Jersey, enabled the maintenance of a service to St. Malo until the end of December 1939.

The Needles passage was closed to commercial shipping from 1 September, with all traffic diverted via Spithead. Access to Southampton was only permitted in official daylight hours even though schedules of sailings were constantly upset by weather conditions and the impact of war in the Channel. Dispensation was given for Channel Islands and Le Havre sailings to pass through a special night opening of the 'gate'.

War was declared on Sunday 3 September 1939. For a time life continued much as normal, and the impact was most keenly felt on the shipping services. Sailings were hit by more stringent controls on travel and the rapid implementation of service reductions. The last Weymouth boat trains ran on 5 September, with the down service arriving at 2:20 a.m. on the 6th. Great Western passenger services from Weymouth closed down on instruction from the Immigration Office after the 2:30 a.m. departure on 9 September, and the *St. Julien* returned with 114 passengers, the *St. Patrick* following light. The port was deemed unable to deal with freshly imposed passport and exit permit examination requirements. The *St. Julien* was requisitioned on 9 September and departed for Avonmouth on the 12th. A week later *St. Helier* sailed from Weymouth to Fishguard to cover the *St. Andrew* on the Rosslare service. The *Roebuck* and *Sambur* were retained to maintain the Weymouth cargo operation Henceforth all Channel Islands mail, passenger and parcels traffic was to be shipped via Southampton, which also became the base for requisitioned steamers of the Great Western, London, Midland & Scottish Railway (LM&SR), London & North Eastern Railway (L&NER) and Southern fleets.

The Southampton passenger service was reduced to a thrice-weekly operation from 11 September and vessels began to appear donned in grey war paint. The *Lorina* was transferred to government service and replaced by the *Hantonia;* the *Isle of Guernsey* was the next to depart on 23 September. The remaining operation faced blackouts on ships, in sheds and on the quays which, coupled with constant challenge by military forces, made working conditions extraordinarily difficult. All passengers were required to be in possession of valid passports and exit permits, and the resultant checks created significant delays in the ports. Baggage was liable to examination by officials in addition to undergoing the normal customs examination. Ship operators had to apply to H.M. Customs before bunkering could be undertaken, and vessels were limited to the amount of fuel required for a normal round-trip with a small margin in reserve. The Southern imposed restrictions on the number of passengers in order to give an added measure of safety. All passengers were required to obtain a boat embarkation ticket in addition to their normal rail and boat ticket, with the number of tickets being issued for each sailing being within the revised capacity. The service to the Islands was maintained outwards by night from Southampton, with a daytime return crossing, but shortening daylight hours after 15 November necessitated night crossings in both directions; departures from the Islands changed to 3:00 p.m. from Jersey and midnight from Guernsey on Mondays, Wednesdays and Fridays.

The fleet was further reduced on 16 November, when the *St. Helier* was requisitioned to serve as a transport vessel. The service continued despite these wartime difficulties. The departure time of the *Brittany's* sailing from St. Malo for Jersey was moved to 12:00 p.m. on Thursdays from 3 October and then to 9:00 a.m. on Fridays from 17 November. Between 18 November and 2 December the *Isle of Jersey* went to Glasgow for boiler cleaning, whilst on 30 November the *Normannia* grazed Platte Ledge when entering St. Helier at 3:52 p.m. Heavy fog caused the arrival at Southampton of the 22 December departure from the Islands, scheduled for 8:00 a.m. on the 23rd, to be delayed by 48 hours until Christmas morning. The *Brittany* acquired war paint during the Christmas holiday, whilst she laid-over in St. Malo before being withdrawn on 27 December.

There was still substantial cargo business on offer. At the outbreak of war the Jersey tomato season was at its peak and between September and December 1939 1,158,324 packages, representing 7,240 tons were carried to Southampton. In the same period 213,645 packages of tomatoes, 55,906 packages of flowers, 12,962 packages of vegetables, and 278 cattle were shipped from Guernsey.

Restrictions were placed on the planting and export of flowers from Guernsey so that land could be given over to the production of foodstuffs, including potatoes for the use of islanders and for export. Normally Guernsey produce was distributed throughout England, southern Scotland and Wales, Belfast and Dublin, but it became clear that if reasonable deliveries were to be made they would have to be restricted to the principal towns. An agreed split of destinations between the Weymouth and Southampton routes was established, but the irregular arrival pattern of steamers meant that they often ended up being loaded with traffic irrespective of final destination.

In planning cargo shipments for the 1940 season it was evident that the use of Southampton as a commercial port would be restricted by the military authorities and the withdrawal of the Weymouth passenger service permitted a greater tonnage to be handled there. The country was divided into three areas for distribution purposes - Southern Division, Northern Division and South Wales Division - with apportionment based on the percentage of traffic carried by the companies in the 1939 season. This gave the Southern approximately 12,000 tons to transport for the season, principally for London, Southern stations, and L&NER (Great Eastern section) stations via London.

On 9 January 1940 the *Normannia* collided with *HM Trawler M39* at 6:35 a.m. when inbound into Southampton. Later that day the *Isle of Sark* struck a buoy when berthing in St. Helier and damaged a propeller, requiring her to be dry docked to allow it to be changed two days later. The *Brittany* was transferred to Folkestone on 22 January and replaced on the 24th by the *Hantonia*. She relieved the *Isle of Sark* for three trips in February and took the place of the *Normannia* on the Island routes from early May.

There was still optimism for the forthcoming tourist and growing seasons. On 21 February a letter by 'Publicity' in the Guernsey Evening Press noted that the 'air services and railways have intimated that they will have no difficulty in bringing visitors to Guernsey in large numbers every week throughout the holiday season'. It was observed that many workers in the Midlands were now enjoying wage levels far in excess of their peacetime standard, with substantial overtime from wartime work leaving them with a surplus to spend on holidays. The paper reported that the Island was to make a bid for summer visitors by distributing a six-page brochure to convey 'her attractions as an Island of Beauty of Rest and of Pleasure.' It was anticipated that transport by sea and air could be provided for up to 3,000 visitors weekly.'

The Jersey Morning News reported a member of the States Tourism Committee remarking 'Everything is pointing towards a visitor season becoming a fact, providing, of course, that nothing really serious happens in the meantime'. The Jersey Tourism Committee suggested that the island offered ' the ideal resort for wartime holidays. Happily our Island is far removed from the theatre of war. The bays with their eternal sands, sea and sunshine, together produce an atmosphere of peaceful tranquility, strangely different from the rest of the world'.

This optimism was encouraged by the withdrawal of administrative controls on passengers to and from the Islands from 15 March following representations to the Home Office by the Island authorities, but the restrictions were reintroduced in June when it was suspected that refugees from France might be entering the UK through Jersey.

On 4 March the *Fratton* made a special crossing from St. Malo to Guernsey with a consignment of over 100 tons of wood from Rumania to make tomato and flower boxes for the export trade. These would normally have been sourced from the Baltic, but wartime conditions made this impossible.

The *Isle of Sark* collided with an unknown steamer near Spit Refuge buoy on 14 March but was able to continue her crossing to the Islands and maintain her subsequent programme of voyages. She became the first vessel to be fitted with armaments - a twelve-pounder gun. During April and May degaussing equipment was fitted to the *Hantonia*, *Isle of Sark*, *Lorena* and *St. David*. The *Ringwood*, *Minster*, *Fratton* and *Haslemere* were also equipped between trips to and from the Islands. *Brittany* returned from Folkestone to Island service on 20 April, followed by *Isle of Guernsey* on 23 April and *Dinard* the following day. Rail fares and charges were increased by ten per cent on 1 May. On 4 May the *Normannia* was requisitioned by the government.

The first loadings of the 1940 potato season were disappointing when twenty-five tons were shipped on the *Porthmorna* to Weymouth on 14 May. Farmers considered there was no incentive to dig early during dry weather, as it was in their interests to wait for rain to swell the crop. There was evidence of a farmer protest against early digging at a fixed price. By 18 May just 238 loads of potatoes had been shipped against 6,162 in 1939. The States Agricultural Committee placed adverts suggesting that it might prove necessary to curtail sailings, and some farmers agreed to begin digging from 20 May.

The Le Havre route was closed on 19 May as German forces pressed deeper into France, with the *St. Briac* making the last sailing, and traffic was then routed through St. Malo until 28 May. The Jersey-St. Malo service was increased from fortnightly to weekly, and sailed directly from St. Malo to Southampton.

On 20 May the *Coral* left Jersey for Southampton with 2,255 packages of potatoes, a weight of 113 tons. From then until the middle of June shipments were regular and increasing. The following day *Sambur* sailed for Weymouth with 337 tons (6,626 packages), and on 22 May *Ringwood* sailed for Southampton with 275 tons. The pattern of sailings for the following week was established as: -

Mon: Southampton, & Liverpool (Newhaven if necessary)
Tue: Weymouth, Newhaven, Poole and Holyhead
Wed: Weymouth (386t), Southampton (295t), Cardiff (371t) and Portsmouth (430t)
Thu: Weymouth, Newhaven and Poole
Fri: Weymouth, Southampton, London, Liverpool and Holyhead
Sat: Weymouth, Poole, Holyhead, Cardiff and Newhaven

The **St Patrick** arriving at Weymouth. *(Author's collection)*

On 23 May the cargo vessels *Tonbridge*, *Deal* and *Hythe* were transferred from Dover to Southampton, followed by the *Whitstable*. As the need for vessels to support the evacuation from Dunkirk became clear on 29 May, a signal was put out stating 'all available Southern Railway steamers of 1,000 tons gross with a range of 150 miles are required for immediate government service'. The *Whitstable* returned to Dover, along with the *St. Briac* and *Hythe* for 'special service', and the *Brittany* and *Roebuck* were requisitioned and sent straight Dover.

In June every available ship was pressed into service to lift the Jersey potato and the Guernsey tomato crops, which promised record offerings. The tomato season was late, but crops were heavy and good prices were being returned to the Guernsey growers. Whilst hoteliers and boarding house keepers initially anticipated receiving some visitors from the UK, it became increasingly apparent that the outlook was rapidly worsening.

On 6 June the announcement of a drop in prices the following week caused intense congestion at the Jersey Weighbridge. Between 6 and 8 June the *Roebuck* was recalled for one more trip to Guernsey, returning with 380 tons of tomatoes and on 9 June the *Sambur* returned to Weymouth with tomatoes. Both the *Roebuck* and *Sambur* were then requisitioned for war service with the L&NER's *Sheringham* brought in to deputise. On 7 June *Hythe* and *Whitstable* came back into service only to be taken over again, along with *Ringwood* on 9 June. *Ringwood* was returned on 14 June.

The final sailing between Southampton, Jersey and St. Malo took place on 14 June when 114 passengers were carried on the *Hantonia*. Paris fell, and all rail communication to St. Malo was suspended from the same day. The *Hantonia* returned directly to Southampton on 16 June with 650 passengers on board. Cars were not accepted on the sailing to maximise passenger space, and owners were seen selling their vehicles or even giving them away on the quay. The British government asked the Islands for help in evacuating St. Malo, and eighteen yachts sailed from Jersey to assist. St. Malo was occupied from 17 June.

The *Train Ferry No 1* arrived in Jersey on 17 June loaded with government stores, whilst sister vessel the *Train Ferry No 3* was loading a cargo of Bofors guns in Southampton earmarked for the defence of the Islands. When it became clear that demilitarisation of the

Islands was imminent, the *Train Ferry No 3* sailed without her cargo.

The *Sheringham* was sent from Guernsey to Alderney on 17 June with instructions to take off men of military age and child evacuees, as the previous day the men of the British machine gun training centre on the island had been instructed to leave and destroy their equipment, but she returned almost empty. The *Staffa*, the normal supply ship between the two islands, was now strikebound with the crew refusing to work so close to the combat zone. After considerable confusion, it was left to a flotilla of six small cargo boats to effect the evacuation.

By 18 June German forces had taken Cherbourg and on 19 June the British government considered the Islands indefensible, and began the process of withdrawing military personnel and material back to the UK. A government voluntary evacuation scheme was announced on the same day, and women, children and men of military age were advised to leave the Islands and were given priority in the evacuation arrangements. The Home Office gave little direction on what this meant, so in Guernsey this was interpreted as a general instruction with immediate effect with departures to begin the following day; in Jersey the Bailiff A M Coutanche advised people to stay. Families had a matter of hours to decide their course of action. The entire population of Alderney, around 1,500 people, chose to leave, 8,000 of 50,000 left Jersey and 17,000 of 40,000 left Guernsey. Demilitarisation was completed on 20 June and the last submarine telephone cable link from Britain to France was cut.

All available ships were requisitioned for the evacuation of service personnel from the Islands and St. Malo. The *Train Ferry No 1* took personnel and supplies back to Southampton. The *Brittany* brought back members of the Army Technical School who had been training in Jersey, together with military personnel and their families back from both Jersey and Guernsey. The *Biarritz* and *Malines* carried military personnel to Southampton and Weymouth respectively. Produce traffic was abandoned as there were no vessels available for the loading of potatoes, and cargo vessels were employed to evacuate residents from Jersey. Thousands of packages were left on the quaysides awaiting shipment, but these were left behind as steamers concentrated on the passenger evacuation.

The *Hantonia* took the mail service from Southampton on 19 June and was retimed to return from Jersey at 7:00 a.m. and Guernsey at 9:15 a.m. on the 21st. The evacuation effort was stepped up significantly on 20 June. Many passenger and cargo vessels assisted in the evacuation, including: -

19 June	Alderney > Weymouth	*Glen Tilt*
	Jersey/Guernsey > Southampton	*Biarritz*
	Guernsey > Poole	*Guernsey Queen*
	Guernsey > Southampton	*Train Ferry No 3 (from Jersey)*
	Jersey > Southampton	*Train Ferry No 1*
20 June	Guernsey > Weymouth	*Antwerp, Batavier IV, Felixstowe, Haslemere, Sheringham*
	Guernsey > Southampton	*Biarritz, Corinia*
	Jersey > Weymouth	*Farfield, Malines, Ngatira, Perelle, Porthmorna, Rye, Stork, Suffolk Coast, The Baron, West Coaster*
	Jersey > Southampton	*Archangel, Autocarrier, Coral, Hodder*
	Islands > Southampton	*New Fawn*
21 June	Guernsey > Weymouth	*Deal, Doggersbank, Duke of Argyll, Duke of York, Fratton, Friso, Glen Tilt,*

		Gorecht, Sheringham, Tonbridge, Viking, Zeus
	Guernsey > Plymouth	Saxon Queen
	Jersey > Weymouth	Atlantic, Brittany, Caribia, Despatch II, Dominence, Felspar, Hondsrug, Jaba, Minster, Pinguin, Ringwood, Wega , Whitstable
	Jersey > Southampton	Shepperton Ferry
	Jersey/Guernsey > Southampton	Hantonia, Isle of Sark,
22 June	Guernsey > Weymouth	Antwerp, Biarritz, Maidstone, Princess Astrid, Rye, Sheringham
	Guernsey > Southampton	Malines
	Islands > Weymouth	Courier, Joy Bell III, Madeleine Kamiel, Present Help, Vestal
23 June	Alderney > Weymouth	Alnwick, Camroux IV, Empire Jonquil, Stork, Suffolk Coast

Weymouth, which had typically handled two Channel Island sailings a day, was faced with some 58 arrivals and 25,484 passengers over three days from the morning of 20 June, many on vessels which were not equipped for handling passenger traffic.

All vessels could recount similar tales of changes of plan, the loading of large numbers of evacuees, and delays in disembarking at Weymouth. The *Brittany* left Southampton at 9:45 p.m. on 20 June and arrived in St. Helier at 9:34 a.m. on the 21st. After loading with 914 evacuees, *Brittany* left Jersey at 1:30 p.m. and arrived in Weymouth Bay to anchor at 9:41 p.m. She was not able to berth until 11:46 a.m. on 22 June and completed disembarkation at 2:27 p.m. Leaving Weymouth at 12:10 p.m. on 24 June, she returned to Southampton.

The *Haslemere* left Guernsey at 2:00 p.m. on 20 June carrying around 350 child evacuees and a handful of adults, berthing at Weymouth at 9:00 p.m. before returning to Southampton. She then undertook another round trip between 23 and 25 June. The *Minster* was also in Guernsey on 20 June loading cargo, when she was requisitioned and sent to Jersey at 5:21 p.m. Leaving St. Helier at 6:00 a.m. on 21 June with around 500 evacuees she sailed directly to Weymouth, arriving at 5:45 p.m. On 25 June the *Minster* left Weymouth at 9:53 a.m. and sailed to Guernsey, where she arrived at 5:24 p.m. and loaded produce. Leaving Guernsey at 9:00 p.m. on 26 June the *Minster* arrived in Southampton at 8:55 a.m. on 27 June and was laid up.

The *Ringwood* was engaged on the cargo service in Guernsey on 20 June when she was requisitioned and sent to Jersey. She left at 4:30 p.m. and arrived in Jersey at 7:00 p.m. On the following day she left Jersey at 4:14 p.m. with 603 evacuees, berthing at Weymouth at 2:30 p.m. to disembark before returning to Southampton.

The *Tonbridge* was held outside Weymouth for thirty hours awaiting entry into the harbour, with one nurse on board and children sleeping in cattle stalls; food was brought out to the ship whilst she waited.

One evacuee's tale was recounted by Charles Ammon MP in a written question to the Home Secretary: - 'The evacuation arrangements, such as they were, were deplorable. I came over on the *Antwerp*, a troopship licensed to carry (and lifebelts provided for) 700, and there were 2,000 men, women and children aboard, to be chased by a submarine halfway across. We reached Weymouth at 5 p.m. and came alongside at 9.30 p.m., and there we were left without food or drink until the next day, when people started fainting in all directions and officialdom woke up at last.'

A short train awaits passengers from the *St Patrick* as she prepares to berth at Weymouth. *(Great Western Railway)*

The port struggled to cope with the huge number of short-notice arrivals. Children were dispersed across the country with many ending up in Cheshire, Lancashire, Scotland and West Yorkshire. One sick child died during the evacuation, and one was born. In the confusion of evacuation passengers became separated from their baggage and huge quantities remained at Weymouth to be identified and cleared through customs.

The Guernsey Evening Press reported: -

'The scenes in the town this morning will never be forgotten by any Guernseyman. Thousands thronged the narrow streets making last-minute arrangements for evacuation. Nowhere in the town could a suitcase be purchased. Many shops closed their doors as it was found that although it was easy to dispose of their goods, no money was forthcoming.'

[*Guernsey Evening Press, 20 June 1940*]

The following day the Guernsey Star reported

'Six thousand people, including nearly all the children of school age, have left Guernsey.'

[*Guernsey Star, 21 June 1940*]

The Southern continued to operate despite the deteriorating military situation and hostile enemy activity in the exposed passage across the channel. Some twelve sailings were made from the Islands between Sunday 23 June and Friday 28 June

The *Brittany* was returned to the company on 25 June, too late to play a role in the evacuation. The UK Ministry of Food was anxious to secure as much a possible of the potato crop and the *Deal, Maidstone* and *Whitstable* were sent to Jersey. The L&NER *Felixstowe* joined the Weymouth fleet on 26 June, but in the event did not sail to the islands.

The *Ringwood* sailed overnight with general cargo for Guernsey on 27 June and completed her discharge in St. Peter Port by 6:00 p.m. on the 28th. The *Isle of Sark* left Southampton at 7:17 p.m. on 27 June with 259 passengers for Jersey and Guernsey, arriving without incident in St. Helier at 6:29 a.m. on the 28th. The political decision to demilitarise the islands had not been publicly communicated, so German forces used reconnaissance flights to observe defence capability and look for signs of surrender. At 10:15 a.m. a hostile plane was observed above the harbour whilst the *Isle of Sark* was completing passenger embarkation. She left for Guernsey and Southampton at 10:32 a.m. and when halfway between the islands observed another enemy plane passing over from the Guernsey direction. The *Isle of Sark* reached St. Peter Port at 12:25 p.m. with 484 passengers on board, almost all of whom were travelling to Southampton. As the ship's departure was not scheduled until after nightfall, passengers were allowed to land in Guernsey, provided they returned to the ship by 8:00 p.m.

As passengers were assembling to board the *Isle of Sark* at 6:55 p.m three Heinkel He111 aircraft appeared from an easterly direction. and dropped a salvo of bombs on the pier. As further planes appeared, Capt. Golding, Master of the *Isle of Sark,* sent out radio messages to the Southern and the naval authorities in Portsmouth advising them of the attack. The planes flew over the harbour three at a time, dropping a large number of bombs and machine-gunning vehicles waiting with their loads on the White Rock. The only defence available on the Island was on board the railway vessels. The *Isle of Sark's* twelve-pounder gun and four Lewis guns went into action and fought off dive bombing and low-level attacks, thus limiting the damage to the harbour and the ships. *Ringwood* and *Sheringham* were in the harbour loading tomatoes and also went into action to defend the harbour. *Ringwood's* master was ashore in the Old Harbour at the time and reported an 'exciting and dangerous passage' back to his ship. There was no damage to the ship but AS Cooke, who was ashore at the time of the attack, sustained bullet wounds and was taken to hospital. Passengers took shelter on the lower landing level of the Jetty and only one, a French refugee, was injured and detained in hospital. The attack caused the complete destruction of a large number of vehicles loaded with tomatoes which were awaiting shipment on the White Rock, in the mistaken belief that they were military vehicles, and considerable damage was done to shore facilities; casualties in Guernsey were heavy, with thirty four killed and thirty injured. A number of small craft anchored in the harbour were sunk.

The public clock on the weighbridge at St. Peter Port stopped at two and a half minutes to seven. A simultaneous raid took place in Jersey, with heavy bombing and machine gunning. Again, lorries lined up on the quay and loaded with potatoes for export were an immediate target and Norman's store and warehouse was set ablaze; eight people died in the raid.

The Guernsey raid ceased at 8:00 p.m. and Capt. Golding was instructed to sail as soon as circumstances permitted. He decided to remain until 10:00 p.m. to allow passengers time to rejoin the ship and for remaining Guernsey-originating passengers to reach the quay. Thirty-eight of the forty-nine railway company staff on Guernsey were evacuated.

Last to board was the Southern Railway's ticket checker, Mr. Prince, who left the island without returning home to collect luggage or personal effects. The *Ringwood* sailed for Southampton at 9:54 p.m. followed by the *Isle of Sark* at 10:05 p.m. with 647 passengers on board. Large numbers of planes were heard passing overhead on three occasions during the channel crossing, but *Isle of Sark* docked safely at Southampton at 8:30 a.m. on 29 June with *Ringwood* following at 9:21 a.m.

The *Hythe* left Southampton for the Islands on the night of 28 June, but was recalled shortly after her departure. The *Felixstowe* was loading cargo for Jersey, but her sailing was also cancelled.

The railway companies appealed to government departments for assistance in further evacuations and the withdrawal of staff, but this could not be provided. There was thus a temporary end to the service.

On 30 June a German pilot landed on Guernsey to establish that it was not defended, and that evening a number of transport planes brought in a Luftwaffe platoon. The following day Jersey was occupied after surrender ultimatums had been dropped from aircraft. The BBC broadcast a statement that 'all communication with the Channel Islands has been temporarily suspended ... all letters and parcels for the islands should not be posted pending further announcement'.

Five days later, the *Deal* (with 404 tons of potatoes), *Maidstone* (with 429 tons) and *Whitstable* (with 426 tons) were still unloading at Stonehouse Pool, Plymouth as the wagon stabling accommodation was insufficient to permit the discharge of two vessels simultaneously.

In the period between the outbreak of hostilities and the suspension of service, the Southern steamers conveyed 62,654 passengers, 61,375 tons of cargo, 17,401 bags of parcel post and many thousands of parcels. The total quantity of traffic conveyed on the Island services by passenger and cargo boats through Southampton comprised 29,302 tons and 115,381 parcels. In the same period 1,694,068 packages of tomatoes (compared to 1,675,149 in 1939), 199,417 packages of flowers, 47,068 packages of vegetables, and 109 cattle were shipped from Guernsey. The total potato traffic conveyed from Jersey during the period of operation was 6,824 tons. In June 1940 - despite cancellation of many shipments - 954,603 packages were transported, compared to 812,326 in 1939.

The Channel Island fleet was now available for other duties.

CHAPTER SEVEN

Channel Island ships at war 1939-1945

'Friday, 31st May, saw her once again in Dunkirk Harbour, and on this occasion she embarked sixteen hundred French troops. They were fated to make an interesting passage. While the St. Helier was coming out in the dusk, H.M.S. Sharpshooter, a mine layer engaged on transport work, went sharp across her bows and the inevitable collision took place. The St. Helier herself was not too badly damaged, but it was different with the Sharpshooter, whose Captain had to request the St. Helier to keep steaming into her. So for forty minutes, in the one spot in which such a performance was least desirable, the St. Helier with one engine at half speed, pushed her bow into the broken side of the mine layer which otherwise would certainly have been swamped and sunk. By this time it was quite dark and enemy planes, aware that something was not going quite according to plan, commenced to drop flares and bombs in the vicinity. Nevertheless, neither vessel had been hit when a tug came out to attend to the Sharpshooter. Misfortune, however, was abroad that night, and no sooner had the tug taken the Sharpshooter in charge than the Princess Eleanora, in normal times a well-known pleasure steamer, picking her way through the confusion, crashed into the St. Helier on the starboard bow. Fortunately things might have been worse, for the resulting damage was not sufficient to prevent either vessel from pursuing its course, although the Princess Eleanora came out of the encounter minus a paddle box. For the French troops on board, these occurrences had not been the most favourable prelude to the coming cross-Channel trip. While the St. Helier was working her engines

slowly ahead to keep her bow well into the broken side of the Sharpshooter, they had been used to trim the ship, large numbers of soldiers being moved sometimes to one side and sometimes to the other as the tide swung the vessel. Nevertheless the St. Helier was by now heading for home, and they were inclined to congratulate themselves that the worst had passed, when the St. Helier ran over a submerged wreck. At that, the French troops are said to have shrugged their shoulders in a fashion suggestive at once of astonishment and resignation. They had come to the conclusion that there were no limits to the possibilities. However, the luck of the Great Western steamships held good, and nothing further of an unfortunate nature took place'.

[Dunkirk and the Great Western]

The *Isle of Jersey was* requisitioned as early as 25 August 1939 to be sent to the Harland and Wolff yard in Belfast for conversion into a hospital carrier. She returned for installation of 'domestic' items at the Southern workshops in Southampton and then sailed under sealed orders on 1 September to support the home fleet in the north of Scotland, based at Scapa Flow.

After the declaration of war the *Isle of Guernsey* sailed from Southampton to Cherbourg on 4 September to carry troops forming part of the initial British Expeditionary Force. The *Lorina* and the *St. Julien* were requisitioned for initial use as troop carriers; the *Lorina* made her first crossing from Southampton to Cherbourg on 11 September, and the *St. Julien* followed on 12 September, leaving Weymouth for Avonmouth to undertake two troop sailings to St. Nazaire. The *Isle of Guernsey* was requisitioned as a hospital ship and left Southampton on 23 September to undergo similar conversion work to the *Isle of Jersey*. The *St. Patrick* was requisitioned a week later for work as a troop ship between Avonmouth and France until 11 October, when she returned to the Fishguard route. The *St. Julien* moved to Southampton on 5 October for conversion as a hospital ship, and was repainted white with red crosses to operate between Newhaven and Dieppe. The following day the *Isle of Guernsey* sailed under sealed orders from Southampton to return injured service personnel to Newhaven. The *St. Helier* was requisitioned on 16 November to serve as transport between Southampton and Cherbourg.

The *Isle of Jersey* was actively engaged in war operations during the early part of 1940, particularly during the period of fighting in Norway. On 7 May the Commander-In-Chief of the Home Forces signalled a special message to the *Isle of Jersey* stating 'The expeditious manner in which you have responded to the many calls made on you in the last few days is very much appreciated.'

The *Normannia* was added to the requisitioned fleet on 4 May 1940.

The *St. Julien* began to evacuate troops from Boulogne to Southampton on 21 May, later transferring to Dieppe. As the situation in Belgium deteriorated, plans were drawn up for an evacuation by sea, and the *St. Helier* was identified as one of ten ships immediately available for the task, with the *Lorina* and the *Normannia* on the stand-by list. The *St. Helier* had been engaged on troop and stores sailings between Southampton and Cherbourg, but was diverted to Folkestone on 22 May. On 25 May, the day before the formal evacuation of Dunkirk was invoked, the *St. Helier* was attacked by nine planes and kept alongside the Dunkirk quayside rather than risk being sunk in the harbour approaches. Capt. Pitman survived days of aerial attack by 'steering towards the spot where the last bomb fell'.

The *Isle of Guernsey* left Dover on 26 May for Dunkirk with the *Worthing,* as the latter was one of the few vessels with the relevant charts. Although sporting Red Cross markings, both vessels came under fire from enemy guns at Gravelines, although medical staff on board assumed this was French shelling practice, and reportedly carried on with their afternoon tea. The *Isle of Guernsey* arrived safely in Dunkirk, leaving the same evening at

The *Isle of Jersey* was painted in clear hospital ship colours of white and red to denote her wartime role. *(Ferry Publications Library)*

10:00 p.m. with 346 stretcher cases, despite being fitted out for just 203. She arrived with the *Worthing* in Newhaven via Dover at 5:00 a.m. the following morning before leaving again at 12:00 p.m.

The *Lorina* arrived in Dover from Southampton at 2:00 p.m. on 29 May and left for Dunkirk 30 minutes later. She arrived in the port at 7:30 p.m. during an air raid over the town, harbour and approaches. She was attacked by a flight of about twenty planes and hit by four salvoes of bombs and eventually sank in shallow water. Survivors were transferred to a destroyer and landed at Dover at 4:00 a.m. on 30 May. Eight of the *Lorina's* crew of forty-nine were killed and four wounded.

After leaving Dover at 5:00 p.m. on 29 May the *Isle of Guernsey* observed an airman descending by parachute and took steps to save him. AS J. Fowles climbed down a rope ladder to help, just as the vessel was attacked by ten enemy planes at 8:20 p.m. Fowles lost an arm in the rescue but was awarded the DSM. The *Isle of Guernsey* eventually berthed at 11:30 p.m. entering between the breakwaters with the port lit up by the fires from burning oil tanks and equipment. She left Dunkirk at 2:15 a.m. being shaken repeatedly by the explosion of bombs falling on the quay and in the water, and arrived at Dover at 7:00 a.m. on 30 May with 490 wounded on board, but was ordered to Newhaven and reached there at 11:15 a.m. It was recorded that all the ship's crew displayed great courage under most difficult conditions. On 1 June the *Isle of Guernsey* sailed for Weymouth at 4:00 p.m.

The *St. Helier* left Dunkirk on 30 May during a heavy air raid with 2,000 French troops on board, but collided with the inbound minesweeper *HMS Sharpshooter,* hitting her at right angles, and continued for a distance with the wooden vessel impaled on her bow to prevent her sinking. After 40 minutes the tug *Foremost 22* came to the rescue and took *HMS Sharpshooter* in tow. *St. Helier* was then hit by a paddle steamer the *Princess Eleanor,* which left her starboard paddle box hanging over the bow of the *St. Helier.* There was still time for the *St. Helier* to strike a submerged wreck before arriving safely at Folkestone at 6:45 a.m. on 31 May.

The *Roebuck* was requisitioned on 29 May and went straight to Dover. There was no time for 'de-gaussing' so she headed to Dunkirk without being demagnetised. The *Roebuck* reached La Panne on 31 May having left in such haste that she had no charts for the evacuation. The destroyer *Wolsey* hit her in the stern, but both vessels were able to proceed. Unable to take troops on board without docking due to an offshore wind, the *Roebuck* proceeded into harbour despite coming under shellfire. She loaded 570 troops and 99 wounded over improvised boarding ramps, and returned at 3:35 p.m. to reach Dover four hours later, but was unable to berth until 7:00 a.m. the following morning.

The *St. Julien* came under heavy shelling whilst loading at Dunkirk, despite her Red Cross insignia, and the master described his crew as 'getting shaky', but they assisted in carrying stretchers aboard and reached home safely. Meanwhile Guardsmen cut free the lifeboats from the wreck of the *Lorina* and used them for evacuation from the beach.

The following day *St. Helier* remained on the Mole at Dunkirk for seven hours under fire. Despite the stress and fatigue of the operation, Capt. Pitman refused the order to stand down and returned for another trip on 2 June, supplemented with ten naval personnel as many crew were completely exhausted. The *St. Helier* took the last consignment of men from Dunkirk before the Senior Naval Officer signalled 'BEF is evacuated' to the Admiralty at 11:30 p.m. She had carried 11,700 men in eight trips between Dunkirk and Dover. Capt. Pitman and his First and Second Officers each received the DSC, and the ship's quartermaster the DCM, for their part in the evacuation.

Some 20,000 British forces remained further west in France, and plans were drawn for a series of evacuations. On 5 June the *St. Helier* attempted to withdraw the Highland Division from St. Valery en Caux, but could not locate her escort vessel and withdrew after becoming suspicious when encountering a small boat displaying lights and full of cheering men. The *Guernsey Queen* was on standby for the evacuation and was assisting at Veules, at 4.00 a.m. on 11 June when she came under fire from the battery at St. Valery en Caux and was hit by a shell on her starboard side.

The *Sambur* was requisitioned on 9 June with no time for 'de-gaussing'. The *Roebuck* and *Sambur* headed to St. Valery en Caux, unaware that the evacuation attempt had been completed. They approached on 13 June but were unable to locate their naval escort vessel. A French fishing vessel advised them that it was safe to approach which they did, noting that the *Train Ferry No 2* was anchored close inshore, but they retreated when within 1½ miles of the port as the coastal batteries opened up. The *Roebuck's* hull, bridge and deck were holed and the ship sustained three casualties. The *Sambur* was also badly hit with two crewmen killed.

As the withdrawal effort moved westwards, the *St. Helier* crossed to St. Malo to take off 2,545 British and French troops on 17 June, despite the local pilot refusing to assist in her approach to the port. The following day the *St. Julien* attempted to take wounded from Brest but had to retreat after coming under bombing and machine gun fire, and on 20 June the *St. Helier's* attempts to withdraw troops from La Pallice, were thwarted as she was bombed on her approach and withdrew unharmed.

After German forces occupied the Islands, the rest of the railway fleet was available for other duties. On 8 August the *Isle of Guernsey was* transferred to naval commissioned service and refitted at Penarth; she remained under the white ensign with her Southern crew until 22 September 1943.

The *Roebuck* was repaired at Cardiff to be employed as a barrage balloon escort vessel for a period from 22 October 1940. She operated with the *Sambur* as convoy escort vessels in English Channel

Following her eventful final departure from St. Peter Port, the *Isle of Sark* left Southampton on 3 February 1941 to provide relief for the *St. Patrick* on the Fishguard-

In the latter stages of the war the situation in the Channel Islands became desperate as rations were reduced and starvation took hold. The International Red Cross chartered the *Vega* for relief work in 1939, and she made six life-saving trips from Lisbon to Guernsey and Jersey between December 1944 and June 1945 loaded with supplies. *(Ferry Publications Library)*

Rosslare route until 16 March, when she was laid up at Milford Haven, moving on to Bideford on 24 April. She remained there until 20 December when she was chartered for naval commissioned service. The *Isle of Sark* was fitted with surface warning radar for training purposes and remained in war service until the Pacific war had been concluded in 1945. She was released from military service on 12 December 1945 but was not redelivered until 24 June 1946 after reconditioning.

The *St. Julien* spent time at Scapa Flow and around the Clyde before sailing for the Mediterranean with the *St. Andrew* on 25 June 1943. She steamed 30,000 miles and carried 90,000 patients before returning to Penarth in April 1944.

The Fishguard-Rosslare route was a perilous journey. The *St. Patrick* survived two attacks from enemy aircraft but her luck ran out at dawn on 13 June 1941 when a hostile aircraft again attacked, some 15 miles from Fishguard on an overnight passage from Rosslare. Four bombs hit the cross-bunker fuel tanks forward of the funnel which exploded, blanketing the superstructure in a sheet of flame. The *St. Patrick* immediately broke in two and the crew showed extraordinary heroism as they faced the task of evacuating passengers from the two halves of the vessel. Stewardess Owen was noted as displaying exceptional courage in her efforts to ensure the safe egress of her passengers. The *St. Patrick* sank within six minutes. Passengers clung to floating seats and liferafts in the water, as it had proved impossible to launch the lifeboats. Some sixty-six of her complement were saved, but twenty-eight were lost, including eighteen crew, her master, Capt. Fereday and his youngest son, who had been accompanying him during his holidays. The *St. Patrick's* pennant was later washed ashore and recovered. Miss Owen was awarded the Lloyds Medal and the George Medal, the only woman to receive both honours, Chief Engineer Cyril Griffiths received an OBE for rescuing an unconscious passenger, Second Engineer Frank Purcell an OBE for rescuing three from the engine room, and Radio Operator Norman Campbell who continued to broadcast an SOS message until water reached the boat deck, was awarded an MBE

The *St. Briac* was attached to the Fleet Air Arm training school at Arbroath, but became the next loss, when she hit a mine and sank off Aberdeen on 12 March 1942 with the loss of thirteen of her crew and thirty forces personnel.

As the war began to take a more positive turn and plans were formulated for the invasion of Europe, the *Isle of Guernsey* arrived at Leith on 28 September 1943 for refit and conversion to an LSI (Landing Ship Infantry) which involved removal of her lifeboats to be replaced by Landing Assault Craft. The *St. Julien* took part in the Anzio landings in January 1944. The GWR's *St. David* was bombed and sunk on 24 January 1944 when carrying injured troops off Anzio, despite sporting hospital markings. Ninety-six on board were lost.

The *Isle of Guernsey* arrived back in Southampton from Leith on 12 February 1944 after her conversion, and took part in a series of preparatory exercises for the D Day landings alongside *Isle of Jersey*. The *Isle of Guernsey* sailed to the south west coast to unload troops onto beaches in simulated war conditions, facing a smokescreen and dummy bombs, whilst guns were in action throughout the exercise. She took part in gunnery exercises in the channel and was engaged on night manoeuvres with the Royal Navy.

The *St. Helier* also operated as a troopship and later carried internees to the Isle of Man, then operated as a depot ship at Dartmouth supporting motor torpedo boats. She was converted into an infantry assault ship, capable of carrying six landing craft and 180 troops in readiness for a role as an assault ship at D Day.

On D Day, 6 June 1944, the *Isle of Guernsey* was one of the first vessels to arrive off the Normandy beaches carrying Canadians who landed at Bernières. She was now designated as a LCI (H) – an infantry carrier with hand-operated davits. Three of the ship's landing craft were blown up by mines as they tried to penetrate the beach defences. She was the second vessel to enter the mulberry harbour at Arromanches. In total she made thirteen

A general view of the main street of St Peter Port, Guernsey, showing people queuing for the stocks of British food which have just arrived following liberation. *(Imperial War Museum)*

Generalmajor Siegfried Heine confirms the unconditional surrender of German troops in Guernsey aboard HMS Beagle on 9 May 1945. *(Ferry Publications Library)*

trips to the landing beaches, before serving at Oostende and then on a regular troop service between Newhaven and Dieppe.

The *Dinard, St. Helier* and *St. Julien* also acted as troop carriers during the landings. Dinard was badly damaged when she hit a mine off Juno beach on 7 June, but was able to return to Southampton for repairs. The *St. Julien* also struck a mine on 7 June but returned to Southampton with assistance; a 10ft square hole was found between the waterline and keel. The *HMS Brittany* acted as a Royal Navy auxiliary net layer, setting out moorings for the liberty ships supplying allied forces. She later sailed to Cape Town and Mumbai.

The *Isle of Jersey* spent most of the war at Scapa Flow, supporting the northern fleet in her role as a hospital carrier, with a short interlude supporting the Normandy beaches. She returned to Southampton for a refit and minor alterations on 10 May 1944 prior to taking part in preparatory exercises for the D Day landings. She made her first trip as a troopship to the Normandy beaches on 8 June 1944 and between then and 11 July she completed eleven round trips, bringing back 1,963 hospital cases. On 17 July 1944 the *Isle of Jersey* left Southampton for Aberdeen to be dry-docked, before resuming duty with the northern fleet on 7 August. As the *Isle of Jersey* left Orkney for the final time at the end of the war, Capt. Golding sailed past the base and through the fleet anchorage, flying the signal 'Goodbye Orkney Islands' from the Yardarm. Messages were received in response from the Fleet Officer, Orkney stating: -

'On your departure from Orkney for the last time I wish to express my appreciation of the admirable services you have rendered to the European war to the Home Fleet and its base. The medical facilities afforded by the *Isle of Jersey* have always been of the highest order and the smooth cooperation with the Merchant Navy officers and men has been outstanding. *Isle of Jersey* has carried out many perilous journeys during the war and it is hoped that she may soon return to her peaceful Channel Islands runs. Goodbye and good luck'.

Wartime remembrance

THIS TABLET IS ERECTED TO THE MEMORY, AND RECORDS THE NAMES OF THOSE MEMBERS OF THE CIVIL POPULATION WHO LOST THEIR LIVES AS THE RESULT OF AN ENEMY AIR RAID ON JUNE 28ᵀᴴ 1940.

ANQUETIL, BASIL T.
BATISTE, WALTER J.
BOUCOURD, CLIFFORD H.
BREHAUT, ALICE.
BREHAUT, GEORGE E.
CAMBRIDGE, HERBERT W.
COLLENETTE, FRANCIS T.
DE GARIS, FRANK A.
DE JAUSSERAND, LILIAN M.
DE JAUSSERAND, SAMUEL.
FERBRACHE, OLIVE M.

GILLMORE, FREDERICK R.
HEAUME, GERALD A.
HOBBS, HAROLD F.
INGROUILLE, HENRY.
LE CHEMINANT, HAROLD G.
LE MAITRE, HERBERT W.
LE NOURY, PIERRE.
LE PAGE, FRANK J.
LE PAGE, FRANK J.
LE PAGE, ROY.
MAHY, JOHN W.
MARQUIS, ALFRED.

MAUDUIT, MARCEL F.
NORMAN, CECIL G.
RENOUF, JOHN R.
ROBERT, AMY L.
ROBERT, DAISY M.
BARRE, JOHN E.
BARRE, WALTER.
STITCHMAN, CHARLES.
TARDIVEL, JOHN F.
WALKER, JOHN W.
WAY, JOSEPH E.

IT ALSO COMMEMORATES ALL GUERNSEY CIVILIANS WHO, IN THIS ISLAND OR ELSEWHERE, DIED IN CONSEQUENCE OF HOSTILITIES DURING THE SECOND WORLD WAR 1939 — 1945.

Top: Commemorative plaque in St Peter Port to record those members of the civilian population who lost their lives during the air raids on 20 June 1940 as the *Isle of Sark* prepared to leave the Island for the last time prior to occupation. *(Author)*

Right: Wartime service of the Southern Railway fleet is preserved in a series of plaques at the National Railway Museum in York. *(Author)*

Below left: Plaque in St Helier to commemorate those who evacuated from Jersey. *(Author)*

Below right: Plaque in St Helier to mark the hostile raid on the harbour on 20 June 1940.

S.R.
"BRITTANY"
WAR SERVICE
1940
CHANNEL ISLANDS EVACUATION
1941 — 1945
ROYAL NAVAL AUXILIARY
INDIAN OCEAN
MEDITERRANEAN
HOME WATERS
ATLANTIC OCEAN

Evacuees From Jersey
1939 - 1945
Remembering those who left Jersey, those who came back after the war ended and those who sadly did not return

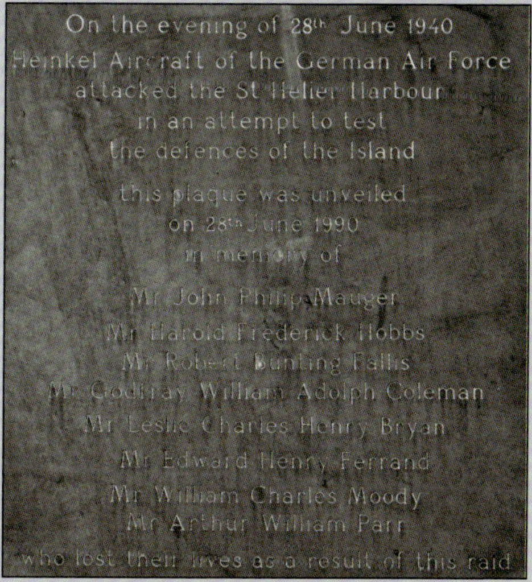

On the evening of 28ᵗʰ June 1940 Heinkel Aircraft of the German Air Force attacked the St Helier Harbour in an attempt to test the defences of the Island

this plaque was unveiled on 28ᵗʰ June 1990 in memory of

Mr John Philip Mauger
Mr Harold Frederick Hobbs
Mr Robert Bunting Falls
Mr Godfray William Adolph Coleman
Mr Leslie Charles Henry Bryan
Mr Edward Henry Ferrand
Mr William Charles Moody
Mr Arthur William Parr
who lost their lives as a result of this raid

CHAPTER EIGHT

Liberation and nationalisation 1945-1959

'It was 1:30 a.m. in mid-Channel. Under the pounding from the engines, the great coil of hawser in the stern of the ship quivered like jelly. A little girl, covered in a blanket, was crouched against the hawser, her head resting near the rusty capstan. She opened her eyes wearily. Sleep was impossible for long in these conditions. She yawned and looked up at the stars, for there was no cover over her head. Other passengers were huddled under lifeboats, sprawled on the cargo hatch. Men, women, children. But this was no scene from some immigrant ship of the bad long ago taking pioneer families out to America or Australia. This happened last week. And I witnessed it. On a HOLIDAY ship the British Railways steamer Isle of Sark taking 850 passengers overnight from Southampton to Jersey'.

[Daily Mirror, HELL on a HOLIDAY ship, 19 August 1955]

On the afternoon of 8 May 1945 Churchill announced that 'our own dear Channel Islands will be freed today'. After almost five years of occupation the Islands were about to be liberated. German forces surrendered unconditionally the following day, 9 May, as *HMS Bulldog* landed in St. Peter Port and a pinnace visited St. Helier to accept their surrender. The *St. Helier* made a brief return to Guernsey with 'Operation Nest-egg' reinforcements, sailing from Plymouth on 11 May before returning to Southampton and sailing to Jersey on the 16th.

The post war restoration of shipping services took time. Railway ships had supported the war effort and undergone significant conversion to serve their new purpose, and there was an ongoing requirement to repatriate service personnel and equipment from around the world. Each vessel required substantial work to bring it back to passenger condition at a time when shipyards were faced with an unprecedented peacetime order book. Some ships would not be coming back; the Southern fleet had been reduced through the loss of the *Lorina*, *Normannia* and *St. Briac*, and the Great Western had lost the *St. Patrick* and *St David*.

Channel Islands Airways, in which the Southern and Great Western had raised their shareholding to fifty per cent in 1942, resumed their flights from Croydon on 21 June. Two days later the freighter *Haslemere* arrived in Jersey. The Southern passenger service recommenced from Southampton when the *Isle of Guernsey*, still painted in her wartime grey livery with yellow funnels topped in black, and flying both the Southern and Great Western house flags, sailed for the Islands on 25 June. She operated six return sailings until 9 July then returned to the Newhaven-Dieppe route. The *Isle of Guernsey* was replaced by the *Hantonia*, which had freshly completed an overhaul after her wartime duties. The *Dinard* joined the *Hantonia* in late July to operate the passenger service through the summer months, before returning to Dover when the *Isle of Jersey* resumed her sailings from 9 October, after her post-wartime refit at Green & Silley Weir on the Thames. After serving in the US navy as a supply ship, the *Whitstable* was brought back into service from Southampton, making her first call at Jersey on 23 July.

THE NEW T.S. "FALAISE"
SOUTHAMPTON, ST. MALO AND CHANNEL ISLANDS SERVICES
SOUTHERN RAILWAY

The Southern Railway celebrates the entry into service of the *Falaise* in 1947, shortly before she passed to British Railways ownership. (*Author's collection*)

The *Sambur* sporting Great Western colours at St Peter Port. She served the Islands for nearly forty years and was the first Great Western ship to reach Jersey after Liberation in 1945. *(Ambrose Greenway collection)*

The Southern ordered a cargo vessel and a passenger ship from Wm. Denny & Bros, to replenish their losses. Whilst the latter was said to be for the Channel Islands services, the losses to the company's fleet had been from other routes. In the event the new vessel was placed on the Southampton-St. Malo service to cover the loss of the *St. Briac*, and the return of the *Dinard* to Dover.

The Great Western had no passenger vessels immediately available at the end of the war, pending their return from government service and refit to peacetime condition. The terminal facilities at Weymouth also required remedial work before the passenger service could re-commence. The company chose to order two passenger ships from their traditional supplier, Cammell Laird of Birkenhead, to replace the loss of the *St. Patrick* and the *St. David*. One of the new vessels was earmarked to provide seasonal support for the Weymouth service.

The *Sambur* arrived in Weymouth on 14 September, being the first Great Western vessel to return. She took up a twice-weekly sailing schedule to Jersey from 18 September, calling alternately on her outward and return journeys in Guernsey. The *Roebuck* was discharged from military service and returned to Weymouth on 13 October making her first sailing on 17 October.

The return of the fleet proceeded too slowly to provide capacity for returning evacuees alongside the military personnel who were needed to remove wartime munitions and structures and restore the Islands to a peacetime state. A military corvette service supplemented scheduled sailings from 1 January until 5 October 1946, when more of the cross-channel fleet had been released by the government. Ships used included the *Empire Lifeguard,* the *Empire Peacemaker* and the *Empire Rest,* all former *Castle* class frigates that had been converted into ocean-rescue ships. These additional services operated from Southampton, and were managed by the Southern, which also supplied officers and other personnel.

The link between Jersey and France re-opened from 15 January 1946 with the *Autocarrier,* which had been added to the Southampton fleet. Granville was initially used as the French destination port, as St. Malo was still recovering from wartime damage, and it was not until 16 April that services were restored there by the *Autocarrier.* In April 1946 the keel for the replacement vessel for the *St. Patrick* was laid down at Cammell Laird, Birkenhead.

Before the war all railway company shipping services at Southampton had used the Inner and Outer Docks but on 10 April 1946 the *Whitstable* docked at Berth 32, Itchen Quays, and shortly afterwards the cargo services moved to Berths 20-23 in the Empress Dock, where they were to remain.

The first Great Western first passenger ship to be released for peacetime service was the *St. Helier,* which had been involved in a collision on 16 July 1945 whilst still on military service and was sent for a six week repair programme. She continued her duties before being sent to Newport for an extensive refit from 20 March to 12 June 1946. On 13 June *St. Helier* returned to Weymouth, allowing her to resume service with the 2:00 a.m. departure on 16 June. The *St. Julien* was discharged from military service in January 1946 prior to an extensive refit at Penarth. The *St. Helier* maintained the service until 1 December, when the *St. Julien* returned to take over for a month, before going to Fishguard for the Irish service.

The Weymouth freight service to Guernsey incorporated a weekly call in Alderney from 14 June; this service lasted until 30 March 1947, when around forty trips had been made.

Isle of Sark makes ready for her arrival in St Helier. *(Dave Hocquard)*

Crowds aboard *Isle of Jersey* ignore the photographer and prefer to view the Needles whilst inbound to Southampton c1950. *(FotoFlite)*

The *Brittany* sits alongside the German-built jetty in St Helier in August 1955. *(Dave Hocquard)*

The *Brittany* returned to Jersey on 5 June 1946 after her post-wartime refit at Harland & Wolff in Southampton, and took up the weekly service to St. Malo the following day; she again offered a full programme of excursions as in the pre-war years, and at weekends assisted on the cross-Channel service. The *Isle of Sark* was the next to return on 25 June allowing her to cover the Southern's 1946 summer service alongside the *Hantonia* and *Isle of Jersey*. The *Dinard* was withdrawn and sent to the Tyne for conversion to be a craned-on car carrier.

The first of the Southern's post war new builds, the passenger vessel *Falaise*, was launched at Wm. Denny & Bros. on 25 October 1946. The *Falaise* incorporated two sets of twin Parson's turbines and two oil fired boilers delivering 20½ knots, and was fitted with Denny-Brown stabilisers and a bow rudder. She could accommodate 1,450 passengers, with 940 in first class, and sleeping berths for 338. Material shortages delayed her sea trials until the following spring.

The Southampton-Le Havre route was restored on 13 January 1947 by the *Autocarrier*, which operated a fortnightly schedule until the *Brittany* took over on 10 March. The cargo vessel *Winchester* was launched for the Southern on 21 March at Wm. Denny & Bros.

The *St. David* was launched at Birkenhead on 6 February 1947. She was soon followed by *St. Patrick,* the largest and last vessel to be built for the Great Western, which was launched on 20 May, St. Patrick's Day, by Viscountess Portal, wife of the company chairman. *St. Patrick* flew the pennant of her namesake, sunk off Fishguard in 1941. Both ships incorporated twin sets of Parson's turbines with steam generated by three Babcock and Wilcox boilers. Each could accommodate 1,300 passengers but neither was fitted with stabilisers. The design of the *St. Patrick* fulfilled the dual-purpose brief for her planned deployment on the Channel Islands and Rosslare routes. She had a smaller car deck and fewer cabins than the *St. David*, creating extra space for more lounges, dining and smoking saloons, and reflecting the high passenger capacity requirements of the summer daytime crossings to the Islands. A two-class vessel, she had first and third class dining saloons, and an open plan first class lounge. The main vestibule featured an elaborate wooden inlaid map of Great Western rail and sea routes. She cost £578,791.

In positive developments for the Southern the *Hantonia* was released to return to the Le Havre service on 2 June 1947. The new £560,000 *Falaise* sailed on her maiden voyage from Southampton to St. Malo on 14 July thereby restoring the full complement of pre-war Southern passenger services. She was unable to dock in St. Malo as the lock had been destroyed during the 1940 retreat, so anchored in the River Rance whence passengers were ferried ashore by vedettes. The service operated twice-weekly, which allowed *Falaise* to provide a direct service to Jersey at weekends, her first call being on 19 July.

In a small move that was to have more significant consequences later, Commodore Cruises Ltd. was registered as a London-based passenger shipping company in March 1947. The company operated a succession of former Royal Navy Fairmile B craft on excursions along the southeast coast of England and made its first venture across the Channel on 9 September 1947 when *Red Commodore* was chartered to Sark Projects Ltd. to serve Alderney and Sark from Guernsey. The company operated under its own name from Guernsey in 1948 and was successful in securing a monopoly contract from the Sark Chief Pleas in 1950.

Britain's railway companies were in dire straits at the end of the war, with both infrastructure and equipment suffering from the effects of wartime traffic levels, insufficient maintenance, no investment and the impact of enemy action. This situation applied to the marine fleet just as much as the railway network. The election of a Labour government in 1945 was a prelude to nationalisation of key private industries including

The *St Julien* was a stalwart of Island sailings from Weymouth from 1925 until 1960. Seen here in British Railways colours. *(Author's collection)*

The *St Patrick* catches the morning light in St Helier prior to conversion to a one-class ship. The GWR crest is still visible on her bow. *(Dave Hocquard)*

coal, steel and transport; Channel Islands Airways was one of the first, becoming part of British European Airways on 1 April 1947. The Southern and Great Western's astute investment was not allowed to profit from the 1950s boom in air travel; the two companies had sown the seeds of the decline of sea carryings. The Transport Act 1947 received the Royal Assent on 6 August, triggering the transfer of the majority of Britain's railways and their associated shipping services to the British Transport Commission (BTC). Unlike Docks and Inland Waterways, shipping operations were not deemed worthy of a separate Executive within the new structure, with Sir Cyril Hurcomb, chairman of the BTC, noting on 29 September 1947 that 'The operation of existing steamer services should continue to be linked with the Railways, of which they are in effect a projection across the narrow seas'.

The *Brittany* was holed and put out of action for the rest of the season on 28 August, when she struck rocks at Gorey whilst undertaking a 'Round the Island' excursion from St. Helier. At the end of the summer, the *Falaise* took over the Saturday mail sailing from Jersey, and made her first call at St. Peter Port on September 6 1947.

The first of the Great Western new-build vessels, the *St. David*, arrived in Weymouth for a trial operation to the Islands on 3 September, in anticipation of the arrival of her sister *St. Patrick* in 1948. She had entered service on the Irish Sea during the summer season, and the company deemed it prudent to understand how a vessel of her design would handle Island waters. She arrived on her maiden voyage on 4 September, and remained on the service for four weeks, but was not to return after her trial. The Southern's new cargo ship, the *Winchester,* made her first call at Jersey on 2 December.

Despite the late start to the season, 1947 proved to be a good year for the Weymouth service, with 121,887 passengers and 1,940 cars carried and an additional 23,400 inter-island travellers. Passenger figures were nine per cent higher than had been achieved in

1938, making it the best year on record. There was clearly a strong appetite for holidays after the restrictions of the wartime years.

On 1 January 1948 the independent railway companies and their shipping operations were formally nationalised, being vesting into the British Transport Commission (BTC), supported by a Railway Executive. The network was divided into six regions with the former Southern becoming the Southern Region, and the Great Western constituting the Western Region. The BTC inherited a fleet of 122 ships and an urgent need to replenish wartime losses, and quickly developed a five-year plan to bring the fleet back to its pre-war strength. Common ownership brought wider opportunities for the sharing of resources between routes, as they were no longer prescribed by company allegiance. The BTC was, however, concerned at the relationship between the old companies and their preferred suppliers of new build vessels and sought to open out tenders to a wider range of yards. From the Islands' perspective there was little outward evidence of change, as they remained served by two routes delivered by different Regions.

The post war investment programme was now coming to fruition, and the *St. Patrick* took 115 passengers on her maiden voyage from Weymouth on 4 February. She still sported the Great Western colours with a red funnel and company house flag, as the BTC had yet to determine liveries for the nationalised undertaking. The *St. Patrick* continued on the Weymouth station until the end of the season on 26 October, and then went to Fishguard to act as the winter relief vessel.

Both Regions resumed programmes of excursion sailings. On her return to Weymouth in 1948 *St. Patrick* acted as the summer seasonal vessel; this enabled a resumption of the excursion programme, with the *St. Helier* released to inaugurate day trips to Guernsey from Weymouth on 21 July and Torquay on 18 August 1948 for £1 5s. The *St. Helier* also filled in with a series of coastal cruises from Weymouth, but these only lasted for two seasons. At Southampton the *Falaise* took over the programme of shoulder season long-weekend cruises to France and the Islands from the *St. Briac*.

Management of the Weymouth fleet was transferred from the Western Region to the Southern Region on 1 November 1948 and the marine operation followed in July 1949. By now the *St. Julien* and the *St. Helier* had lost their distinctive Great Western red funnels, being repainted with the buff and black of the new nationalised enterprise. The new colours reflected those of the old Southern, with the removal of the white line between the black hull and the red boot top. The BTC also determined that the new house flag should reflect the railway network logo comprising a golden lion holding a railway wheel astride a crown, all set on a blue background. At 10.00 a.m. on 4 April all ships of the new British Railways fleet, with the exception of the F&RR&HCo-owned *St. Patrick*, hauled down their old house flags and raised the new standard.

Three new vessels came to the Islands in 1949; the *Worthing* offered an inter-island excursion on 28 April and then conveyed a party to Southampton on the 29th for the F.A. Cup Final. The second became a more regular visitor. The *Falaise* now ran thrice-weekly on the Southampton-St. Malo route and could no longer fit in her trip to Jersey, so the *Isle of Thanet* sailed from Dover each weekend to operate a Friday night service to Guernsey, omitting Jersey as she was too long to enter St. Helier. Another Dover ship, the *Hythe*, was transferred to the Southampton fleet in May 1949.

Reports surfaced in the media on 31 August that a 4,000-ton ship was to be built to serve the Islands, but these proved to be inaccurate. A new vessel was under consideration, but it was for the Southampton-Le Havre route to replace the *Hantonia*. This was further disappointment for the Islands after the earlier announcement of the *Falaise*.

The *St. Patrick* sustained damage to her hull when grounding at St. Helier during gale conditions on 17 September 1950, forcing her to be withdrawn and sent to Penarth for repairs.

One of the advantages of the new nationalised enterprise was the ability to overcome the former parochial approach to ship deployment and permit greater inter-play between different route resources. The *Duke of York* spent the 1950 summer season at Southampton and opened a twice-weekly service to Cherbourg, and also covered the weekend sailing to Guernsey. However the Cherbourg service continued to underperform, and the *Duke of York* was not to return. In another break with the past, management of the Western Region service from Fishguard to Rosslare was transferred to the London Midland Region bringing both Wales-Ireland routes under common control, but leaving the Western Region with no cross-channel ferry routes and breaking the historic links between Weymouth and Fishguard.

The railway companies owned many of the ports around Britain at the time of nationalisation, and these were placed under a separate body to the BTC. Southampton Docks were transferred to the Docks & Inland Waterways Board on 1 September 1950, although control and operation remained in the hands of the British Railways Docks and Marine Manager.

Passenger steamers temporarily moved to Berth 46 in the Ocean Dock at Southampton in autumn 1950, whilst improvements were made to their normal berths 7-9 in the Outer Dock. Meanwhile in Jersey the mailboat berths were brought together with the switch of the Weymouth berth from the New North Quay to a position astern of the 'Southampton' berth, with the Southampton cargo vessels taking their place. Meanwhile at Weymouth, a project to reconstruct the cargo stage to create additional space was completed in July 1951. It proved flexible enough to accommodate the loading of both railway wagons and motor vehicles.

The new lock at St. Malo opened in time for the 1951 season and an extra ship was placed on the Southampton route to accommodate the anticipated increase in passengers. The *Princess Maud* was brought from Holyhead to operate two sailings each week to St. Malo and the weekend service to Guernsey. The *Normannia,* the new ship for the Southampton-Le Havre route, was launched at Wm. Denny & Bros. on 19 July 1951, and delivered to the BTC in January 1952. In a nod to history, as her namesake had been the first double reduction geared vessel to operate on the channel, the new *Normannia* was the first with high speed Pametrada-design turbine units coupled to the twin shafts via double reduction gears. On trial she reached 21 knots, but had a service speed of 19½ knots. *Normannia* had capacity for 780 first class and 630 third class passengers and sailed from Southampton on her maiden voyage on 3 March 1952, replacing the *Hantonia*.

After working with British Channel Island Shipping (BCIS), a subsidiary of Coast Lines, to take cargo to Alderney, the Commodore Shipping Company Ltd was registered as a company in Guernsey on 22 March 1952, with BCIS acting as managers. On 25 June *Island Commodore (I)* sank at moorings in St. Peter Port and was replaced three days later by the *Silver Commodore*, which came from Newhaven to supplement *Fleet Commodore* and *Arrowhead* on the Guernsey-Alderney and Guernsey-Sark services. *Arrowhead* also provided a range of freight services to the Islands from France and southern England, including Portsmouth.

The *Dinard* returned from Dover to the Southampton-St. Malo route on summer weekends in 1952. She was joined from Dover by the *Isle of Thanet,* which again operated a Friday night sailing from Southampton to Guernsey, returning by day, thence back to Dover. This pattern continued up to the 1958 season.

The year saw the construction of a new hard runway at Jersey Airport, which allowed

A tight fit aboard the *Isle of Sark* on 14 July 1959 in the days before ro-ro services. *(Dave Hocquard)*

larger aircraft to operate, and prompted a major increase in the volume of air traffic. Initially it appeared that the railways would fight back aggressively against air competition. On 27 January 1953, following exploratory talks between British Railways and Island officials, the States of Jersey agreed in principle to the deepening of St. Helier Harbour, if British Railways were to go ahead with plans to build three ships similar to the *St. Patrick*. British Railways invited tenders for construction of the vessels, but in July it was stated that no decision had been taken. The project then lay dormant, but in May 1954 a new cargo stage opened at Weymouth.

In February 1955 Commodore's *Arrowhead* was joined by her sister ship the *Channel Trader* to meet increasing demand, sailing for the Island Shipping Company Ltd between Portsmouth and Alderney, Guernsey and Jersey.

British Railways refined their position in 1955 to say that two new ships would be provided for the Weymouth service, but this news came with a proposal to close the Southampton route. Again this proved premature. It was clear that action needed to be taken, as on board standards were falling behind modern expectations, especially with increasing air competition. The *Daily Mirror* published a feature article on 19 August sub-headed 'Eight hours of misery on a cross-Channel trip to the Channel Islands' which gave a sensationalist account of the crossing. Island officials and British Railways representatives met in Jersey on 8 November, and mutually agreed that St. Helier Harbour would be deepened and approval sought from the BTC for new vessels to replace the *St. Helier* and the *St. Julien*. In Guernsey at a similar meeting the following day, it was stated that two new cargo ships would also be commissioned. It was to be another two years before the order for these vessels was placed.

The *Hythe* made her last call at Jersey on 23 August 1955 before being withdrawn to be broken up. She was replaced by the newer *Brest* from the Newhaven-Dieppe route.

Damage inspection under way at low tide in St Helier on 7 September 1957 after the *Isle of Jersey* hit rocks off Elizabeth Castle. *(Dave Hocquard)*

After a period without significant operational incidents, the year ended with a collision between the *Haslemere* and the *Winchester* in the Solent. The *Haslemere* had left Jersey at 4:55 p.m. on 1 December under the command of Capt. Hewson, with two passengers and a crew of twenty-six, making a full speed passage for Southampton. Later that evening Capt. Denny took the *Winchester* from Southampton for Jersey at 11.24 p.m. with one passenger and a crew of nineteen. The two vessels were due to pass in the Solent, which was blanketed by dense fog with little wind and a calm sea, but both vessels maintained full speed, closing in at 25 knots. Although aware of each other's presence, they had difficulty identifying their relative positions by radar. Capt. Denny expected the *Haslemere* to turn to starboard near Sconce Buoy to head up the Solent, but his radar suggested that the *Haslemere* was not taking this course. On the *Haslemere,* Capt. Hewson thought that the *Winchester* was south of the mid-channel, and altered his course to port to reach the north side of the channel; a position maintained up to the collision. Neither vessel slowed despite the conditions, and although the *Winchester* sounded her whistle repeatedly after leaving Southampton, *Haslemere* did not until she heard two fog signals from the *Winchester;* two long blasts were blown in reply, the second almost at the moment of sighting.

At 1.09 a.m. on 2 December the stem of the *Winchester* came into contact with the starboard quarter of the *Haslemere* about 5 cables from Sconce Buoy. Both vessels were damaged in the collision. The Court concluded that navigation of both the vessels was improper and dangerous in the weather conditions but assigned the graver faults to Capt. Hewson, whose licence was suspended for eight months; Capt. Denny was suspended for six months. The *Pentland Firth* was chartered in to cover the period of repairs to both vessels.

The first half of the 1950s saw the seasonal tourist trade to the Channel Islands grow considerably. Jersey figures illustrated that, whilst sea travel experienced a thirteen per cent growth in four years, air travel expanded by ninty-seven per cent over the same period, growing from thirty-seven per cent market share to fifty-one per cent, and surpassing sea carryings for the first time in 1955. Air was not to relinquish this dominant position again.

In February 1956 the *Arrowhead* was lost off Exmouth and the *Snider* was chartered as replacement. She was capable of supporting both refrigerated and general cargo exports from Alderney. Her operation was taken over by Alderney Tramp Shipping Company Ltd and Commodore's interest in cross-channel services was temporarily over.

The long trailed announcement that the BTC had approved the construction of two passenger and two freight vessels for the Island services came on 9 November 1956. Initial speculation suggested that one passenger ship would be allocated to

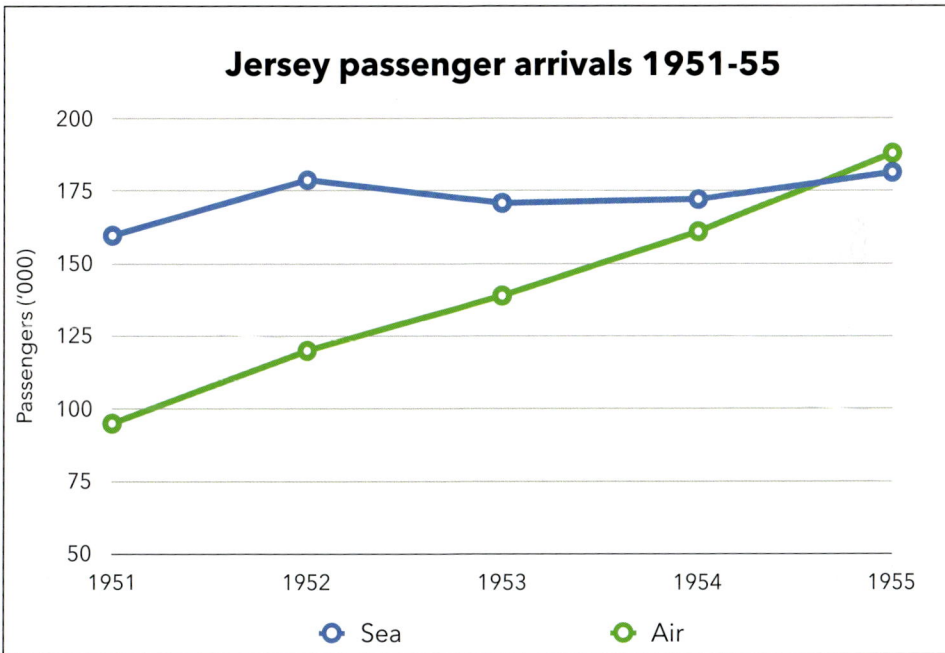

Jersey passenger arrivals 1951-55

Southampton and the other to Weymouth. On 30 November the States of Jersey agreed to spend £280,000 on the deepening of St. Helier Harbour although there were no formal agreements in place. Weymouth Corporation also invested some £40,000 during 1958 to extend the mail boat berth in anticipation of the arrival of the new vessels. A year after the initial announcement, the BTC finally placed an order for two new passenger vessels with J Samuel White of Cowes, and two cargo vessels with Brooke Marine of Lowestoft. The combined investment was £3.5m. At £1.5m, each passenger vessel was nine times the original cost of *Isle of Jersey* and twice the price of the 1952 *Normannia*.

The cargo business was still substantial, with both Southampton and Weymouth dispatching eighty to ninety wagons of tomatoes by rail daily during the season.

The centenary of sailings from Weymouth was marked on 17 April 1957 with a telegram to Capt. Newton, master of the *St. Julien,* and the ship was dressed overall on arrival in the Islands.

The *Isle of Jersey* struck a rock on Elizabeth Castle and was holed when entering St. Helier harbour after an overnight crossing from Southampton on 7 September 1957. Once inside the harbour, the *Isle of Jersey* collided with a Dutch timber boat, which was not damaged. A defect with the steering mechanism was blamed. Passengers were transferred to the *Isle of Guernsey* and the *Isle of Sark*.

Growth in traffic on the Dover Straits, which was aided by the re-introduction of no-passport day excursions, coupled with more stagnant volumes on the Island routes, led to the *Isle of Thanet's* Friday night summer sailing to Guernsey being withdrawn after the 1958 season. Further cutbacks followed in the autumn, with both the Le Havre and Islands routes being reduced by one sailing each week from Southampton and Weymouth. This allowed the *Brittany* to be withdrawn for the winter, with the *Falaise* and the *Normannia* remaining to cover both routes. The Jersey-St. Malo sailing was undertaken by the *Normannia*, which arrived in Jersey every Thursday as part of a twice-weekly winter schedule from Southampton. These changes were intended to bring substantial economies to the costs of the shipping services. The *Normannia* made her first call in the Islands on 13 November 1958, with the *Falaise* following on the 25th: -

'Following heavy squalls of rain and hail, the many black clouds cleared for the sun to shine brilliantly for the first arrival in Jersey on November 13 of the 3,500 ton British Railways mail steamer *Normannia*. The *Normannia* with Capt. H G Le Huquet in command entered St. Helier Harbour from Southampton and Guernsey at 9:29 AM. On the Pier Heads to watch *Normannia's* arrival was a large number of interested people many with cameras to record the event. The ship presented a striking site as she came into view steaming across St. Aubin's Bay, and as she turned Elizabeth Castle breakwater moving towards the harbour entrance the huge white superstructure glistened in the sun. This large boxlike superstructure gives the *Normannia* a rather ungraceful appearance somewhat similar to the *Falaise*, which is well known locally. Captain Le Huquet brought the *Normannia* into harbour in fine style. Within minutes the ship was tied up in her berth having turned and backed quickly down the harbour. Soon the 94 passengers were moving down the gangway and preparations were started for than *Normannia's* departure for St. Malo at noon. A reporter commented 'first impression is of size, space and comfort in every respect. There is no question but that the accommodation is excellent'.
[*The Jersey Weekly Post 14 November 1958*]

From 1 January 1959, in a reverse of their 1948 decision, British Railways' Weymouth shipping manager assumed responsibility for the management of both the Weymouth and Southampton operations. The Weymouth route then took on a longer summer schedule and the Southampton winter schedule became weekly. The *St. Patrick* did not return to Fishguard at the end of the 1959 summer season and was retained to offer an enhanced winter service from Weymouth; the sailing was extended from Jersey to St. Malo at weekends. Not all news at Weymouth was positive, as on 26 September the last 'Channel Islands Boat Express' took the traditional Great Western route from Weymouth to London Paddington. Henceforth connecting rail services to London would operate via Southampton.

With four new ships under construction, the older steamers were gradually withdrawn. The *Whitstable* was the first to leave, being sold for scrap in May 1959, followed by the *Haslemere,* which was sent to Rotterdam for breaking up in August. Chartered tonnage was used as an interim measure, including the SNCF's *Brest,* pending arrival of the new vessels.

The names of the new freighters perpetuated the nomenclature of the old GWR vessels. The *Elk* made her maiden voyage from Southampton on 6 August, which allowed the *Ringwood* to be withdrawn after making her final trip on 9 October. On 31 October the *Moose* paid her first call in Jersey. On the same day the *Isle of Jersey* made

Isle of Jersey in steam and resting on the bottom alongside in St Helier. *(Dave Hocquard)*

her last seasonal call at her namesake island and a large gathering watched her leave, believing it to be her last trip. Although British Railways denied this at the time, the crowd was to be proved right.

From 3 November the 9:15 p.m. train from London Waterloo to Southampton was extended through to Weymouth on Tuesdays and Fridays to connect with winter sailings. These were operated by *St. Patrick* and *Normannia*, with *St. Helier* and *St. Julien* laid up in Weymouth. The winter cargo service from Southampton was cut back to a single weekly round-trip. Passenger traffic was forced to use Weymouth, as the new cargo vessels did not have passenger accommodation. During passenger vessel overhaul periods the cargo ships ran from Weymouth, with the *Winchester* also taking her turn.

In another break with the past, ownership of the *St. Patrick* was transferred from the F&RR&HCo to the BTC on 17 December. Her traditional Great Western red funnel was painted out, but she retained the GWR crest on her bow.

After ceding much of the Island passenger business to the airlines that they had helped foster, the stage was now set for the railway services to mount a comeback, with investment in four new ships about to come to fruition. The outstanding question was how the new resources would be deployed.

CHAPTER NINE

British Railways 1960-1978

'The *Caesarea*, 3,800 tons, first half of the British Railways £3 million answer to the impact of air competition on sea travel between the British mainland and the Channel Islands, took the water today at J Samuel White's yard…. Probably no other channel service operated by British Railways ships has been so hard hit by air competition than that between the mainland and the Channel Islands. This has posed a problem for Southern Region, British Railways, and its advisors, the southern area board of the British Transport Commission. The *Caesarea*, Roman name for Jersey, has been designed with the new standards of comfort and safety to meet this problem. The existing ageing ships on the service have little sheltered seating in daylight on a trip which takes nine hours and which is frequently beset with bad weather. There is insufficient sleeping accommodation for night crossings. The air trip takes about one hour….'

[*Daily Telegraph, 30 January 1960*]

The new decade started positively on 29 January 1960, with the launch and naming of the *Caesarea* at Cowes by Lady Coutanche, wife of the Bailiff of Jersey. Sir Philip Warner, the Chairman of British Railways' Southern Region, alluded to the commercial problems facing the Channel Island services but looked forward positively in his address at the ceremony: -

'This ship and her sister will help to eliminate the present heavy financial losses on the Channel Isles services. We just could not let this service run down. It was an act of faith to build them and we made a good decision, although at really great expense, £1,500,000 for each ship. But I think we ought to be able to provide a better service than in the past'.

This act of faith was narrowly backed by Weymouth Corporation, who approved a plan for improvement works to the port facilities in February. A third railway track was to be added at Weymouth Quay, together with new two-storey offices and additional siding space.

The *Caesarea* at 4,174 tons was then the largest passenger vessel to operate to the Islands, with capacity for 1,400 passengers and a crew of seventy-eight. She was powered by two Pametrada steam turbine engines and double reduction gears to achieve 19 knots and was 322ft in length with a beam of 51ft, optimised for the harbours of St. Peter Port and St. Helier. Her single class accommodation was spread across three passenger decks and included several lounges, two cafeteria/bars, and a 110-seat restaurant.

The *St. Patrick* returned to service painted in the full British Railways livery on 27 February 1960 after being relieved during overhaul by the *Normannia*. The ageing *Isle of Jersey* was sold in March, sailing to the River Tyne to be converted for employment in the Middle East pilgrim trade. As the *Libda* she headed for Tripoli, where the new venture proved unsuccessful and she was broken up at La Spezia in 1963.

The concerns expressed by British Railways about financial losses on the Island routes led to speculation about their future, as the order for two new vessels did not sit comfortably with continued operation of a smaller fleet from both Southampton and Weymouth. The strategy was eventually announced on 4 June; the new Channel Islands operation would: -

- use fewer but bigger ships;
- concentrate all the passenger ships on the shortest sea route, using only one mainland port, namely Weymouth;
- introduce a one-class, comfortable standard for all services; and
- not carry cargo on passenger ships, to avoid delays.

The fleet would be reduced to the *Caesarea*, *Sarnia* and *St. Patrick* from summer 1961, generating an estimated annual saving of £209,000. Passenger services were to be consolidated onto the old Great Western route even though they were under Southern Region control, a decision that did not go down well in Southampton. It was feared that this would place pressure on the viability of remaining railway services to Le Havre and St. Malo. Southampton's airport was also under threat from the Ministry of Aviation and there were concerns that all the city's links with the Channel Islands could be severed. The South Eastern Area Transport Users Consultative Committee (TUCC) launched an Inquiry into the proposals, which was held in September 1960. The Inquiry concluded in October with approval for the proposed service changes, signalling the end of Southampton as the primary passenger port for the Islands.

Shipping services suffered further, when the Post Office transferred all mail, except printed material and parcels, to air transport from 18 July, in a move designed to improve services. Mail by air was nothing new, but the decision finally severed the long-standing importance of the daily arrival of the mail boat in the Islands.

Lady Arnold, wife of the Bailiff of Guernsey, launched the second new vessel, *Sarnia*, at Cowes on 6 September, marking the end for three veteran members of the fleet. The

The launch of the *Caesarea* on 29 January 1960. *(Ferry Publications Library)*

Restaurant on board the *Sarnia,* from a 1961 publicity brochure. *(Author collection)*

St. Helier undertook her last sailing on 14 September with an excursion from Torquay to Guernsey, and went to Weymouth to await a decision on disposal. The *St. Julien* took her last daylight service from Weymouth on 24 September, returning on the 27th. Capt. Goodchild presented her name pennant for preservation in the Castle Cornet museum in St. Peter Port. Then the *Isle of Sark* completed her duties after arriving in the Islands on 29 October, sailing empty back to Southampton to be laid up prior to sale. The winter schedule was operated by the *St. Patrick,* with the *Isle of Guernsey* acting as reserve for both the Southampton and Weymouth stations.

The *Caesarea* arrived for the first time in Weymouth on 12 November, and four days later a party of 200 press and invited guests boarded her from a special Pullman train at Weymouth Quay to sail to Southampton. *Caesarea* sailed from Southampton at 1:15 a.m. on 18 November under the command of Capt. Newton, the former master of the *St. Patrick,* and arrived in St. Helier at 9:30 a.m. to be formally met by Sir Alexander Coutanche and a large crowd at the pier heads. The *Caesarea* operated a short cruise for invited guests and was then opened up to the public. The Jersey Evening Post described the new arrival: -

'*Caesarea* has two continuous decks, main and upper, with the promenade deck, boat deck and navigating bridge deck above the upper deck. The lower deck extends forward and aft of the machinery spaces. All exposed weather decks are sheathed with teak and the hull below the main deck or bulkhead deck is subdivided into watertight compartments by means of 11 watertight bulkheads. A cellular double bottom is fitted throughout, except in way of the fore and aft peaks and aft shaft tunnel. All double bottom tanks are arranged for the carriage of water ballast or freshwater. Furnace fuel oil, diesel oil, distilled water are carried in deep tanks above double bottom freshwater in wing tanks at the aft end of the engine room. The hull form was decided after a series of model resistance and self-propulsion tests, carried out at the national physical laboratory.

The *Caesarea* has a balanced rudder aft and the bow rudder, to enable the vessel

The *Sarina* dressed overall at St Helier. *(Ferry Publications Library)*

to navigate stern first when entering port. These are operated by rotary vane type steering gears of AEG manufacture, the power being supplied by hydraulic pumps driven by electric motors. Control from the bridge in each case is electric.

Propulsion is by two single casing steam turbines, of Pametrada latest design, impulse type with ahead and astern elements incorporated on a single rotor shaft, each driving a three bladed 'Novoston' alloy propeller through articulated locked train double reduction gearing. Steam for domestic services, bunker heating etc. and supply to the distiller, the latter providing make-up feed for the main boilers, is supplied by two oil fired Spanner boilers working at a pressure of 60lb per square inch.

There is one class of accommodation for 1,400 passengers. Passengers are carried on all decks except the navigating bridge deck. There are private cabins for 62 passengers in one and two berth cabins on the lower deck forward and two cabin-de-luxe on the promenade deck. There is a seating accommodation for all passengers. The public rooms are on the main, upper hand promenade decks and there are two 22 berth sleeping lounges aft on the lower deck.

The Captain's day cabin and bedroom are on the navigating bridge deck. The deck and engineer's officers' cabins mess room and toilets are in the deckhouse on the boat deck, and the accommodation for stewards, catering staff and deck and engine room ratings is on the main deck. General cargo is carried in the fore hold and general cargo and cars in the forward and after between decks. The cold room, preparing room and refrigerated machinery room is also on the lower deck.

The public rooms have been specially planned to provide modern décor and ease of maintenance. The internal decorations and furnishings are the latest in the design and comfort. There has been a widespread use of teak in the décor. Plastics have

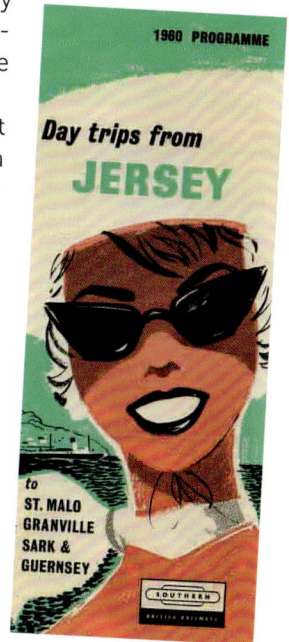

1960 PROGRAMME

Day trips from JERSEY

to ST. MALO GRANVILLE SARK & GUERNSEY

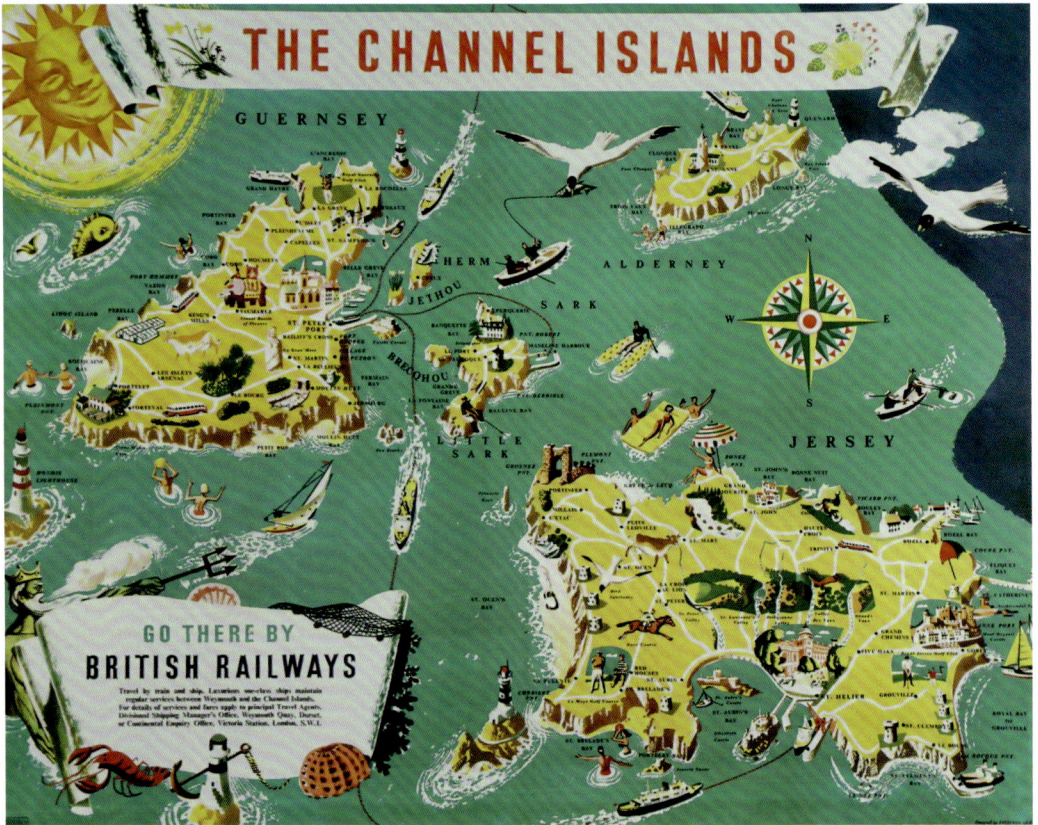

THE CHANNEL ISLANDS

GO THERE BY
BRITISH RAILWAYS

been freely used. There are many armchairs in the lounges, which are of even brighter colours that other public rooms. Extensive use has been made of black and white colouring and also of grey to provide neutral backgrounds underfoot and on the ceilings. Heating is provided by a Thermo Tank system and ventilation is provided for all passengers and crew. Maximum precautions have been taken against fire hazard in excess of present statutory requirements.

Life saving apparatus includes six fibreglass lifeboats with built in buoyancy. Two of these boats are propelled by diesel engines and four by hand mechanical propelling gear. In addition to the boats, 45 inflatable life rafts are installed on special launching ways.

The catering facilities are of the latest. There is a restaurant, cafeteria and bar with the most modern equipment. They have an easy to maintain decor and furnishings. Important considering the service in which she will be engaged, the *Caesarea* is fitted with the Denny Brown stabilisers of the latest type, which reduced rolling greatly in rough seas.'

[*Jersey Evening Post, 20 November 1960*]

The *Caesarea* went on public display in St. Helier on 19 and 20 November, when some 18,200 people visited her. She sailed for St. Peter Port the following day, arriving at 9:30 a.m. for another public open day before returning to Southampton. Her first scheduled sailing was on 2 December. *St. Patrick* was released to Mountstuart Dry Dock in Cardiff for a £90,000 refit, which included conversion into a one-class ship and an upgrade to her facilities to match the standard of the new vessels, but lack of space precluded her being fitted with stabilisers. She did not return to service until 21 April 1961. The *St. Helier* and the *St. Julien* were sold to Van Heyghen Frères in Ghent for scrap, although the *St. Julien* was initially utilised as an accommodation ship. The *Isle of Sark* followed her sisters for scrapping in Ghent in March 1961.

Commodore Shipping changed hands in July 1960 when the company was purchased by Mansfield Markham. He set about transforming the business with a move towards offering high speed services and opening routes to France. In December 1960 Commodore Shipping acquired the *Linger* from Mansfield Markham for £11,500 to operate a high-speed service to Sark.

The Guernsey Tomato Marketing Board was established in the winter of 1960-61 to manage the packing, shipping and marketing of the entire Guernsey crop. A large labour-saving packing shed was built in Guernsey, which was used to palletise trays of fruit for the English markets. The Board signed a three-year transportation contract with British Railways and chose Weymouth as the English terminal for the service. The Southampton-based *Elk, Moose* and *Winchester* were employed to fulfill this contract, so the Weymouth-based *Sambur* and *Roebuck* were dedicated to carrying the remainder of the cargo, often to Southampton, being joined by chartered tonnage at peak times. Palletisation was also eventually adopted for exports from Jersey, and British Railways was able increase its share of this business with the reduced rates that this process offered all parties.

With completion of the harbour works at Weymouth in May 1961 all was set for the transfer of services. The *Isle of Guernsey* made her final crossing from Southampton on 12 May, arriving in the Islands the following morning and, after disembarking passengers and unloading cargo, sailed back to Weymouth, thus ending a railway passenger shipping link that dated back to the start of the South Western Steam Packet Company services on 1 May 1842. The new one-class service was inaugurated on the same day from Weymouth by the *Caesarea* and the *St. Patrick,* with the *Isle of Guernsey* retained in the fleet until 10 June. A new railway timetable was introduced with a dedicated 'Channel Islands Boat Express' adorned with roof-boards on the carriages offering a fast service from London Waterloo. This service operated from Monday to Saturday, with Sundays added in July and August, and offered identical 10hr 35min journeys in each direction between London and Jersey: -

London Waterloo	dep	8:10 a.m.	Jersey	dep	9:00 a.m.
Weymouth Quay	arr	11:40 a.m.	Guernsey	dep	11:15 a.m.
	dep	12:30 p.m.	Weymouth Quay	arr	3:15 p.m.
Guernsey	arr	4:30 p.m.		dep	4:00 p.m.
Jersey	arr	6:45 p.m.	London Waterloo	arr	7:35 p.m.

Additional weekend night sailings were offered in each direction, with two arrivals on Saturday afternoons in Weymouth at 2:15 p.m. and 3:30 p.m. but the overnight sailings were not well patronised. With the service now reduced to one class accommodation the return fare from London was lowered to £5 15s 6d. The new arrangements placed significant pressure on the station facilities at Weymouth Quay, with Saturday departures at 2:45 p.m., 3:00 p.m. and 4:00 p.m. for London Waterloo, at 4:15 p.m. for Birmingham and Cardiff and 4:30 p.m. for London Waterloo. The second vessel was timed to arrive at 3:30 p.m. and occasionally missed connecting to the 4:15 p.m. departure, leaving passengers with a difficult onward journey.

The Weymouth fleet was augmented on 13 June by the arrival of the *Sarnia* with a press trip from Southampton under Capt. Cartwright; she sailed on to Guernsey, where she met her sister *Caesarea* on the 14th. The *Sarnia's* first scheduled sailing was on 17 June. Her arrival saw the *St. Patrick* relegated to operate extra sailings and excursions as the reserve vessel. The *Isle of Guernsey* returned to Southampton to be laid up prior to sale and scrapping at Van Heyghen Frères, Ghent in November 1961.

The *Sarnia* ended the year on a low note when she hit the quay wall in St. Peter Port and damaged her hull on the starboard side on 9 December, requiring her to be taken out of service for repair. But the service changes had resulted in an eleven per cent increase in passenger carryings to 200,955 on a three-ship fleet, compared to 181,385 on six vessels in 1960, endorsing the strategic decision to focus on Weymouth with a smaller fleet.

Commodore Shipping purchased the goodwill of the Alderney Tramp Shipping Company Ltd in April 1962 for £100, and utilised the *Orselina* on a three year charter to resurrect their interest in cross-channel services. In May the company took *Allen Commodore* on bareboat charter from Allen Shipping Line to operate from Portsmouth. At the same time Jack Norman (of Guernsey Contractors Ltd and J&D Norman haulage) and A G Norman (Builders Merchants) joined the Board, bringing with them a substantial volume of cargo business. The *Elly Jensen* was chartered to start a service to Shoreham, replacing the *Orselina,* which was relegated to operate a bulk cargo service.

The *Sarnia* was allocated to the Folkestone-Boulogne service for a short period of cover for the *Canterbury* in April 1962, but returned for the start of the summer service on 12 May. The summer season schedule was relaxed slightly, with added port time in Guernsey to improve punctuality.

The *Brittany* was withdrawn from service and laid up in Southampton at the end of the Jersey-St. Malo operating season on 29 November, amid rumours that she might not return. It was known that British Railways were keen to close the service, but the Jersey authorities tried to secure the deployment of the *St. Patrick* for a limited service in 1963,

The *Sarnia* eases off the Albert Quay at St Helier as she prepares to depart on 12 September 1967. *(Ambrose Greenway)*

The *Winchester* outbound from Southampton on 7 June 1963. *(Nick Robins)*

with a reduced number of inter-island calls. The *Brittany* did not return, and was sold the following March for use in Finland. In a further cost reduction exercise, the winter connecting boat trains were withdrawn; as some eighty-seven per cent of Island business was carried between May and September, this was a less contentious issue.

In the meantime Commodore Shipping began a car and cargo service to St Malo in September 1963 with the *Orselina*. The *Norman Commodore*, a sister of the *Allen Commodore*, was purchased for the Shoreham link, and the *Allen Commodore* was retained on the Portsmouth service.

More significant changes occurred on 1 January 1963, when the BTC was disbanded and full responsibility for the railway system was vested in the British Railways Board. Marine posts were transferred to the Shipping & International Services Department, for which a board member was made responsible. Whilst the operating Regions retained responsibility for the operation of shipping services, the new department was tasked with instilling a more commercial approach. At the same time there was a significant increase in fares on the Channel Island services.

British Railways duly deployed the *St. Patrick* on the Jersey-St. Malo service in 1963, with additional sailings to Weymouth at weekends. At the end of the season the winter sailings were reduced to twice-weekly and the passenger fleet dropped back to two ships. The *St. Patrick* moved to Southampton after her last trip from the Islands on 10 October, to relieve the *Normannia* and the *Falaise* when they were transferred to the short sea routes. The *St. Patrick* took up the Le Havre route on 5 December, after a refit, and maintained that route until it was closed on 10 May 1964.

British Railways increased their rates significantly when the contract for the Guernsey tomato export trade was tendered at the end of the initial three-year period in early 1964, resulting in half the tonnage being allocated to the Shoreham service of Commodore Shipping. The *Heenvliet* and *Guernsey Coast* were chartered by the Guernsey Tomato Board for the Shoreham service and managed by Commodore Shipping. A new cargo service was also opened to Rainham, Kent using *Allen Commodore* and *Norman Commodore*, but they proved too large and were replaced by a smaller vessel.

The loss of half the business reduced the number of British Railways cargo ships required to maintain the services and the *Sambur* made her final trip from the Islands on 29 March 1964 before being laid up in Southampton, and towed away for scrapping in the Netherlands on 10 June. The run down of British Railways facilities at Southampton continued with the closure of the marine workshops. The last Channel Islands passenger vessel maintained at the yard was the *Sarnia*, and the workshops closed on 15 May after completion of work on the *Hampton Ferry*.

In the same month, the entrepreneur Mr. N.S. Cowasjee founded Jersey Lines, and purchased the *Sir Richard Grenville* from Devon Cruising Ltd. renaming her *La Duchesse de Normandie*. She had previously been the Great Western's Plymouth tender, and had completed her railway service on 31 October 1963. *La Duchesse de Normandie* began operating a Guernsey-Jersey-St. Malo route with a certificate for 550 passengers, although Jersey Lines was eventually to operate to a variety of French ports including Granville, Paimpol and Cherbourg. She was refitted by Willoughby's at Millbay to make her fit for sea-going duties and add capability for carrying twenty cars on deck.

In a move that was eventually to have far-reaching consequences for the Islands, Peter Dorey, manager of Onesimus Dorey & Son, and Jack Norman, CEO of Commodore, created a new company to be called Condor Ltd, on a ²/₃/¹/₃ shareholding. Seeking to exploit the uncertainty following withdrawal of the *Brittany*, the founders looked for a vessel to operate a fast passenger-only service from France to the Islands and purchased a PT50 hydrofoil for £200,000 from the Italian shipyard Rodriguez, having originally gone to the yard to buy a smaller PT20 craft. The vessel, designed to reach a top speed of 33 knots, became the first in what was to prove an enduring line when it was named *Condor I*. The new daily services between St Malo, St Helier, and St

La Duchess de Normandie leaves St Helier; her squat shape betrays her origins as a Plymouth-based tender vessel for the GWR as the former *Sir Richard Grenville*. (Dave Hocquard)

Peter Port were introduced on 1 May, and the craft made a trip to Torquay at the end of the season.

The *St. Patrick* transferred to open the summer Southampton-St. Malo service after closing the Le Havre route, whilst still maintaining the service from Jersey and also offering Weymouth-Guernsey day excursions. Competition on a route that British Railways had wanted to close was now intense.

The two-ship Weymouth service was supplemented during the summer months by the French Railways cargo vessel *Brest*, which carried vehicles in tandem with the mailboats. *Caesarea* sustained slight damage after striking a rock approaching St. Peter Port on 29 July, but was able to continue in service.

The *Guernsey Coast* was sunk off Cap de la Hague with the loss of one crewman on 6 August after colliding with the Liberian Steamship *Catcher*. The collision took place shortly after 2:45 a.m. when the *Guernsey Coast* was on passage from St. Peter Port to Shoreham with a crew of ten and a cargo of 292 tons of tomatoes under Capt. Healy. The *Catcher* was a steamship of 7,238 tons gross, 441ft in length by 57ft in beam, heading from Antwerp to San Juan, Puerto Rico. She was Liberian owned and her owners refused to assist with the subsequent Inquiry.

The *Guernsey Coast* had left St. Peter Port at 8:15 p.m. on 5 August and encountered poor visibility during the crossing. There was dense fog at the change of watch at 2:00 a.m. Capt. Healy was on the bridge keeping watch on the radar, although he was not qualified to do so, and there was a man at the wheel. The vessel was approximately 26 miles north and east of Cape De La Hague. The navigation of the *Guernsey Coast* was described by the Inquiry as 'deplorable', as she proceeded at excessive speed in foggy conditions and failed to slow even when she heard fog signals from the *Catcher*. Capt. Healy failed to detect the approach of the *Catcher* on a conflicting course.

The stem of the *Catcher* struck the port side of the *Guernsey Coast*, penetrating nearly to the midship line at a right angle. The *Guernsey Coast* heeled to starboard and quickly began to settle in the water. The crew had donned lifejackets and mustered on deck when the alarm was sounded. The quickest way to abandon the vessel was to board the *Catcher*, whose bows were towering above the impaled port side of the *Guernsey Coast*. The crew of the *Catcher* assisted the evacuation by lowering rope ladders, with all the crew of the *Guernsey Coast* quickly saved except Capt. Healy and the acting Chief Engineer. The latter, assisted by the acting Second Engineer, stopped the engines and the oil lubricating pump and reached the foot of a ladder beside Capt.

Enjoy a weekend in the Channel Islands

Departures every Friday from London 21 October 1966 to 3 March 1967 (except Dec. 23) including all travel, full board and accommodation in hotel and coach tour of the Island on Sunday

JERSEY from **£12 10s**
GUERNSEY from **£11 10s**
for further details please ask for folder

British Rail | Southern Region

A fine view of the *Caesarea* with the distinctive coat of arms to the fore. *(Ferry Publications Library)*

Healy when the *Guernsey Coast* heeled over to starboard and sank within seven minutes of impact. Capt. Healy was recovered by a boat from the *Catcher*, but the acting Chief Engineer could not be found. The Court found Capt. Healy culpable for the sinking and suspended his certificate for twelve months.

The *St. Patrick* completed the Southampton-St. Malo season on 27 September and the service closed, the last of the railway company-operated passenger services from Southampton. The *St. Patrick* sailed the following day for Newhaven, to be overhauled before heading for a new role on the Dover Straits. The cargo service continued until 19 December when the *Moose* arrived in Jersey from St. Malo for the last time. The *Roebuck* was diverted from her normal duties at the end of 1964, to be used in the filming of the film 'The Heroes of Telemark' in Poole and Weymouth Bay.

At the end of the year, British Railways introduced a new corporate image with the name truncated to British Rail, and a new double arrow symbol applied to the fleet, accompanied by house colours of monastral blue, pearl grey and flame red. The ships' hulls were painted in blue, with a thin white dividing line above the light brown bottom, while the superstructure was grey, with funnels in red, with a white double arrow, surmounted by a thin black top. The *Winchester* returned from overhaul in December 1964 in the new colours. The grey superstructure was quickly deemed to be a hazard in poor visibility, and by February 1965 those vessels already in the new colours had had their superstructures repainted white. The *St. Patrick* was the first of the passenger ships to receive the new livery, losing her GWR stem badge in the process. The new image was first used on 16 January, when 'British Rail Shipping Services' replaced 'British Railways Southern Region' on all island advertisements.

The start of 1965 saw the introduction of a simplified timetable, with a consistent 8:15 a.m. departure time from Jersey throughout the year, with an overnight winter service from Weymouth and a daylight operation during the summer.

The *Roebuck* sailed for the last time from Guernsey to Weymouth on 27 February and was laid up until 29 July, when she was sold for scrapping to Lacmots of Queenborough. This ended the last Great Western connection with Weymouth. The *Winchester* was transferred from Southampton to replace the *Roebuck* on 1 March.

Commodore began to take steps to consolidate their position as an increasingly important freight carrier. In February they chartered the *Eilenburg* directly from her builders in Germany and the following month Jack Norman took control of the company from Mansfield Markham. The purchase of Channel Transporters (Portsmouth) Ltd, a significant force in the Jersey potato and tomato trade, followed and on 1 April Commodore acquired the Channel Stevedores operation in Portsmouth. The *Orselina* was withdrawn from the St. Malo service in April. From the beginning of May the company acted as its own agents in Jersey, withdrawing from a contract with J. G. Renouf. In June, both the *Norman Commodore* and *Fleet Commodore* were withdrawn, and on 27 June Commodore closed their Rainham link to concentrate on Portsmouth. In August *Mignon* joined the Commodore fleet, but *Allen Commodore* was sold as she proved unsuitable for the service. Commodore also chartered the *Friendship* for one year with the option of a second year. The company signed an agreement to lease Mile End Quay in Portsmouth, which was renamed the Albert Johnson Quay, and switched its operations from the Camber Quay.

Jersey Lines equipped *La Duchesse de Normandie* with a hydraulically operated scissor vehicle lift in April 1966. This extended the ramp some 20ft above the afterdeck level, with a strengthened drop-flap added to allow vehicles to drive on and off, and improve her ability to cope with large tidal ranges. The £4,000 cost was considered worthwhile in eliminating damage caused by craning and reducing turnaround time in port. Cowasjee observed that this was the first ship to operate a drive on/drive off service in St. Helier and St. Peter Port.

A National Union of Seamen strike began on 16 May with the objective of reducing the working week from fifty-six to forty hours. The *Elk* and the *Moose* were quickly strike-bound on Nos. 23 and 29 berths in Southampton, and the dispute continued until 1 July. Consolidation of the services had stabilised the decline in passenger carryings. but demand for vehicles was increasing. The SNCF cargo vessel Brest was chartered between 10 July and 10 September to operate a car carrying service in tandem with the passenger fleet. 'Cheap-weekend specials' were introduced in the autumn to help boost winter traffic.

French Line CGT chartered the *Lisieux*, which had just been displaced from the Newhaven-Dieppe route, to operate a St. Malo-Jersey service between 10 July and 2 October, with a weekly call in Weymouth. The service operated from St. Malo to Weymouth on Thursdays, with a day trip from Weymouth to Guernsey on Fridays, followed by a Friday night sailing to St. Malo. British Rail acted as agents for CGT. The

La Duchesse de Normandie leaving Southampton on 27 May 1968. *(Nick Robins)*

service was not a success and was not repeated after the first season.

The *Caesarea was* transferred to Dover from 14 December to operate the Golden Arrow service for a period of six weeks.

JERSEY LINES
1969
SCHEDULE

"LA DUCHESSE DE BRETAGNE"
THE FASTEST SHIP IN THE CHANNEL SERVICE

PASSENGERS AND CAR FERRY
DRIVE ON — DRIVE OFF

UNITED KINGDOM
CHANNEL ISLANDS & FRANCE

Jersey Lines introduced their second vessel, *La Duchesse de Bretagne*, formerly the *Brighton* displaced from the Newhaven-Dieppe route, in May 1967. Reputed to be the fastest vessel on the South Coast with a top speed of 24 knots, she was refitted for Islands service at Antwerp, before entering service from Torquay. Fitted with drive on/drive off ramps on each quarter, the vessel could carry twenty cars and 1,450 passengers. Her advertised schedule included excursions from Southampton, Weymouth, Torquay and Plymouth to the Islands. British Rail objected to this competitor being in breach of the terms of sale agreement, but the matter was resolved with Jersey Lines confirming that all advertised schedules would be operated. Cowasjee forecast that she would carry 75,000 passengers in the next four months at a reception on board *La Duchesse de Bretagne* on 5 May.

The new Weymouth passenger terminal and £250,000 customs hall was brought into use in June, and officially opened on 31 July, easing the processing of inbound passengers. On the upper level, new offices provided an improved working environment for staff. The British Rail vessels were now carrying 220,000 passengers to the Islands through the port each year. The continued growth in vehicle carryings again resulted in the charter of the *Brest*

The former Newhaven-Dieppe French registered *Lisieux* at No 1 berth in St Helier for the start of the short-lived CGT service to St Malo on 10 July 1965. *(Dave Hocquard)*

between 3 July and 10 September, and this supplementary service was subsequently extended until 7 November.

La Duchesse de Bretagne discontinued sailings from Weymouth to the Islands in July, as the sale agreement restricted her to carrying overflow passengers and cars when the railway ships' capacity had been filled. Jersey Lines replaced the Weymouth schedule with day excursions from Torquay to Cherbourg, and on 10 August opened a service from Southampton to the Channel Islands and St. Malo. At the end of the season Jersey Lines announced that *La Duchesse de Bretagne* had carried 80,969 passengers and 1,529 cars since entering service, and forecast 100,000 passengers for 1968.

Commodore took on a larger container vessel from August 1967 with the charter of the *Carsten*, which was later joined by her sister *Nincop*. The fleet was expanded further from January 1968 by the charter of the *Athene*. Noting the success of the Commodore operation, British Rail proposed major changes to their cargo business in October, with plans to switch to a container operation despite a requirement for significant investment in containers, ships and port facilities. The freight business now seemed destined to receive the investment already afforded to passenger services.

Control of the Southern Region's shipping services passed to the Shipping & International Services Division, which took over the shipping activities of the British Railways Board from 1 January 1968.

The Albert Johnson Quay opened in Portsmouth on 7 February after a £500,000 development and Commodore were granted a twenty-one year lease on the facility. The expanded shore capacity allowed the tomato traffic to be transferred from Shoreham. Commodore reached agreement with British Channel Island Shipping for the transfer of their cargo service to the Albert Johnson Quay in Portsmouth on 10 May 1968, thereby closing the London link after 115 years of operation. This latterly operated from Tower Pier in London to the London berth at Victoria Pier, St. Helier.

A classic view of the *La Duchesse de Bretagne*. (FotoFlite)

The cargo vessel ***Commodore Goodwill*** outward bound to Jersey from Portsmouth. *(FotoFlite)*

In April 1968 the acceleration of rail journeys facilitated by electrification of the line from London Waterloo to Bournemouth, allowed the departure of the boat train from London to be put back to 09:55 from Easter Monday 15 April, thus giving passengers longer time to connect into the service. The departure from Weymouth was retimed to 13:30 with arrivals in Guernsey at 17:30 and Jersey at 20:00. The late arrival time in Jersey brought initial opposition from hoteliers as guests arrived late for their evening meals, but the service was an immediate success, with overall traffic to Jersey increasing by twenty-five per cent, and Guernsey by thirty-seven per cent. The situation was helped further by a sixteen per cent increase in air fares. This led to the issue of sailing tickets to control demand, and passengers were turned away on a number of occasions. Solutions considered to address growing demand included possible use of the *St. David* as a third ship, but extra sailings of the *Caesarea* and the *Sarnia* proved a more pragmatic remedy. The *Elk* and the *Moose* were utilised to transport cars from Weymouth during the season whilst owners travelled on the passenger vessels, obviating the need for a charter of the *Brest*.

Caesarea sustained hull damage and was holed when she hit an obstruction approaching Weymouth on 22 August 1968. She was sent to dry dock at Southampton for repair with *St. Patrick* returning to cover. Traffic figures for the first season of the accelerated British Rail service showed a healthy increase of 80,897 passengers to 382,224, while accompanied cars increased by 2,468 to 12,287.

In August the single deck cargo vessel *Commodore Clipper (I)*, formerly the *Clipper*, entered service for Commodore Shipping after being purchased for £39,000. The Company withdrew the *Nike* in September, whilst the tween decker *Commodore Goodwill (I)*, formerly the *Goodwill*, joined the fleet in November after purchase for £70,000.

Meanwhile *La Duchesse de Normandie* reopened the Jersey-St. Malo route with *La Duchesse de Bretagne* on 22 May 1968, with the Southampton service following shortly after. However the season was interrupted when *La Duchesse de Normandie* suffered propeller damage and had to go to Southampton for repairs. The end for Jersey Lines came rapidly when the Company was actioned in the Royal Court of Jersey to pay a Dutch Company £3,304 on 16 November. The Sunday Mirror reported that Cowasjee had liabilities of £400k and that payments to creditors would be three shillings in the pound. A defiant Cowasjee stated that the company would bring *La Duchesse de Bretagne* back for the 1969 season, but this did not happen and further proceedings followed. *La Duchesse de Bretagne* was arrested in Southampton and sold to Harry Pound, who towed her to Portsmouth to await a buyer but she was sold for scrapping in April 1970. Condor exploited the absence of Jersey Lines and chartered a seasonal PT50 craft as *Condor 2* from Rodriguez for the 1969 season.

The Shipping & International Services Division was incorporated as a wholly owned subsidiary of Sealink (UK) Ltd on 1 January 1969. Plans to introduce the container freight business moved slowly, in part because of a reluctance in the Islands to install the shore facilities required to handle large containers. In June British Rail, recognising that the scale of investment was significant, agreed to share equipment with Commodore Shipping. The plans gained momentum after the Executive of the Shipping & International Services Division familiarised themselves with the issues when they visited the Islands in October 1970.

Commodore bought the Portsmouth-based road haulier A. Burnett & Sons (Transport) Ltd. to give them a foothold in UK haulage, and withdrew the *Eilenburg* in May. In July they purchased the interests of Thomas Allen in Jersey and Guernsey when they elected to withdraw from the Island business; this included British Channel Island Shipping companies in Guernsey and Jersey. After Mansfield Markham sold his shares to finance companies, Jack Norman was elected chairman of Commodore on 8 August. The company ordered two new German-built freighters in the name of Channel Transporters (Portsmouth) Ltd. to take advantage of UK government grants. On 30 September Commodore closed their services to Alderney and Sark and between the islands. *Island Commodore (1)* was sold to the Isle of Sark Shipping Company.

In November the new brand name Sealink was launched, encompassing the joint shipping fleets of British Rail, SNCF and the Zeeland Steam Ship Company. At the end of the year Sealink was able to celebrate a forty-eight per cent increase in Weymouth passenger business in just two years.

The *St. Patrick* sailed from Folkestone to Guernsey and Jersey on 8 May 1970 to undertake a short programme of day excursions to St. Malo, before returning back to Dover on 11 May. The Newhaven-Dieppe route vessel *Villandry* also operated day excursions from Le Havre and Cherbourg to Jersey over the Whitsuntide weekend.

British Rail announced a new volume-based charging system for flower traffic for the 1971 season, mirroring the structure applied by airlines. This increased some rates by 156 per cent, bringing an end to the dedicated flower boats. The *Winchester,* which had spent most of her career carrying this traffic from Guernsey, could not be adapted for the switch to containers. She made her farewell visit to Guernsey on 29 December 1970, and was withdrawn and sold to Chandris Cruises, who renamed her *Exeter* and sent her to Piraeus for conversion to a cruise ship. She enjoyed an extended period of operation as the *Radiosa*, before being broken up in 1995 in Greece. The *Winchester's* cargo duties were picked up by the *Selby,* operating mainly from Southampton from the start of 1971. *Selby* suffered a difficult introduction to the route, as she ran aground in gales off Jersey on passage from Southampton in January 1971 and had to be towed by the Newhaven tug *Meeching* to Marchwood for repair. Commodore Shipping's *Carsten,* which was then operating on the Portsmouth route, was chartered in to cover her absence.

The *Falaise* and *Maid of Kent* lie alongside at Weymouth. *(Ferry Publications Library)*

The experimental hovercraft *VT1* visited Jersey on 4 January 1971, taking four hours for the 124-mile crossing from Gosport. Built by Vosper Thornycroft at Portchester, this prototype craft spent a month on trial between Jersey and France, including a maiden flight to Dinard covering the thirty-six miles in 1 hour 15 minutes in a Force 7 gale, but the vessel was not a success and was scrapped in Portsmouth in 1973.

In a busy month for Commodore, *Island Commodore (II)* was launched on 29 January and *Norman Commodore (II)* delivered the following day.

It was announced in February 1971 that the new British Rail containerised freight operation would operate from Southampton, with Guernsey tomato traffic remaining at Weymouth. Two new ships were to be built for the service, to be joined by either the *Container Venturer* or *Container Enterprise*, with the *Elk* or the *Moose* retained for the tomato trade. Within six weeks the location of the English terminal had been switched to Portsmouth, precipitating the end of the Islands' historic links with Southampton.

Growing passenger traffic during summer months prompted the introduction of more overnight crossings from Weymouth, but the ships were not equipped to carry high volumes of sleeping passengers. Additional seating was installed in the *Caesarea* and the *Sarnia* early in 1971, so that 870 numbered seats could be provided under cover, and from May these were allocated through a reservation system overcoming the unseemly scenes on boarding; a ceiling of 1,000 passengers was placed on night crossings so that every passenger had a seat or berth for the crossing. On 30 April 1971 the *St. Patrick* again sailed from Dover to Jersey for a short programme of excursions to St. Malo, before returning on 8 May.

With British Rail committed to the containerisation project and two new container ships, it came as a surprise when it was announced in December that these would be operated under a pooling arrangement with Commodore Shipping under the trading

Top: The *Normannia* first visited the Islands on 13 November 1958 and was converted to carry cars in early 1964. She is pictured on 5 April 1976 after the conversion. *(Kevin le Scelleur)*

Bottom: The *Caesarea* leaving Weymouth for the Islands, with the *Falaise* at the linkspan. *(Ferry Publications Library)*

name of Brit-Comm. This would introduce a daily service from Portsmouth to both Islands operating with a fleet of four ships, two from each company. The service was planned to start on 1 May 1972, but port facilities in Guernsey and Jersey were not fully ready until 2 October, so one vessel from each company operated until then.

The *Guernsey Fisher* entered service on 6 January 1972, with the *Jersey Fisher* following on 20 February, both under a five year charter from James Fisher & Sons Ltd of Barrow. Their arrival ended the charter of the *Lune Fisher*. The new combined lo-lo fleet provided sufficient freight capacity to allow the general cargo service from Weymouth to end in April 1972, although the port retained the Guernsey tomato trade.

Attention turned to providing a more economical solution to the transportation of accompanied cars. An initial British Rail report supported the introduction of a ro-ro service, but this had to be matched by agreement at the ports to provide the necessary shore facilities. The States of Jersey authorised a £1 million investment in a 240ft ramp, capable of taking vehicles weighing in excess of twenty tons but the States of Guernsey initially decided not to invest in ramp facilities. This decision was noted in Weymouth, where there was an agreement to provide similar facilities, subject to these being reciprocated in the Islands. The new service was therefore planned to operate from Weymouth to Jersey for the 1973 season, using either the *Falaise* or the *Normannia*.

The *Caesarea* sustained propeller damage after they became caught in lobster pots at St. Peter Port during foggy conditions on 19 July; she was sent to Falmouth for repair. The *Maid of Kent* sailed directly from Folkestone to Jersey to provide cover, arriving at 10:15 on 20 July. She operated three round trips to Weymouth before returning to Folkestone for her scheduled services, dropping passengers from the Islands in Newhaven en route.

The *Elk* made the final railway company sailing from Southampton to the Islands on 29 September 1972. On the same evening, *Guernsey Fisher* sailed from Jersey for Portsmouth, to take up the new Brit-Comm service from 2 October. The *Moose* was retained to carry cars from Weymouth, before being withdrawn with the *Elk* on 8 October; the *Selby* remained in service until 21 October. All three vessels were then quickly sold; the *Elk* and the *Moose* to the Valmas Shipping Co for service in Greece. The *Nasim* (formerly the *Elk*) was lost in February 1976 and the *Agios Dionyssios* (formerly the *Moose*) was sold at end of 1995.

Harbour dues in St. Helier were raised by fifteen per cent in October, as preparatory works began in parallel for the installation of ro-ro ramps in St. Helier and Weymouth. The following month the Jersey Harbours and Airport Committee took delivery of a new multi-purpose vessel the *Duke of Normandy*, designed to assist large vessels entering and departing from St. Helier.

The *Caesarea* damaged her fuel tanks on 9 March when she ran aground entering the harbour at St. Helier and was taken out of service for inspection. The ro-ro ferry *Holyhead Ferry I* was fortuitously en route from Dover to Holyhead so deputised with a sailing from Weymouth to Guernsey on 11 March, returning the following day without visiting St. Helier as she was too large to enter the harbour. Guernsey thus sampled a British Rail ro-ro vessel even though no facilities were available. New ramp facilities were completed in Jersey at the north end of the Albert Pier adjacent to the cross wall separating the drying and tidal areas, ready for the summer season. No. 4 and No. 5 berths were allocated for stern loading ro-ro ships to berth to their starboard side, requiring vessels to swing on entering the pier heads and move astern to their berth.

The *Normannia* visited Jersey for a chartered excursion from St. Malo on 26 April, but it was the *Falaise* that was to be allocated to the Island ro-ro service. She was released from duties at Newhaven by the arrival of the *Senlac*, and headed to Holyhead for

The stern-loading *Falaise* at Weymouth on 13 August 1973. She was to suffer an abrupt end to her career the following summer. *(Nick Robins)*

alterations and a refit in readiness for her Channel Island duties. The *Falaise* had been converted into a stern loading car ferry in 1965 with capability for carrying 100 cars but with her passenger capacity reduced to 700. She made a trial run to Jersey on 25 May, another voyage on 30 May, and her first scheduled crossing on 1 June under Capt. Picot; the start of a new era for the Islands. The *Falaise* made one round trip daily, leaving Jersey at 07:30 and returning from Weymouth at 15:30. 25,000 cars were carried during her first season and the numbers of passengers travelling by sea to Jersey grew by 50,000 to 320,000 in 1973, demonstrating the demand for a car ferry service.

The maiden season of the *Falaise* was marred by repeated engine problems, with many cancellations and rescheduled trips, leading to passengers and the Island authorities questioning her suitability for the route. But overall the first summer and the switch to ro-ro proved successful. British Rail made their experiment permanent after the initial seven months of operation, with two weekly-calls added in Guernsey where cars had to be craned from the stern ramp due to the lack of ramp facilities. The States of Guernsey reacted quickly, announcing an investment of £175k in a new linkspan to accommodate car traffic from 1974.

The *Falaise* operated two winter sailings, leaving the *Caesarea* or the *Sarnia* to operate the weekend sailing. *Normannia* returned to take over the winter service from 18 December to allow the *Falaise's* engine problems to receive attention. Using the *Falaise* and the *Normannia* on the winter schedule forced significant changes to the Royal Mail contract, as there was no provision for the carriage of mail. The mail traffic was therefore containerised and shipped via Portsmouth, with the passenger ships losing the right to fly the Royal Mail pennant and the historic title of Royal Mail Steamer. The *Caesarea* took the last mail sailing to the Islands on 5 October, returning with the final outward mail on 8 October. The *Normannia* was to remain on the Weymouth station until March 1974.

Although Southampton no longer featured in the Channel Island schedules, a new

The *Svea Drott* was drafted in at short notice to cover for the ailing *Falaise* in August 1974. Her performance was sufficiently impressive for British Rail to purchase her as the *Earl Godwin* in December 1974. *(Ferry Publications Library)*

The *Caledonian Princess* - initially built for the Stranraer-Larne route - was transferred from Fishguard to replace the *Falaise* from 1975. She was converted to a one-class vessel at Immingham in 1976 and remained on Channel Island routes until July 1981, being withdrawn and sold in 1982. *(Kevin Le Scelleur)*

Divisional office was established in the old South Western Hotel to control operations from Portsmouth and Weymouth, as well as a new service between Weymouth and Cherbourg that was planned to begin in April 1974.

The *Normannia* returned to Dover on 15 March 1974, but was soon required back to cover for *Falaise* between 29 April and 20 May. *Sarnia* suffered turbine problems on 29 April and was then off service until 15 May.

The new ro-ro ramp in Guernsey was inaugurated by the *Falaise* on 26 June 1974, and thenceforth her schedule called there twice-weekly, with the remaining time spent on the direct Weymouth-Jersey route. A new 'Night Flyer' product utilising the 00:30 sailing from Weymouth to Jersey, arriving in St. Helier at 06:00, enjoying a 15 hour stay ashore, before returning at 21:45 to arrive back at 05:00, proved to be a popular initiative to boost travel. The bargain fare of £8 included a bottle of spirits and 200 cigarettes. Optional extras included a 95p supper and a coach tour of the island.

On 28 June the *Sarnia* suffered a recurrence of her turbine problems and was withdrawn from service for ten days. The *Maid of Orleans* was drafted in to cover for her absence between 29 June and 7 July. Despite her extended refit earlier in the year *Falaise* continued to suffer from boiler problems on her intensive schedule. Although it had been intended that she continue in service for the season, she was withdrawn on 14 August after a very late arrival in Weymouth. On the same day British Rail announced that the *Caledonian Princess* would replace her in 1975, providing extra capacity for the growing demand for commercial freight on the ro-ro service. *Falaise* sailed to Holyhead for repair on 21 August. The cargo fleet was used to carry cars for a short period, until the arrival of the chartered *Svea Drott* on 19 August; she maintained the service, including a visit to Southampton on 8 September when gales made Weymouth inaccessible, until the *Caledonian Princess* could be released on 26 September. With twin turbines fed by two Babcock & Wilcox boilers, the 1961 built *Caledonian Princess* could reach 20 knots, and twin rudders, a bow thrust unit and bow rudder made her a very manoueverable vessel. She continued until 26 October when the *Normannia* arrived for the winter season. The scale of repairs required by the *Falaise* proved unjustifiable and she was sent directly from Holyhead to Bilbao for breaking up on 24 December.

The winter schedule of 1974-5 saw the *Normannia* operate alone, as both classic passenger ships were laid up. British Rail turned to a more permanent arrangement with the *Svea Drott* as replacement tonnage for the *Falaise*; she had impressed during her charter and was purchased in December 1974, and named *Earl Godwin* after the Earl of Wessex and father of King Harold. *Earl Godwin* went to Harwich where her engines were removed for machining and re-bedding, and then to Holyhead to replace her cabins with seating accommodation, fit a new bow door and add stabilisers in the largest conversion project ever undertaken at the port. Conversion for Island service in time for the 1975 summer service proved ambitious; the *Caledonian Princess* was therefore brought in to replace the *Normannia* on 15 July. By then the *Normannia* had completed 170 consecutive round trips on the Island routes - the longest unbroken spell by any Sealink vessel. On 15 and 26 September the *Caledonian Princess* caused damage to a number of vessels whilst approaching No. 5 berth in St. Helier during strong south-westerly winds.

The high operating costs of the *Caesarea* and the *Sarnia* relative to their diesel powered cousins prompted British Rail to consider withdrawing them. The *Caesarea* completed her last full season before transferring to the short sea routes to replace the *Maid of Orleans*, with her final sailing being the 08:15 from Jersey to Weymouth on 6 October 1975. The occasion was marked with a small reception hosting the Lieutenant Governor during her call in St. Peter Port; the signal station hoisted flags to mark

The *Caledonian Princess* shortly after conversion to a one-class ship in 1976. *(Dave Hocquard)*

A heavily loaded and freshly painted *Earl Godwin*; note the 'reverse' British Rail logo on her port funnel, a unique feature of the Sealink fleet. *(Miles Cowsill)*

The *Earl Godwin* leaving Weymouth in 1976 – one of the longest lasting Channel Island vessels of the modern era, she is laid up in 2018. *(Miles Cowsill)*

'farewell' on her departure.

The number of car ferry calls in Guernsey was raised to three for the 1976 season, and there was sufficient demand for vehicle space to justify a full ro-ro operation, using the *Earl Godwin* and the *Caledonian Princess,* with the *Sarnia* retained to provide extra peak capacity. The *Earl Godwin* arrived for trials in Guernsey direct from refit at Holyhead before taking up her first sailing with the 08.30 from Jersey to Guernsey and Weymouth on 1 February 1976, the first time since 1897 that a maiden sailing had begun in the Islands. Her arrival allowed the *Caledonian Princess* to be withdrawn to be altered for the multi-purpose service. She went to Immingham for an extensive £426k conversion into a one-class ship, with new lounges, tea bar, a television lounge and the addition of 570 seats for night crossings.

The *Earl Godwin's* early service was problematic; by 23 March she had suffered generator problems for the third time in two weeks and was taken out of service for repair. The *Sarnia* and the *Normannia* covered the schedules until 6 April, during a very busy Easter period, despite a dockers strike in Jersey that closed the harbour to vehicles for a week. When the *Earl Godwin* returned in April she found herself strikebound by a crew sit-in over manning levels.

The *Caledonian Princess* returned on 12 May to begin the new multi-purpose service, albeit largely in the old schedule, although the evening sailing from Jersey sailed directly to Weymouth. The *Caledonian Princess* sailed at 00:30 from Weymouth to Jersey, returning at 08:00 to Guernsey and Weymouth, whilst *Earl Godwin* sailed at 13:30 from Weymouth. The *Sarnia* operated supplementary weekend services to both Islands during the summer coupled with Wednesday day excursions to Guernsey.

The *Caledonian Princess* went to Holyhead to undertake winter relief duties on 14

Viking II was launched for Thoresen Car Ferries' Southampton-Le Havre services in 1964, but was acquired by British Rail in 1977 as the *Earl William* following the successful introduction of *Earl Godwin*. *(FotoFlite)*

The future *Earl William* awaits conversion to Channel Island service at Holyhead. *(Dave Hocquard)*

Conversion complete, the *Earl William* is a fine sight as she arrives at St Peter Port. *(John Hendy)*

December. Even with limited winter capacity, ro-ro freight traffic was growing on the multi-purpose sailings, although Bob Norman of Commodore Shipping was quoted as saying "The future lies in containers, not trailers, the present split being 95% lo-lo and 5% ro-ro". British Rail's increasing confidence in ro-ro marked a strategic shift away from the lo-lo venture at Portsmouth, and plans for a dedicated ro-ro operation from Portsmouth to replace the Brit-Comm arrangements began to take shape. The City of Portsmouth had opened up the Continental Ferry Terminal in 1976 to handle a new Brittany Ferries service to St. Malo and a Townsend Thoresen route to Cherbourg, and it was partly to deter these operators from considering Channel Island operations that gave impetus to British Rail's plans. A new build vessel could not be justified, so Lloyd's Leasing acquired the *Viking II*, a sister of the *Earl Godwin*, on behalf of British Rail from Townsend Thoresen in December 1976; she arrived at Holyhead on 22 December for the lengthy conversion process. Meanwhile the Sealink dredger *Landguard* was chartered by Weymouth Council to extract 35,000 cubic metres of spoil from the harbour over a period of six weeks from the end of February 1977.

March saw the completion of projects to lengthen the *Island Commodore* and the *Norman Commodore*.

The *Sarnia* enjoyed a stay of execution and represented British Rail under Capt. Barker at the Spithead naval review marking the Queen's Silver Jubilee on 28 June 1977. The autumn was marked by a succession of final sailings for the British Rail fleet. The *Sarnia*, having carried over three million passengers during her Weymouth career, made her last scheduled sailing between the Islands and Weymouth on 4 September, although she returned to Guernsey on charter on 10 September. *Sarnia's* final farewell from St. Peter Port was watched by a large crowd and Capt. Evans was given a message from Harbour Master Capt. Wolley which stated: -

'Farewell to an old friend. Best wishes to you and all on board, from the Harbour Master and staff at St. Peter Port'.

The *Earl William* prior to removal of the British Rail logos from her funnels. *(FotoFlite)*

EARL WILLIAM

LONDON

Her departure left a full multi-purpose service operated by the *Earl Godwin* and the *Caledonian Princess*. The *Jersey Fisher* made her last call in the Islands as a British Rail ship on 29 September, being handed over to Commodore Shipping, who renamed her the *Commodore Challenger*. The *Guernsey Fisher* completed service when she left St. Peter Port on 27 October, thereby closing the British Rail cargo service, although the Guernsey tomato traffic still justified a seasonal charter to Weymouth. British Rail dissolved the Brit-Com Agreement on 31 October in favour of operating their own ro-ro service from Portsmouth. The closure of the British Rail container service effectively also brought the Royal Mail contract to an end, as although trailers were used for a trial period, the Post Office found they preferred the transport of parcels by containers, and the 137-year old contract was terminated in 1978. Commodore signed a contract with the Royal Mail on 17 May 1978, and thereafter was entitled to fly the Royal Mail pennant. Meanwhile 'Sealink' became the brand name for British Rail Shipping Services in the Islands.

The new service from Portsmouth Continental Ferry Port was planned to start with the *Earl Godwin* on 31 October, as the freshly named *Earl William* was delayed at refit. The start was postponed until 8 November following industrial action by the crew of the *Earl Godwin*, who disputed manning and wage levels and 'sat in' on the vessel on the ramp at Weymouth. The initial Monday-Friday service established the pattern for future services by leaving Portsmouth at 23:00, for Jersey via Guernsey arriving at 08:30, returning at 09:50 via Guernsey, and arriving back in Portsmouth at 18:50. On Friday nights the *Earl Godwin* sailed directly to Jersey and then spent the weekend in Guernsey, as the Weymouth vessels occupied the berths in St. Helier. The first weekend sailings met stormy conditions in the Channel, and both the *Caledonian Princess* and the *Earl Godwin* found themselves storm-bound in St. Peter Port. The *Earl Godwin's* night sailing from Portsmouth on 11 November did not arrive in St. Peter Port until 18:00 on the 12th. The *Caledonian Princess* arrived five hours late from Weymouth at 11:40 on 12 November and was forced to remain in port until 08:00 on the 13th before she could head to Jersey. Even then she could not berth in St. Helier until late afternoon. The *Earl Godwin* did not leave for St. Helier until midday on 13 November, having transferred her passengers to the *Caledonian Princess*.

The *Earl William* finally entered service on 16 January 1978 with the 23:00 sailing from Portsmouth, marking the transformation of the Island services to a full ro-ro operation. The new pattern was an immediate success, with loadings from Portsmouth running at double initial expectations, so a Saturday sailing was added to the schedules on a year-round basis from 1 April. This necessitated changes to the Weymouth schedule to aid punctuality of the *Earl William;* the Weymouth vessel sailed directly to Jersey then back to Guernsey, before returning light to Jersey to lay over.

Whilst the Portsmouth service settled into the new schedule, the Weymouth route was beset by problems. The *Earl Godwin* was sent to Immingham for overhaul after her service at Portsmouth, but found herself trapped by an industrial dispute with lock gate operators. The *Normannia* was transferred to operate the Weymouth service until 31 March, but more capacity was needed as the seasonal traffic grew, and the *Viking Victory,* a sister of the *Earl Godwin* and the *Earl William,* was chartered from Townsend Thoresen between 3 and 29 April. As the *Caledonian Princess* also required a visit to dry dock in April, the *Normannia* returned to support the service but was only able to carry vehicles due to a major oil leak in her accommodation, so the *Caesarea* was brought back from Dover to offer passenger capacity. Services settled down to normality with the return of the *Caledonian Princess* on 1 May and the *Earl Godwin* on 5 May. The *Caesarea* and the *Normannia* made their final trips from the Islands to Weymouth on 6 May. The

A third vessel in the successful 'Viking' series on the Channel Islands route was *Viking Victory*, on charter from Townsend Thoresen in April 1977. *(Ferry Publications Library)*

Sarnia left Weymouth for the last time on 24 May 1978 bound for Immingham and conversion into a floating supermarket, to operate between Ostend and Dunkirk for Channel Cruise Lines Ltd. In June the *Normannia* was sold to Red Sea Ferries of Dubai as a pilgrim ship. Both ventures were to prove troubled.

Shore facilities improved in Portsmouth when the *Earl William* became the first vessel to use the second vehicle ramp at the Continental Ferry Port from 5 June. The port facilities were enhanced with an extension to the terminal, and Derek Shorter was noted as saying that "The opening of the new berth is a statement of Sealink's faith in the long term viability of the Portsmouth route". Meanwhile a second £850k ro-ro ramp was ordered for St. Helier in May.

The 1978 summer timetable reflected the growing confidence of the Sealink operation and gave the Islands an unprecedented level of service, with three multi-purpose sailings each day, seven days a week - a giant step forward from the era of cutbacks. The services were truly transformed.

Development of Condor craft

Top: The pioneer *Condor 1* entered service for Condor on 1 May 1964 and steadily developed traffic between the Islands. She remained with the company until 1976. Photographed on 9 July 1974. (*Condor Ferries/Kevin Le Scelleur*)

Middle: *Condor 2* supplemented *Condor 1*'s capacity from the 1969 season after Jersey Lines went out of business. She stayed for two seasons but returned in 1981, when she was photographed on 16 August. (*Condor Ferries/Kevin Le Scelleur*)

Bottom: *Condor 5* entered service on 2 June 1976, and was photographed on 27 July 1976. She served Condor until October 1992 and was subsequently sold. (*Condor Ferries/Kevin Le Scelleur*)

Above: *Condor 3* joined the fleet in April 1971 and operated with Condor until December 1979. (*Condor Ferries/Kevin Le Scelleur*)

Left: *Condor 4* was acquired in 1974 for the French day trip market and spent 16 years with the company. (*Condor Ferries/Kevin Le Scelleur*)

Below: The Marine and General Engineering Yard at St Sampson's plays host to the winter overhauls of *Condor 5* and *Condor 4* on 11 December 1982. (*Dave Hocquard*)

CHAPTER TEN

Privatisation and competition 1979-1986

'Travel the Starliner service to the Channel Islands

This brand-new overnight travel experience connecting Portsmouth and the Channel Islands is on the most luxurious ferry operating out of Britain providing the highest standard of service.

You have your own en suite cabin with virtually every facility that is now offered by a top class hotel. Join the ship in time to have your evening dinner on board before she sails. The next morning choose between a continental breakfast brought to your cabin or a full English breakfast in the ship's restaurant before disembarking fully refreshed.

With dinner on board the main course varies from Roast Fillet of Beef Chasseur from the hot table to Trout Chambertin from the cold table...'

[Sealink British Ferries' Starliner brochure, 1985]

O n 1 January 1979 the shipping division of the British Railways Board was transferred into the ownership of Sealink UK Ltd, a wholly owned autonomous subsidiary of the Board. In addition to the shipping assets employed on the Island services, the transfer included the railway's forty-four per cent interest in George Troy and Sons Ltd in Jersey, and a twenty-five per cent holding in Guernsey Stevedores. The new division inherited a strong trading surplus and was well placed to compete with its private sector rivals around the country.

The troubled start to the Portsmouth route continued when the *Earl William* became entangled with chains from a buoy moored near Portsmouth on 19 January 1979, bending her propeller shaft and causing significant damage to her propellers. The growing importance of the route for freight traffic was evident in the immediate transfer of *Earl Godwin* to cover both the *Earl William's* repairs and her subsequent planned refit period at Falmouth, leaving the Weymouth route without a service for five weeks. The *Caledonian Princess* did not return to re-open the Weymouth service until 1 March.

Tragedy struck on 14 August 1979, when a freak storm of force 10 winds and 50ft waves hit contestants in the 605 mile Fastnet yachting race, leaving fifteen crew members dead - the worst disaster in the history of ocean yacht racing. Amongst those who lost their lives was Peter Dorey, grandson of Onesimus Dorey, who had purchased the Onesimus Dorey & Sons share in Condor in 1964. His shares passed to his wife Kathleen, who had named the first Condor vessel in Italy in 1964, and she took over the running of the company.

1980 was marked by the second world fuel crisis, as OPEC raised prices dramatically following reductions in supply from Saudi Arabia and post-revolution Iran. Fuel shortages led to queues at petrol stations, and from April passage times of sailings on the Weymouth route were extended by fifteen minutes to reduce fuel consumption, and Sealink simultaneously introduced a £4 vehicle surcharge. Peak season weekend capacity was increased by changing the Weymouth schedule, so that the vessel arriving in Jersey on Saturday morning operated a return sailing to Weymouth rather than remaining in port over the weekend, ending a long standing tradition.

The *Earl William* was withdrawn from service for repair in May after suffering another engine failure, with the *Free Enterprise II* chartered from Townsend Thoresen to provide cover. The *Free Enterprise II* quickly proved inadequate for the freight business, so the *Earl Godwin* returned to maintain the Portsmouth service, and the *Free Enterprise II* went to

Free Enterprise II covered for the *Earl Godwin,* when she was transferred to Portsmouth to cover for *Earl William's* engine problems, seen at Weymouth in May 1970. *(Miles Cowsill)*

Free Enterprise II entering St Helier. *(Dave Hocquard)*

The *Viking 4* was completed in June 1973 and operated for Viking Line from Mariehamn and Stockholm before joining the Sealink fleet as *Earl Granville* in 1981. *(Ferry Publications Library)*

The *Earl Granville* suffered a torrid time during her first season of operation in 1981. *(FotoFlite)*

Weymouth on 21 May 1980 to operate alongside the *Caledonian Princess;* she remained there until 11 June.

Meanwhile work continued in developing harbour facilities at St. Helier, with the heavy-lift vessel *Stahleck* being used to install the second linkspan in June. The *Solidor* became the first ship to use the new ramp.

The Portsmouth service proved increasingly popular despite the operating problems of the *Earl William*, and this encouraged Sealink to look for a larger vessel to allow the route to continue to grow. Restrictions on the ship size that could be handled in St. Helier proved a significant constraint, but Sealink acquired the 1973-built Finnish vessel *Viking 4* through Williams & Glyns Industrial Leasing, completing the deal on 25 August. There were initial concerns about her manoeuverability in port, as she was 4ft longer than the *Caledonian Princess*, but her garage deck offered significantly enhanced vehicle capacity. *Viking 4* underwent an extensive £10 million refit and modification programme at her builders Jos. L. Meyer Yard at Papenburg, Germany. Two 12-cylinder diesel engines were fitted, together with new stabilisers and an additional bow door to act as a collision bulkhead. The number of sleeping berths was reduced from 280 to 170, with forward cabins being replaced by reclining seats. *Viking 4* emerged as the *Earl Granville*, being named after Lord John Carteret, the one-time bailiff of Jersey who became Earl of Granville in 1744.

With a conservative government in power in the UK, the issue of privatisation of public utilities was high on the agenda. Whilst the full break up of British Rail was deemed too ambitious at this stage - and was not to be enacted for over a decade - steps were taken to divest the Board of some of its 'non-core' activities. Sealink UK Ltd was seen as a prime candidate for privatisation, and proposals were announced in the

The *Earl Granville* mid-channel on her late morning sailing from Guernsey to Portsmouth *(FotoFlite)*

House of Commons on 14 July 1980.

By the end of 1980, Sealink recorded a fifteen per cent year-on-year increase in passenger traffic on the Island routes, carrying a record 890,000 passengers, 98,000 vehicles, 20,000 commercial vehicles and 10,000 trade cars on the combined Portsmouth and Weymouth routes. This success was not matched in the Group as a whole, which made a substantial loss as the end of the pooling agreement on short sea routes with Townsend Thoresen resulted in heavy price competition at a time of deep recession.

Sealink began to consider the future development of the Island services as part of their preparation for life in the private sector. Although the *Earl Granville* would offer enhanced capacity from Portsmouth, the *Caledonian Princess* was approaching twenty years old so further investment was likely to be necessary. Plans were announced in January 1981 for the construction of two new ships for the Island services. Work was scheduled to start in 1985 but in the event the proposals were overtaken by the politics of privatisation.

The *Earl Granville* undertook sea trials after her refit on 23 February 1981, and arrived in Portsmouth for the first time on 20 March. After a VIP familiarisation trip, which included champagne receptions for Island dignitaries on 26 and 27 March, she commenced her scheduled service on 29 March with the 23:00 departure from Portsmouth. The new Portsmouth sailing schedule was: -

Portsmouth	dep	23:00
Guernsey	arr	06:00
	dep	06:30
Jersey	arr	08:20
	dep	09:50
Guernsey	arr	11:45
	dep	12:15
Portsmouth	arr	18:50

Loading of ro-ro vessels at Portsmouth was a significant logistical challenge. With *Earl Granville* berthing bow-in in St. Peter Port and stern-in at St Helier, traffic had to be loaded in two halves, with freight used to counter-balance an in-built list to the vessel. The majority of freight carryings were on trailers which were driven on and off by stevedores with tractor units, but smaller operators such as Breakwell's and Sayers chose to ship accompanied vans.

The *Earl Godwin* was sent to operate on the Heysham-Douglas route for Sealink's Manx Line operation from 25 March to 9 April, before returning to Weymouth to support *Caledonian Princess*. The introduction of the *Earl Granville* released the *Earl William* for refit before she resumed service from Weymouth on 3 May, the day after the *Caledonian Princess* had departed from the Islands for the last time, seemingly the end of the steam turbine era. The *Caledonian Princess* was overhauled at Avonmouth before heading to Dover to replace the *Caesarea*, which had recently been sold.

1981 was difficult for growers and farmers in the islands, with an outbreak of foot and mouth disease affecting cattle in Jersey, and the rising cost of heating oil hitting the Guernsey tomato industry. With increasing volumes of traffic being carried by lorries and trailers on the ro-ro service, it became clear that the charter of cargo tonnage was no longer justifiable for the growing season, and 1981 proved to be the last season of operation.

The *Earl Granville's* first season was marred by a succession of operational problems. She suffered a generator failure on her crossing from Portsmouth on 10 June, forcing her to anchor to allow repairs to be undertaken, eventually arriving in Jersey six hours late with

100 passengers on board. Three days later the *Earl Granville* suffered an engine failure, missing her outward Guernsey call and arriving in Jersey on one engine. A difficult month worsened when fire was discovered in the *Earl Granville's* domestic boiler three hours after leaving Portsmouth on 22 June, some twelve miles south of Isle of Wight. She returned escorted by a tug and two lifeboats, arriving back in Portsmouth at 05:30. 377 passengers, fifty-nine cars and nine freight vehicles were disembarked through the stern door and transferred to Weymouth. The fire caused £200k damage to the central heating system and electrical equipment and the *Earl Granville* was sent for repair to Husband's Yard in Southampton, remaining off service until 16 July.

The *Earl William* was transferred from Weymouth to cover the Portsmouth schedules during the *Earl Granville's* absence, and there was an unexpected return for the *Caledonian Princess,* when she returned from Dover to maintain the Weymouth services. The *Earl William's* stay at Portsmouth also proved eventful. After suffering engine trouble and running at slow speed for two days she struck a rock on the eastern side of St. Helier harbour on 5 July and sustained two gashes on her hull near the keel. After a full inspection she was cleared to return to Portsmouth, but further engine trouble forced her back to St. Helier, having only reached Corbière. The *Earl William* then sailed directly to Falmouth for dry dock repair. Sealink were now in desperate straits approaching the peak of the season. The *Viking Trader* was chartered from Townsend Thoresen to provide freight capacity, arriving in the Islands for the first time on 7 July, but she subsequently suffered a bow visor failure. The *Earl Siward* made a rare appearance for three days from 11 July, breaking her seasonal transfer from Holyhead to Newhaven to help out. At 369ft she was then the largest ferry to have used the inner harbour at St. Helier.

The *Earl William* returned to traffic on 15 July, followed by the *Earl Granville* on the 17th, but the operational difficulties continued. On 20 July the *Earl Granville* hit the linkspan in St. Helier during a normal stern-first approach, displacing it backwards by several feet and buckling plates and girders. Several cars were craned off the stern of the ship, as Emeraude Ferries' *Solidor* occupied the harbour's second linkspan. The *Earl Granville* dragged the linkspan back into position and then turned within the harbour to move stern-in to the forward berth, now vacated by the *Solidor,* and discharge the remaining deck load. The *Earl Granville* then sailed for Guernsey to avoid the falling tide and collect passengers for Portsmouth. Her troubles were not yet over; fire broke out in pipework lagging whilst returning to Jersey to collect Portsmouth-bound passengers, and the ship hove-to off Grosnez whilst it was brought under control. After inspection by the fire authorities in Jersey the *Earl Granville* eventually sailed for Portsmouth at 20:15. Temporary repairs were made to the linkspan in St. Helier and the ramp remained operational in this state for the rest of the summer season before a permanent repair could be effected.

On 5 October the *Earl William* struck a rock in the vicinity of Dog's Nest Beacon whilst entering St. Helier, sustaining damage to her plating and an 18ft hole in her hull; 440 passengers were transferred to the *Earl Granville*. The *Earl William* was sent to Le Havre for repairs as in addition to the hull damage, her main engines and gearbox required realigning; she did not return until 20 December. *Maid of Kent* was brought in from Dover to substitute on the Weymouth-Guernsey run from 3 October but she was too big to enter St. Helier; her final sailing left St. Peter Port at 19:04 on 30 October. This proved to be the final Sealink steam powered passenger service, as the *Maid of Kent* was sent for lay up and sale at Newhaven on her return to Weymouth. Meanwhile the *Earl Granville* hit severe seas off the Isle of Wight on 9 October necessitating hospital treatment for twelve passengers and a stewardess, and causing damage to sixty cars on her car deck.

The Island services incurred a loss of £1.5m for the 1981 season, largely due to the additional costs incurred by the fire damaged *Earl Granville* and the grounding of the *Earl*

The *Earl Siward* arriving at Weymouth in July 1981 whilst covering the Channel Island operations for three days. *(Ferry Publications Library)*

William. Sealink announced cutbacks on the Weymouth route for the 1982 season as early as June 1981, with the Portsmouth services receiving increasing prominence in the schedule. This was confirmed in September with the Weymouth winter and spring sailings trimmed from three to two per week, a reduction of fifty-one departures for the route. Services were suspended for six days in January 1982 when crews went on strike in sympathy with colleagues in Newhaven, who faced proposals to close the Dieppe route. Problems for travellers were compounded by poor weather conditions, and there were long delays by air.

The popular 'Night Flyer' promotion was re-introduced from Weymouth on 11 June 1982, offering a return trip on overnight sailings in each direction for £19.50 including a litre bottle of spirits and two bottles of wine. An optional Island coach tour could be taken for an additional £3.95. The 125th anniversary of rail-sea services between London and the Islands via Weymouth was celebrated on 24 May 1982, but a strike by train drivers resulted in cancellation of the boat train and the calling off of a reception in Weymouth.

The 1982 season was largely uneventful after the operational disruption of the previous year. The *Earl William* struck La Platte Beacon off the end of Elizabeth Castle breakwater at St. Helier whilst on passage from Weymouth to Jersey on 20 November. She was not holed, but suffered damage to internal pipework and for some 70ft along the hull below the water line. Passengers were transferred to the *Earl Granville* sailing to Portsmouth, and the *Earl Godwin* was recalled to provide cover for *Earl William* until 6 December. The collision was ascribed to a 'navigational error'.

Towards the end of the year there were two positive developments in the proposed provision of new vessels for the Islands. The Sealink business plan for 1983 to 1987 proposed significant investment in a large multi-purpose vessel capable of accommodating 2,000 passengers and 480 cars for the Island services. The proposal envisaged this being commissioned in 1987-88, with a sister vessel to follow in the early 1990s. Meanwhile on 25 November, Commodore Shipping announced their own plans to operate a car ferry from the UK with capacity for 800 passengers and 150 cars.

The year saw a ten per cent fall in Sealink carryings to 800,000 passengers, but there was a balancing rise of twelve per cent in vehicle traffic to 110,000 cars, and 150,000 tonnes of freight was shipped. Preparations for the new season began early when *Earl Granville* visited Weymouth for ramp trials on 16 December in anticipation of the introduction of a new sailing pattern for summer 1983. The year started with severe gales around the Islands and services were often disrupted by late arrivals. The *Earl Granville* incurred bow visor damage on 20 January and sailings on 21 January were cancelled to allow repairs to be carried out.

An experimental twenty-one wagon trainload of Metro and Mini cars was delivered direct from British Leyland at Longbridge to Weymouth Quay on 8 March to be driven onto the *Earl Godwin*. A further train operated through to Weymouth Junction with cars driven through the streets to the berth as the tramway was blocked, but these experiments were not repeated. Fuel oil for the fleet had been delivered by train to Weymouth Quay during the summer season for a decade since the gradual withdrawal of steam turbine vessels, but this practice ceased on 16 September 1983. The 1983 season did, however, see the reintroduction of a connecting rail service from Bristol.

The summer 1983 schedule introduced a complex ship interchange between the Weymouth and Portsmouth routes, with the *Earl Granville* and the *Earl William* operating weekend sailings from both ports. From 2 July the *Earl Granville* left Portsmouth at 23:00 on her normal Friday night schedule to the Islands, but returned to Weymouth on Saturday morning to arrive at 14:30 and undertake a round trip to Cherbourg, before heading back

The *Earl William* at Weymouth Harbour pending her late afternoon sailing to St Peter Port. *(Miles Cowsill)*

The **Earl Godwin** backs out of Weymouth Harbour. *(Miles Cowsill)*

to the Islands overnight, returning to Portsmouth on the Sunday. The *Earl William* operated the reverse pattern starting in Weymouth on Friday nights, and sailing back from the Islands to Portsmouth to cover the *Earl Granville's* Saturday night schedule, before returning from the Islands on Sunday to Weymouth. The service was an immediate success with 12,700 passengers and 2,500 cars carried on the first weekend of operation, but it placed significant strain on the vessels and increased the possibility of delays being transmitted between the two routes.

Two significant milestones were celebrated in July 1983. Sealink celebrated the carrying of their one-millionth car from the UK at a reception in Jersey, where the Bailiff, Sir Frank Ereaut, was noted as saying that the service "was a lifeline without which the islands could not exist". Condor's four millionth passenger was presented with a bottle of champagne by Kathleen Dorey. The company had prospered by building inter-island links between Guernsey, Jersey, Sark and St. Malo with a fleet of fast craft. Condor became a full subsidiary of the Commodore Group on 28 August when the company acquired the remaining 2/3 stake, and David Norman was appointed Managing Director.

The Bonus Breakaway Holiday product achieved 60,000 bookings in the first eight months of 1983, with 58,000 'Night Flyer' bookings in the same period. But September saw extreme weather conditions forcing the cancellation of sailings, with hundreds of passengers becoming stranded in Jersey and being accommodated in parish halls and schools across the island.

The reality of inadequate shore facilities supporting the new ro-ro product was acknowledged in a report presented to the States of Jersey, which recommended construction of a new £15m ro-ro ferry terminal to the west of the Albert Pier, with two berths and a marshalling area for freight.

Meanwhile Sealink's management team set a target of mid-1984 for privatisation of the company. This decision was to have profound consequences for the Islands. The services had been integrated with the operation of connecting rail services since the opening of the railway to Southampton in 1840, and had benefitted from being part of a much larger enterprise. The services enjoyed the economies of scale provided by national marketing, sales, procurement and technical support networks, vessels could easily be transferred between routes when the need arose, and route profitability could be considered alongside the financial contribution that passenger traffic made to the wider railway network.

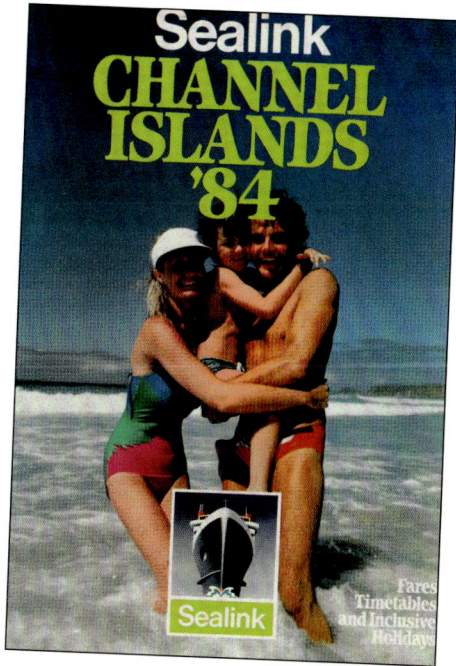

As the Sealink business evolved to carry increasing numbers of cars there was less dependence on the rail passenger, weakening the links with the parent company. But a move to the private sector would switch the corporate focus to shareholder value and profit, requiring each route and port to make a contribution. The Channel Islands were amongst the biggest loss makers of all the services operated by Sealink at privatisation; in 1983 the Portsmouth route lost £951k after interest, the Weymouth route £11k. Yet the Weymouth services had the group's second highest average passenger load of 702 passengers per sailing (Holyhead-Dun Laoghaire was top with 705 passengers per sailing; Portsmouth-Channel Islands services averaged 528). Services to Jersey and Guernsey had finite traffic potential because of the size of the islands, their resident population and the volume of hotel bed stock. Further, direct air competition was easier and more intense than on other routes that, coupled with easily accessible car hire, limited the growth of the motorist market. Sealink had an unprotected monopoly to the Islands, and there were growing rumours of a rival operation.

The financial issues facing the Channel Islands services were laid bare in January 1984, when Derek Shorter, Sealink's Channel Islands Shipping Manager, suggested that the company was not interested in a new terminal in St. Helier to handle bigger vessels, as this would increase the burden of harbour dues in Jersey, already around £1m each year. There would be little point in providing large ship facilities on one island if the other did not follow suit, as there were economies of scale in serving both Islands with the same fleet. Warning that any private owner of Sealink would expect a reduction in dues during the loss making winter months, he expressed a preference to retain operations within the inner harbour at St. Helier with investment focused on existing shore facilities. Shorter suggested that any attempt to bring competition to the routes would be strongly resisted.

The 1984 season saw an established pattern of connecting rail services linking with sailings to the Channel Islands, directly to Weymouth Quay and at Portsmouth via a bus link with special baggage facilities from Portsmouth Harbour station to the Continental Ferry Port.

London Waterloo	d	09:40	19:50	20:05	Jersey	d	08:00	09:50	21:55
Portsmouth Hbr	a		21:24		Guernsey	d	10:30	11:55	18:30
Portsmouth CFT	d		23:00		Weymouth Quay	a	15:00		06:00
Weymouth Quay	a	12:48		23:13		d	15:30		06:45
	d	13:30		23:30	Portsmouth CFT	a		18:50	
Guernsey	a	18:00	06:00	09:45	Portsmouth Hbr	d		19:53	
Jersey	a	20:30	08:20	06:15	London Waterloo	a	18:51	21:25	10:11

The short-lived connecting services from Bristol were withdrawn from 16 December 1984.

The *Earl William* encountered bad weather on passage from Guernsey to Jersey during winter gales on 23 January 1984; she was unable to enter St. Helier and a trailer carrying electrical equipment tipped over, crushing two cars. The *Earl William* returned to St. Peter Port but gales prevented her from berthing so she sailed on to Portsmouth. The *Earl William* was again stranded on 6 February, this time by bow thruster failure and bad weather in St. Peter Port.

The Sealink fleet began to appear without the railway 'double arrow' logo on their funnels in preparation for privatisation. The *Earl Granville* returned from refit with her dummy funnel painted plain red on 22 February. The following month Sealink unveiled a new corporate identity, giving ships a white hull with a two-tone blue trim and a gold 'SL' insignia on the funnel, but this was not applied to the Channel Islands fleet for the 1984 season. However a new corporate house flag incorporating the 'SL' insignia was hoisted across the fleet.

Rumours of competition for Sealink continued to spread. On 2 May 1984 Brittany Ferries confirmed that they had held discussions with the States of Jersey, but no decision on establishing a service had been made. There was little to prevent a prospective operator from commencing a service as spare linkspan slots were available in both Islands and the Jersey Authorities indicated they were prepared to permit a competing operation. Brittany Ferries, working in partnership with Huelin Renouf and Mainland Market Deliveries (MMD), contemplated use of the *Pen-ar-Bed*, but this French vessel was deemed inadequate by the UK Department of Trade, who required a reduction in her freight capacity if she was to be registered under the British flag. The proposals were put back to the 1985 season.

In July 1984 Torbay Seaways announced their intention to operate a twice-weekly summer ro-ro service from Torquay in 1985 with a reduction to a weekly frequency in winter, using a vessel capable of carrying around 600 passengers and fifty cars. This would also take freight, which was deemed essential to underpin any ferry service.

The process of privatisation gathered pace, as the UK government was keen for a quick sale. The financial portents were not good. Potential bids from major ferry operators European Ferries and P&O were ruled out because competition concerns could delay the process, and the potential value of the company was depressed by poor trading conditions experienced in the first half of 1984. The eventual contenders were Sea Containers, Common Brothers and a consortium led by executive directors of Sealink, but only Sea Containers submitted a compliant bid. The UK government accepted their £66 million bid on 19 July 1984; only £34.1m of this was payable up-front. British Ferries Ltd was formed as a holding company to own Sealink UK Ltd, which was formally taken over on Friday 27 July 1984. The new company would trade as Sealink British Ferries. The umbilical link

The *Ailsa Princess* had been a regular on the Weymouth-Cherbourg route from 1982, and visited the Islands for berthing trials whilst in pre-privatisation livery in October 1984. She was later renamed *Earl Harold* and painted in the new Sealink British Ferries white livery. *(Miles Cowsill)*

between mainland railways and ferry services to the Islands had been severed after 142 years; the services were once again wholly in private hands.

James Sherwood, President of Sea Containers, wrote to staff outlining the new company's vision and plans on a route-by-route basis. For the Channel Island services he noted: -

'This is the main problem child of the company. These services are expected to lose more than £1 million in the current year. Something must be done urgently to bring them into the black. We don't yet have all the answers but we are considering the operation of a new more economic freight-only ship on the Portsmouth/Channel Islands route. We think daytime services only on Weymouth/Channel Islands may allow us to do away with passenger cabins and carry more people enjoying improved on-board facilities. Fares will probably have to go up and substantial economies must be achieved both afloat and ashore'.

Sherwood outlined his intention to make a public issue of shares in Sealink British Ferries within three to five years, stating that he wanted to be able to say to the public 'Look at our excellent record of on-time departures. Look at our lack of stoppages due to industrial disputes. Look at our terrific on-board comfort and service'. These, he maintained, were the foundations for a successful company. However, Sherwood's plans were not predicated on there being competition for his Channel Island services.

These plans came to fruition on 8 August when Channel Island Ferries formally announced the start of their new service. The company would operate on a year-round basis with a vessel capable of carrying up to 500 passengers and cars, with a commitment to carry freight throughout the year. Brittany Ferries' involvement enabled the charter of a

After their winter 1983-4 refits, Sealink vessels returned without the distinctive 'double-arrow' logo on their funnels, in readiness for privatisation. The *Earl Granville* approaches Portsmouth in July 1984. *(Author)*

vessel to the company, shared the costs of the reservation system, strengthened their position in Portsmouth and placed pressure on any Sealink plans for expansion on the Western Channel. Huelin Renouf was an established player in the Island freight business, dating back to 1851 and had extensive distribution interests in the Islands and a lo-lo service from Portsmouth. MMD's shareholding was more discrete, as they were heavily dependent on existing freight capacity as the biggest customer with Sealink British Ferries. This led to robust exchanges when their involvement became understood. Channel Island Ferries would commence operations in April 1985, when Brittany Ferries would make a suitable vessel available, to be manned by British officers and crew. The company claimed their service had been 'greeted with enthusiasm and considerable backing from all the official bodies controlling ferry services into and out of the islands ... and given residents the security of their own freight and passenger lifeline'.

Against this background James Sherwood visited Jersey and Guernsey on 14 and 15 August 1984 to outline his plans to the authorities and local staff. Initial thoughts were that the *Earl William* would be transferred to the Mediterranean and based in Venice, to provide a new link to Istanbul in connection with Sea Containers Venice Simplon Orient Express rail service.

Ramp times for St. Helier for the 1985 season were published at the end of September and demonstrated that the aspirations of both Sealink British Ferries and Channel Island Ferries could be accommodated alongside the French services of Emeraude Lines on a year-round basis.

There was widespread surprise in early October when Sealink British Ferries announced a radical change to their proposals. Instead of reducing the Portsmouth service to a freight-only operation, £5 million was to be invested in the conversion of the *Earl Granville* and the *Earl William* to provide a high quality daily overnight service in each direction between Portsmouth and the Islands, with a new daytime link to Cherbourg. The press release claimed: -

'We aim to bring an overnight Starliner service from Portsmouth which will be the Orient Express of the sea, with an exclusive environment, excellent restaurants and very high quality ships with sumptuous cabin accommodation'.

Portsmouth was identified as the best-connected port for freight traffic due to its strong road connections, and Cherbourg was envisaged as a new growth area for traffic to the Islands. The vessels would receive major internal refits to provide quality overnight facilities for 400 passengers, all accommodated in cabins. On daytime crossings the vessels would operate with a maximum of 800 passengers. In a letter to the Jersey Transport Advisory Council, James Sherwood stated the company was: -

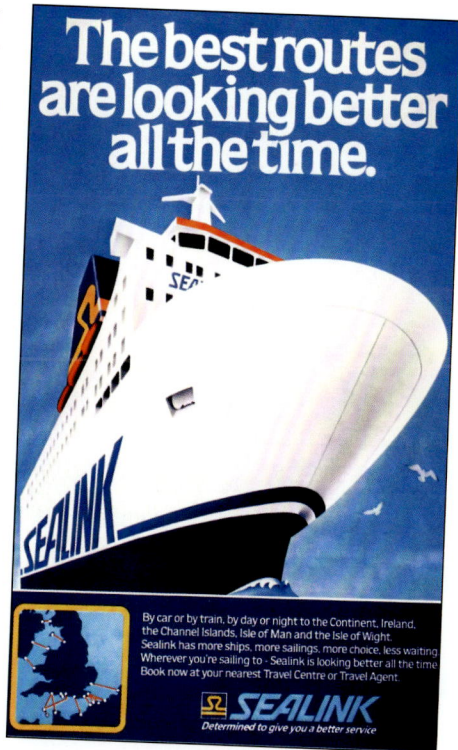

The best routes are looking better all the time.

By car or by train, by day or night to the Continent, Ireland, the Channel Islands, Isle of Man and the Isle of Wight. Sealink has more ships, more sailings, more choice, less waiting. Wherever you're sailing to - Sealink is looking better all the time. Book now at your nearest Travel Centre or Travel Agent.

Ω SEALINK
Determined to give you a better service

'spending £5 million to upgrade two ships on Portsmouth/Channel Islands and the two ships on Weymouth/Channel Islands. The plan is to concentrate foot passengers and motorists on the Weymouth service because of the excellent rail connections at Weymouth and the desirable short steaming time. This route will be daytime only (Sunliner) and will allow passengers to leave home on the mainland in the morning and be in their Channel Island hotels in time for supper. Return travellers will leave the hotels in the Channel Islands early in the morning and be home on the mainland that evening. Fares on the route will be economical. No sooner had we announced a capital investment programme in increased services, the Channel Islands' Governments announced that they would allow another operator in to compete with us. Unfortunately the trade will not support two operators so I feel the Channel Islands will suffer because of this decision. We have always operated winter services at great loss in return for competitors not being allowed on the Weymouth/Portsmouth routes so we shall be under no obligation to provide such sailings in the future'.

In reality, a competitor did not need the States' permission to operate if there were linkspan slots available, provided they met the relevant operating standards, although it was evident that Channel Island Ferries had received encouragement from the States.

Following the announcement that she would work in tandem with the *Earl Godwin* on the Weymouth sailings, the *Ailsa Princess* visited the Islands for berthing trials, being the largest vessel then to berth in St. Helier when she loaded a cargo of trade cars on 15 October. The *Ailsa Princess* was painted in the new Sealink British Ferries livery whilst wintering at Weymouth, and then sent to Glasgow for fitment of a new bow thrust to improve her manoeuverability.

Channel Island Ferries chose to match Sealink British Ferries' 1984 standard return fare of £56 for the 1985 season and offered overnight 2 berth cabins for £14, but the new

Brittany Ferries' *Benodet*, a sister of *Earl Granville* operating on the Plymouth-Roscoff route, was chartered to Channel Island Ferries for their new service. *(FotoFlite)*

Sealink British Ferries' fare structure was very different. The Portsmouth route, aiming at a more up-market clientele, would be charged at a single fare of £59, which included a buffet dinner, ensuite luxury cabin with television (with no extra charge for single occupancy) and a full English breakfast. In comparison the return air fare from Southampton was around £68. The peak return fare via Weymouth was fixed at £58.

The *Earl Godwin* ran aground in thick fog on rocks east of the Elizabeth Castle breakwater on 15 October 1984. Some 240 passengers donned their life jackets as a precaution, but the *Earl Godwin* was eventually re-floated with assistance from the States' tug *Duke of Normandy*, and proceeded to her berth, before heading to Holyhead for repairs. This left the *Earl William* to cover the winter Weymouth programme alone.

Torbay Seaways' plans for the 1985 season suffered a major setback when the Torquay authorities voted against construction of a new linkspan, fearing congestion from lorries queuing for the service. Managing Director Graham Thompson maintained that the company would still provide a service to the islands from the south west in summer 1985, later announcing that they would introduce Britain's first hydrofoil service from April 1985 with period return fares at £45, compared to the £58 charged by Sealink for a journey of twice

the duration.

Martin Miller, the newly appointed sector director for Sealink British Ferries, criticised facilities in Jersey saying that 'passengers will travel in style from Portsmouth, and at present, stumble off at Jersey to what can only be described as a not very good environment. The facilities are small and not inviting and there is no nice connection between the ship and dispersal area'. He proposed that, as British Ferries had made a £5 million commitment to the Channel Islands, the States should respond by upgrading facilities.

James Sherwood's 1985 New Year message to staff reiterated the threat that the company was no longer obliged to offer loss-making winter services to the Islands if a competitor was permitted to operate. Meanwhile preparations for the revised Sealink British Ferries service began to take shape. In early January the *Earl William* headed to Aalborg, Denmark for her refit and the *Earl Granville* followed on 26 January, with the *Ailsa Princess* returning to cover the Portsmouth single-ship schedule.

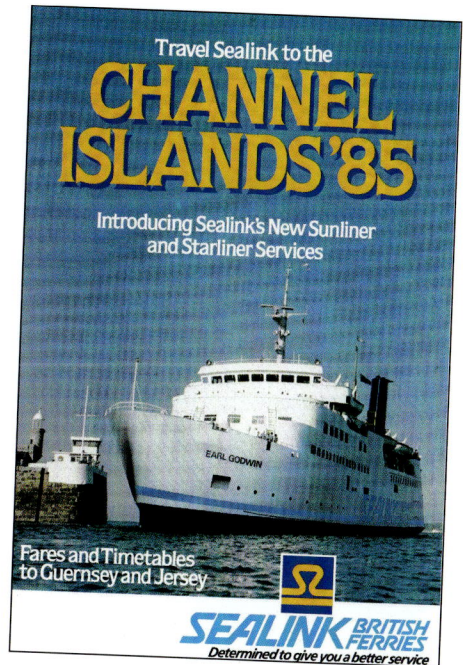

Travel Sealink to the
CHANNEL ISLANDS '85
Introducing Sealink's New Sunliner and Starliner Services

EARL GODWIN

Fares and Timetables to Guernsey and Jersey

SEALINK BRITISH FERRIES
Determined to give you a better service

When Senator Bernard Binnington, President of the Harbours and Airports Committee, was interviewed in the Jersey Evening Post on 12 January 1985, he maintained that plans for new berths outside the existing harbour must go ahead to allow larger ships to operate to Jersey 'because fewer and fewer ships fit the present harbour. We are strictly limited by the space we have available, and in order to safeguard the continuity of shipping services in the foreseeable future, we need to make provision for taking larger ships which, in turn will bring economies of operation'.

Extensive investment in existing facilities was therefore unlikely whilst this debate continued, thwarting Sealink British Ferries' ambitions for shore facilities to match the quality of the new service.

The scale of competition from Channel Island Ferries' grew significantly when Brittany Ferries chartered the *Benodet*, a sister of *Earl Granville*, to the company. The *Benodet* offered significantly more capacity than the original company aspirations had suggested was required. After completing a season on the Roscoff-Plymouth service, the *Benodet* was sent to St. Malo for a £1.15m refit and overhaul. She was renamed the *Corbière* and re-registered in Nassau in the Bahamas. Capt. Wilkinson was appointed Senior Master and became responsible for recruiting and training the two crews, who were to work on a two-weeks-on, two-weeks-off basis. *Corbière* would carry 250 cars, with berths for 230 passengers, and an additional 170 reclining seats. Her schedule was fitted around berth availability at Portsmouth, so she sailed from Jersey at 19:30, Guernsey at 22:15 and arrived in Portsmouth at 08:00 using the Brittany Ferries berth before departing again at 10:00, the reverse of the Sealink British Ferries winter schedule. The company would create 106 jobs for British officers and crew on *Corbière* with ship management provided by Denholm, and up to 140 shore roles, forty-eight of which would be in the islands and ninety-two in Portsmouth, where the reservations team were to be based. 140,000 passengers and 16,000 freight vehicles were targeted for the first year of operation, representing twenty per cent of the sea market. In the post-privatisation era, the company was able to offer

The *Corbière* makes a fine sight in
her first operational season.
(FotoFlite)

The inauguration ceremony for the first Channel Island Ferries sailing from Jersey on 27 March 1985. Actor Terence Alexander prepares to cut the ribbon, prior to driving his white Rolls Royce on board *Corbière*. Senior Master Douglas Wilkinson looks on. *(Ferry Publications Library)*

through fares with British Rail from the outset.

As a new company, Channel Island Ferries was free to establish themselves on a 'low cost' basis with no legacy of union restrictions and the associated costs inherent in the more traditionally manned, unionised and British-flagged Sealink British Ferries operation. The new company was therefore able to operate with lower manning and wage levels.

In the first quarter of 1985 the number of sea passengers to the Islands fell by thirty-three per cent year-on-year before either of the new operations had a chance to make their mark.

Channel Island Ferries emphasised their different approach, marketed as 'The Better Way', by launching the new service from the Channel Islands. The *Corbière* attracted 8,000 visitors to a public open day in Jersey prior to the maiden sailing on 27 March 1985. The first passenger boarding the 19:30 departure to Portsmouth via Guernsey was actor Terence Alexander from the popular BBC television series 'Bergerac', in his trademark white Rolls-Royce after officiating at the inauguration ceremony. On arrival in Portsmouth at 08:15 the following morning, the *Corbière* was met by the Lord Mayor John Marshall, his Lady Mayoress Louisa Taylor and round-the-world yachtsman Chay Blyth for a champagne breakfast in the carvery restaurant, before she took passengers south on the first 10:00 departure, an excusable 40 minutes late. The *Corbière* arrived back in Jersey on schedule at 17:45.

The *Corbière's* entry into service was marred by a dockworkers union dispute concerning freight shipments belonging to MMD. Portsmouth Stevedores, a company owned by MMD, had won the shore-handling contract against competition from two established companies based in Portsmouth. MMD went to the High Court for an injunction against the union as the *Corbière* arrived on her inaugural sailing. There were ugly scenes in St. Helier with Jersey stevedores acting in sympathy with their Portsmouth colleagues.

The *Corbière* dressed overall on her maiden crossing. *(Dave Hocquard)*

The *Earl William* in the new Sealink British Ferries white livery sported for the 1985 season on the Starliner service. *(Ferry Publications Library)*

Sealink British Ferries' ambitions to launch the Starliner operation at the end of March were thwarted by a national shipyard strike in Denmark, which stranded both the *Earl Granville* and the *Earl William* at the Aalborg yard. The company was forced to charter the Rederi AB Gotland ferry *Thjelvar* to cover the Weymouth-Cherbourg service to allow the *Ailsa Princess* to continue at Portsmouth. The *Earl William* was the first refitted vessel to return to Portsmouth on 23 April 1985 and she inaugurated the Starliner service the following evening, a month later than scheduled. The *Earl Granville* followed to Portsmouth on 29 April and, after overcoming generator problems, operated the first Bateau de Luxe daytime departure to Cherbourg and the Islands on 30 April. The service launch was very low key and considerably more hurried than had been planned, in consequence of the late return of both ships.

The *Earl William* and the *Earl Granville* had undergone a dramatic transformation, masterminded by leading yacht interior designer Jennie Macleane. Gone were the rows of reclining seats and on board facilities servicing everyone from 'Bonus Breakaway' day trippers to Islanders taking their cars away. In their place were en suite cabins fitted out with televisions, luxury toiletries and writing paper, buffet restaurants with a daily selection from lobster to roast beef, and hotel-like lounge seating areas. The quality of onboard service received special attention with all staff undergoing extensive training. All of this came at a price - both for Sealink British Ferries and its customers. But the delayed launch was just the start of an uphill battle, as overnight crossings could be fully booked with as few as 100 passengers on board, limiting fare income and on board spend. And there was a strong corporate push for the Starliner operation to be a flagship service for the group, leading to substantial extra costs for a broad menu in the buffet restaurant irrespective of the number of passengers, and complimentary luxuries such as toiletries and notepaper. Whilst freight volumes could be maintained, rates were under threat, with largest customer MMD having a conflicting interest in Channel Island Ferries. The management team had a fight on their hands.

A competition was held in Weymouth schools to rename the *Ailsa Princess*, and the newly christened *Earl Harold* opened the 'Sunliner' service with the *Earl Godwin* on 24 May. The pattern of sailings saw dedicated direct departures to Weymouth by the *Earl Godwin* from Guernsey at 07:15 and the *Earl Harold* from Jersey at 07:30, returning directly at 13:15 to Guernsey and 15:15 to Jersey, with the vessels laying over in the Islands at night.

Torbay Seaway's attempt to add to further competition for Channel Island business ran into difficulty during the maiden voyage of the *Star Capricorn* on 6 May 1985. The vessel found itself unable to rise onto its foils on leaving Torquay, and returned to port to offload sixteen day excursion passengers to lighten the load. On the return sailing from Jersey, *Star Capricorn* was forced to seek shelter from bad weather in St. Peter Port. On 28 June she collided with a whale some twenty miles north west of Platte Fougère on passage from Guernsey to Torquay, and had to be towed back to St. Peter Port by the French tug *Abeille Languedoc*.

In May the States of Jersey considered their investment in the 'West of Albert' development

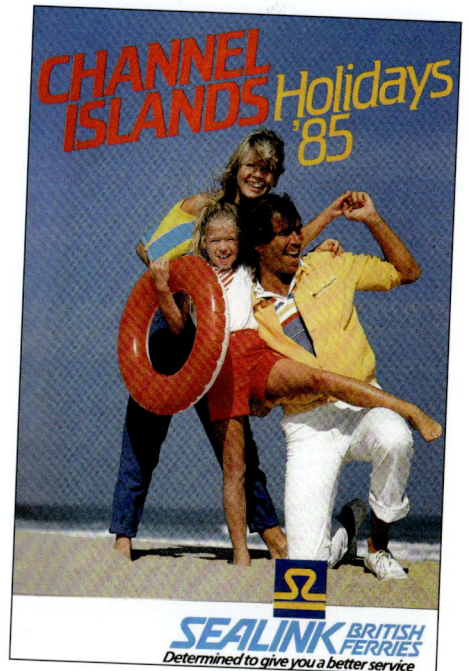

CHANNEL ISLANDS Holidays '85

SEALINK BRITISH FERRIES
Determined to give you a better service

Facilities on board *Earl Granville* and *Earl William* were transformed in readiness for the launch of the Starliner services to the Channel Islands. The new theme also reflected the ships' visits to Cherbourg as part of their daily rotation.

Top: The Bayeux Lounge on the *Earl William*. *(Miles Cowsill)*

Bottom: The Conquerer Bar on the *Earl William*. *(Miles Cowsill)*

The Sealink Weymouth operation was branded as the Sunliner service in 1985, with a daylight sailing pattern to balance night departures on the Portsmouth route. This resulted in the loss of considerable volumes of low-value excursion traffic.

Top: The *Earl Harold* was dedicated to the Jersey-Weymouth-Jersey service in 1985. *(FotoFlite)*

Bottom: The *Earl Godwin* was dedicated to the Guernsey-Weymouth-Guernsey service in 1985. *(FotoFlite)*

The **Star Capricorn** had a brief and troubled season of operation for Torbay Seaways. She is seen on a trial arrival in Jersey on 5 May 1985. *(Dave Hocquard)*

project, in a debate that lasted two days. There was no opposition, and the largest capital project ever undertaken by the States was given the green light.

The delayed start to Sealink British Ferries' services gave Channel Island Ferries the bonus of a full month operating with just the *Ailsa Princess* in competition. By the end of June, in figures disputed by Sealink British Ferries, the company claimed it had carried eighty-five per cent of passenger traffic and eighty per cent of passenger vehicles on the Portsmouth-Channel Islands route. Sealink British Ferries pointed out that the 'Starliner' product was aimed at a very different market, with inclusive meals and cabins. The 'Sunliner' service from Weymouth was, however, proving more successful, but the late evening arrival time of the sailings in both islands was not popular with either holidaymakers or hoteliers. During June the *Corbière* changed her schedule for two days to provide a link to St. Malo whilst Brittany Ferries' *Prince of Brittany* was withdrawn from service.

Sealink British Ferries misfortunes continued on 2 July when the *Earl Granville* suffered propeller shaft problems caused by a failed bearing, which plagued the vessel over the next week. The *Earl Granville* was eventually taken out of service at Portsmouth on 9 July and sailed to the Vosper repair yard in Southampton for the fitting of a replacement shaft bearing, returning to service three days later. Channel Island Ferries also suffered in July when one of the *Corbière*'s starboard propeller blades was damaged after making contact with an unknown object. She was sent to Southampton for repair, and a spare was used to replace the damaged blade with the vessel out of service for less than 24 hours.

A third brochure reprint was delivered to Channel Island Ferries in July 1985, and the company made inroads into the trade car shipments that supported the Islands' car hire businesses. MMD switched a proportion of their freight traffic to support their investment in *Corbière*, and Sealink British Ferries countered by encouraging the growth of Ferryspeed and Channel Express to replace lost business.

Torbay Seaways struggled to make the right impact with the *Star Capricorn,* as almost thirty per cent of planned sailings were cancelled. The company cut the number of scheduled sailings by withdrawing the Sunday service from 20 August, and searched for a conventional vessel to replace the *Star Capricorn*. They settled on the former Caledonian MacBrayne side-loading vessel *Hebrides,* which had capacity for 300 passengers and thirty cars. She undertook ramp trials in early December in readiness for the 1986 season, when she would return as the renamed *Devoniun*.

By the end of August Channel Island Ferries claimed to have carried 68,000 passengers, attracting eighty-three per cent of the Portsmouth-Jersey market, but were coy about the Guernsey figure, where their journey time was less competitive. Sealink British Ferries countered with a claim of eighty per cent share of the freight market, but faced mounting losses on their Channel Island services, with the budgeted £3 million profit now projected to be a £7 million loss for the year. Sector Director Martin Miller assessed the reality of the situation by stating there was only sufficient business for one operator.

Drastic change was needed, and Sealink British Ferries revised their plans for the 1986 season. The two-ship Portsmouth service was to be retained but with a significant reduction in fares, moving away from the fully inclusive price structure. Passengers would be able to book a daytime fare from Portsmouth to Guernsey and Jersey via Cherbourg that gave an arrival in Guernsey at 17:45, some 3 hours 30 min ahead of Channel Island Ferries. The Weymouth service faced a reduction to a single-vessel operation using the *Earl Godwin*, with the *Earl Harold* to return to the Irish Sea. Some 250 voluntary redundancies were sought. In the event, the *Earl Harold* was retained on the Channel Island service and the *Earl Godwin* transferred to cover the Weymouth-Cherbourg route.

Symbolic of the changing relationships between rail and sea, British Rail operated the last Channel Islands Boat Train from Weymouth on 15 September, ending a tradition of dedicated rail connections that dated back to 1857. The numbers of passengers travelling via Weymouth to the Islands fell from 368,850 in 1983 to 155,780 in 1985; the switch to daytime crossings to balance the overnight services to Portsmouth had eliminated the high volume but low revenue Bonus Breakaway traffic.

The Sealink British Ferries livery was changed locally to drop 'Sealink' for the 1986 season, here seen on the *Earl William* on her early morning arrival in Guernsey. (Miles Cowsill)

The *Earl Granville* inward to Porstmouth from Cherbourg. *(FotoFlite)*

The *Corbière* operated on a daytime schedule from Portsmouth, which was less attractive to freight operators than the night alternative. (*Miles Cowsill*)

The *Earl Harold* in her 1986 season British Ferries livery. (*Miles Cowsill*)

The Channel Island Ferries winter schedule changed from 17 November to offer an overnight sailing from Portsmouth on Sunday nights at 23:00, arriving in Guernsey at 06:30 and Jersey at 09:00, instead of the Monday morning departure, but maintaining the normal schedule back from the Islands on Monday evenings. This enabled the company to offer day trip opportunities to the Islands. The pattern continued until 5 May 1986.

The *Corbière* went to Rotterdam for refit and improvements to her passenger areas in the autumn, with Brittany Ferries supplying the *Cornouailles* to substitute with a French crew and Channel Island Ferries catering team. In December the company announced similar schedules for 1986, but with the daily operation brought forward to 6 May rather than June and a new standby return fare of £28. The company had set a (revised) target of 130,000 passengers for their first year and stated they were well on target and expected to carry 100,000 by the end of 1985. Chairman Ian Carruthers, was reported as saying: -

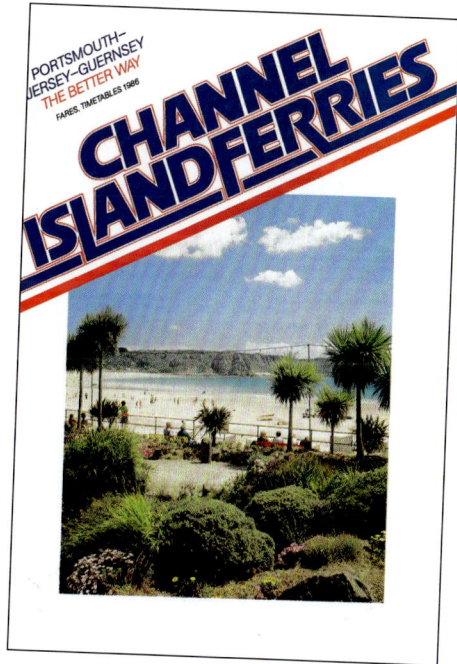

'nearing the end of the first successful year of the companies operation, we have succeeded in breaking into an existing market, establishing a reputation for consistency and consequently witnessed a dramatic growth. Our formula of providing high standards of service at value for money prices works and is obviously what our passengers want. We intend to maintain this policy in the future and promote the many advantages of sea travel with Channel Island Ferries to the motorist or foot passenger, who either traditionally or for the first time wants to take a holiday break in the islands'

In his New Year message to employees, James Sherwood described the Channel Island routes as a 'fiasco' and described the 'dreadful circumstances' of a company 'fighting for survival'. He envisaged a 'bloodbath' on the Cherbourg route as Brittany Ferries developed the Caen route and expanded operations from Poole, but believed the new pricing policy would discourage Channel Island Ferries from continuing their service. The reported losses prompted representatives of the Jersey Transport Advisory Committee to travel to London to meet Sherwood to discuss their concerns for the future.

The problem for both Sealink British Ferries and Channel Island Ferries was that passenger demand was in freefall. Portsmouth originating arrivals in Jersey fell to 52,794 in 1985, a thirty-eight per cent drop from the previous year's single ship service, despite the two-ship Sealink British Ferries operation and the arrival of Channel Island Ferries, and Weymouth

The *Corbière* inward to St Peter Port passes her former fleet partner the *Prince of Brittany*. (FotoFlite)

The *Earl Godwin* sailing light to Guernsey from Jersey. *(Miles Cowsill)*

originating arrivals fell to 87,665, down by thirty-nine per cent. There was a modest four per cent rise in the number of vehicle arrivals, from 24,244 to 25,108. In contrast the number of passenger arrivals by air in Jersey rose by eleven per cent to 616,835. Air travel's market share grew from seventy one per cent to eighty per cent. Yet peak daily sea capacity had risen from 3,350 with the *Earl Godwin*, *Earl Granville* and *Earl William* in 1984, to 4,050 with the *Corbière*, *Earl Godwin*, *Earl Granville*, *Earl Harold* and *Earl William* in 1985, despite the much reduced passenger capacity of the *Earl Granville* and the *Earl William*.

During the annual refit programme from early January until 14 March 1986, Sealink British Ferries offered a one-ship service from Portsmouth, and Cherbourg calls were suspended. Ships re-appeared sporting a revised 'British Ferries' identity, replacing Sealink British Ferries on the side of each vessel. This was a local initiative, frowned upon centrally but not over-ruled, that sought to distinguish the standards of the vessels on the Channel Islands services from those of the rest of the group.

The *Earl Granville* was used to promote the company's ships and facilities on her return from refit. In February she hosted a Channel Islands holiday exhibition in Portsmouth, then on 19 February sailed to berth alongside HMS Belfast in the Pool of London for a four-day exhibition. Passenger and freight services to the Islands were promoted to the travel trade and invited guests, alongside other Sealink routes, with the *Earl Granville's* car deck converted to a fairground complete with a traction engine, freight trailers, exhibition stands and a replica of the Bayeux Tapestry. Weymouth sailings were suspended for a week from 17 February to permit the *Earl William* to cover the *Earl Granville's* Portsmouth schedule, an action described by the Mayor of Weymouth & Portland as 'shabby and disastrous'. The *Earl Harold* resumed the Weymouth service on 24 February, covering until the *Earl Godwin* returned from refit on 3 March, then returned to operate the full service from 26 March.

The new fare strategy reduced Channel Island Ferries' Portsmouth market share to fifty-three per cent up to the end of April, but with Sealink British Ferries' losses for 1986 projected to be around £6 million the situation could not continue. Both companies were now suffering from increased air competition, and the market showed no signs of recovering significantly from the 1985 position. Sealink British Ferries considered three options to improve their financial position: -

1. To withdraw completely - this would worsen the situation as the company would be left with ships and facilities but no revenue
2. To rationalise services and continue with a reduced operation – but Channel Island Ferries had no intention of withdrawing and it would not be possible to match their operating costs
3. To enter into a joint venture with Channel Island Ferries - considered the only viable option

In May, senior representatives of Channel Island Ferries and Sealink British Ferries met to consider the way forward. An offer of financial compensation to persuade Channel Island Ferries to withdraw from the market was rejected. By the summer, Sealink British Ferries was clawing back market share, finding itself increasingly restricted by the reduced passenger capacity of the Portsmouth fleet, and maintaining a strong dominance of the freight market, albeit still with financial losses. The pressure on both companies was increasing. Talks moved to consider consolidation, and a merger of the two operations was eventually agreed. Initial proposals to announce this in mid-September were put back to avoid this becoming an issue during the National Union of Seamen elections.

Following growing speculation Sealink British Ferries and Channel Island Ferries announced their intention to form a new joint company on Tuesday 30 September 1986. To be called British Channel Island Ferries (BCIF), the joint venture was intended to ensure

Tower Bridge opens to allow *Earl Granville* under Senior Master Paul Baker to berth in the Pool of London on her promotional visit on 19 February 1986. (*Ferry Publications Library*)

The *Earl Granville* swings off her berth at Portsmouth on a morning departure to Cherbourg and the Islands in 1986. (*Miles Cowsill*)

the long-term viability of the services in the face of increasing air competition and mounting losses. The new company aimed to capture a larger market share for sea travel, noting that this had dropped from thirty per cent to twenty-two per cent between 1984 and 1985, representing a fall in volume from 730,000 to 470,000 passengers.

BCIF would start operations from Portsmouth the following day (1 October) utilising the *Corbière* and the *Earl Granville* on charter from their respective parent companies, with a winter sailing schedule of day and night sailings to both Islands. The Weymouth route would operate with the *Earl Harold* from 15 May to 26 September, thereby accommodating seventy per cent of the passenger traffic on this route. The loss-making service from Portsmouth to the Channel Islands via Cherbourg would cease leaving the *Earl William* surplus to requirements. The new company was to be registered in Jersey and fifty per cent owned by each of the two partners. The Board comprised three voting directors from each shareholder and up to four non-voting directors, including the managing director. The acting chief executive of BCIF and joint managing director of Channel Island Ferries was to be Colin Carter and his deputy Martin Miller, former director of Sealink British Ferries' South West division.

Colin Carter was reported as saying: -

'This is a very positive and far-sighted move. It enables us jointly to address ourselves to providing the travelling public with the best quality service at competitive prices. From today, the whole question of competition is no longer between ferry operators, but between services by sea and air. By combining forces in this way, we will be in a much stronger position to encourage tourism to the Islands. And, equally important, it will, of course, mean better scheduling for freight in both directions and for Island residents wishing to travel to the mainland.'

Charles Lenox-Conyngham, Chairman and Chief Executive of Sealink British Ferries, responded: –

'In the past, no ferry service to the Channel Islands has ever made an adequate return and, in particular, in the past two years there have been severe doubts whether our services could continue. This joint venture removes the uncertainty from both our staff and our customers, and should provide us with a viable base for the next two years until the opening of the new port in St. Helier. We hope then to be able to introduce larger and so more economic ships.'

At a meeting at 11:00 on 30 September Sealink British Ferries advised the trade unions that they were withdrawing their Channel Islands services from Portsmouth and Weymouth with immediate effect, and all staff employed on these routes would be made redundant from Saturday 4 October. A total of 630 staff were given notice, made up of 193 shore staff including twenty one staff in Guernsey and twenty nine in Jersey, and 121 ships officers and 316 ratings. Just eleven redundant shore staff were offered jobs on new terms in BCIF.

The rapid implementation of the announcement forced the trade unions to respond quickly. Officers and crew of the Sealink British Ferries fleet went on immediate strike with sit-ins on the *Earl William* in St. Peter Port, the *Earl Godwin* in Weymouth, the *Earl Granville* in Cherbourg and the *Earl Harold* on arrival at Portsmouth, having been diverted from Weymouth as the *Earl Godwin* blocked the berth. The strike spread to other Sealink British Ferries routes, adding to the financial pressures on the company.

After a five-vessel summer service, the islands were reduced to a single-ship operation. The *Corbière* could easily handle the autumn passenger traffic, but freight capacity was severely reduced. With the *Earl William* blocking the linkspan in St. Peter Port, Guernsey was served by disembarking passengers without using the linkspan, with car traffic diverted to Jersey and shipped back using Torbay Seaways' side-loader *Devoniun*, which discharged directly on the quay. The crew of *Earl William* eventually prevented the *Corbière* landing passengers, forcing them to be transferred into St. Peter Port by boat.

Closure of Sealink British Ferries services led to a strikebound fleet as crews protested over job losses and proposed cuts in pay and benefits. *Earl Godwin, Earl Harold* and *Earl William* are laid up at Weymouth. *(Barry Watts)*

An usual view of the *Breizh-Izel* in BCIF livery leaving Ouistreham whilst covering for Brittany Ferries' operations. *(Miles Cowsill)*

BCIF gave notice that they would suspend the service to Guernsey if this blockade continued, and the service was withdrawn for five days from 13 October before agreement was reached with the trade unions; the *Earl William* then sailed to Weymouth to join the rest of the strike-bound fleet. Redundancy notices were withdrawn on 14 October and a complex agreement reached to settle the dispute at other Sealink British Ferries ports, but the company was unable to reach any accord with the unions that would allow the *Earl Granville* and the *Earl Harold* to join the BCIF joint venture.

The differential in salary levels proved to be the main issue. Under the joint venture it was necessary to bring Sealink British Ferries' ship operating costs, particularly on the *Earl Granville*, close to those of the *Corbière*. This would require seafaring and shore staff to be re-employed on new conditions far inferior to those they enjoyed under Sealink British Ferries' employment. Channel Island Ferries would not agree to incorporate the old arrangements into the joint venture, and would not charter the *Earl Granville* on anything other than bare-boat terms; this stance posed insurmountable difficulties for any agreement between Sealink British Ferries, NUMAST and the NUS.

A winter freight-only service from Weymouth was considered as a means of resolving the dispute, but it became increasingly clear that Sealink British Ferries could not meet the agreed terms. The ongoing industrial dispute threatened the stability of Sea Containers, which had purchased Sealink with loans and was generating insufficient cash to pay interest on the borrowed money. The joint venture was at an impasse, with just the *Corbière* operating under the new arrangements.

Meanwhile Condor took advantage of the limited capacity available and employed the *Condor 7* to provide an alternative service to Weymouth for affected travellers. Such an operation was already being considered for the 1987 season, and the preparatory work permitted a nimble response to the issues involved in establishing a new service. The service proved popular and carried 18,000 passengers in 18 days of operation, convincing Condor that a regular schedule would be a viable proposition for the following season.

Frustrated at the lack of progress with the joint venture and facing growing concerns at the lack of capacity, Channel Island Ferries took out a High Court injunction against Sealink British Ferries, suing them for failure to provide two vessels on bareboat charter to BCIF. In court, Sealink British Ferries' QC described the legal agreement which set up the new company as being a 'ghastly muddle', with none of the three signatories having a common understanding of what the agreement stood for. He claimed that the strike had prevented Sealink British Ferries from fulfilling their obligations and argued that, when the dispute was settled in mid October, the agreement with the officers union NUMAST put it out of their power to provide the two vessels on the agreed terms. The case centred on interpretation of a 'force majeure' clause in the agreement that stated: -

> ' A party shall not be liable in the event of the non-fulfilment of any obligation arising under this contract by reason of act of God, disease, strikes, lock-outs, fire and any accident or incident of any nature beyond the control of the relevant party'.

In what proved to be a landmark interpretation of force majeure clauses, the judge held that the settlement between Sealink British Ferries and the unions represented 'a completely new causative event in their disablement from performing the joint venture agreement', and that Sealink British Ferries' entry into that settlement agreement, 'far from being an act beyond their control, represented a genuine choice on their part'. He noted that the strike could well have been easier to settle if Sealink British Ferries had avoided the 'tragic miscalculation' represented by their 'brutal' introduction of the agreement without prior consultation. He considered that it would be the 'most unjust if Channel Island Ferries had had to bear the brunt of Sealink British Ferries' improvidence in this regard'.

Judgment in favour of Channel Island Ferries was upheld in the Court of Appeal, and Channel Island Ferries compulsorily purchased Sealink British Ferries' fifty per cent interest in BCIF in January 1987. Sealink British Ferries was banned from operating direct services to the Channel Islands for a minimum period of twelve months, to give BCIF a free hand. Further, the authorities in Jersey banned Sealink British Ferries from using St. Helier for twelve months.

Legal wrangling between the two companies continued until 1991, with Sealink British Ferries claiming repayment of loans made at the time of the proposed merger and BCIF counter-claiming for financial losses during the period of disrupted services. Legal fees had outweighed the sums in question by the time judgment was made in favour of BCIF.

The period of intense and bitter competition had ended, leaving BCIF with a near monopoly, with just the fledgling Condor operation and Torbay Seaways as seasonal competition. Channel Island Ferries had wildly exceeded their expectations for the new service; David had beaten Goliath. Sea passenger carryings had stabilised at their new lower level in 1986, but BCIF now faced the new challenge of providing a credible service for 1987 with the original business plan in tatters.

CHAPTER ELEVEN

British Channel Island Ferries and Condor 1987-1998

'An Island based Company.

1988 will be British Channel Island Ferries' fourth year of operation, and the company looks forward to the New Year with confidence. As an Island-based company, British Channel Island Ferries is run with Islanders' needs very much in mind. We are proud to have operated throughout 1987 with a remarkably high reliability record – 99% of sailings operated as scheduled – and to have received much praise for the courtesy and helpfulness shown by our Officers, Crews and Staff.

Last year we carried more than 300,000 passengers to and from the mainland. This year, with extensive improvements to the Portelet and a full six-month season on the Weymouth route, we look forward to welcoming even more Islanders aboard our ships'.

[British Channel Island Ferries brochure, 1988]

The collapse of the joint venture left BCIF's 1987 proposals for a two-ship Portsmouth operation complemented by a seasonal Weymouth service in tatters, with two of the three planned vessels no longer available to the company. The *Corbière* continued to maintain her old Channel Island Ferries schedule, with a 10:00 daytime sailing from Portsmouth to Guernsey (16:30-18:00), then Jersey (19:45-22:00) before an overnight return crossing, arriving in Portsmouth at the slightly earlier time of 07:00, but there was to be no second passenger vessel for the route. Sealink British Ferries' offer to charter the *Vortigern* was rejected as she lacked cabin accommodation. Instead, the *Breizh-Izel* was chartered from Brittany Ferries to offer additional freight capacity, sailing opposite the *Corbière*.

The final chapter for the Sealink British Ferries' Channel Islands fleet was marked at Weymouth on 27 March when the *Earl Godwin* left for lay-up on the River Fal, with *Earl William* later leaving for a temporary role as a prison ship at Harwich. The company continued to run a seasonal Weymouth-Cherbourg service with *Earl Harold* until 1989. The *Earl Granville* was retained at Portsmouth to maintain the Cherbourg service.

The BCIF Weymouth service was scheduled to start from 15 April 1987, with an overnight departure and daytime return crossing to balance the Portsmouth operation, but finding a suitable vessel proved difficult. Eventually Marlines' *Baroness M* (formerly the Normandy Ferries' *Lion*) was secured and renamed the *Portelet,* with Capt. Perkins appointed as Senior Master. The *Portelet* had already benefited from an extensive refit in Greece, in which ninety-six four-berth ensuite cabins had been added during 1985. She arrived in Weymouth on 5 April to be stored, before heading to Portsmouth to cover the *Corbière's* four-day refit in Southampton. The *Corbière* returned with additional passenger seating installed on her port side, and sporting her new corporate identity with the word 'British' appearing above the old Channel Island Ferries logo on her hull. The *Corbière* and the *Portelet* offered combined daily peak capacity for 2,190 passengers, substantially below the 3,800 of the previous season, and the lowest since resumption of full services after the war.

The *Portelet* returned to Weymouth on 15 April ready to commence service that evening, but a Department of Transport inspection found issues with her new aft cabins. The sprinkler system was inadequate in one third of the cabins, requiring *Portelet* to sail with a reduced passenger certificate pending completion of the necessary remedial works.

The new BCIF livery was a simple adaptation of the former Channel Island Ferries approach, with the word 'British' added above. The **Corbière** enters St Peter Port. (*Miles Cowsill*)

The *Portelet* was built as the *Lion* for Burns & Liard's Ardrossan-Larne route and was later employed by P&O between Dover and Boulogne. She joined Marlines as the *Baroness M* prior to her charter to BCIF. *(Ferry Publications Library)*

The *Portelet* operated from Weymouth for two seasons for BCIF in 1987-8. She soon found herself in direct competition with Condor. *(Miles Cowsill)*

The *Portelet* turning in the harbour at St Peter Port for Jersey during her first season. (*Miles Cowsill*)

Brittany Ferries' *Cornouailles* was chartered to sail in tandem with *Portelet* to offer additional capacity for Easter traffic. The works were completed after the Easter peak with the *Cornouailles* maintaining the service. It was an inauspicious start for the Weymouth service, drawing heavy criticism despite the problems that the company had encountered in providing any service at all.

Respected industry commentator John Hendy wrote in Sea Breezes that BCIF was:

'undoubtedly scraping the bottom of the barrel, but so few ships are able to operate into Jersey that perhaps they had no alternative'.

The *Portelet* returned to establish a pattern of night sailings at 22:45 from Weymouth, arriving in Guernsey (06:45-07:15) then on to Jersey (09:15-10:30), before offering a daytime return crossing to Guernsey (12:30-13:00) and Weymouth, where she arrived at 18:00. This seasonal service operated until 27 September, with *Portelet* laid up in Weymouth for the winter. She carried 138,000 passengers and 28,000 cars in her first season.

David Donhue joined the company as Managing Director, bringing a wealth of experience from a career with Townsend Thoresen.

Meanwhile, invigorated by the success of their short-notice autumn operation in 1986, Condor signed an agreement to operate a seasonal service from Weymouth to the Islands between 10 April and 17 October, using the *Condor 5* and the *Condor 7* as appropriate. The service started from St. Malo, where the vessel was berthed overnight, and ran via Jersey and Guernsey to and from Weymouth.

Commodore purchased the *Commodore Goodwill (II)* in May 1987; she replaced the *Commodore Enterprise* but surpassed her with capacity for sixty per cent more containers, despite being just one metre longer and having broadly the same crewing costs. The new vessel allowed the *Commodore Enterprise* to be sold.

The *Corbière* was the victim of a hoax on 9 August, when police in St. Helier were advised that a bomb had been placed on board the vessel. She had just departed at 17:30 for Guernsey and returned to port to enable a search to be made. No bomb was found and the *Corbière* sailed again at 21:00 making up time on the crossing to Portsmouth. Later that month the freight vessel *L Taurus* undertook ramp trials in both Guernsey and Jersey, in anticipation of operating a freight-only service from Poole for Torbay Seaways Freightliner. The company envisaged running to the Islands four times weekly throughout the year, twice to both Guernsey and Jersey. *L Taurus* made her first scheduled visit to Guernsey on 30 September.

The first full season of Weymouth operation proved successful for Condor, with 46,200 passengers carried, and on 2 September the company announced their intention to meet increasing demand by introducing a 41m 400-seat catamaran to the route from 15 June 1988. In the event their intended craft was delayed, and the company purchased *Condor 8* to offer increased passenger capacity.

On the night of 15-16 October 1987 the 'great storm' saw hurricane-force winds sweep through the Channel and across the south of England. The *Corbière,* under the command of Capt. McNeil, sheltered off Alderney in 105 mph winds but was struck by extreme waves causing damage to some forty cars, and displacing several trailer loads. On arrival in Portsmouth, some seven hours behind schedule, the car deck was a scene of devastation.

For the following season BCIF changed their Portsmouth schedule to operate overnight with the *Corbière* from Portsmouth to the Islands from 3 January 1988, departing at 21:30 and sailing direct to Jersey (07:00-09:00), returning via Guernsey (11:00-12:30) to arrive back in Portsmouth at 19:00. This provided a better schedule for freight customers, with overnight deliveries to the Islands counter-balanced by access to the UK produce markets

Now sailing in Commodore colours, the former **Pride of Portsmouth** after her renaming as **Norman Commodore** (III). (*Dave Hocquard*)

The *St Edmund* spent a decade operating on the Harwich-Hoek route for Sealink before serving in the Falklands war. Her charter to BCIF followed a period operating in the Mediterranean for Cenargo as the *Scirocco*. *(FotoFlite)*

Shorn of any external branding, *Earl Granville* undergoes refit work alongside in Southampton. *(Ferry Publications Library)*

An as yet unnamed *Rozel* in dry dock at Southampton being refitted and repainted in January 1989 in readiness for BCIF service. *(Ferry Publications Library)*

The *Sirocco* is assisted by tugs as she enters dry dock on 8 January 1998. *(Ferry Publications Library)*

the following day. The Weymouth schedule reverted to a daytime 13:00 departure to Guernsey (17:30-18:30), and on to Jersey (20:30-22:00) before returning overnight to Weymouth for 06:45 the following morning. The *Corbière* underwent her annual refit at Falmouth between 11 and 26 March resuming her regular schedule on 27 March. The *Portelet* was brought out of winter hibernation to cover her sailings during this period.

The *Earl Granville* returned to visit Guernsey on a twice-weekly schedule for Sealink British Ferries from 30 March 1988, a symbolic extension of the Portsmouth-Cherbourg service following completion of the one-year ban. However, the company was still prohibited from visiting Jersey. Condor added a number of calls at Alderney to their Weymouth service in 1988, utilising the *Condor 5*.

The *Portelet* was re-chartered by BCIF for the summer season and some £200k was spent adding 300 Pullman seats around the ship to counter criticism of her facilities. She commenced her summer season of Weymouth sailings on 6 April, but services were disrupted by an NUS strike from 4 May, which began with the *Portelet* but soon spread to the *Corbière* and the *Earl Granville*. The *Breizh Izel* was brought in from Brittany Ferries to maintain the freight service, but the industrial action was short-lived and crews returned to work from the evening of 6 May.

On 19 August 1988 BCIF announced that services from Portsmouth and Weymouth would be consolidated to operate solely from Poole from 2 January 1989, claiming that this would reduce the passage by up to two hours, thereby narrowing the differential with Condor. This was true for the Portsmouth route, but a lengthening of crossing times compared to Weymouth. Poole, advertised as the 'Clearway Port', was seen as a large and uncongested port with good facilities and accessibility, and was already a base for shareholder Brittany Ferries. With Condor taking increasing market share at Weymouth, the move would allow the company to consolidate the fleet and eliminate the need for a seasonal vessel. However BCIF suggested it was considering the retention of a freight-only

Torbay Seaways' side-loading *Devoniun* was flexible enough to provide relief services during the blockade of St Peter Port in 1987. *(Miles Cowsill)*

The *Corbière* closed the Portsmouth service for BCIF and initiated sailings from Poole pending the arrival of *Rozel*. The pair are seen at Poole in February 1989. *(FotoFlite)*

An early morning view at St Helier as the *Rozel* leaves for St Peter Port during her first season with the company. *(Miles Cowsill)*

service from Portsmouth.

The 8,987 ton *Scirocco* was chartered from Cenargo to replace the *Corbière* for the 1989 season. As the renamed *Rozel*, she would be the largest vessel ever to operate to the Islands, with capacity for 1,300 passengers and 296 cars, cabin accommodation for 671 passengers, and seating for a further 982. The *Corbière* was destined to go back to Truckline Ferries for the Poole-Cherbourg service. In a further tidying up of the fleet, *Portelet* was returned to her owners on completion of her Weymouth season on 1 October. In December BCIF secured a charter of the multi-purpose *Cornouailles* from Brittany Ferries to replace the freighter *Breizh-Izel*, offering winter freight capacity and a summer daytime passenger service from Poole, with an overnight return crossing from the Islands. The *Breizh-Izel* moved from Portsmouth to Poole on 24 December, and was laid up until 3 January 1989.

The BCIF move to Poole was not well received by the freight community, who had established shore infrastructure to support the Portsmouth service and valued the easy access to the motorway network offered by the port. In October BCIF shareholder MMD approached Commodore Shipping with a view to establishing a joint ro-ro freight service from Portsmouth; these discussions expanded to consider closer integration between the two companies. A new joint company, C&M Shipping, was formed in Guernsey, and discussions were held with Sealink British Ferries, who also had an interest in the commercial opportunities presented by BCIF's departure from Portsmouth. Plans were quickly formulated to replace the BCIF Portsmouth freight capacity. In a separate move, Commodore Shipping purchased the *Hamburg* to bolster their container business as the *Commodore Clipper (III)* on 28 December. After refit in Rotterdam she arrived in Guernsey

ROZEL
NASSAU

BRITISH
CHANNEL ISLAND

The BCIF livery on the *Rozel* was amended to incorporate a second blue stripe on the hull. *(FotoFlite)*

The diminutive *St Julien* provided short lived competition to Condor from Weymouth for Weymouth Maritime Services in 1989.(*Miles Cowsill*)

on 9 March 1989, but proved too large to be efficient, and was eventually put out to charter from March 1990.

Emboldened by BCIF's withdrawal from Weymouth and their own fifty-nine per cent year-on-year growth to 73,500 passengers in 1988, Condor announced plans for a £5m investment in *Condor 9*, a 450 passenger 35 knot vessel to be built by Aluminium Shipbuilders in Portchester, with delivery scheduled for April 1990. This would be the largest catamaran of its type in the world.

The *Corbière* took the last BCIF sailing from the Islands into Portsmouth on 2 January 1989 and sailed light to Poole in readiness for the first departure at 21:30 that day. The *Scirocco* arrived from the Mediterranean on 8 January for a £1 million refit including internal alterations to her passenger areas. After her refit the newly named *Rozel* sailed to Poole then on the Islands for berthing trials, which gave the opportunity to open her up to the public. The *Rozel* made her maiden voyage on 21 February with the 21:30 sailing from Poole, after the *Corbière* had arrived from the Islands with her last passenger sailing for the company.

The *Rozel* sailed straight into some of the worst storms of the winter, but quickly proved her worth. The *Corbière* continued to operate in freight-only mode until the arrival of the *Cornouailles* on 10 May, renamed the *Havelet* after a £2m refit at Brest. The *Havelet* was fitted with a new sun deck, restaurant and bar, with enhanced retail facilities and an additional 120 reclining seats. Her car deck acquired a telescopic ramp to facilitate access to the upper car deck. The *Havelet* offered a morning freight-only sailing from Poole and an overnight return until 25 May, when the sailings were timetabled for passengers until the end of September.

The 1989 BCIF peak season schedule was therefore as follows: -

Condor fleet development

Top: *Condor 8* joined the fleet in May 1988 and proved a mainstay of the inter-island and St Malo services. *(Miles Cowsill)*

Middle: The similarities between the BCIF and Condor liveries are evident as *Condor 5* passes Rozel in St Helier. *(Miles Cowsill)*

Bottom: *Condor 8* and *Condor France* pass on the approached to St Helier on 8 June 1996. *(Dave Hocquard)*

The unusual sight of two Brittany Ferries vessels in St Helier; *Reine Mathilde* prepares to replace *Armorique* as cover for the damaged *Rozel*, as *Condor 7* departs for Weymouth. *(Robert Le Maistre)*

		Rozel	Havelet
Poole	dep	21:30	10:00
Guernsey	arr	06:30	15:15
	dep	07:00	17:00
Jersey	arr	08:30	19:00
	dep	10:00	22:00
Guernsey	arr	12:00	
	dep	12:45	
Poole	arr	17:45	06:30

The Elizabeth Harbour was formally opened by the Queen in St. Helier on 25 May; the new berths could handle vessels up to 130m in length, which was matched by the facilities at St. Peter Port in Guernsey, thereby increasing the permissible length of vessels on the Island routes.

The new C&M Shipping freight service from Portsmouth commenced from 3 January 1989 with the *Earl Godwin* in freight-only mode, managed under contract by Sealink British Ferries. On 20 March the *Pride of Portsmouth* replaced the *Earl Godwin* under a three-year charter to Mainland Transport (Holdings) Ltd, the holding company of MMD. The links between Commodore and MMD were consolidated from 1 August when Commodore took full control of the MMD Group. Sadly Commodore chairman Jack Norman, who had been the driving force behind the company and a major shareholder in Condor Ltd, died on 2 September, aged 77.

At Weymouth the seasonal Condor service began on 10 April 1989 with the arrival of the *Condor 7,* and capacity from the port was further enhanced from 5 May when new operator Weymouth Maritime Services commenced operations with a 23:30 sailing of the *St. Julien,* chartered from Scandilines of Norway. The vessel left Weymouth on Mondays,

Torbay Seaways Freightliner provided freight competition from Poole for BCIF using the *L Taurus*, until they were bought out in April 1990. *(Nick Robins)*

The graceful *Armorique* arrives at St Helier whilst covering for the *Rozel* in September 1990. *(Robert Le Maistre)*

Condor 9's entry into service on 17 August 1990 proved premature, and she was quickly withdrawn but returned in 1991 with an improved ride control system. (*Miles Cowsill*)

Tuesdays, Wednesdays and Saturdays with selected calls at Alderney in the weekly schedule. This operation incurred heavy losses and closed on 3 October when the *St. Julien* was repossessed and the company called in the receivers, even though a winter sailing programme had been advertised. Weymouth Maritime Services' Norwegian officers and crew 'sat in' on the vessel until their wages were paid by Scandilines, and the *St. Julien* left Weymouth on 19 October. Although it was later reported that Weymouth Maritime Services would use the *Smyril* on a return to the Islands in 1990, this did not materialise. Thus ended one of the Islands' shortest-duration mainland services.

The *Rozel* was badly damaged on 26 September when she hit an unknown object and lost a propeller approaching St. Peter Port. Her 234 passengers and thirty-one cars disembarked to continue their journeys with Weymouth Maritime Services or the *Havelet,* whilst divers were called to inspect the damage. The *Rozel* sailed direct to Falmouth for repair but the damage was sufficiently serious for her to be out of service for three months. The *Armorique* was initially chartered from Brittany Ferries from 28 September to provide cover, and was later replaced by the *Reine Mathilde*. The latter was pinned against La Collette Marina wall in St. Helier on 28 November whilst trying to berth in 85 mph winds, highlighting the vulnerability of the Elizabeth Harbour to any prevailing southwesterly wind.

The *Pride of Portsmouth* was chartered by C&M Shipping to replace *Earl Godwin* on their new freight service from Portsmouth in March 1989. (*Miles Cowsill*)

The chartered *Commodore Clipper IV* replaced the *Juniper* from January 1991 and was to stay with Commodore until September 1996. (*Miles Cowsill*)

Condor 9 (FotoFlite)

In October the States of Jersey passed regulations to permit licensing of the use of linkspan ramp facilities in St. Helier. These gave a measure of protection to companies prepared to make a year-round commitment to the provision of services, and prevent seasonal operators from creaming off profits. Weymouth Maritime Services was identified as the first company potentially impacted by this control, with their failure to provide a winter service likely to be taken into account in applications for future services.

The switch to Poole initially proved a success for BCIF and the company recorded a twenty per cent rise in passenger carryings to 499,022 for the year. But Condor was also growing, and carried 85,191 passengers, giving the fledgling operation a significant seventeen per cent share of the total market by the year-end 1989. In a move to capitalise on business growth and build further shoulder season traffic, BCIF extended its two-ship operation to start in early April 1990 and operate through to late October; fifty-five per cent of annual business was now carried in these periods, reflecting a changing holiday market. The only schedule change was a 15-minute earlier arrival in Weymouth for the *Havelet*. The company marketed a 'French Connection' service in conjunction with Brittany Ferries and Emeraude Ferries to offer a Poole-Jersey, Jersey-St. Malo, St. Malo-Portsmouth round trip in 1990.

The newly enlarged Commodore Group now had access to the wharfage, warehousing and road haulage operation of MMD and the ro-ro operation from Portsmouth was proving very successful. In February 1990 the company announced a withdrawal from the lo-lo business, switching solely to ro-ro services from March 1991. Preparatory work for a two-vessel operation went better than expected and this change was brought forward to August 1990.

BCIF fought back against the Commodore operation by purchasing their Poole freight competitor, Torbay Seaways Freightliner and the *L Taurus* on 10 April 1990. This was made through the BCIF Isle of Man subsidiary Aubreyville Ltd, which also owned the Huelin Renouf fleet. The ship made her last journey as *L Taurus* on 15 June, and was renamed the *Sylbe,* to be employed on an intermittent freight service to the Islands under the banner 'Channel Island Freight'. BCIF sought to make inroads into road haulage operations and invested in a fleet of curtain sided trailers to Island specifications, building on experience of Channel Island Ferries in this area.

In a parallel move Huelin Renouf purchased Torbay Seaways passenger operation on 11 April, consolidating their links with the West Country, and continued to operate the *Devoniun* on the Torquay-Alderney-Guernsey-Jersey routes for the full 1990 season. The service was not a great success and in October the *Devoniun* sailed to Ipswich for a major engine overhaul and a £800k refit, prior to an eventual sale on 24 May 1993 to Falcon Maritime Inc. of Monrovia, who renamed her *Illyria*.

Although the *Condor 9* was delayed from her anticipated April 1990 delivery, Condor announced their intention to move into the vehicle market by building a large car carrying wave-piercing catamaran for the cross-channel service for the 1992 season. BCIF Chairman Colin Carter responded that "these things (catamarans) are not yet proven and 1992 is a long way off". Conseilleur Berry of the Guernsey Transport Board welcomed the proposal and suggested that the two companies were not in direct competition as they operated from different ports for different customers. Following completion of fitting out at Southampton, the *Condor 9* undertook successful sea trials off the Isle of Wight and then arrived in St. Peter Port at 22:45 on 11 August. She sailed to St. Malo two days later, and undertook her first trial crossing between Jersey and Weymouth in 2hrs 37mins on 14 August. On board were eighty fare paying passengers from the out-of-service *Condor 7*, who were transferred to the new craft for her non-scheduled sailing. *Condor 9* entered service on 17 August after minor modifications to her water jets in St. Sampson's harbour,

Condor 10 employs a very similar livery to that used by BCIF, with red and blue stripes on a white hull. *(FotoFlite)*

but soon encountered problems in rough seas. Her bow rode too high and the craft lifted up over waves before crashing down into the troughs, giving an uncomfortable ride to passengers and throwing considerable spray and water over the vessel. A number of leaks were found around the windows and the radar mast, which damaged the electrical circuitry of the vessel. *Condor 9* was withdrawn from service after three days and returned to her builders. After comparative trials with *Condor 7* off Alderney, a new ride system was identified as the solution to the problem and the vessel was kept out of service until this was fitted for the 1991 season.

The £40m contract for the larger vehicle-carrying craft was due to be signed in September, but Condor delayed the order until the technical problems with *Condor 9* had been resolved. There were also problems with *Condor 7*, which had suffered engine problems on 23 July and was withdrawn for three days at the height of the season. To add to concerns, *Condor 8* damaged her starboard engine whilst inbound from Sark to Jersey near Corbière on 22 August; she completed her trip on one engine, before being withdrawn from service for three days for repairs. The Weymouth service continued until 30 October.

August marked the end of Commodore Shipping's lo-lo service to the UK after the company chartered the *Juniper* to run opposite the *Pride of Portsmouth* for the first six months of ro-ro operation. She made her first visit to the Islands on 30 July. The *Commodore Goodwill (II)* left the fleet on 24 August and the St. Malo service was switched to ro-ro operation on 18 September. Huelin Renouf purchased the *Island Commodore* and renamed her *Huelin Dispatch*. Commodore replaced the *Juniper* with the chartered *Commodore Clipper (IV)* in January 1991, as she had not delivered the capability expected. At the same time the ship management contract with Sealink British Ferries was terminated, being handled internally in Guernsey until December, when management of the *Pride of Portsmouth was* transferred to Goliat Shipping A/S in Norway, who already

Freight competition; BCIF's *Sylbe* lies opposite Commodore's *Jupiter* in St Helier on 20 August 1990. *(Dave Hocquard)*

managed the *Commodore Clipper (IV)* at much lower cost. The *Pride of Portsmouth* was renamed the *Norman Commodore (III)*.

Works to repair the base of La Platte beacon in St. Helier were completed in December 1990, but a fault with navigation equipment on the *Pride of Portsmouth* led to her colliding with the structure and knocking it over on 21 February 1991. An £80k replacement beacon was completed in late October 1991.

Condor's 1991 season started on 23 March when *Condor 9* returned with a new ride control system. *Condor 7* moved to inter-island sailings after operating the last cross-channel hydrofoil service on 7 April with *Condor 4* and *Condor 5* acting as relief vessels, pending sale. The start of the season proved slow to pick up, with the Gulf War having an impact upon bookings but Condor began to take a significant proportion of the sea business, carrying 125,000 passengers during the year. Such levels of abstracted business in both the passenger and freight markets could not be ignored, and BCIF announced in the late summer that it had not exercised an option to purchase the *Rozel* and instead would charter the smaller former Brittany Ferries vessel *Reine Mathilde* for the next two years. The vessel would be renamed the *Beauport*. Whilst this was seen as a stop-gap move for the company pending a longer-term decision, it marked a turning point. As if to reinforce this, Jersey harbour master Capt. Roy Bullen expressed his belief that the future for passenger transportation by sea lay with wave piercing catamarans not larger superferries.

The *Rozel* made her last sailings to the islands in January 1992 and the *Beauport* entered service in February after a £1m refit. Commodore's freight business was healthy enough to consider plans for new ro-ro tonnage, and the company entered discussions with a broad range of shipyards and finance houses in May.

Condor had another successful year with a twenty-five per cent growth in passenger carryings to reach 20,000 in July 1992, and a 10,000 year-on-year passenger increase in the first five months of operation. Condor managing director David Norman announced plans on 24 August to introduce two car-carrying wave-piercing catamarans to compete directly with BCIF from spring 1993. On the same day, TNT Shipping and Development took a fifty per cent financial stake in Condor, with Australian Chris Butcher becoming executive chairman. The bigger financial and technical resources now open to the

The *Beauport* replaced *Rozel* as BCIF's passenger vessel from February 1992. *(John Downs)*

The *Beauport* backs out of St Peter Port with a sailing for Poole. *(John Bryant)*

The *Purbeck* sailed for both BCIF and Commodore, seen here during her short operation for Commodore during 1994/5. *(FotoFlite)*

company helped facilitate the order for the 580 passenger, eighty-four car carrying *Condor 10* from Incat in Tasmania. *Condor 4* and *Condor 5* were passed to Commodore Shipping. After considering proposals from nineteen shipyards, Commodore placed an order with Royal Schelde in October for a new £18m freight vessel capable of carrying 94 x 12m units for delivery in May 1995.

Meanwhile in December 1992, Island Ferries initiated a service between Weymouth and Alderney using the Norwegian *Trondenes* carrying twelve passengers, twenty-five cars and 128 tonnes of freight per crossing. The service lasted until September 1993.

Above: Interior photos of the refurbished *Havelet* in 1990. *(Miles Cowsill)*

The *Havelet* was another Brittany Ferries vessel that saw employment on Island services. As she backs out of St Peter Port the *Baronness de Serk* heads for Sark. *(Miles Cowsill)*

The original BCIF business case had been predicated on a monopoly of services to the Islands, but the company now faced competition on two fronts. The gamble of moving to Poole hit the core freight business, exacerbated by Commodore Shipping's new focus on ro-ro and their takeover of largest customer MMD. The intermittent freight service with the *Sylbe* had dwindled and she spent much of her time laid up in Poole before being taken out of service at the end of 1992, and sold in spring 1993. Meanwhile Condor's upcoming investment in two car-carrying catamarans would further hit passenger and vehicle carryings. Condor was able to offer competitive journey times of 2hrs 15mins from Weymouth to Guernsey and 3hrs from Weymouth to Jersey, substantially below those of BCIF from Poole. When Condor announced a fare-freeze for 1993 the financial stress on BCIF mounted. At the end of the season and facing another downturn in carryings, BCIF announced a reduction in services for the 1993 season.

Both rival operations were comparatively 'low cost' compared to BCIF'S multi-purpose ferries, and Condor was able to exploit summer profits without maintaining a winter service as there was no Service Level Agreement requiring them to operate year-round. Commodore meanwhile was not encumbered by any obligations to the passenger business and could concentrate on being a dedicated low cost freight operation. Being 'low cost' had been the core of the original Channel Island Ferries proposition when attacking Sealink British Ferries. The predator had become the prey.

In the event Condor's search for a second vessel with a suitable ride control system for cross-Channel operation proved too difficult. *Condor 10* began a 27-day delivery voyage from Tasmania on 21 January and undertook ramp trials in March before opening the car carrying service on 1 April 1993 alongside the passenger only *Condor 9*. BCIF was able to

Commodore Clipper off the Isle of Wight. *(FotoFlite)*

The *SeaCat Isle of Man* had a short but eventful charter to Condor, rescuing passengers from the stricken *St Malo* off Corbière on 17 April 1995. *(Ferry Publications Library)*

maintain their two-vessel operation, with twice-daily sailings during the summer season. The two companies entered a destructive price war, which lasted through the summer. At the end of the season BCIF was facing a £3m loss and a Condor service extended through the winter months. BCIF announced that the charter of the *Beauport* would not be renewed and that, in further retrenchment, it would operate with the *Havelet* in 1994, backed by a charter of the freighter *Purbeck*. The *Beauport* undertook her final sailing for BCIF on 31 October.

In December the *Norman Commodore (III)* caught fire in the English Channel. She proceeded to St. Peter Port, where the Guernsey Fire Brigade attacked the fire through the stern door, but the blaze spread to the accommodation decks and cargoes of butter and chocolate before it could be extinguished. Damage to the vessel was estimated at £1.5m and the *Norman Commodore (III)* remained out of service until June 1994.

1994 opened with a surprise announcement from BCIF when on 7 January company chairman Colin Carter advised shareholders that the company would cease operating passenger and freight services from 22 January. Simultaneously Condor announced that they had bought the passenger business, and Commodore the freight operation. The pincer movement had worked. The *Havelet* left the Islands for the last time as a BCIF vessel on the evening of 21 January and the takeover was completed the following day.

This was the end of an era. In less than a decade Channel Island Ferries had broken the historic monopoly, and now the successor company had ceased trading. Henceforth a Channel Island based company controlled passenger and ro-ro freight services to the Islands, and a new dependence on fast craft as the mainstay of UK and French passenger links was beginning.

The new regime started on 22 January 1994 with Commodore operating freight sailings

The *Havelet* was rebranded with the Condor Ferries logo following the takeover in 1994. *(Anthony Meads)*

Condor 11 powers away from St Peter Port for Weymouth. *(FotoFlite)*

Passengers crowd the open decks to watch the photographer as **Condor 12** makes the most of calm sea conditions heading across the Channel. *(FotoFlite)*

from Portsmouth and Condor the passenger services now solely focused at Weymouth. The *Purbeck* was chartered by Commodore to cover sailings until the arrival of the *Island Commodore (III)*, and Condor chartered the *Havelet* from BCIF for a three year period to operate an overnight schedule from Weymouth with a daytime return crossing. This commenced from 6 March and enabled Condor to offer better reliability than could be achieved solely with *Condor 10*. The integration of BCIF schedules took longer than anticipated, and Condor was late publishing its schedules and fares for the 1994 season, which eventually appeared in a simplified banded fare structure, with modest changes to the 1993 levels.

Commodore soon encountered operational difficulties. Within days of her return to service after the English Channel fire, the *Norman Commodore (III)* suffered a total engine control failure whilst entering St. Peter Port on 14 June, and collided with, crushed and sank the *Herm Trident VI*.

TNT's fifty per cent shareholding in the Condor business was transferred to Holyman Ltd in 1994. In its first major expansion move after floating on the Australian Stock Exchange in April, Holyman signed a AU$40m contract with Incat Tasmania for the construction of a new 78m car and passenger carrying wave piercing catamaran.

Condor 10 struggled to cope with increasing volumes of traffic through Weymouth, and Condor began to look for a bigger vessel for the route. The new Holyman vessel was named *Condor 11* at her launch in Hobart, Tasmania on 21 July, and the accompanying press release suggested that the vessel 'may be chartered' to Condor from spring 1995. Circumstances were to dictate otherwise, as *Condor 11* ran aground on Black Jack Reef, Hobart during sea trials in October, whilst travelling at 36 knots under the command of Incat Managing Director Robert Clifford, badly damaging her hulls. Salvage crews took eight weeks to recover the stricken vessel, which returned to Hobart for substantial repairs, delaying her introduction until May 1995.

More positively, Commodore confirmed an order for a second new freight vessel on 14 November for delivery in March 1996. A pooling arrangement between Condor and Channiland led to rationalisation of services on the St. Malo-Jersey-Guernsey-Sark route, releasing *Condor 9* for charter to *Viking Line,* who renamed her *Viking Express* for service between Helsinki and Tallinn, before she was chartered in the Caribbean for the winter.

Private Equity firm 3i took a 1/3 stake in Condor with a €50m investment during 1995. Condor adopted the name Condor Ferries for a new corporate identity, with a revised blue and red livery for the vessels. The repairs to *Condor 11* forced the company to find another vessel for the start of the 1995 season and the *Seacat Isle of Man* was chartered from March until May pending delivery of the new vessel.

On Easter Monday 17 April 1995 the Channiland fast ferry *St. Malo* struck La Frouquie, 900 metres north of La Corbière lighthouse at around 10:00, whilst on passage from Jersey to Sark. Whilst visibility was good, there was a westerly force five wind with a spring tide ebbing to the west, and sea conditions were moderate to rough. The *St. Malo* rapidly took on water and sent out distress signals. She was quickly helped by a number of boats and helicopters, including the *Seacat Isle of Man,* which ensured there were no fatalities. Some of the 307 passengers stepped on to a flotilla of rescue boats, others were winched into helicopters and more than 100 leapt into life rafts amid waves up to four feet high. More than fifty people suffered injuries, many suffering from broken legs and ankles as they abandoned the vessel. The *St. Malo* was beached in St. Aubin's Bay, to be assessed by divers.

In the subsequent Inquiry the master was found guilty of a 'reckless act'. The report concluded that Capt. Penean failed to stop the craft when he realised he was off course while negotiating the inshore passage between Corbière lighthouse and the outer-lying

Sisters **Commodore Goodwill** and **Island Commodore** line up on the ro-ro berths at St Peter Port. *(Ferry Publications Library)*

Commodore Goodwill and *Island Commodore* pass each other off the Cherbourg Penisular. *(FotoFlite)*

Condor Express at the Elizabeth Terminal in St Helier. *(Miles Cowsill)*

reef. The UK marine accident investigators considered that the evacuation system and equipment aboard the *St. Malo* were inadequate. The channel was closed following the accident, but Capt. Bullen, Harbour Master at St. Helier, was happy that passenger ferries should continue to use it in the future once steps had been taken to mark the rock site.

Condor 11 eventually entered service on 18 May, but proved to be an unpopular craft and incapable of meeting the tight planned schedules, with port calls frequently exceeding the scheduled 30 minutes by up to an hour. She suffered a large number of cancellations in bad weather and generated widespread scepticism about the ability of fast craft to operate in winter weather; her charter was not renewed. *Condor 11* made her last journey to the Islands on 31 October after a final fortnight of operation characterised by a series of cancellations due to strong winds; she was redeployed to Cat-Link in Denmark. Condor chartered *Condor 12* for the summer 1996 season.

The *Island Commodore (III)* entered service in June 1995, releasing the *Purbeck* for charter. Over 2,000 people visit her in September during an open day in Guernsey, which coincided with the announcement that the name for the second ro-ro freight vessel would be the *Commodore Goodwill*, the third Commodore vessel to carry this name. The *Commodore Goodwill (III) was* launched at Royal Schelde Yard, Vlissingen on 11 November, and named by Mrs Seyna Sonnichsen, wife of the Chairman of Goliat Shipping, thereby completing a £38m ship replacement programme for Commodore. The vessel was towed out of an underwater building dock to an adjacent fitting-out berth, so that the 210 ton bridge and officers' quarters section could be lifted into position. The *Norman Commodore (III)* made her final journey to the Islands on 8 December and was sold to Fosen of Norway. The *Commodore Clipper (IV)* and the *Island Commodore (III)* offered an accelerated winter freight service before the *Commodore Goodwill (III)* entered service on 1 March 1996, releasing the *Commodore Clipper (IV)*.

Emeraude Ferries' **Solidor 2** reflected at St Malo pending her sale. *(Miles Cowsill)*

Condor 8 remained on the St. Malo link. *Condor 9* returned from charter to operate a short programme of excursions from Torquay until 30 September when she was laid up in Guernsey, pending overhaul in Portsmouth. *Condor 10* was still surplus to requirements, and on 27 October sailed from Portsmouth to Weymouth and thence to a charter in New Zealand. Condor's winter service was left to the *Havelet,* after a £650k refit which included the fitting of outer fenders and inner casings and sealing her bow door to bring her up to the safety requirements of the International Maritime Organisation.

The £I.8 million scheme to expand storage space at Elizabeth Harbour in St. Helier and enable the handling of the next generation of larger wave-piercer ferries began on 8 January 1996. The *Solidor 2* and the *Havelet* were confined to the Albert Pier for three months whilst the initial work took place.

The Jersey Harbours & Airport Committee rejected Condor Ferries' application for a licence to run a high-speed service between Jersey and St. Malo, and the company shelved plans to supplement their UK fast ferry service with an additional catamaran. The *Havelet* was employed as additional capacity for a further year, sailing overnight from Weymouth at 22:30, arriving in St. Helier at 07:30 the following morning. She returned from St. Helier at 08:30, calling in Guernsey at 10:30 and leaving for Weymouth at 11:15 for a 16:15 arrival. For the 1996 season the *Havelet* operated alongside another chartered 5Im Incat wave piercer *Condor 12,* which was delivered from Tasmania on 3 April. *Condor 12* could carry 674 passengers and 155 cars, on twice-daily schedules from Weymouth to Guernsey and Jersey, departing at 07.00 and 16.10. The direct crossing to Guernsey was scheduled at 2 hours 30 minutes with an arrival in Jersey some 75 minutes later. The *Havelet* was sent for refit once *Condor 12* came into service. Meanwhile *Condor 9* operated a full season of Torquay-Guernsey excursions.

Condor Ferries ordered a new £23m 84m Incat catamaran for the 1997 season, with the

The *Condor Vitesse* at Poole pending her afternoon sailing Jersey. *(Ferry Publications Library*

Condor 12 deemed only a short-term capacity solution. Rather than tempt fate by continuing numerical craft naming, the new vessel was to be named *Condor Express*. Condor Ferries applied to operate her in wave heights of over 3m, the then restriction for this type of craft, as they planned to use *Condor Express* on a year-round basis, heralding the end of traditional passenger ferry operations to the Islands. Condor also reviewed their English port strategy and concluded positive discussions with the Poole Harbour Commissioners to transfer Weymouth services there from the 1997 season. Reiterating the advantages previously lauded by BCIF, Condor claimed that Poole would enjoy better road access, although crossing times would be longer due to the slow approach into the harbour.

The *Havelet* was withdrawn from service at the end of the season to correct defects under the Safety of Life at Sea (SOLAS) regulations, leaving a full fast craft operation for the winter services. *Condor 12* maintained the winter schedule despite protests from the Islands. The *Havelet* returned to act as a standby vessel from November on completion of the remedial works. In the meantime the new build *Condor Express* was launched in Tasmania on 24 November.

An 18-month feasibility study concluded that conversion of the freight vessels *Island Commodore* (III) or *Commodore Goodwill* (III) to carry passengers as ro-pax vessels was impractical, so Commodore investigated the possibility of building a new purpose built ro-pax ship capable of carrying 300 passengers and eighty-five cars. The two sister companies entered discussions on the provision of year-round services with the Jersey Transport Authority and the Guernsey Transport Board, seeking exclusive rights to the linkspans in Jersey for fifteen years, whilst aiming to secure funding for the new ro-pax vessel. Condor also sought access to a Jersey berth to allow them to compete with Emeraude Line on the St. Malo route.

Condor Express arrived in Poole on 15 January 1997 after a 12,000-mile delivery journey from Australia. She operated the Weymouth service from 31 January, releasing *Condor 12* for overhaul, pending her transfer to operate on the Holyman Sally Ramsgate-Oostende service, where she was renamed *Holyman Rapide*. On 28 February *Condor Express* operated the final inbound service from the Islands to Weymouth, before departing empty to Poole. She commenced services on the new route the following day, with a schedule based on departures at 06:15 and 15:40 from Poole to Guernsey (2hr 30min) and Jersey (3hr 45min via Guernsey).

Condor Express suffered multiple teething problems during her first year of operation, resulting in many cancellations, with no back-up service available. A petition in Guernsey in favour of the restoration of services with a conventional craft amassed some 8,500 signatures. There was strong criticism of the service offered by Condor, and a number of coach companies were said to be contemplating withdrawing their business. The Jersey Transport Authority noted that 'poor performance arose because of technical problems with frequent breakdowns and delays. Difficulties were compounded by the failure of the company to provide the standard of customer care expected when dealing with passengers generally, and in particular those affected by the disruption of service caused by technical problems'. Condor Managing Director Rob Provan took exception to the criticism claiming that Condor Express had carried 128,300 passengers and 30,831 cars in the 1997 season, rises of twenty-four per cent and twenty per cent over 1996, and pointing out that air carryings had been stagnant in the same period. He denied any lack of communication or customer care, stating that he knew of no other ferry company that went to such lengths to look after their passengers.

Condor 9 operated services to the Islands from St. Malo from 1 May to 6 October, with a daytime connection onward to Poole. Channiland withdrew from the service and their vessel St. Malo was chartered by Condor as the Condor France. On 30 July Condor announced their intention to return to Weymouth in 1998 with a new service to Guernsey and St. Malo using Condor 10. There would be no call in Jersey, as the Jersey Transport Authority still refused Condor a licence to operate on the route, in order to provide protection for Emeraude Lines. The re-introduction of a Weymouth service would offer the shortest passage time to St. Malo, but also had the advantage of blocking the port to potential competitors.

Commodore celebrated fifty years of service in September with open days using Island Commodore (III) in Jersey on 7 September and Commodore Goodwill (III) in Guernsey the following Sunday. Later that month Purbeck was withdrawn from service.

At the end of the summer Condor released operating statistics for March to September 1997, recording the arrival time in Poole after each round-trip, demonstrating just how difficult the first season of operation of Condor Express had been: -

79 per cent of round trips reached Poole arrived within one hour of schedule
16 per cent were delayed by more than one hour
5 per cent were rescheduled due to tidal conditions
1 per cent were cancelled by weather
2 per cent were cancelled by technical issues

Condor met with the Jersey Transport Authority on 10 October to explain the pattern of breakdowns to Condor Express. They outlined how they intended to rectify the engineering problems afflicting the vessel, including fitting new inter-coolers to correct an inherent design fault, installing a new design of cylinder heads as thirty-five had to be replaced during the 1997 season, fitting new cam shafts to replace two that had failed, and welding to reduce vibration in the engine compartment. But the patience of the Jersey Transport Authority and Guernsey Transport Board had been pushed too far. On 15 October they announced their intention to invite tenders from operators interested in operating services to the Islands from the UK. Condor reacted quickly, placing advertisements in Island papers outlining the benefits of their operation, and offering free tickets for an inter-island trip to sample the service. They also initiated a public petition to support their right to continue operations.

Condor 8 was sold to Canadian interests in October, renamed the *Wavemaster*, and loaded on to a heavy lift ship at St. Malo on 27 November for her trip across the Atlantic. *Condor 9* completed her season on the St. Malo-Jersey route on 3 November, but four days later the Guernsey Transport Board followed their Jersey colleagues and banned Condor from carrying cars to St. Malo, again to protect Emeraude Lines' services. *Condor 10's* service from Weymouth would be passenger-only.

The New Year period saw all sailings cancelled between 30 December 1997 and 9 January 1998 due to both bad weather and vessel technical issues. *Condor Express* was sent to Liverpool for refit on 9 February and replaced by the *Rapide,* the former *Condor 12.* The *Rapide* suffered from a succession of engine problems in February and March resulting in more delays to sailings.

Condor 10, operating as *The Lynx* on her winter charter to Trans Rail, suffered significant wave damage to her bow whilst on passage from Wellington to Picton on 16 March, requiring extensive repairs at Incat, Tasmania. Condor reacted quickly, and on 20 March announced cover for *Condor 10* by the charter of *Condor Vitesse,* a sister of *Condor Express. Condor Vitesse* opened the Weymouth-Guernsey-St. Malo route on 1 May.

Channel Hoppers began a service with the *Varangerfjord* in late May, operating with a strict wave height limitation of one metre. This was raised to 2.5m from 13 June. Sailings left Portsmouth at 08:30 for Jersey, arriving at 13:00 and returning at 17:30, with an Alderney call at weekends.

The Jersey Transport Authority and Guernsey Transport Board placed adverts in Lloyd's List in February inviting tenders from passenger and car ferry operators interested in providing a year-round service between the Channel Islands and the United Kingdom from 1 January 1999. The successful tenderer was required to provide a service which would meet the requirements of holidaymakers and Channel Island residents, and specifications laid down by the Island authorities in respect of frequency of sailings, fares, standard of vessels etc. Nine companies expressed an initial interest but only three were to submit tenders - Condor, Hoverspeed and P&O European Ferries.

There was very strong interest in the bid process as it unfolded, with well-attended public debates with the tendering parties that strongly favoured the P&O European Ferries bid in straw polls. Conversely a Channel Television telephone poll came out strongly in favour of Condor. P&O European Ferries brought their Austal fast craft *Superstar Express* on trial to St. Helier and St. Peter Port, and held open days for the public. Condor engaged in an extensive advertising campaign to position themselves as the local candidate. They prepared a critique of the bids that was widely used by the States, pointing out that the proposed P&O European Ferries conventional vessel (*Pride of Bruges*) was a sister of the *Herald of Free Enterprise*, and questioning the capabilities of the proposed rival fast craft in Island waters.

The Jersey Transport Authority summarised the three submitted tenders: -

'Condor is proposing to use two fast ferries - *Condor Express* and *Condor Vitesse* with a back up passenger only carrying vessel *Condor 9*. The company will invest in a new conventional vessel carrying cars and freight to be operated from January 2000. There will be no direct sailings to Jersey. The services will be split between three ports: Weymouth for early morning and late evening fast ferries, Poole for other fast ferries and Portsmouth for the conventional vessel. In the winter there will be one sailing five days a week and in the summer three sailings daily. From

The *Condor Express* inward from Weymouth in the Little Russel approaching St Peter Port. *(Miles Cowsill)*

January 2000 the Ro/Pax would operate daily. Fares for 1999 would be at the 1998 level raised by three per cent. Day excursion fares would be available to Channel Island residents as well as United Kingdom residents. The capacity of *Condor Express* and *Condor Vitesse* will be 750 passengers and 185 cars. *Condor 9* would carry 450 passengers, and the conventional vessel would have capacity for 500 passengers and 41 four-berth cabins. The maximum daily capacity would be 2,250 passengers and 555 cars in 1999, with an additional 500 passengers with the conventional vessel in the year 2000. The earliest start would be 07:00 from Weymouth and 08:15 from Jersey. The latest arrival would be 23:55 in Weymouth and 23:10 in Jersey.

Hoverspeed is proposing a year round fast ferry from Weymouth, an extra daily conventional ship operating from June to September, and possibly a second fast ferry operating between June and September, if demand justified it. Operating out of Weymouth the company would invest in Terminal improvements at that port. Under option 1, which involves the year-round fast ferry service, with a seasonal conventional ferry service, all fast ferry services would be via Guernsey and the conventional ferry would be direct to Jersey and back via Guernsey. With option 2, which involves the introduction of an additional seasonal fast ferry service, one of the fast ferries operating between June and September would be direct to Jersey and back via Guernsey. Fares would be largely unchanged from their current level. There would be a discount on the conventional ship and parity for United Kingdom and Channel Island traffic, but with a discount for Island residents on brochure and promotional fares. The fast ferry *Super Seacat* would have a capacity of 770 passengers and 175 vehicles and the conventional ferry would have the capacity of 1,000 passengers and 160 vehicles. Under option 1 (excluding the seasonal fast ferry) the maximum capacity would be 2,540 passengers and 510 vehicles per day. The earliest start would be 07:00 from Weymouth and 11:30 from Jersey. The latest arrival would be

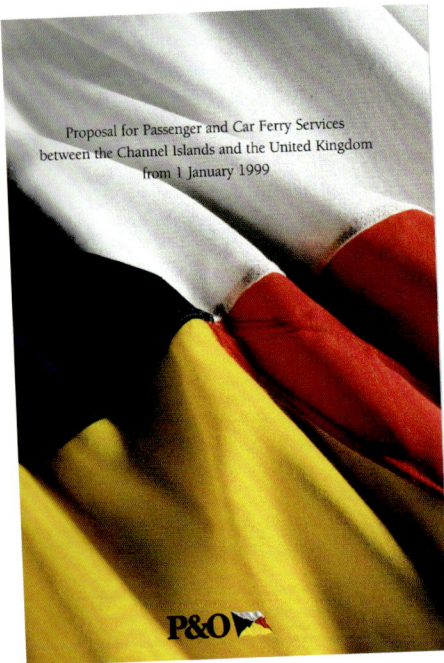

Proposal for Passenger and Car Ferry Services between the Channel Islands and the United Kingdom from 1 January 1999

P&O

23:59 in Weymouth and 19:50 in Jersey. There would be a fast ferry daily year-round and, in the summer, there would be two fast ferry services daily plus one conventional ferry. In the winter months the conventional ferry would provide permanent back-up.

P&O European Ferries is proposing two seasonal fast craft - one covering the period March to November and the other covering the period April to September. In addition there would be one conventional vessel year round. The fast craft each have a capacity of 900 passengers and 200 vehicles and the conventional vessel a capacity of 1,000 passengers and 330 cars (or freight vehicle equivalent). The conventional vessel would have 100 four berth cabins. All services will operate via Guernsey and the proposal includes a link to St. Malo. The proposals are based using Portsmouth that appears to have a disadvantage in terms of travel time at sea. An alternative proposal is put forward involving using Weymouth and excluding St. Malo but this is not considered by the Company to be its preferred option. The brochure fares proposed would be the same as the 1998 level. There would be a discount for travel on the conventional vessel, and a range of incentives for off-peak travel. Fares available to United Kingdom passengers would also be available to Channel Island passengers. There would be a daily service in winter and summer. In the summer months the maximum capacity would be 2,800 passengers and 730 vehicles per day. In the summer months the earliest start would be 07:00 from Portsmouth and 08:00 from Jersey. Latest arrival would be in Portsmouth at 21:20 and Jersey at 19:35. There would be one service daily using the conventional vessel in January, February and December, two services daily using the conventional vessel and a fast craft in March, October and

P&O European Ferries brought their Austal fast craft *Superstar Express* for ramp trials in the Islands as part of their bid for the services in 1989. She is pictured here off Noirmont Point, Jersey. *(Dave Hocquard)*

Pride of Bruges was P&O European Ferries' intended ro-ro vessel in their bid for the Island services, offering capacity for 1,326 passengers and 350 vehicles. She was near-identical in dimensions to the **Rozel.** *(Miles Cowsill)*

November, and three services daily between April and September involving the conventional vessel and two fast craft'.

The Jersey Transport Authority noted that Emeraude Ferries were apprehensive about the P&O European Ferries proposal to operate to St. Malo. There were concerns at the impact of both the P&O European Ferries and Hoverspeed bids on Commodore's freight services, but this should have been expected if the authorities wanted anything other than a fast craft operation.

The Jersey Transport Authority placed great weight on the Jersey Tourism Committee's strong support for the Condor bid, as tourism accounted for eighty per cent of passengers. Their analysis noted that Weymouth and Poole offered fast crossing times and good catchment areas compared to Portsmouth, and considered the latter to be too far away as a fast ferry port. The potential for day trips from Weymouth and Poole was seen as a market segment capable of significant growth from the 30,000 trips in 1997. Condor's new conventional ferry was deemed commercially viable as it would replace an existing freight ship under the same corporate flag; they contrasted this with the P&O European Ferries and Hoverspeed offers of 'old ships in need of refitting'. Doubts were raised as to whether the P&O European Ferries conventional craft would fit into St. Helier. The Condor offer of Incat catamarans was judged to be based on tried and tested vessels, compared to the Austal craft proposed by P&O European Ferries and the Hoverspeed *SuperSeacat*, which had wave height operational restrictions. Whilst P&O European Ferries was seen as having the best distribution network, 'the experience and dedication of Condor, coupled with the accessibility and responsiveness of their local management, and the respect they held as business partners', was seen as important by Jersey Tourism. They noted that Condor would be run by a Channel Island owned company with a business focus on the Islands, compared to the P&O European Ferries and Hoverspeed bids which would form only one

The *Island Commodore* provided matched freight capacity to *Commodore Goodwill*, but could not be converted to ro-pax capability to meet Condor's passenger back-up requirements under their new contract with the States, and was replaced by *Commodore Clipper* in 1999. *(Miles Cowsill)*

part of their larger portfolios.

The Guernsey Tourist Board identified the key factors they felt should determine which sea carrier should be chosen to operate the UK service: -

1. continued provision of a fast ferry operation on a twelve-month basis
2. the reliability of the vessel and quality of service on offer
3. the shortest possible travelling time between the UK and the Channel Islands
4. a schedule which allows for the development of the day trip market
5. a range of ports accessible to the southwest and southeast England markets, seen as fifty-seven per cent of the UK market
6. marketing resources of the company dedicated to the UK-Channel Islands route and, above all
7. the same carrier should provide sea passenger services to Jersey, Guernsey and the UK.

The Guernsey Tourist Board's view was that the islands should only risk changing operators if another carrier would offer a substantially better service than Condor. They considered this was not the case, based on the evidence of the tenders. Although it was noted that Condor had major problems during the last year, these appeared to have been surmounted. The decision to go to tender appeared to have had the desired effect of jolting the company to provide a first class service in 1998. Members of the Tourist Board (chaired by Geoff Norman, director of Commodore, who played no part in the proceedings) gave this view their unanimous support. In contrast, the Guernsey Hotel and Guest House Association backed the P&O European Ferries bid.

On 1 June the Jersey Transport Authority announced they were in favour of Condor by a majority vote, but the Guernsey Transport Board supported the P&O European Ferries tender, albeit after a tied vote of two for Condor and two for P&O European Ferries, with the President revealing he would have voted for P&O European Ferries. It was clearly not practical for the two Islands to be served by different operators, and no bids had contemplated a single island service, so a compromise was needed. The stalemate drew derision in both islands. Guernsey Tourist Board Vice President Carol Fletcher said the Board was very disappointed with the Transport Board decision, 'at the end of the day the Tourist Board wants the best service in terms of customer care and quality' [*Guernsey Evening Press 3 June 1998*]. Condor were reported to have threatened to sue the States if they were forced out of the Harbours [*Guernsey Evening Press, 2 July 1998*].

On 11 June the two States' Boards met in Jersey to resolve their different perspectives; Conseilleur Febrache replaced Conseilleur Walters, thereby giving the Guernsey contingent a Condor majority and an overall majority between the two islands in favour of Condor. On 19 June the Guernsey Transport Board reversed their decision and announced they were now totally in support of the Condor proposal. Final representations were made by both Condor and P&O European Ferries, but the decision to appoint Condor was ratified by the States of Jersey on 30 June and States of Guernsey on 1 July when they were asked to 'approve, in principle, that permission be granted to Condor Ferries Limited, for a period of three years commencing 1st January 1999, to enable that company to operate passenger and car ferry services between Jersey and the United Kingdom'.

A new Service Level Agreement (SLA) was then approved by the Jersey Transport Authority that included, inter alia: -

- Guarantees of performance with recompense to travellers where the performance guarantee is not met
- The provision of a conventional vessel from October 1998
- The provision of satisfactory management and staff resources at each port
- A detailed customer care document with plans for delayed passengers
- Independent evidence of the ability of the company to fund the investment of the purchase of a new ro-pax vessel, the purchase of *Condor Vitesse* and the buy-out of Holyman (then still a fifty per cent shareholder in the Company)
- Arrangements to ensure that the conventional vessel will maintain sufficient spare capacity to be able to cope with disruptions to fast ferry services

The Jersey Transport Authority made it 'very clear' to the new Chairman of Condor Ferries that if the service fell short of what was expected during the three-year period of the permit it would not be renewed.

Given the criteria that were eventually used to evaluate the bids, which placed greater emphasis on local knowledge than operational reliability or quality, many were bewildered as to what the purpose of the tendering competition had been, other than to bring Condor to heel. A competition initiated because of frustration at repeated operational problems and poor customer service attracted companies with strong reputations in both fields, but was settled by a fear of change. Condor played on their Island credentials and proposed a joint ro-pax investment with Commodore, whereas Hoverspeed and P&O European Ferries were seen as threats to the Commodore freight business, even though freight carryings were essential to underpin the costs of the back-up capability of a conventional vessel. There could only be one winner on these terms and the opportunity for change was lost. The States were at a crossroads and their decision ensured that the Islands' fortunes were now inextricably linked to Condor and fast craft.

CHAPTER TWELVE

Twenty years of Condor 1998-2018

'Condor Liberation: one month to go!

The first sailing of the state-of-the-art Condor Liberation is just one month away.

Condor Liberation – the first ferry of its kind in Northern Europe – marks a new era in sea travel, and with hundreds of passengers already booked to travel on her inaugural sailing from Poole to the Channel Islands on Friday 27 March, it's going to be quite an event.

Spaces on the first sailing, which departs at 09:30, are selling fast, and anyone wishing to travel and enjoy this once-in-a-lifetime opportunity should book now.

Condor Ferries has already seen a 14% increase in bookings for travel in Spring to Guernsey and Jersey, with passengers keen to be amongst the first to sail on this fabulous new ship. There is also strong demand for summer travel as holidaymaker's (sic) make their plans for a summer escape.

With a trimaran (three-hull) design, Condor Liberation offers greater stability and better sea-keeping ability, providing a smoother, more comfortable and reliable crossing for passengers. The new ship has also undergone a comprehensive customisation programme and sports the new company brand identity, featuring three new colours - dark blue, pink and gold.

Inside, the fast ferry offers an impressive new Duty Free shop, Adore, children's play area, plus a range of eating and drinking outlets. Passengers can also choose from three new seating lounges, including two upgrade areas: Ocean Plus seats in the Horizon lounge, where the floor to ceiling windows offer panoramic views; and the Ocean Club lounge with its all-leather reclining seats and first-class at-seat steward service'.

[*Condor Ferries press release, 27 February 2015*]

Having successfully overcome the challenge to their Island services, Condor set about the process of restoring their reputation and delivering the commitments made in the new SLA. The *Havelet* was purchased in September 1998 for the year-round service from Weymouth and as short-term disruption cover for *Condor Express,* pending delivery of a new ro-pax ferry to replace the *Island Commodore* and the *Havelet.* A new fast craft service was planned for the summer 1998 season to link Weymouth and St. Malo via Guernsey. Whilst *Condor 10* was the preferred vessel for this service she was required her elsewhere, so *Condor Vitesse* was procured for the new route. She operated at half her capacity to leave standby accommodation available for any passengers affected by potential issues with *Condor Express.*

The *Condor France* made her last journey between Jersey and St. Malo on 12 September before being sold and renamed the *Acacia.* In a strategic 'U' turn, Weymouth was added back into the schedules in October 1998. The company's new customer care credentials were soon tested when the *Havelet* encountered storm conditions during a 16 hour crossing from Weymouth to Jersey on 24 October. Ten cars were damaged, causing the company to review their policy of not chaining down cars on the vehicle deck.

The autumn also proved a difficult operating period for Channel Hoppers, who lost many sailings during the months of September and October, but were still able to claim carryings of 20,000 passengers in their first operating season. The *Varangerfjord was* arrested in Portsmouth for non-payment of harbour dues on 27 October, but was released after payment.

Condor Vitesse completed her first season's scheduled service and, after a period of cover for *Condor Express,* was chartered to New Zealand's Tranz Rail on 2 November to replace *Condor 10,* and renamed *The Lynx* for the journey south. In November the *Havelet* was arrested by the Maritime Safety Agency in Weymouth after a routine inspection found thirty-five faults on the vessel. She was released back to service after the faults were corrected.

In the severe New Year gales of 1999 Condor was able to operate the *Havelet* for the passenger services, and *Commodore Goodwill* joined her on 6 January after overhaul in Spain. Both vessels suffered only slight delays during the inclement weather that followed through January and February.

The summer 1999 season saw Condor operate three sailings daily using *Condor Express* and *Condor Vitesse* from 30 April to 17 October, leaving Weymouth at 07:00 and Poole at 12:55 and 19:40. The *Condor 9* returned from New Zealand to operate twice daily sailings between Jersey and St. Malo, replacing *Condor France.* For the first time since 1964 Condor did not operate a service to Sark.

Channel Hoppers proposed ambitious plans to run to the Islands from Southampton, Torquay and St. Malo from 27 March, using a Boeing Jetfoil on a new Southampton-Alderney-Jersey-St. Malo schedule; *Varangerfjord* was scheduled to operate the Torquay-Alderney-Cherbourg link. But the company failed to secure a charter of the *Princess Clementin,* resulting in *Varangerfjord* operating alone, initially from Southampton. After pressure from the authorities in Torquay her programme was revised to incorporate a Torquay-Jersey-Alderney-Southampton-Alderney-Jersey-Torquay routing on Wednesdays, Fridays and Sundays. Day trips from Devon proved popular in the summer season but the Southampton leg was dropped at the end of August, following alleged non-

The *Havelet* found employment with Condor pending the arrival of the new build *Commodore Clipper.* Here she passes Noirmont Point inbound to Jersey. *(John Downs)*

The *Commodore Clipper* on her launch day at the Van der Giessen-de-Noord yard on 8 May 1999. *(Martijn Nobel)*

payment of harbour dues. Towards the end of the year Channel Hoppers faced legal action from the Norwegian owners of the *Varangerfjord* over unpaid fees. Police were called in to search for the missing Managing Director after a series of complaints to the Trading Standards Authority. Channel Hoppers became another short-lived footnote to the Island story.

Emeraude Lines introduced a new Westamarin-built 300 passenger, thirty-five car catamaran between Jersey and France from 1 May. Emeraude purchased the craft from Elba Ferries of Genoa for FF38 million and spent a further FF10 million on refurbishment and modifications, including extension of her passenger spaces to accommodate 420 people. The twelve year old twin-hulled craft, formerly the *Elba Express,* was renamed the *Solidor 4.* She enabled the company to increase its sailings, doubling the capacity arriving from France each day. *Solidor 3* and *Solidor* 4 operated from St. Malo to Jersey each morning, with one returning to France and the other going on to Guernsey. The investment supported Emeraude's exclusive agreement for vehicle ferries between the Channel Islands and France in the face of the challenge from Condor. *Solidor 4* was plagued by poor sea-keeping capabilities and mechanical problems, being unable to reach

Cruise across by Traditional Ferry

Relax and enjoy the experience

If getting there is half the fun for you, choose our traditional ferry the 'M.V. Havelet'. It takes a leisurely 9 hours to reach Guernsey and 12 hours to get to Jersey - time well spent aboard this delightful ferry. When you reach your destination you'll be well and truly in the holiday mood, relaxed and raring to go.

You can enjoy a drink in the Compass Bar, and on daytime summer crossings - drinks and snacks at the Islander Bar out on the sundeck. Whatever you do, don't miss the many bargains on sale in the duty-free shop and perfumery. Children will have a great time in the play area, and for a small extra charge there's even a Cinema.

Travel in comfort

For night crossings there are a number of private cabins available complete with hand basins, and some with private shower and w.c., or you can stretch out in a reclining seat in one of two comfortable Pullman lounges, one equipped with television. You'll get a great all-round view in the 'Panorama' Forward Lounge.

With your car

Travelling with your own car is strongly recommended, allowing you to take a lot more luggage, and you can explore the delightful lanes and countryside of the Islands to the full.

Great on-board facilities

The whole family will enjoy their cruise aboard the 'M.V. Havelet', it has so much to offer. Like the Wheelhouse Coffee Shop for hot and cold snacks or full meals. Or how about something a bit special in the Clipper Restaurant, with its value for money menu.

Commodore Goodwill on the west berth in Elizabeth Harbour, St Helier as Emeraude Lines *Solidor 4* leaves for St Malo. (Miles Cowsill)

Commodore Clipper in St Peter Port. The distinctive Commodore Lion on her funnel was adopted from the house flag of the Lion Shipping Company, who at one stage owned the *Commodore Queen*. (Miles Cowsill)

Guernsey in anything over force four conditions. The company substituted *Solidor 3* on these occasions. Finally in September 1999 Emeraude Lines secured a five year Service Level Agreement with the Jersey Harbour Authorities for passenger and car-carrying services between Jersey and St. Malo.

The £30m 500 passenger capacity new ro-pax *Commodore Clipper* was delivered to Condor Ferries on 25 September, and replaced the *Island Commodore (III)* and the *Havelet* as the back up vessel for the fast craft fleet. She was the first new conventional ship for the Island services since the *Caesarea* and *Sarnia*. Major works costing £4.25m were required to accommodate her at Portsmouth Continental Ferry Port, including a 200m quay wall, berth dredging to a depth of 6.5m, land reclamation, and a two lane integrated bridge and pontoon linkspan.

The *Island Commodore (III)* left the Islands for last time on 26 September and was sold as a cable-laying vessel for a reported £24m. The *Commodore Clipper* entered passenger service on 18 October, operating a six-day schedule from Portsmouth leaving at 09:30 for Guernsey, where she arrived at 16:00, then on to Jersey for 20:00, before sailing overnight to arrive back in Portsmouth at 06:30. *Commodore Goodwill* operated her freight schedule on the reverse pattern with an evening departure from Portsmouth, returning by day. The *Havelet's* role as back-up vessel was now complete and she was laid up in Weymouth, surplus to requirements. *Condor Vitesse* left Falmouth on 9 November for the 21-day journey to New Zealand to resume her winter charter for Tranz Rail between Wellington and Picton, where she replaced *Condor 10*.

Condor Vitesse and *Condor Express* received praise from the Island authorities for a significant improvement in punctuality and reliability during 1999. Of the 1,172 scheduled crossings between January and September there were no technical cancellations, with thirty-five (three per cent) cancelled due to weather and fifty-nine (five per cent) delayed by more than one hour.

Top: The forward Quiet Lounge with panoramic views on *Commodore Clipper*. *(Ferry Publications Library)*

Bottom: The food service area on board the *Commodore Clipper*. *(Ferry Publications Library)*

The *Condor Vitesse* displays her Incat hull number (44) on the bow and sports both Condor Ferries and Brittany Ferries logos on her hull during her period of operation on the Poole-Cherbourg route. *(Kevin Mitchell)*

The new berth at Portsmouth Continental Ferry Port opened to accommodate the *Commodore Clipper* and *Island Commodore* on 8 March. The old linkspan was then allocated to fast craft use. Condor increased the number of sailings between Poole and St. Malo for the summer 2000 season with an evening departure from Jersey to St. Malo and an 05:00 return crossing, although this reduced the time available for vessel maintenance and repair. *Condor 9* was utilised to operate two round trips daily between St. Malo and Jersey.

The *Havelet* was sold to Prekookeanska Plovidba, the parent company of Montenegro Lines, and she sailed from Weymouth for the last time on 25 August 2000. She was renamed *Sveti Stefan* and allocated to the Bar-Bari service in the Adriatic.

For the summer of 2001 Condor Ferries concluded an operating agreement with Brittany Ferries to run a Poole-Cherbourg fast craft service utilising *Condor Vitesse*. Both companies marketed the vessel, and the Brittany Ferries logo was added to her livery. Known as the *Vitesse* by Brittany Ferries, she became *Normandie Vitesse* from 2005. The service comprised a morning round trip from Poole to Cherbourg, leaving the afternoon for *Condor Vitesse* to operate a Poole–Guernsey–St. Malo round trip on Mondays, Wednesdays and Fridays, and a Poole-Jersey-Poole service on Tuesdays, Thursdays and Saturdays. *Condor Express* remained to focus on the Poole/Weymouth-Channel Islands services and *Condor 9* was utilised on two daily round trips between St. Malo and Jersey.

Condor Ferries set up direct competition for Emeraude Lines' *Solidor 5*, by launching a car carrying service from St. Malo to the Islands in 2002, replacing the passenger-only service operated by *Condor 9*. *Condor 10*, which at the time was laid up in Hobart, was brought back to begin the service, arriving in March. Later in 2002 the Commodore Group, the parent company of the Condor Ferries shareholding, whose subsidiary companies also included Commodore Shipping and Commodore Express, was sold to a management buyout backed by Dutch bank ABN AMRO for €225m with the bank taking the majority

With Brownsea Castle in the background, *Condor Rapide* makes the mandatory slow progress out of Poole Harbour as she approaches Sandbanks in August 2010. *(Kevin Mitchell)*

shareholding. Any semblance of 'local control', so important in the tender process four years previously, was now lost. The year saw passenger carryings on the English routes climb to 548,000, the best performance since 1984.

An economic study for Weymouth and Portland Council in 2002 recorded that Condor made a direct contribution of some £7.73m to the local economy. This included £255k of net income for the council from the harbour, £4.35m in wages to 104 full-time and 255 seasonal staff who lived in the borough, with £1.55m going to local companies for ferry maintenance and a further £1.12m of indirect tourism spend. Councillors were debating a £1.2m proposal to redevelop the ferry terminal prepared by property consultants Donaldsons. But the Council was not in a position to keep Condor in the town at any price.

For Summer 2003, Condor Ferries' corporate identity was renewed, using the same font as that chosen for the Brittany Ferries service in 2002. This was the first year of four in which passenger carryings declined, falling back to 525,000.

The management involvement in the buy-out of the Commodore Group proved short lived but highly lucrative, when the group was sold to the Royal Bank of Scotland venture capital arm for €360m in 2004, representing a profit of €135m in just two years. The entire group was rebranded Condor Ferries and the Commodore name disappeared, albeit retained in ship names. Commodore Express was renamed Condor Logistics, whilst both the *Commodore Goodwill* and the *Commodore Clipper* were repainted with the new Condor Ferries' logo.

Condor 10 sustained damage whilst berthing at the East Berth at Elizabeth Terminal in St. Helier on 24 October 2004; she had been operating on three engines after becoming entangled with a length of rope on leaving St. Malo. She sailed to Guernsey for repair and was out of service until 29 April 2005. Condor lost business across all UK routes in 2004 resulting in a twelve per cent downturn in passenger carryings to 463,000.

The early Easter in 2005 was marked by a period of poor weather. *Condor Express* ran

Condor 10 arrives in St Helier in a revised Condor livery. Note the flags of Guernsey, Jersey and St Malo below her bridge. *(John Downs)*

the Island service until 23 April, when she was replaced by *Condor Vitesse*, but she suffered technical problems and was replaced by *Condor Express* after two days of operation. *Condor Vitesse* returned on 29 April. Condor continued to experience technical issues with both *Condor Vitesse* and *Condor Express*, but *Condor 10* operated well to St. Malo.

In November *Solidor 5* was taken out of service with damaged stabilising foils and sent to Cherbourg for repair. The Board of parent company Sogestran was unable to find a replacement vessel and cancelled all sailings. Financial problems had escalated due to aggressive pricing action by Condor on entering the market, resulting in a loss of €8m in the two years since they took over the company. The result was bankruptcy, leaving Condor Ferries without any car-carrying competition on the French routes. Concerns were raised in the Islands that without any form of States control Condor Ferries could exploit it's near-monopoly of services to raise fares.

2005 saw a 3.9 per cent increase in Condor's inter-island traffic, against a backdrop of a further nineteen per cent fall in business on the UK route to 373,000 passengers, the lowest level since 1967.

Condor experienced a largely trouble-free season in 2006, running from Weymouth only on mid-season Mondays, Tuesdays, Wednesdays and Fridays, adding a Poole-Channel Islands sailing on Thursdays, Saturdays and Sundays, and during the high season. *Condor Vitesse* sailed directly from Poole to Jersey on Sundays, Thursdays and Saturdays, thence to St. Malo, and from Poole to Guernsey then St. Malo on other days. *Condor 10* operated the Jersey-St. Malo link, but volumes were down around fourteen per cent year-on-year. To add to the company's problems, there was a further twelve per cent fall in traffic on the English routes to 330,000 passengers. Condor Ferries replaced their Polish deck and engine crew on Portsmouth route vessels with Ukrainians in an effort to reduce operating costs.

Winter weather conditions forced many cancellations of Condor services in early 2007, and the *Commodore Clipper* was required to offer two additional Sunday sailings to clear the backlog. There were only limited winter sailings between Jersey and St. Malo utilising *Condor 10,* with one round trip sailing on Thursdays, Fridays and Sundays and two on Saturdays.

The States of Jersey had agreed as early as 28 March 2006 that there should be an SLA in place for each passenger and car ferry operator on sea routes to and from Jersey. The Islands' governments worked with the Regional Council of Brittany to find another company to compete on the St. Malo route in the absence of Emeraude Lines. The Jersey Minister for Economic Development signed an SLA with HD Ferries Ltd on 13 March 2007 for services between Jersey, St. Malo and Guernsey for a twelve-month period until 14 March 2008. HD Ferries was a subsidiary of Howe-Davies Transport and Travel Services Company, part of the UK based software specialist 2morrow Group. The SLA was prepared after consultation and HD Ferries were required to maintain a permit for the use of the ro-ro ramps in St. Helier and agree to operate a minimum of one passenger and car carrying ferry.

The chosen vessel was *HD1*, an Incat K-series catamaran with capacity for 400 passengers, capable of 45 knots but restricted by the UK Maritime Coastguard Agency to operate in wave heights less than 2.5m, although 3.4m was approved by the Bahamian authorities, where she was registered. The Jersey Evening Post noted that the Deputy Harbour Master had supported this view, and that 'Condor Ferries had submitted that its rival ship should be restricted to the lower wave height'. Chris Howe Davies of Howe-Davies stated that "commercial pressure from competing operators may have been a factor" in the decision.

The company employed a number of staff from the former Emeraude Lines operation, and set itself a target of 100,000 passengers for the first operating season. Two days after

Relationships between Condor Ferries and HD Ferries were frequently strained; *HD1* overtakes *Commodore Clipper* as they head out of St Peter Port. *Commodore Clipper* has been repainted in the new Condor Ferries livery. *(Gary Bembridge)*

Condor Express on the berth at Poole in September 2012. The linkspan is wide enough to permit the use of two ramps to speed discharge and loading of the vessel. This was to prove an insurmountable obstacle at Weymouth. *(Kevin*

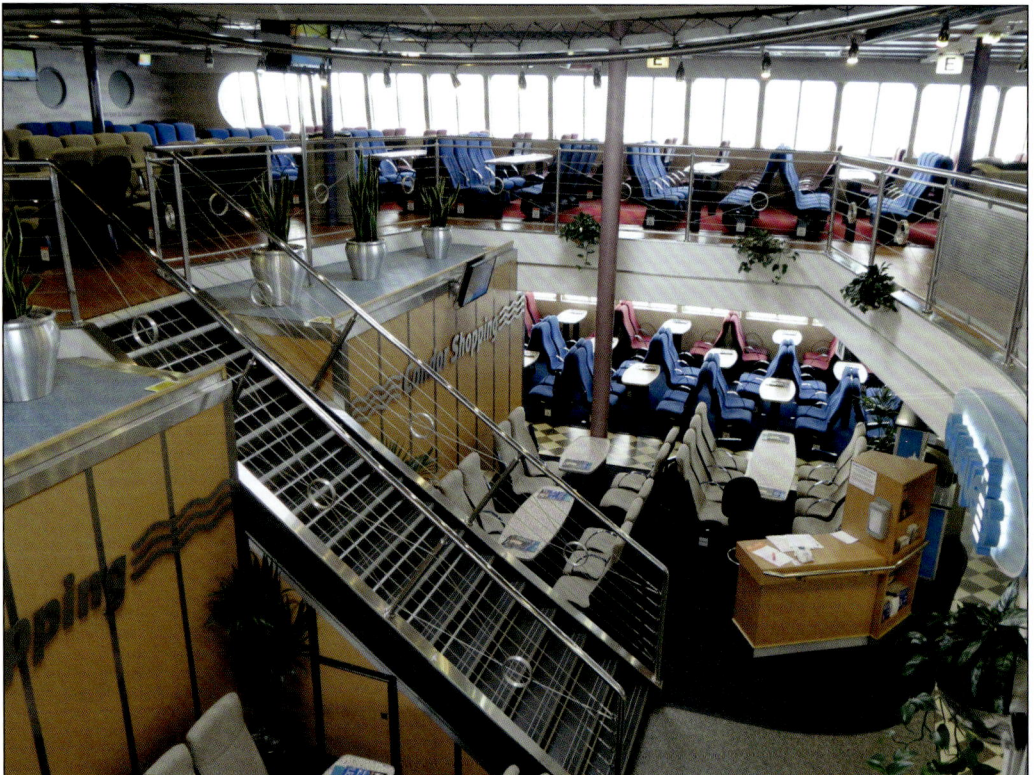

Interior view of the two deck arrangement of passenger accommodation on *Condor Vitesse*. *(Kevin Mitchell)*

Condor 10 at Weymouth with her Condor logos painted out in April 2011. She left Weymouth for Korea in October 2011. *(Kevin Mitchell)*

the SLA was signed, HD Ferries operated their first sailing to St. Malo. *HD1* suffered from an engine failure on her initial departure on 15 March and sailings were cancelled 'for operational reasons' the following day.

On 11 May *HD1* twice attempted to get into the outer harbour at St. Helier in adverse weather, and on the third attempt collided with *Commodore Goodwill* as it was manoeuvering. No passengers were on board at the time. A harbour department pilot was on board the HD ferry, although the *HD1's* master was in control. The ship's master was suspended from duty after the collision while an investigation was carried out.

The difficult first season got worse for HD Ferries at 23:55 on 28 July. *HD1* had planned to berth on the east berth in Elizabeth Harbour, but this was still occupied by *Condor Express,* following delays to her loading operation. The decision to berth at the less suitable west berth was made by the master in conjunction with port control, as this was preferable to waiting outside the harbour during worsening weather conditions. *HD1* had a Jersey pilot on board. Whilst berthing at the west berth *HD1* made contact with the *Condor Express,* which was still loading. There were no reported injuries to passengers or crew of either vessel. *HD1* suffered penetration of the hull on her port side about 0.7m above the waterline, affecting three longitudinal compartments, with distortion of her shell plating and structure in a further two compartments. *Condor Express* sustained superficial damage to her starboard bow but this was deemed not to affect the seaworthiness of the vessel and there was no influx of water. The damage prevented *HD1* from being operated in more than 2m-height waves, and the SLA was suspended for a short period.

Condor Ferries reacted strongly to the two incidents and initiated a public relations battle with a press release on 3 August stating that a 'so-called 'low-cost' company' should not be authorised to provide 'low-secured services'. HD Ferries retaliated, equally strongly, that they would need more than two collisions with Condor Ferries' ships to prevent them from operating low-cost services to France, recalling their wish to set up on a long-term basis.

HD Ferries began sailings to Cherbourg on Mondays and Fridays from 6 August, omitting a planned call in Alderney, but there was a poor public response. The company's woes continued on 16 August when *HD1* collided with a fender at St. Malo and was withdrawn until 25 August for repairs. In September HD Ferries announced that it would not operate the planned winter service citing high fuel costs and the general economic conditions. The States of Jersey responded by indicating that it would be unlikely to grant a ramp licence to HD Ferries again. On 2 October, HD Ferries announced that the company would lodge a complaint against Condor Ferries for libelous remarks in their earlier press release, but this was not followed through. The HD Ferries season finished on 6 November.

Condor Ferries also found the economic circumstances difficult and introduced their autumn schedule earlier than previous years due to poor levels of advance bookings. The *Commodore Goodwill* suffered a bow thruster failure and collided with the entrance to La Collette yacht basin in St. Helier whilst berthing during heavy sea conditions on 10 December. Her starboard propeller and shaft was damaged and the vessel had to be dry docked in Falmouth to enable repairs. Brittany Ferries' *Coutances* was chartered to cover for the *Commodore Goodwill*. The *Commodore Clipper* then collided with newly repaired piles on the new jetty at St. Peter Port whilst docking at No. 2 berth in 40 knot south easterly winds, but suffered little damage. Passenger carryings on the English routes recovered by four per cent by the year-end to 344,000 after four years of decline.

The *Commodore Goodwill* did not return to service until 2 January 2008, but it was soon evident that further repairs were needed and she went to Falmouth for the installation of a new gearbox on 6 February, with the *Triumph* brought in to cover but she had difficulty sustaining the scheduled timings. *Commodore Goodwill* sailed directly from Falmouth to Guernsey to resume sailings on 18 March. *Condor Vitesse* struck the harbour wall when berthing in St. Malo on 22 March, damaging her port side hull aft and holing the vessel. She was sent to Weymouth for permanent repairs, not returning to service until 9 April. Then *Condor Express* experienced engine problems and was out of service for a week from 13 April.

HD Ferries recommenced their St. Malo service on 29 March 2008 with *HD1,* and announced a proposal to establish a link to the UK. They withdrew the Cherbourg service, offering a direct link from Guernsey to St. Malo instead, but this was also was dropped after two months. In May *HD1* carried commercial vehicles for the first time, and HD Ferries invested in a cargo shed in St. Malo to handle this business.

The ownership of Condor Ferries changed hands again on 1 September 2008, when the £4.6bn Macquarie European Infrastructure Fund II (MEIF II) acquired Admiral Holdings, owner of the Condor Group, in a deal approved by the Jersey Competition Regulation Authority. The €390m transaction included both Condor Ferries and the Condor Logistics freight forwarding division. The majority of investors in MEIF 11, which also then owned the Isle of Man Steam Packet Company and Wightlink Isle of Wight Ferries, were described as European pension funds holding long-term investment perspectives. Macquarie viewed the company as a 'mature, essential service business with a leading market position'. Condor Chief Executive Rob Provan said this was "a good deal for the company. The business is stable and it is very important to have owners interested in the long term". There were strong local rumours of cost cutting in the company and a possible withdrawal of vessels. Some 900 staff were employed at the peak of the season, reducing to 600 in the off season. It was pointed out that *Condor Express* was only fully utilised at weekends between May and August. But the next move worked strongly in Condor's favour.

HD Ferries ceased operations on 7 September 2008, giving just four days notice of

Condor Rapide gains speed as she heads out past Old Harry Rocks on leaving Poole Harbour for Guernsey in October 2011. *(Kevin Mitchell)*

Condor Vitesse sported the distinctive 25th Anniversary stripes from 2012, here seen in Weymouth Harbour in July 2013. *(Kevin Mitchell)*

closure. The company blamed rising fuel prices and a lack of business but also claimed that they would return for the 2009 season. Meanwhile *HD1* was sent to Newhaven to be laid up, but was also put up for sale for £10m. It had been a difficult year for all the smaller island operators, as the summer was characterised by bad weather. HD Ferries announced in February 2009 that they would not resume services that summer, citing the size of the passenger market as being insufficient to sustain two companies competing on the French route. The company openly criticised the States of Jersey for failing to provide assistance and create competition in a market dominated by Condor. In the view of the Jersey authorities it was very unlikely that HD Ferries would be granted a ramp permit again, leaving Condor Ferries with a total monopoly. In November 2009 *HD1* was sold to the Korean company Dae A Express Shipping and renamed *Moon Flower*.

Mechanical problems on *Condor 10* resulted in her operating at reduced speed until 1 July 2009, and Condor began to look for a replacement vessel. The season was largely uneventful until the autumn gales arrived. Almost all weekend sailings were lost over an extended period between 28 October and 4 December. On 30 November, for example, *Condor Express*, *Condor Vitesse* and *Condor 10* were all storm-bound in Jersey. Between 22 December 2009 and 2 January 2010 there were no fast craft crossings due to weather conditions, with the service maintained by the *Commodore Goodwill* and *Commodore Clipper*. With a need to increase revenues, Condor Ferries increased the price of a cabin on overnight crossings from £70 to £110. At the same time the company began to recruit more Eastern European staff to replace French and British employees on board their fleet.

Condor introduced *Condor Rapide, a* sister vessel to *Condor Express* and *Condor Vitesse* on 13 May to replace *Condor 10*. She initially replaced *Condor Express,* which had been running the Weymouth service on three engines since the end of March due to a cracked engine block, visiting St. Malo for the first time on 14 May. *Condor Express* went to

Cherbourg for repair, leaving *Condor 10* in service until 2 June, when she returned to Jersey from St. Malo and was sent to Portland to be laid up for sale. At this time both *Condor Express* and *Condor Rapide* were running on three of their four engines. *Condor Express* was repaired on 6 June, and four days later *Condor Rapide* resumed running on four engines.

On 16 June the *Commodore Clipper* was nearing Portsmouth Harbour on a crossing from Jersey when fire broke out on the main vehicle deck. The blaze originated in a refrigerated trailer unit, which was being powered from the ship's electrical supply. The *Commodore Clipper* was able to berth in Portsmouth, but whilst the crew contained the fire they could not extinguish the flames. Given the difficulties of fighting a fire on the vehicle deck, the fire brigade required freight lorries to be removed before attention could be given to passengers, resulting in some having to wait up to twenty hours before disembarking the vessel. The report by the Marine Accident Investigation Branch (MAIB) said berthing at Portsmouth was: -

> 'significantly delayed through ineffective co-ordination between shore agencies and because of equipment defects. Once alongside, the high density of cargo and constraints in the design of the vessel limited access to both fight the fire and to disembark the passengers. As a consequence, freight trailers had to be towed off the vessel before the fire could be extinguished'.

The MAIB was concerned that no single person or organisation had taken responsibility for the whole incident, but the report noted that the Port authorities and Condor Ferries had made operational changes to prevent a similar occurrence.

The summer season saw further operational difficulties for Condor Ferries, with the *Condor Vitesse* operating on three engines for a week in late June, *Condor Express* running on two engines for a short while in late July, and at various times in early August *Condor Vitesse* was experiencing repeated bearing trouble on her port outer engine and *Condor Rapide* was running on three engines. In late August *Condor Express* was transferred to cover the Poole-Cherbourg route for *Condor Vitesse*, which switched to the less intensive Weymouth station. It was clear that the *Condor Vitesse* was in need of significant repairs, so in September *Condor 10* was brought back from her lay up at Portland. *Condor Rapide* also needed a new engine to return to full operational service; she was sent to Portsmouth for major overhaul on 1 November after completing her St. Malo season. *Condor Vitesse* ran between Jersey and St. Malo on three engines at a maximum speed of 23-25 knots until 16 December, when she went to Weymouth for repair. *Condor Express* operated at weekends on the Weymouth service. *Condor Rapide* took over the St. Malo service after her new engine was fitted.

The intensive service was clearly causing fleet reliability problems and Condor Ferries contemplated a full rescheduling of services for the 2011 season. The winter 2011 schedule saw just one weekly fast craft sailing from Weymouth on Saturdays. The *Commodore Clipper* received an extensive internal upgrade in her ten-year survey.

On 28 March 2011, *Condor Vitesse* sailed from St. Malo for St. Helier with 200 passengers on board, at reduced speed because of poor visibility. As weather conditions and visibility improved the vessel accelerated to full speed. Traffic was observed to be minimal and radar sensitivity was particularly good in calm conditions. Less than an hour into the voyage the *Les Marquises* a fishing vessel from Granville, was detected by radar to starboard but went unobserved by the bridge team. *Condor Vitesse* passed the south east Minquiers buoy to port and was between Plateau des Minquiers and Iles Chaussey at 06:42 when she collided with *Les Marquises*. It was not immediately clear what had happened, but a bilge alarm suggested hitting a substantial object. A passenger reported witnessing a collision, and a search and rescue operation began immediately. Visibility was now poor, which hampered the operation.

Condor Vitesse returned to the area of the collision and launched rescue boats, one of which found two survivors from the sinking wreckage. They boarded *Condor Vitesse*, suffering from cold and minor injuries, but the boat's skipper was missing. Another French fishing vessel found him unconscious and injured; he was attended by a volunteer nurse travelling as a passenger on *Condor Vitesse* and then transferred to the Jersey lifeboat, but was later pronounced dead. *Condor Vitesse* continued at slow speed to St. Helier, where the passengers and vehicles were discharged and the vessel taken out of service.

The subsequent Inquiry noted that the 45mph collision split the *Les Marquises* in half, killing Capt. Philippe Lesaulnier, and concluded that the collision occurred because visibility was restricted, the radar lookout on both vessels was ineffective, the speed of *Condor Vitesse* was probably too fast for the conditions, and the level of alertness in watch keeping lapsed as she left the restrictions of the St. Malo approach channel.

Capt. Le Romancer and First Officer Tournon were later charged with manslaughter and received 18-month and 12-month suspended sentences respectively from a court in Coutances. The trial heard that an investigation by France's BEA maritime authority found the pair had been having 'almost continuous conversations unconnected with the operations of the vessel'. They were ordered to pay £6,800 in damages to the fishing boat captain's widow, £2,550 to each of his children and £1,700 to each of the other two surviving fishermen who had been on the boat. Condor Ferries did not face prosecution. The Coutances prosecutor appealed, suggesting that the sentences were not severe enough. But after doubts were raised as to whether or not the radar on *Condor Vitesse* was functioning correctly, Tournon's sentence was overturned. Le Romancer's conviction was upheld.

Condor Express ran on two engines between St. Malo and Jersey after a fishing line became entangled in her engines on 4 April. She was out of service for five days, but further engine problems saw her not running on normal services until 2 May. Meanwhile the Brittany Ferries insignia was removed from *Condor Vitesse*.

Both States Authorities expressed concerns over the reliability of the three Incat craft and threatened Condor with a licence review if they could not be improved. To balance this view, they praised the *Commodore Clipper* for the improved on board service following her overhaul. After a difficult spring period the summer season proved largely uneventful, with few operational problems. The new operating pattern, which increased Poole sailings to 242, proved more successful for Condor Ferries than in 2010 and passenger numbers on the English routes grew by five per cent to 369,000, the third consecutive year of growth. Weymouth remained the dominant port with 228,000 passengers; it had consistently been the busiest English port since 2005. There was often congestion in Jersey, as three vessels, including the *Commodore Clipper*, were scheduled to arrive within minutes of each other.

Condor 10 was sold to Korean interests in October and sailed from Weymouth for her 5,000-mile delivery voyage. *Condor Rapide* again suffered engine problems during the autumn and sailings were disrupted by severe gales.

In February 2012 large cracks were found appearing in the quayside at Weymouth, forcing all high-speed services to operate from Poole whilst £4m of repairs were carried out. All three Condor Ferries craft were back in service over the Easter weekend, but between 18 and 25 April all fast sailings were cancelled due to bad weather, with traffic transferred to the *Commodore Clipper*. *Condor Rapide* operated on the St. Malo-Jersey-Guernsey run until 9 May, when she alternated on the service with *Condor Express*.

Condor Express has a variation of the 25th Anniversary stripes applied to her hull in 2013, with blue replacing the yellow stripe on *Condor Vitesse*. *(Kevin Mitchell)*

It was reported in April that Ukrainian crew members employed by Condor Ferries were paid £2.35/hour. The company defended this position by saying staff received other benefits, and stressed that freight rates would rise if these wages were increased. The RMT trade union began a lengthy campaign to draw attention to these low wages, and initiated a series of protest rallies in Portsmouth.

Condor Ferries celebrated the 25th anniversary of their cross-channel services in 2012. *Condor Vitesse* was repainted with three coloured stripes - yellow, red and blue - added to her livery, with the figure "25" inscribed on her bow. She was welcomed into St. Helier by a water cannon salute from the States tug *Duke of Normandy* on 11 April. On board was Capt. Dumont, who took the first sailing from Weymouth on 10 April 1987.

The positive mood was enhanced by an improvement in performance between April and June, when Condor Ferries operated 1,312 sailings across their network; forty-six sailings were lost on the northern route representing seventy per cent of all lost sailings. Eighty-five per cent of all sailings arrived within fifteen minutes of schedule. Ninety-nine per cent of conventional ferry sailings operated on time. The summer was to prove to be a generally trouble free season. In July *Condor Vitesse* was taken out of service for engine repairs, but the August bank holiday weekend saw a forty-nine per cent increase in Condor bookings over 2011.

The closure of the Condor Logistics operation was announced on 4 October, following changes to low value consignment tax relief which affected many Channel Islands freight businesses. There were 110 job losses in the UK, fifty in Jersey and twenty in Guernsey. The road haulage arm of the business was sold to Paul Davis Haulage from 1 January 2013. After a period of growth passenger carryings fell by six per cent in 2012 to 346,000, precipitated by the forced withdrawal from the Weymouth, the port of choice for the majority of passengers.

Brittany Ferries decided not to renew the joint Poole-Cherbourg service in 2013. However, the company continued to provide stevedores to handle the weekly *Commodore Clipper* summer call in Cherbourg.

In January 2013, James Fulford was appointed CEO of Condor Ferries and announced a

Commodore Goodwill (FotoFlite)

Condor Express shorn of her Condor Ferries logos in anticipation of her sale to Seajets, leaves Weymouth with the 13.30 sailing to Guernsey on 23 March 2015 - the last commerical departure from Weymouth. *(Kevin Mitchell)*

thorough review of operations from the UK to fully understand the business requirements of all parties. Maintenance costs of the three fast craft were reported to be of order of £5m per year, and the company stated that any future fleet investment would require to be underpinned by a long term operating agreement with the Island authorities. Meanwhile both *Condor Express* and *Condor Rapide* were repainted with a similar scheme to the *Condor Vitesse's* anniversary livery. The yellow stripe on *Condor Vitesse* was replaced in blue on *Condor Express* and green on *Condor Rapide*.

Winter conditions caused problems for the *Commodore Goodwill* whilst approaching the berth in St. Peter Port on 6 February. A sudden squally increase in wind to around 45 knots blew the ship hard to the south. The master elected to turn the vessel outside the port but as he decided to abort the manoeuver the combined effects of wind and inshore tidal flow forced the vessel against the Castle Cornet Breakwater. A subsequent check by the crew confirmed that there was no water ingress, and the *Commodore Goodwill* proceeded to St. Helier, where more detailed examinations were undertaken.

The completion of eighteen months of work to repair the quay wall at Weymouth allowed Condor Ferries to resume services from the port on 17 July 2013. Upgrade work comprised re-piling of the 1930s quayside with steel sheeting capped with concrete and new fenders, with the former Sealink linkspan refurbished, although it was still not wide enough to handle the twin stern ramps of a fast craft. Scour protection was laid on the seabed to counter the forces from the ship's water jet. The car ferry terminal was renovated, with a bistro and coffee shop added to the facilities. Both Islanders and the Weymouth catchment population welcomed the return of the service, and Condor Ferries noted an increase in business. The Company raised confidence by talk of the purchase of a new vessel to operate from the port to replace both *Condor Express* and *Condor Vitesse*. The transfer to Poole had cost Condor Ferries a reported additional £1m in fuel costs based on the extra thirty minutes passage time.

After carrying freight to and from the Islands for almost eighty years, latterly with a two-ship lo-lo operation from Southampton and Cherbourg to Jersey, Guernsey and Alderney using the *Huelin Dispatch* and the *Huelin Endeavour*, and being prime shareholders in Channel Island Ferries, Huelin Renouf filed for bankruptcy on 22 August resulting in the loss of nearly 100 jobs.

Condor Vitesse was withdrawn for repairs at the end of the season on 14 October. Reports began to circulate that Condor Ferries was interested in purchasing a new £50m prototype trimaran vessel that had been launched in January 2010 at the Austal yard in Henderson, Australia as the *Austal 102*, but for which no buyer had been found. In November Condor Ferries launched their 2014-15 timetable, allowing passengers to book up to 16 months in advance of travel for the first time. A commitment to Weymouth was made clear in the sailing schedule.

Condor Ferries signed an 'option to purchase' contract for the *Austal 102* in January 2015, set at ten per cent of the vessel value. Austal expected to complete the transaction in the first half of the year, substantially reducing the debt on their books and eliminating the holding costs of the vessel. From Condor Ferries' perspective the investment was justified by making financial savings through reducing the UK-based fleet from two to one fast craft, but the Macquarie Fund required a long-term user agreement with the Island authorities as a prerequisite to capital investment. Given the track record of fast craft operation, the new vessel would need to operate with a higher degree of reliability than her predecessors if she was to be the sole craft on the UK routes. Negotiations with the Islands were protracted and put back the transaction date, leading to pressure from Condor on the States to permit them to meet a June deadline.

Bad weather in January and February 2014 saw many sailings cancelled. On 6 February Condor employees on *Condor Rapide* went on strike in St. Malo. The crew raised the Breton flag and demanded the Bahamian registered vessel be transferred to the French register. All sailings from St. Malo were cancelled, with passengers forced to travel via the UK. Sailings did not resume until 19 February, with the company stating not only had it lost £500k through the action, but also that it did not have the funds to meet employees' demands.

As Condor considered consolidation of their UK operation, it became clear that Weymouth was unable to handle the proposed new craft without significant investment. Although the No. 3 berth had been rebuilt, Condor rejected using this for a larger vessel, favouring the No. 1 berth. But this required a £10m investment to accommodate the twin stern doors of the larger vessel, and the Council did not have these resources available. The Dorset Echo emotively accused Condor of holding Weymouth to ransom by threatening to abandon the port and move operations elsewhere, and launched a petition calling on Condor to show their support for the town. Council executives met with the Transport Secretary in an attempt to secure government funding for the works to No. 1 berth, but this was not forthcoming.

In an extended interview with the Dorset Echo on 9 June 2014, James Fulford said that the company was looking to upgrade its vessels and invest in a safe, efficient and up-to-date fleet to keep the Channel Islands connected and supplied into the future. He noted that *Condor Express* was launched in 1996 and *Condor Vitesse* in 1997, and they were coming to the end of their lives. Condor was looking to buy a £50m 102m high-speed trimaran that would have twenty per cent more capacity, offer a far more comfortable ride and be able to sail in adverse weather to replace the existing vessels. However investor

Commodore Clipper offers additional passenger capacity covering for the stricken *Condor Liberation* during a rare visit to Poole on 31 March 2016. *(Kevin Mitchell)*

funding to buy the new ferry could only be unlocked if Condor received the certainty of a new Channel Islands operating licence. A decision on this agreement, which was anticipated to last up to ten years, was expected at the end of June. If successful, the new ferry would begin sailings from Easter 2015, replacing the dual sailings from Weymouth and Poole. Berth No. 1 near the Weymouth Harbour entrance was the only suitable location for the new ferry. Whilst Portland had been considered it was discounted due to the constraints of the road network.

The *Commodore Clipper* grounded on a charted, rocky shoal in the approaches to St. Peter Port at 15:15 on 14 July. The grounding caused a noisy, shuddering vibration that reverberated throughout the ship, but the crew did not check for damage, no external report was made and no safety announcements were made to the passengers. The vessel continued its passage into the harbour. Once alongside in St. Peter Port, cargo discharge, reloading and a lifeboat drill went ahead as planned. However, a pre-planned diver's inspection of the hull discovered damage including significant raking and breaches of the hull, resulting in flooding of double-bottom void spaces forcing the *Commodore Clipper* to be withdrawn from service. The *Toucan* was chartered in her place from 29 July and made her initial call in St. Peter Port, leaving the *Commodore Goodwill* to focus on traffic to and from Jersey.

The subsequent MAIB investigation concluded that the bridge team did not appreciate the navigational risk at very low tide, the accuracy of chart data, and the effect of the ship 'squatting' in shallow water at speed. The electronic navigation system was not being utilised effectively because safety settings were not appropriate to the local conditions, warnings were ignored and the audible alarm was disabled, leading to the crew not acknowledging that the ship might have grounded. The report noted that the repetitive nature of ferry operations could induce a degree of complacency when planning regular journeys. As the responsible authority, Guernsey Harbours did not have an effective risk assessment or safety management plan for the conduct of navigation in its statutory pilotage area. Condor Ferries fully accepted the findings of the report and chartered the *Arrow* from the Isle of Man Steam Packet Company to provide additional cover for the *Commodore Clipper* from 2 August until she returned to service on the 24th.

A new ten-year operating licence was agreed between Condor Ferries and the Jersey authorities on 31 July, as a precursor to investment in the *Austal 270* craft. The non-exclusive operating licence allowed the company to operate passenger, vehicle and freight services until 2024. The Guernsey government also agreed to extend a 'memorandum of understanding' with Condor until 2024, but the Jersey authorities negotiated a 'get-out' clause that could be enacted after seven years if expectations were not being met. Both governments agreed not to pro-actively seek an alternative provider to Condor Ferries for the provision of ro-ro services to the Islands. The two governments agreed a common aim for sea links, namely: -

'To maintain and develop year round, long-term, reliable, robust and reasonably priced roll on/roll off passenger, car and freight ferry services. These services should be of sufficient quality and frequency to meet the travel needs of Island residents, the business community and tourists'.

The agreement divided services between the Northern Route to Portsmouth, Poole and Weymouth, and the Southern Route to St. Malo. The strategically important Northern Route was seen both as the Islands' main freight supply and logistics link for the 'just in time' economy and for the visitor economy and local residents. The Southern Route made a substantial contribution to Jersey's visitor economy and a smaller, but valuable contribution to Guernsey's as well as providing local residents with lifestyle and leisure opportunities. The Islands' requirements were not expected to substantially change in the foreseeable future, although achieving growth, particularly in the leisure market, was an ongoing aim. The Islands' needs were, therefore, best served through a service network delivered via a combination of vessels with the capability to provide the 'Designated Services'. The agreement laid down specific requirements in respect of journey times, frequency, and capability. The specification comprised: -

Northern Route
Freight: five sailings per week using a vessel capable of operating (including port manoeuvering) in at least 40 knot winds and at least 3.5m significant wave height and with adequate external power for at least 40 refrigerated vehicles

Passenger and vehicle: seven sailings per week in peak season, two in winter, with a journey time of no longer than five hours (including intermediate port call) using a vessel capable of operating in at least 3.5m significant wave height, with the provider licensed under the pet passport scheme

Ro-pax: five sailings per week with one rotation per 24 hours, using a vessel capable of operating (including port manoeuvering) in at least 40 knot winds and at least 3.5m significant wave height, with the provider licensed under the pet passport scheme. The ro-pax sailings are additional to the Freight sailings and cannot be satisfied by one sailing covering both Sectors. The vessel provides 'lifeline' services for the Channel Islands in the event of bad weather or other material disruption to normal scheduling and must be certified to carry in the order of 400 passengers and be able to power in the order of 40 refrigerated vehicles

Southern Route
St. Malo-Jersey: twelve sailings per week in peak season, three in winter, with a journey time of no longer than 1.5 hours using a vessel capable of operating in at least 3.5m significant wave height, with the provider licensed under the pet passport scheme

St. Malo-Guernsey: seven sailings per week in peak season, two in winter, with a journey time of no longer than 2.5 hours for direct sailings using a vessel capable of operating in at least 3.5m significant wave height, with the provider licensed under the pet passport scheme

The pattern of traffic between the markets showed that Northern Route Freight and Vehicles were split sixty per cent Jersey to forty per cent Guernsey, and passengers were split fifty-four per cent Jersey to forty-six per cent Guernsey. Southern Route Vehicles were split eighty per cent Jersey to twenty per cent Guernsey, and passengers were split seventy-eight per cent Jersey to twenty-two per cent Guernsey. Inter-Island traffic comprised approximately 10,000 cars and 100,000 passengers, but the split of service between Northern and Southern routes left this traffic in limbo.

A report by Frontier Economics for the States of Guernsey justified the newagreement on the basis that: -

- The ro-ro market to the Islands was small, and implementing different arrangement by both Islands would preclude economies of scale for the operator
- The operation of unprofitable routes was supported through cross-subsidies from profitable activities
- The Jersey agreement included price regulation, minimum frequencies and quality standards
- A joint approach between the Islands improved the bargaining position with Condor
- The long standing relationship between Condor and the Islands created informal but significant mechanisms that could mitigate the scope of opportunistic behaviours which might be missing in the case of other operators.

With the sought after agreement in place, Condor Ferries was able to announce the long anticipated £50m purchase of the Austal 102m craft on 20 August, to replace *Condor Express* and *Condor Vitesse*. This brought bad news for Weymouth, with Condor announcing the transfer of all services to Poole from spring 2015. James Fulford was quoted as saying: -

"I am delighted to announce that we are now proud owners of the *Austal 102*. This represents £50m of investment in our Island services and it will enable us to improve reliability, increase capacity, and give our guests a much greater level of comfort. We plan to introduce the 102 in spring 2015 and, in the months ahead, we will be sharing more details about this superb new ship and announcing ways in which Islanders can be involved in our preparations. Poole is a modern and well-connected port, well liked by our customers. We recognise that this is disappointing news for Weymouth. However, given the need for berth improvements and an Environmental Impact Assessment, Weymouth is not currently in a position to accommodate the 102. Reaching a medium-term arrangement with Poole will give certainty to our

Condor Liberation heads out of Poole Harbour during trials on 26 March 2015. She entered service the next day. *(Kevin Mitchell)*

Condor Liberation leaves St Peter for St Helier in September 2017. The *Europa II* is berthed in the Roads, with passengers coming ashore by tender. *(Author)*

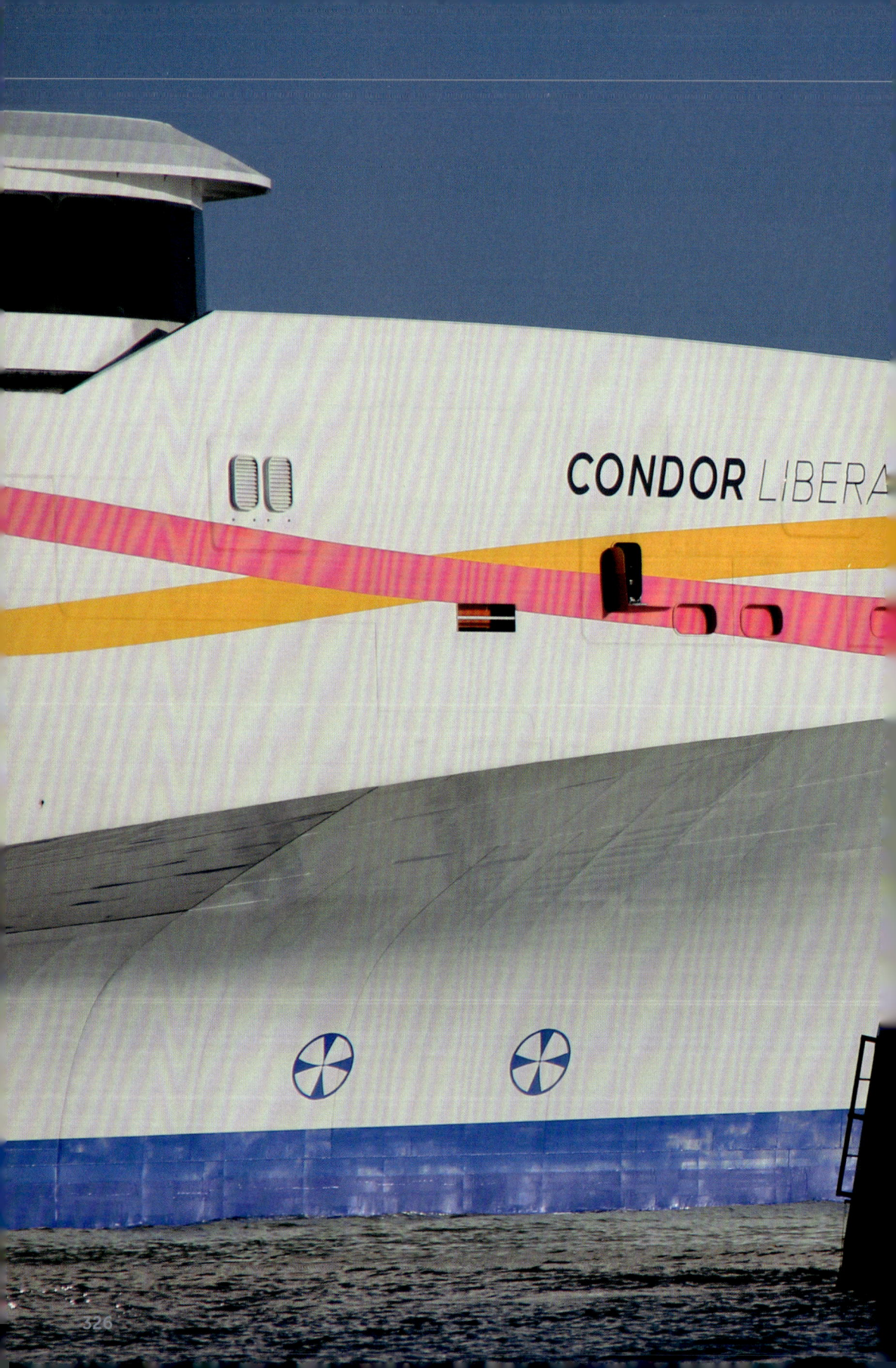

The *Condor Liberation* catches the winter light in December 2016. As a trimaran, her centre hull distinguishes her from previous car carriers in the Condor fleet. *(Kevin Mitchell)*

customers, our Islands, and Poole Harbour Commissioners, while also allowing enough time for Weymouth & Portland Borough Council to establish their long-term plans for their port".

Publication of the 2015 sailing schedule began an intense programme of promotion for the new vessel, now known as the *Condor 102*. Alicia Andrews, Executive Director-Commercial for Condor Ferries was quoted as saying that the new craft would: -

"deliver a whole new on board experience, as well as more comfortable and more reliable travel for passengers sailing to and from the Channel Islands. Passengers will also be able to enjoy day trips to Guernsey and Jersey, with early morning departures from Poole - as well as Inter-Island trips allowing visitors to explore the beauty of both Islands during their stay. It is the Islands sailings which will really capture passengers' imaginations; from the end of March, all journeys to the Channel Islands will be on the new *Condor 102* from Poole, which offers smoother journeys, greater reliability and a superb on board experience including a wider choice of seating, a range of dining, and even shopping facilities for our passengers to enjoy. We are all very excited about the arrival of the *Condor 102* and I'm sure that our passengers will love sailing to the Channel Islands on our new ship."

Condor 102 would offer a choice of three seat classes: *Ocean Traveller* with assigned airline-style seats in an open lounge with access to on board dining and shopping; *Ocean Traveller Plus* in a private lounge with a bar and either airline-style reclining seats or table seating and at-seat charging facilities; and *Ocean Club* in a private lounge with at-seat service and leather reclining seats with tables, and at-seat charging facilities. An outdoor deck area, children's play area, Bureau de Change and range of shopping outlets, including Duty Free completed the facilities. The company stated that the new ship would be more stable than her Incat predecessors, with a capability of operating in higher wave heights. It was claimed that ninety per cent of the 2014 weather-related cancellations would be avoided with the new craft. However Chief Executive James Fulford would not oversee her introduction, as he resigned on 8 September 2014 after eighteen months in the role.

The pre-publicity paid off when tickets for 2015 went on sale on 28 November, the busiest day on record for the Condor Ferries reservations team.

Condor 102 left the Philippines on her delivery voyage on 4 December and arrived in Poole on the 26th to be fitted out by Trimline to Condor Ferries' requirements. The company wasted no time in arranging for the disposal of the *Condor Express* and the *Condor Vitesse*, which were sold to the Greek company Seajets for a reported €9m on 14 January 2015. The *Condor Express* returned to Weymouth following refit at A&P Falmouth on 30 January.

Condor Ferries launched a competition in the Islands to name the *Condor 102*; *Condor Liberation* was selected to commemorate the events of 9 May 1945. New branding was also unveiled, with a core identity based around dark blue, pink and gold. A new Safety Video was recorded in collaboration with the Bournemouth-based Walker Agency; the 'Safety Rap' aimed to provide safety and security information in a creative way, and capture the attention of those who ignored the traditional announcement. However the clip went viral and was ridiculed on social media, and raised public concerns about taking safety seriously, before being withdrawn.

The *Arrow* again substituted for the *Commodore Goodwill* from 2 March during her annual overhaul at Falmouth, and was retained to cover rudder repairs to the *Commodore Clipper*.

The revised stripe livery applied to **Condor Liberation** is shown to good effect as she arrives in St Helier in October 2017. *(Author)*

Sea trials for *Condor Liberation* commenced on 10 March and on the 20th she was named in Guernsey. Three days later *Condor Express* closed the Weymouth service when she arrived back at 23:00 from Guernsey. Some Condor facilities, including the Call Centre, remained until the end of August, when all company operations moved to Poole.

The inaugural sailing of *Condor Liberation* took place on 27 March. The following day she sailed from Poole, bound for Guernsey and Jersey. At 12:52, following completion of the arrival checklist, she was positioned for berthing on No. 2 linkspan at St. Peter Port but gusty conditions forced her to abandon a first attempt to berth and the vessel was repositioned in safe water between the Pier Heads. Permission was gained to berth on No. 2 berth, and the Senior Master planned to back round the turning dolphin at the southern end of No. 1 linkspan, to gain as much distance upwind as possible. The wind gusted to 32 knots as *Condor Liberation* came astern, but the vessel began to set heavily towards the berth once the bow had cleared the dolphin. The Senior Master took evasive action to land the vessel parallel on the berth and across multiple fenders. This was almost achieved but the ship landed heavily on a cylindrical vertical piling. There were no injuries and the vessel remained in a safe condition. Although the damage was small, the hull was breached and *Condor Liberation* had to be taken out of service for a week for repair, but fortunately *Condor Express* was still available. She later collided with the pier at Poole, whilst berthing in windy conditions. The vessel's crew was subsequently cleared of any blame, with unsuitable berth fendering being a contributory factor to the accident.

The incident could not have happened at a worse time in the run up to the busy Easter weekend. *Arrow* was again chartered on 30 March to relieve pressure on *Commodore Clipper,* which operated a Channel Islands-Poole-Channel Islands rotation for the first time on the 31st. On Good Friday, 2 April, *Condor Express* operated a double rotation from Poole, but could not match the planned capacity of *Condor Liberation*.

Condor Liberation returned to service on Easter Sunday, 4 April, after some 6,000 passengers had been disrupted by her absence. *Condor Express* was sent to Weymouth for

The **Arrow** has been sub-chartered from the Isle of Man Steam Packet Company on several occasions to provide cover for freight services. She is now contracted to continue this arrangement on a longer term basis. *(Andrew Cooke)*

lay up. However the problems continued on 11 April when *Condor Liberation* was unable to load twenty-four cars and sixty passengers in St. Helier due to late running and a technical problem with a section of hoistable deck. Embarrassingly, her sailings on Liberation Day, 9 May, were cancelled due to bow thrust issues. By May Condor confirmed that ten per cent of sailings had been cancelled and only sixty per cent had run to schedule. The company announced that it would fund a review of the operation of the *Condor Liberation* in order to assure its customers of her suitability for service to the Islands. But there was to be no further fast craft support as *Condor Express* left Weymouth as the *Champion Jet 2* on 18 May to be reunited with her sister in Greece.

In the peak season Condor proposed daily sailings of *Condor Liberation* on the Northern Route and, where demand commercially viability justified it, a double rotation on Mondays, Fridays and Saturdays. These double rotations allowed boarding for passengers to start from 01:00, and basic sleeping arrangements were offered on the sailing to Guernsey. But it was optimistic to expect that an 03:00 departure time would prove attractive for a fast craft crossing.

	Arrive	Depart	Arrive	Depart
Poole		03:00		14:00
Guernsey	06:00	06:30	17:00	17:30
Jersey	07:30	08:30	18:30	19:30
Guernsey	09:30	10:00	20:30	21:00
Poole	13:00		23:59	

The problems with *Condor Liberation* continued across the summer, with technical issues and weather conditions forcing repeated delays and cancellations. Condor Ferries urged the public 'to refrain from intimidation' following social media complaints about staff, who were bearing the brunt of public anger about her performance.

The independent Holder Report commissioned by Condor Ferries concluded that, whilst the maximum level of heel measured on the *Condor Liberation* during rolling could be disconcerting, it posed no threat to the safety of passengers. The rolling was deemed less frequent than that experienced in similar sea conditions on earlier catamarans, but the angle of heel was greater. The maximum amount of heel recorded during a near gale was 15.5 degrees from horizontal. The report noted that punctuality issues were related more to loading and discharge procedures to achieve the published schedule, than sailing in adverse weather conditions.

On 20 October *Condor Liberation* visited St. Malo for berthing trials. There were more sailing cancellations during the autumn for repair work and on 31 December *Condor Liberation* was hit by the 63 mph winds of Storm Frank whilst moored in Poole Harbour and pierced her hull, forcing more sailings cancellations. She received an extended refit at A&P Falmouth between 13 January and 11 February 2016 and the *Condor Rapide* provided a replacement service outside gales.

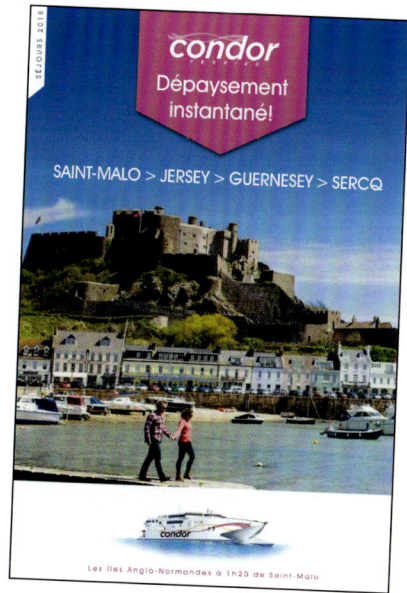

The number of sea passengers on the Northern routes to the Islands in 2015 fell by thirteen per cent to 302,000. Guernsey experienced a serious fall in day visitors of over thirty-seven per cent to 25,100.

In an attempt to ease the burden on *Condor Liberation*, Condor Ferries withdrew her planned double rotations for the 2016 summer season, citing the unpopular early departure time, and the knock on delays to schedules if the craft began to run late. The return to traffic of *Condor Liberation* was plagued by further technical problems ranging from bow thruster failure to filter pump issues, with a succession of sailing cancellations and late arrivals. Between 27 and 29 February all *Condor Liberation* sailings were cancelled with traffic transferred to the *Commodore Clipper,* and *Condor Rapide* operated inter-island services. To add to the pressure on the company, the *Commodore Clipper* suffered a failure to the hoistable ramp to the upper deck on 27 February, stranding vehicles for twelve hours after berthing in Portsmouth at 07:00. Cars were craned off the ramp, which was restored at 20:00. She resumed service on 29 February.

Condor Rapide was overhauled at A&P Falmouth from 1 to 23 March and *Condor Liberation* substituted, including making empty runs from St. Malo to Jersey, where she berthed overnight. The patience of the States was being tested. On 8 March Condor Ferries was given two weeks to issue a plan to improve their service, following breaches of the operating agreement. The following day, the Jersey Chief Minister met with representatives of Macquarie and Condor Ferries to discuss the problems. A similar meeting was sought in Guernsey. Things got worse on 15 March when *Condor Liberation* was halted over safety concerns. Maritime and Coastguard Agency (MCA) staff visited the vessel in Poole and detained her 'after substantial deficiencies were observed by inspectors'. Condor said their operating schedule would be disrupted 'for at least part of the weekend' due to the requirement for re-inspections. It added that engineers were rectifying faults and working on the trimaran's propulsion and steering systems. With *Condor Rapide* away on refit, alternative sailings could only be offered on the *Commodore Clipper* whilst repairs were made. This necessitated a charter of the *Arrow* from 18 March to free the limited space on the *Commodore Clipper* for passenger traffic. On 19 March *Condor Liberation* was cleared to return to service and on the 24th *Condor Rapide* returned from refit.

But the problems did not go away. Between 27 and 28 March Storm Katie brought more

Condor Rapide backs on to her berth in St Peter Port in September 2017. *(Author)*

cancellations over Easter for *Condor Liberation,* and the vessel was damaged on her berth at Poole. Consideration was given to chartering the *Normandie Express* from Brittany Ferries for five days over Easter to act as cover, but the complex administrative requirements involved in setting up a short notice operation prevented the deal being completed in time. Then from 10 to 20 April there were more delays and cancellations of *Condor Liberation* sailings due to problems with the ride control system and engine issues.

Guernseyman Paul Luxon was appointed as CEO of Condor on 1 May. An experienced businessman and politician, he was then Chair of the Jersey Hospitality Association Strategy Group and Minister for the Health and Social Services Department.

In June 2016, Condor Ferries confirmed that patronage on the Northern Route was still decreasing as passengers sought alternative services to *Condor Liberation.* In July Guernsey experienced a twenty-two per cent drop in sea passengers, with Jersey suffering a twenty per cent fall. Sailings of *Condor Liberation* were lost to fuel pump and fuel system faults across the summer. She went to Falmouth for overhaul between 10 November and 9 December. The year ended with mixed results. A dramatic fall in passengers of sixteen per cent to 255,000 on the Northern route overshadowed improvements in reliability and punctuality. 97.9 per cent of all sailings operated, of which 85.6 per cent were within thirty minutes of the scheduled time of arrival, compared with 96.1 per cent and 82.3 per cent respectively in 2015. Paul Luxon said the figures clearly demonstrated the continued resilience of the services. However including freight sailings within these punctuality statistics masked the performance of *Condor Liberation.*

Two significant anniversaries were marked in 2017. Condor celebrated seventy years of providing lifeline freight services to the Islands from the UK. From the inaugural service of Commodore Cruises Ltd in September 1947 the company steadily maintained and adapted its business, whilst the competitive mix changed around it. It now carries eighty per cent of all supplies from the UK, including a mix of temperature-controlled products, heavy and large consignments, unaccompanied cars and passengers. Their reliability is such that businesses can operate on a 'just in time' basis, obviating the need for Island warehouse accommodation. The freight services rarely make the headlines, except when extreme weather disrupts the schedule and creates shortages in the Island shops.

It was thirty years since Condor began their regular passenger service from Weymouth in competition with BCIF. Condor Ferries celebrated this on 28 April 2017, noting that since then they had carried over 14 million passengers and 2.7 million cars, and sailed 5.7 million miles, equivalent to circumnavigating the world 229 times. The company makes a significant contribution to the local economy by employing over 550 people on board its ferries, in its contact centre and in the port operations teams, some of whom had been with the company since the first sailing. Condor has fought hard to protect its monopoly when under threat, and the SLA requirement makes it very difficult for competitors to establish a rival operation.

At the start of the Condor monopoly in 1994 the passenger volume to the Islands stood at 436,000, a fall of some 95,000 from the final year of competition with BCIF, and under half the peak level of 890,000 achieved in 1980. By 2017 this had fallen to 254,000, down forty-two per cent from 1994, and over seventy-one per cent since 1980. The service has adapted to the falls in volume by reducing passenger capacity. The summer 2018 schedule offered space for 1,180 passengers daily in each direction, compared to the 4,050 offered by Channel Island Ferries and Sealink British Ferries in 1987.

Condor Freight continues to underpin the passenger business and has allowed the company to continue operations through the difficult times since the introduction of *Condor Liberation*. The contrast between the reliability of freight services and unpredictability of passenger sailings is stark and it is unclear where the future ownership of Condor Ferries will lie as the Macquarie Fund is wound up. Whatever happens, the future of sea travel to the Channel Islands is unlikely to be as colourful as the past.

A spectacular night-time shot of the **Commodore Goodwill** on her berth in St Peter Port. *(Condor Ferries)*

Commodore Clipper (FotoFlite)

CHAPTER THIRTEEN
Looking back

L ooking back over two centuries of services to the Channel Islands it is easy to conclude that the story is one punctuated by disaster and operational problems. In reality the vast majority of sailings passed unrecorded and without incident, with professional and dedicated crews ensuring a safe passage despite the challenging nature of the sea passage. Yet the Island services have experienced a far higher rate of shipping casualties than comparable services around the British Isles. Most of these were on the southbound journey, where the scope for becoming disorientated in inclement conditions amid the rocky hazards presented by Island geography was at its greatest. It is remarkable how few accidents there were, given the paucity of navigation aids available to crews until comparatively recently. For the bulk of this story masters set sail without any form of echo sounding, radar, radio, or satellite navigation system. Direction finding by means of patent logs, engine revolutions and primitive compasses in some of the most challenging maritime geography in the world placed immense strain on crews for many decades. Advances in navigational aids lagged far behind those in engine technology, ship design and passenger facilities. Accidents still happen, even with the advanced technology of the modern age, and there is no room for complacency even on the most routine and repetitive of trips

The services have been maintained by monopoly providers for most of their history. Periods of competition consistently proved unsustainable, and whilst this often brought a short-term benefit for users there was invariably a poorer service when it ceased. The privatisation of Sealink led to a decade of turmoil and change, with the railway monopoly broken, a race to be the lowest cost operator and the choice of English port changing frequently. For almost 120 years there was little change in the choice of routes available for travel to the Islands, but now neither of the historic links from Weymouth or Southampton is maintained, having been stalwarts of the service for so long. And the passenger market has declined to the extent that there is only room for one operator.

To their credit the railway companies upheld a long track record of investment and rapid provision of alternative tonnage when services to the Islands were disrupted, despite the limited profit potential, and the routes were loss-making for much of their life. The Great Western belatedly invested at Weymouth to challenge the L&SWR and was rewarded with a dominant market share. Replacement tonnage was provided by the Great Western and Southern after their fleets suffered during wartime conditions; British Railways eventually invested heavily to try and achieve financial stability. There was a corporate dedication to maintaining the service, no matter what the operational challenges, without any form of subsidy or SLA to protect services, and fleet investment had no financial protection.

Political involvement in the running of services is a relatively recent phenomenon. Privatisation of railway shipping services by the UK government left the Islands exposed to the vagaries of private enterprise. The States' stood back during the battle between Sealink British Ferries and Channel Island Ferries, and again when BCIF faced Condor, and let the market deliver a dramatic reduction in capacity. When the routes were opened up to competitive tender in 1998 the States preferred the status quo of a 'local' company, believing that established international operators could not better the Condor product. It did not take long for the Island interests to sell out to more remote institutions. This marked a fundamental change from 200 years of service ownership by transport specialists to control by financiers. Condor is likely to have another owner in the coming years, but the track record of the *Condor Liberation* may make this a difficult sale. Close links to Island shareholders are long gone.

The aversion to risk of financial undertakings requires them to seek the kind of

The paths of and inbound *Earl William* and outbound *Caledonian Princess* crossing at Noirmont Point. (*Ambrose Greenway*)

The *Earl Godwin* in her classic Sealink livery prior to privatisation. The end of railway ownership of shipping services in 1984 was to precipitate a decade of competition and change. *(Ferry Publications Library)*

Whilst British Railways and Sealink were able to provide relief vessels from within their fleets, BCIF and Condor often struggled to find alternative capacity when the need arose. The *Havelet* was very much a stop-gap for BCIF. (*Miles Cowsill)*

protection that previous operators could only dream of, before they will consider significant financial investment. In turn the reliability, scale and quality of service has declined to the extent that the States need an SLA to hold the company to account through a controlled level of operation in exchange for service rights. But politicians are not specialists in shipping management, and the States bought into Condor's vision of a single-vessel operation and the reliability of the *Condor Liberation*. In doing so they forfeited any chance of significant future growth in sea passenger carryings.

Freight services underpin the Island economy and the general reliability of such operations with dedicated, purpose-built vessels demonstrates the wisdom of the original investments. Island businesses are dependent on their reliability, having adapted to take this for granted. The capacity and reliability provided by Condor Ferries to the Channel Islands freight businesses contrasts markedly with the service enjoyed by passengers.

Fast craft have been the core of Condor's DNA since the company's earliest days. The Channel Islands are unique around Britain in their dependence on fast craft for the bulk of year-round capacity, despite the severe challenges of weather and sea on their long distance crossings. This narrative is a reminder that difficulties in bedding in new craft are nothing new, and have been experienced by all operators over the years, with even the most popular vessels having had their problems, often for protracted periods of time. Yet the *Condor Liberation* has proved to be a particular problem child. An Island's lifeline route is a challenging place for an experimental prototype craft, especially when there is almost no access to alternative passenger resources. The decline of sea passenger carryings to the Islands has accelerated since the introduced of *Condor Liberation* and customer satisfaction has stagnated. Passenger carryings from England in 2017 fell to a level not seen since the 1960s. It is a sad position to be in after two centuries of journeys by sea to the Channel Islands.

The clean modern corporate identity of Condor Ferries as applied to *Condor Liberation*. (Kevin Mitchell)

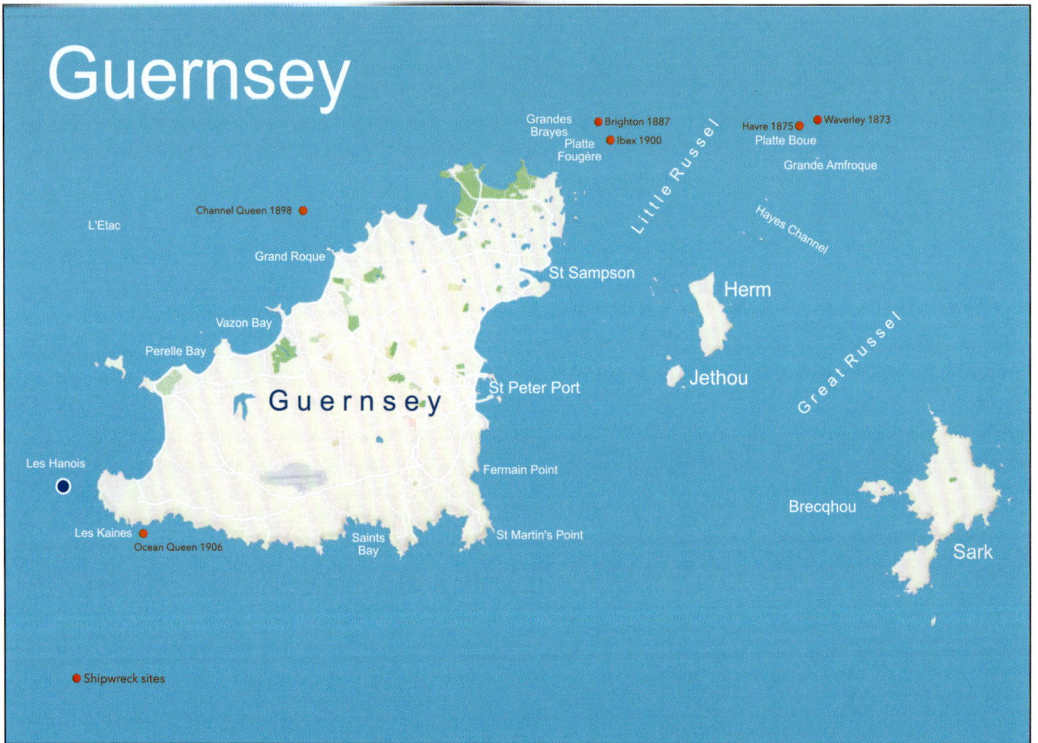

Guernsey

Grandes Brayes
Brighton 1887
Platte Fougère
Ibex 1900
Havre 1875
Platte Boue
Waverley 1873
Grande Amfroque
Channel Queen 1898
L'Etac
Little Russel
Hayes Channel
Grand Roque
St Sampson
Herm
Vazon Bay
Great Russel
Perelle Bay
Jethou
Guernsey
St Peter Port
Les Hanois
Fermain Point
Brecqhou
Les Kaines
Ocean Queen 1906
Saints Bay
St Martin's Point
Sark

● Shipwreck sites

Jersey

Princess Ena 1908
Paternosters
Les Dirouilles
Les Ecrehou

Grosnez Point

Jersey

La Coupe Point

St Ouen Bay

St Catherine's

St Aubin
St Aubin's Bay
St Helier
Gorey

La Corbière
Dispatch 1853
Ibex 1897
Roebuck 1911
Caesarea II 1923
St Brelade's Bay
Metropolis 1861
Caledonia 1881
St Patrick 1932
Express 1859
Paris 1863
Rossgull 1900
Noirmont Point
La Roque Point

● Shipwreck sites

St Peter Port

Salerie

QEII Marina (1989)

St Julian's Pier (1853)

Herm Ferry 9

8

Cambridge Pier (1909)

7

Herm Ferry

Sark Quay

New Jetty (1927)

White Rock Pier

3 4

1

2

5

6

North Esplanade

Victoria Pier

The Quay

Victoria Marina

North Pier

THE POOL

South Pier

Albert Pier

Fish Quay (1987)

Cow Bay

Castle breakwater (1861)

Esplanade

Albert Marina (1875)

Albert Dock

Model yacht pond

Castle Pier (1850)

Castle Cornet

HAVELET BAY

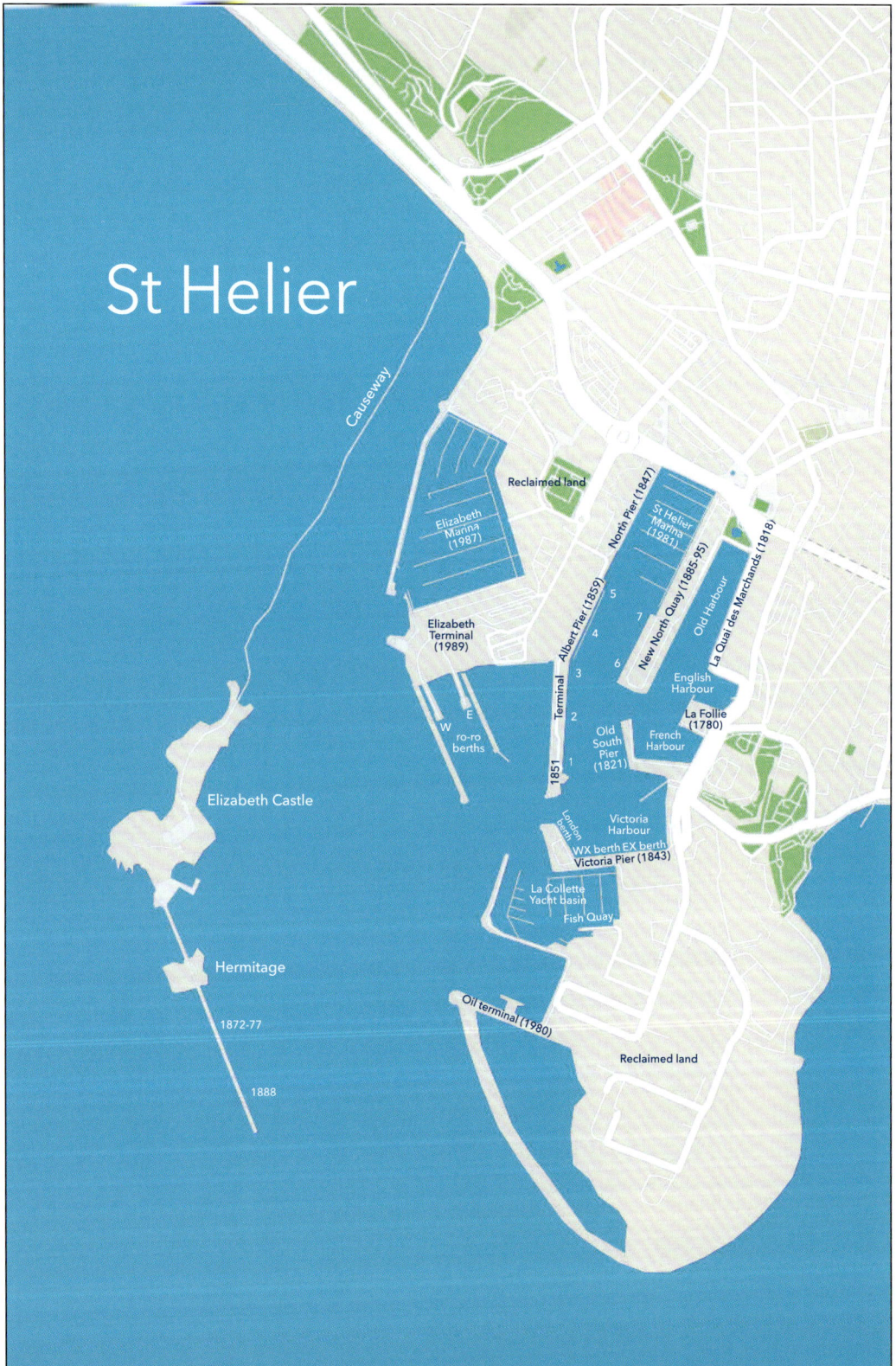

St Helier

Causeway

Reclaimed land

Elizabeth Marina (1987)

North Pier (1847)

St Helier Marina (1981)

La Quai des Marchands (1818)

Elizabeth Terminal (1989)

Albert Pier (1859)

Terminal

New North Quay (1885-95)

Old Harbour

5

7

4

3

6

English Harbour

2

La Follie (1780)

W   E

ro-ro berths

1851

1

Old South Pier (1821)

French Harbour

Elizabeth Castle

London berth

Victoria Harbour

WX berth EX berth

Victoria Pier (1843)

La Collette Yacht Basin

Fish Quay

Hermitage

1872-77

Oil terminal (1980)

Reclaimed land

1888

Poole Harbour

Wareham Channel

Poole Quay

Bay

Hamworthy

North Channel

Middle Ship Channel

Brownsea Island

North Haven Point

Sandbanks

Furzey Island

South Haven Point

Ferry

Haven Channel

Swash Channel

Green Island

LOWER HAMWORTHY

Studland

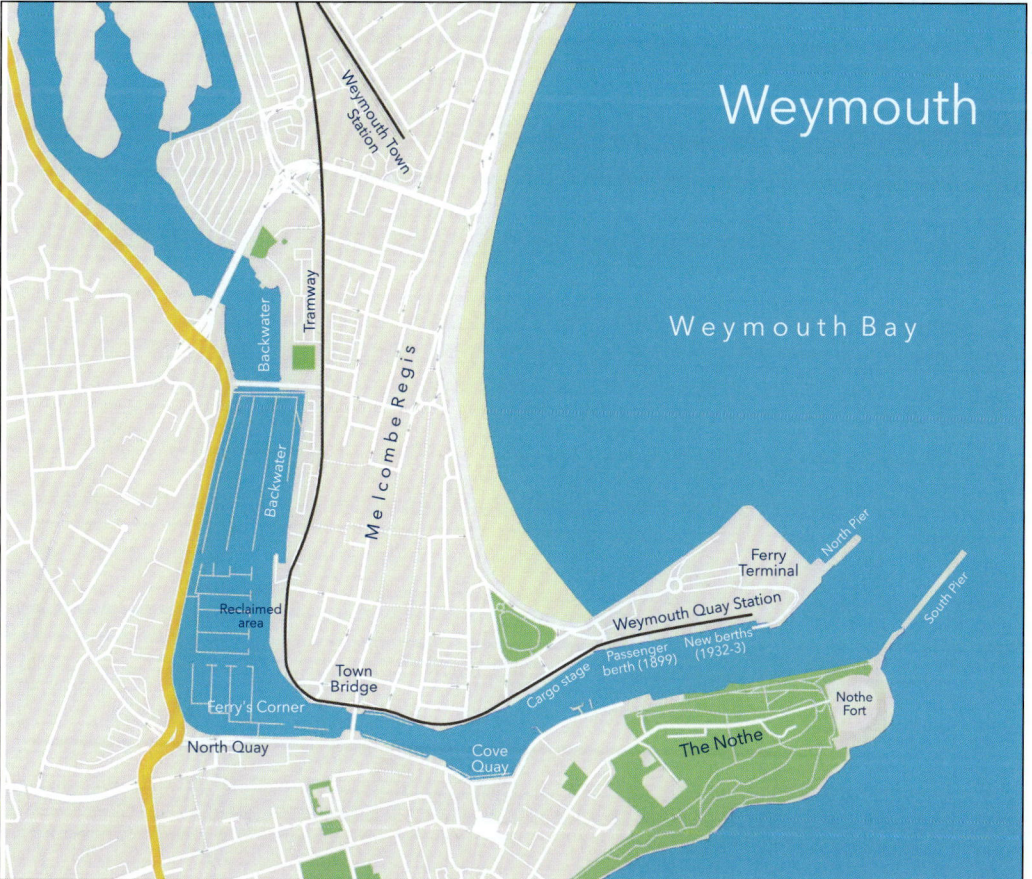

Weymouth

Weymouth Town Station

Backwater

Tramway

Weymouth Bay

Backwater

Melcombe Regis

North Pier

Reclaimed area

Ferry Terminal

South Pier

Weymouth Quay Station

Cargo stage

Passenger berth (1899)

New berths (1932-3)

Ferry's Corner

Town Bridge

North Quay

Cove Quay

The Nothe

Nothe Fort

Southampton & Portsmouth

The *Condor Liberation* leaves St Peter Port for Jersey with Herm in the background. *(Author)*

Condor Rapide (Kevin Mitchell)

Notes

Time
British Rail introduced the 24 hour clock in timetables from 14 June 1965. Sailing schedules are therefore shown in the 12 hour (a.m./p.m.) format prior to this date, and use the 24 hour convention thereafter.

Currency
The modern decimal currency dates back to 15 February 1971. Prior to this date prices were expressed in pounds ('£'), shillings ('s') and pence ('d'). A pound comprised of 20 shillings, and a shilling comprised of 12 pence. There were therefore 240 pence in a pound. Prices are expressed in the currency of the time, but inflation makes comparison difficult. The table is an approximate guide to the modern equivalent of historic prices based on consumer price inflation records.

Year	Modern equivalent of £1
1825	£104.00
1850	£120.00
1875	£108.00
1900	£123.00
1925	£57.90
1950	£33.60
1975	£9.92
2000	£1.65

Measurement
The British Imperial System dates back to the Weights and Measure Act of 1824, which introduced standard definition of the gallon, pound (weight) and yard. A ton (1.016 metric tonnes,) is comprised of 20 hundredweight ('cwt') (50.8kg) or 2,240 pounds. The mile (1,609.34 metres) is made up of 1,760 yards; a yard (0.9144m) is made up of 3 ft or 36 inches. A nautical mile was historically defined as one minute of latitude or 1/60 of a degree. It is defined as 1,852 metres or 1.1508 miles. A cable is 1/10 of a nautical mile. A fathom is a measure of water depth, equivalent to 6 ft. Speed at sea is measured in knots, defined as nautical miles per hour.

Spelling
The modern spellings of St Helier and St Peter Port are used throughout for consistency.

Abbreviations

B&FSNCo - British & Foreign Steam Navigation Co
BCIF – British Channel Island Ferries
BF – Brittany Ferries
bhp – brake horsepower
BR - British Railways
BTC – British Transport Commission
burthen – pre 1836 calculated tonnage
CH – Channel Hoppers
CI – Channel Islands

CIF – Channel Island Ferries
C&M - Cheeswright & Miskin
CSPCo – Commercial Steam Packet Co
cyl - cylinder
ft – feet
g – gross
GSNCo – General Steam Navigation Co
GWR – Great Western Railway (to 1922)
GW – Great Western Railway (1923-47)
HD – HD Ferries
HPM – Henry Maples
hp – horse power
IF – Island Ferries
ihp – indicated horse power
IoMSPCo - Isle of Man Steam Packet Co
JF – James Fisher & Sons
JSPCo – Jersey Steam Packet Company
kt - knots
LB&SCR – London, Brighton & South Coast Railway
L&CISCo – London & Channel Islands Steamship Co
LG&JSPCo – London, Guernsey & Jersey Steam Packet Co
LJ&GSSNCo – London, Jersey & Guernsey Screw Steam Navigation Co
lm – lane metres
LM&SR – London, Midland & Scottish Railway
L&NER – London & North Eastern Railway
L&SWR – London & South Western Railway
L&YR – Lancashire & Yorkshire Railway
m – metres
n - net
nhp – nominal horse power
NSWSPCo – New South Western Steam Packet Co
pc – passenger certificate
PCI&BSSCo - Plymouth, Channel Islands & Brittany Steam Ship Co
PO – Post Office
osc – oscillating
SBF – Sealink British Ferries
SE&CR – South Eastern & Chatham Railway
Sealink – Sealink UK Ltd
shp – shaft horse power
SM&BSSCo – St Malo & Binic Steam Ship Co
SNCF – Societe Nationale des Chemins de Fer
SoESNCo – South of England Steam Navigation Co
Southern – British Railways Southern Region
SR – Southern Railway
SWSPCo - South Western Steam Packet Co
TS – Torbay Seaways
sr – steam reciprocating
Western – British Railways Western Region
W&CISPCo – Weymouth & Channel Islands Steam Packet Co
WS&WR – Wilts, Somerset & Weymouth Railway
WMS – Weymouth Maritime Services

Fleet List

Engines by builder except where indicated

Ada (L&SWR/SR)
Built: Gourlay Bros, Dundee
Completed: 04-1905
Dimensions: 197.5 x 28.2 x 12.5 ft
Tonnage: 529g
Engines: single screw, triple expansion, 93rhp
Speed: 12kt
Cargo steamer built at cost of £13,200 for Honfleur route, with intermittent visits to CI. Worked through First World War and passed to SR in 1923. Laid up at end of Honfleur service in 1932 and sold to Darwen & Mostyn Iron Co for scrap in 03-1934.

Ailsa Princess/Earl Harold (Sealink)
Built: Breda Cantieri Navale, Venice
Launched: 28-11-1970
Dimensions: 369.5 x 57.2 x 12 ft
Tonnage: 3,715g
Engines: twin screw, oil, 2 x 16 cyl Pielstick/Crossley, 14,650bhp
Speed: 19kt
Passengers: 1,200
Cars: 190
Built for Stranraer-Larne route. Transferred to Weymouth-Cherbourg in 04-1982 after extensive refit work at Smith's Dock Co, Middlesbrough. Undertook berthing trials on 8-10-1984 in St Helier before conversion for Sunliner service from 23-4-1985. Renamed *Earl Harold* on 24-5-1985. On closure of CI service maintained the Weymouth-Cherbourg route for 1987 and 1988 seasons. After charter to B&I sold to Aktoploika Maritime, Piraeus, Greece and renamed *Dimitra,* seeing service in Greece and India before being scrapped in April 2010.

Alberta (L&SWR/SR)
Built: John Brown & Co, Clydebank
Launched: 3-4-1900
Dimensions: 280.8 x 35.1 x 14.4 ft
Tonnage: 1,242g
Engines: twin screw, 2 x 4 cyl triple expansion, 254nhp
Speed: 19kt
Built to replace the *Stella* at cost of £67,865. First sailing to CI on 2-6-1900. Improved with poop deck in 1908. Continued to serve CI dur-

ing First World War. Holed on rocks approaching St. Peter Port on 21-7-1920. Major refit at Caledon, Dundee delayed by shipyard strike in 1921. Passed to SR in 1923. Pioneer of Radio Direction Finding equipment in 1927. Withdrawn in 1929 and sold to D Inlessi Fils SA Nav de Samos. Sunk at Punta, Salamis Island on 23-4-1941.

Alderney (L&SWR)
Built: Wigham, Richardson, Newcastle
Launched: 3-1875
Dimensions: 175.0 x 25.2 x 19.5 ft
Tonnage: 422g
Engines: J Shaw & Co; single screw, 2 cyl compound inverted, 90nhp
Speed: 11.4kt
Iron cargo vessel used primarily on Cherbourg, Honfleur and Le Havre routes. Sold in 4-1891 to Dundee & Newcastle Steamship Co. Returned to CI in 1-1913 operating a service from Bristol. Foundered off Malta on 27-12-1914.

Aldershot – see Brittany (II)

Alice (L&SWR)
Built: Caird & Co, Greenock
Launched: 1857
Dimensions: 231.6 x 26.2 x 13.3 ft
Tonnage: 635g
Engines: 2 cyl simple osc, 250nhp
Speed: 12kt
Iron paddle steamer with bowsprit and female figurehead, built as the *Sirius* for the Bee Company of Glasgow to serve in the Baltic. Renamed *Alice* in 1862 and operated as a blockade-runner in the American Civil War. Returned in 1865 to operate a Stranraer-Belfast service for the Caledonian Railway. Purchased by L&SWR with *Fannie* in 1869 and re-boilered in 1874. On CI route between 1879 and 1882. Converted to a coal hulk in Jersey in 1887 and sold for scrap to JJ King, Garston in 1897.

Alliance (NSWSPCo/L&SWR)
Built: Ditchburn & Mare, Blackwall
Launched: 3-1855
Dimensions: 175.5 x 23.7 x 14.6 ft
Tonnage: 168g
Engines: Seaward & Capel; 3 cyl atmospheric,

A solitary crew member watches the photographer as *Earl Harold*, the former *Ailsa Princess*, heads to Weymouth to take up the 'Sunliner' service in 1985. *(FotoFlite)*

225nhp
Speed: 13.5kt
Passengers: 150
Iron paddle steamer built for £19,460 for the Southampton-Le Havre route, sister of *Havre*. First sailing to CI on 7-5-1860. Transferred to L&SWR in 1863. New boiler fitted 1870. Acted as relief vessel on Jersey-France routes from 1876. New compound engines fitted and aft funnel removed by Day, Summers & Co, Southampton in 1878. Re-boilered in 1888 by Day, Summers & Co. Collided with *Wolf* whilst on Cherbourg run on 6-9-1890. Sold for scrap in Netherlands in March 1900.

Alma (L&SWR)
Built: J & G Thompson, Clydebank
Launched: 19-10-1894
Dimensions: 270.7 x 34.0 x 14.6 ft
Tonnage: 1,145g
Engines: twin screw 2 x 4cyl triple expansion, 217nhp
Speed: 19kt
Sister of *Columbia* built for Southampton-Le Havre service. Maiden visit to CI on 1-3-1899 and substituted for *Stella* later that season, but no subsequent visits. Collided with and sank *Cambrian Princess* with loss of 11 crew on 1-4-1902. Re-boilered 1907. Replaced by *Hantonia* in April 1912 and sold to E A Cohan, Southampton. Wrecked off Sakhalin Island 17-6-1924.

Antelope (GWR)
Built: Laird Bros, Birkenhead
Launched: 4-5-1889
Dimensions: 235.5 x 27.6 x 13.1 ft
Tonnage: 672g
Engines: twin screw 2 x triple expansion, 184nhp
Speed: 16kt
Passengers: 413
Steel steamer built new for CI service as part of order for three vessels, first vessels with triple-expansion engines. First sailing from Jersey on 5-8-1889. Hit Cavale Rock off Guernsey on 10-6-1890 and returned to builders for repair, which included shortening of funnels. Heightened again in 1896. Covered for *Ibex* during 1900, but relegated to tender duties at Plymouth from 1903. Covered Plymouth-Brest route from 1910 and sold on closure in 1913 to Greek SA Ionienne de Nav a Vapew and re-named *Atromitos*. Broken up in 1933.

Aquila (W&CISPCo)
Built: J Henderson & Sons, Renfrew
Launched: 1854

Dimensions: 182.0 x 21.4 x 9.7 ft
Tonnage: 264g
Engines: McNabb & Clark; 2 cyl simple osc, 110hp
Speed: 14kt
Iron Paddle steamer, built for North of Europe Steam Navigation Co Harwich-Antwerp service. Chartered to W&CISPCo then purchased in 1857 with inaugural sailing on 17-4-1857. New boilers fitted in 1860 and 1873. Last sailing for W&CISPCo on 28-6-1889 and sold to Alfred Tolhurst, then to Onesimus Dorey for PCI&BSSCo. Operated to CI until 1894, before sold to James Jones of Swansea in 1895 as *Alexandra*. Broken up in 1899.

Ardena (L&SWR/SR)
Built: A MacMillan & Sons, Dumbarton
Launched: 1915
Dimensions: 267.0 x 33.1 x 17.3 ft
Tonnage: 1,092g
Engines: single screw, 4 cyl triple expansion, 350nhp
Speed: 18kt
Built as *HMS Peony*. Purchased by L&SWR for £4,000 and converted by Caledon, Dundee for £117,500 to serve as a cargo and passenger ship. Maiden voyage to St Malo on 6-12-1920 and re-opened Cherbourg route in 1921. Rare visitor to CI. Transferred to SR in 1923. Laid up on closure of the Caen service in 1931 and sold in 1934 to JD Chandris for work in Greece.

Ariadne (SoESNCo/ NSWSPCo)
Built: W Evans, Rotherhithe
Launched: 1-05-1824
Dimensions: 115.0 x 19.2 x 8.5 ft
Tonnage: 133 burthen
Engines: 72hp
Wooden Paddle steamer; first to sail commercially to CI from Southampton on 8-6-1824. Lengthened by 9ft in 1831/2 and acquired by SoESNCo in 1835. Displaced by *Atalanta* in 1836 to operate Jersey-France route for a season before arrival of Camilla. Operated Torquay-CI route from 1843-46 and passed to NSWSPCo in 1847. Scrapped in 1849.

Atalanta (SoESNCo/ NSWSPCo/L&SWR)
Built: Thomas White, West Cowes
Launched: 2-6-1836
Dimensions: 138.1 x 21.9 x 13.0 ft
Tonnage: 380g
Engines: Thames fitted; 2 cyl side lever, 120hp
Passengers: 150
Wooden Paddle steamer; maiden voyage to Channel Islands on 24-8-1836. Lengthened in

1836 and 1851 to reach 160ft. Transferred to NSWSPCo on merger in 1846 and opened Weymouth-CI route in 1850 before returning to Southampton service. Hit by P&O *Sultan* at Southampton on 21-11-1856. Transferred to L&SWR in 1863 and relegated to local trips. Converted to a coal hulk in Jersey from 1869. Scrapped in 1882.

Atalanta (II) (L&SWR/GWR)

Built: Gourlay Bros, Dundee
Launched: 25-4-1907
Dimensions: 170.3 x 32.2 x 15.3 ft
Tonnage: 577g
Engines: twin screw, 2 x 2cyl compound, 200hp
Speed: 14kt
Steel turbine designed as Plymouth tender for L&SWR and transferred to GWR on 10-6-1910 for duties at Fishguard and Plymouth. Sold to Royal Mail SPCo in 1924 and then to P Cottel & Cie in Cherbourg. Scuttled at Le Havre on 11-6-1940.

Autocarrier (SR/BR)

Built: D&W Henderson, Renfrew
Launched: 2-2-1931
Dimensions: 230.0 x 35.6 x 14.1 ft
Tonnage: 985g
Engines: twin screw, 2 x 4cyl triple expansion, 154nhp
Speed: 15kt
Passengers: 120
Steel twin screw steamer built for £49,150; entered service on Dover-Calais route on 30-3-1931 to offer car-carrying capacity to compete with Townsend Bros. Assisted in evacuation of civilians from CI in 1940. Returned after the war to re-open Jersey-France service on 15-1-1946 and thereafter acted as winter relief vessel on the Jersey-St Malo route until 1952. Broken up in Ghent in 1954.

Beauport (BCIF)

Built: Schiffbau Gesellschaft Unterweser AG, Bremerhaven
Launched: 9-2-1970
Dimensions: 119.6 x 18.1 x 4.75 m
Tonnage: 5,464g
Engines: 2 x Pielstick 12PC2V diesels, 9,120kW
Speed: 17kt
Passengers: 1,020; 520 berths
Vehicles: 210
Built as *Prince of Fundy* for Lion Ferry between Portland and Yarmouth. Chartered by BF from 17-4-1978 primarily for Portsmouth-St Malo route as *Prince of Brittany.* Purchased by BF in 1980 as *Reine Mathilde* in 1988. Covered for

Rozel on CI route in 1989. Chartered by BCIF in 1992 and renamed *Beauport* running from 28-1-1992 until 31-10-1993. Laid up, then sold to Stern Maritime Line for service in Mediterranean. Scrapped in India in 2005.

Bertha (L&SWR/SR)

Built: Gourlay Bros, Dundee
Launched: 1905
Dimensions: 182.5 x 28.1 x 12.3 ft
Tonnage: 528g
Engines: single screw triple expansion, 93rhp
Speed: 12kt
Cargo steamer, built for the Southampton-Honfleur route. Sister of *Ada.* Rescued survivors from wreck of *Hilda* in 1905. Worked through war and passed to SR in 1923. Hit quay wall in Southampton on 23-1-1923 and main mast collapsed. Sold to Metal Industries, Rosyth in 1933 for use as salvage vessel to raise wartime fleet in Scapa Flow. Broken up in Belgium in 1948.

Brest (SNCF/BTC)

Built: Chantiers et Ateliers de St Nazaire, Rouen
Launched: 1950
Dimensions: 237.8 x 34.5 x 14.9 ft
Tonnage: 1,038g
Engines: Soc Generale de Construction Méchanique, Las Corneuve; twin screw, 2 x 7cyl, 2,000bhp
Speed: 15kt
Cars: 60
Oil fired steamer, one of three cargo vessels built for SNCF. Jointly owned by SNCF and BTC. Operated as vehicle carrier from Southampton in 1957 and 1958, then Weymouth until 1967. Relief vessel for *Roebuck* and *Sambur.* Sister *Rennes* provided service in 1965. Sold in 1967 to Othon J Metaxos, Lebanon as *Laas IV* and later *Samir.* Later operated in Panama.

Brighton (W&CISPCo)

Built: Palmer Bros & Co., Jarrow, Newcastle
Launched: 1857
Dimensions: 193.5 x 20.9 x 10.0 ft
Tonnage: 286g
Engines: 2cyl simple oscillating, 140hp
Iron paddle steamer, built for HP Maples' Shoreham, London and Newhaven services to the CI on behalf of LB&SCR. Purchased by W&CISPCo in 1858 for Weymouth-Cherbourg service, but continued to call in CI. Reverted to Newhaven service on closure of Cherbourg link. Re-boilered by Thames Iron Works in 1876. Wrecked off Little Russel Channel on 29-1-1887 without loss of life.

Bristol
Built: Bristol
Launched: 1823
Dimensions: 90.1 x 16.1 x 9.5 ft
Tonnage: 130g
Engines: 60hp
Wooden paddle steamer from Bristol & Glamorgan Steam Packet Co used on Southampton-CI route in 1829. Returned to Bristol in 1830.

Brittany (I) (L&SWR)
Built: J Ash & Co, Cubitt Town
Launched: 8-8-1864
Dimensions: 215.6 x 25.6 x 11 ft
Tonnage: 525g
Engines: J Stewart, Poplar; 2 cyl oscillating, 250hp
Speed: 14kt
Passengers: 400
Iron paddle steamer similar to *Normandy (I)*. Last new paddle steamer for L&SWR, primarily for Le Havre route. Maiden voyage from Southampton to CI on 16-11-1864. Re-boilered in 1871 Lengthened to 236ft in 1873 and to 266ft in 1883, with new compound engines by Day, Summers & Co, Southampton. Allocated to CI service until 1889 and then returned to Le Havre. Re-boilered 1893. Sold for scrap to T W Ward in 1900.

Brittany (II) (LB&SCR/L&SWR/SR)
Built: Earle's Shipbuilding & Engineering Co. Hull
Launched: 9-7-1910
Dimensions: 192.0 x 29.2 x 14.2 ft
Tonnage: 631g
Engines: single screw triple expansion, 82rhp
Speed: 12½kt
Built for Newhaven-Caen route and purchased by L&SWR for £15,200 on 3-6-1912. Funnels shortened and masts raked before entering service and arriving in Guernsey on 2-12-1912. To SR and renamed *Aldershot* when *Brittany (III)* delivered on 31-3-1933. Sold in 12-1936 for £2,350 to D. Tripcovitch & Cia in Trieste for Mediterranean service.

Brittany (III) (SR/BR)
Built: Wm. Denny & Bros. Dumbarton
Launched: 12-4-1933
Dimensions: 260 x 39.1 x 14 ft
Tonnage: 1,445g
Engines: twin screw, 2 x 2 stage Parson's turbine, 240nhp
Speed: 16kt
Passengers: 850; 500 1st, 350 2nd
Replaced *Vera* on Jersey-St Malo route from 18-6-1933. Assisted in evacuation of civilians

from CI in 1940, then served at Scapa Flow and in Africa, India, and the Eastern Mediterranean, at D Day and in Bay of Biscay. Returned to Jersey-St Malo route on 5-6-1946. Holed off Gorey during round-the-island cruise on 28-8-1947. To BR on 1-1-1948 Withdrawn 11-1962 and sold in 04-1963 to Alandsfarjan A/B for services in Finland. Broken up 1972.

Brunswick
Built: Rotherhithe
Launched: 1826
Dimensions: 128.5 x 21.0 x 10.5 ft
Tonnage: 218g
Engines: 100hp
Operated from Plymouth and Portsmouth from 1826 to 1856, then sold to Liverpool.

Caesarea (LJ&GSSNCo)
Built: T&W Pim, Hull
Launched: 1850
Dimensions: 133.5 x 20.0 x 13.0 ft
Tonnage: 265 burthen
Engines: single screw, 40hp
Passengers: 60
Introduced to London-CI route arriving in Guernsey on 9-10-1850. Disposed of in 1853.

Caesarea (I) (L&SWR)
Built: Aitken & Mansell, Whiteinch, Glasgow
Launched: 7-1-1867
Dimensions: 187.2 x 24.3 x 13.6 ft
Tonnage: 408g
Engines: single screw, 2 cyl simple, 130 nhp
Speed: 13kt
Iron steamer built for Southampton-St Malo service. Maiden visit to CI on 16-4-1867. Engines compounded and new boiler fitted by Day, Summers & Co, Southampton in 1874. Operated winter service on CI routes from 1875 to 1881, and summer Jersey-France service from 1876 to 1879. Sunk on 27-6-1884 after collision with *Strathesk* off Cap de la Hague.

Caesarea (II) (L&SWR/SR)
Built: Cammell Laird & Co, Birkenhead
Launched: 26-5-1910
Dimensions: 284.7 x 39.1 x 15.8 ft
Tonnage: 1,499g
Engines: triple screw 3 x Parson's direct drive turbines, 6,350nhp
Speed: 20kt
Passengers: 980
Passenger steamer built for the CI service. Sister of *Sarnia (II)*, *the* only L&SWR direct drive steamers, constructed to replace *Frederica* and *Lydia*. Maiden sailing to CI on 24-9-1910. An

unsuccessful design, which proved uneconomic so laid up in winter. Wartime service at Scapa Flow and in Mediterranean, and operated as troop ship from Southampton; refurbished by Caledon in 10-1919. Passed to SR in 1923. Hit rock off Noirmont Point on 7-7-1923 and badly damaged; sold to IoMSPCo and renamed *Manx Maid*. Broken up 1950.

Caesarea (III) (BR/Sealink)
Built: Samuel White & Co, Cowes
Launched: 29-1-1960
Dimensions: 322 x 53.7 x 26.8 ft
Tonnage: 4,174g
Engines: twin screw, geared turbine, 9,000shp
Speed: 19.5kt
Passengers: 1,290 (110 berths)
Final traditional steamer for CI service. Sister of *Sarnia*. Maiden voyage on 2-12-1960. Holed at Weymouth on 08-1968 and grounded in Jersey on 03-1973. Internal improvements made in 1971 to facilitate introduction of reservations system. Final sailing to CI on 6-10-1975, then transferred to Dover and Folkestone. Sold to Hong Kong in 1980. Broken up 1986.

Caledonia (L&SWR)
Built: Cunliffe, Dunlop & Co, Port Glasgow
Completed: 09-1876
Dimensions: 195.1 x 26.3 x 14.0 ft
Tonnage: 539g
Engines: single screw, 2 cyl compound inv, 150hp
Iron steamer built as the *Hogarth* for the Aberdeen Steam Navigation Company's Aberdeen-London service. Chartered, then purchased by L&SWR in 1878 primarily for St Malo route. Maiden visit to CI on 9-10-1878. Struck and sunk on Oyster Rock, St Helier when substituting for *Fannie* on 18-2-1881.

Caledonian Princess (BR/Sealink)
Built: Wm. Denny & Bros. Dumbarton
Launched: 5-4-1961
Dimensions: 331.5 x 57.2 x 12.0 ft
Tonnage: 3,630g
Engines: twin screw, 2 x Pametrada turbines double reduction gearing, 11,500shp
Speed: 19kt
Passengers: 500; 400 1st, 100 2nd ; (1976) 1,400
Cars: 103
Built as replacement for *Princess Victoria* on Stranraer-Larne route. Replaced *Falaise* on Weymouth-Cherbourg route from 1974, then converted at Immingham to multi-purpose role for CI service commencing 12-5-1976. Replaced by *Earl William* and used intermittently

until 16-7-1981, when transferred to Dover. Sold to Quadrini Group in 1982 for use as a floating nightclub on the Tyne. Scrapped in Turkey in 2008.

Calpe (B&FSNCo/ CSPCo/SWSPCo)
Built: McGhie & Hawks, Rotherhithe
Launched: 12-1835
Dimensions: 125.4 x 19.5 x 12.8 ft
Tonnage: 259g
Engines: Seaward; 80nhp
Wooden Paddle steamer built for Spanish service; passed to CSPCo on 8-4-1837 and initially retained on Mediterranean routes. Re-allocated to south coast services in 10-1838 and operated to Le Havre and Plymouth. Transferred to SWSPCo in 05-1842 and used intermittently thereafter. Sold in 1850 and converted to sailing ship. Broken up 1852.

Camilla (Various/SoESNCo/NSWSPCo)
Built: W Evans, Rotherhithe
Completed: 6-1824
Dimensions: 107.8 x 17.9 x 10.0 ft
Tonnage: 102 burthen
Engines: Seaward; 60nhp
Wooden Paddle steamer built for Le Havre service; acquired from GSNCo by SoESNCo and used on Jersey-France services from 31-7-1837 until passed to NSWSPCo in 10-1846 and withdrawn shortly after. Scrapped 1853.

Channel Queen (I) (PCI&BSSCo)
Built: R Craggs & Sons, Middlesbrough
Launched: 13-7-1895
Dimensions: 177.0 x 24.0 x 10.0 ft ft
Tonnage: 350g
Engines: twin screw, 3 cyl, 800ihp
Speed: 16kt
Maiden sailing on 14-9-1895 from Plymouth. Sunk off Guernsey on 1-2-1898.

Channel Queen (II) (L&CISCo)
Built: Goole Shipbuilding & Repairing Co
Completed: 10-1912
Dimensions: 175.0 x 27.9 x 10.9 ft
Tonnage: 670g
Engines: 3 cyl, 109nhp
Operated for L&CISCo from 10-1912 until 06-1920. Sold to Ireland.

Cherbourg (L&SWR/SR)
Built: J & R Swan, Dumbarton
Launched: 1873
Dimensions: 172.6 x 23.1 x 11.9 ft
Tonnage: 386g
Engines: Smith Bros; single screw, 2 cyl com-

pound, 65nhp

Iron steam cargo ship, built for French services. Re-boilered in 1891, refitted and re-boilered in 1909 and fitted with a 'new' 1897 engine in 1921. Passed to SR on 1-1-1923. Sold for scrap to G&W Brunton, Grangemouth 1930.

Chesterfield

Built: Portland
Launched: 1806
Dimensions: 58.3 x 18.9 x 9.5 ft
Tonnage: 85g
Sailing cutter, operated from 11-1806 captured by French in 10-1811.

Chesterfield (II)

Built: Portland
Launched: 1812
Dimensions: 63.3 x 20.0 x 10.1 ft
Tonnage: 107g
Sailing cutter, operated from Weymouth from 11-1812 until 01-1813.

Columbia (L&SWR)

Built: J & G Thompson, Clydebank
Launched: 1894
Dimensions: 270.7 x 34 x 14.6 ft
Tonnage: 1,178g
Engines: twin screw, 2 x 4 cyl triple expansion, 217nhp
Speed: 19kt
Passengers: 153 berths
Built for Le Havre service, sister of *Alma*. First vessel with individual cabins for First Class passengers. Remained on Le Havre route with limited visits to CI, first being on 1-11-1894. Collided with *Vesuvio* in 02-1897. Re-boilered in 1906. Sold in 04-1912 to J.J. Sitges Freres, Alicante as *Sitges*. Taken over by French navy and torpedoed on 24-1-1918

Comet – see Granville

Commerce (PCI&BSSCo)

Built: Ogier, Guernsey
Launched: 26-3-1874
Dimensions: 105.4 x 20.6 x 9.6 ft
Tonnage: 121g
Engines: single screw, 2 cyl, 28nhp
Passengers: 58
Built for Guernsey shareholders for services to St Malo and Plymouth. Re-engined in 1875. Transferred to London-CI route in 1876 but was soon withdrawn. Owned by PCI&BSSCo from 05-1888 and operated from Plymouth until sold on 14-1-1898. Wrecked in 1911.

Commodore Challenger – see Jersey Fisher

Commodore Clipper (IV) (Commodore)

Built: West Bygg 238 A/S, Norway
Launched: 1971
Dimensions: 118.4 x 16.0 x 6.0 m
Tonnage: 6,136g
Engines: 2xWartsila-Sulzer 9ZH40
Speed: 14kt
Passengers: 12
Freight: 636 lm
Built as the Juno for Finska Ångfartygs Ab, and chartered extensively before joining Commodore from 01-1991 to 09-1996 as the *Commodore Clipper (IV)*, replacing the *Juniper*. Subsequently chartered around Northern Europe.

Commodore Clipper (V) (Commodore/Condor)

Built: Van der Giessen-de-Noord, Krimpen a/d Ijssel
Launched: 8-5-1999
Dimensions: 129.1 x 14.7 x 5.8 m
Tonnage: 13,460 t
Engines: 2 x MaK 9M32 diesel
Speed: 18.8 kt
Passengers: 500
Cars: 279
Freight: 1,265 lm
Built for Condor Marine Service with first sailing for Commodore on 27-9-1999. Transferred to Condor in 2005. Fire on vehicle deck during passage Jersey-Portsmouth on 16-6-2010. Fire in engine's oil heating system on 26-4-2012. Ran aground in Little Russel Channel on 14-7-2014. Still in service in 2018.

Commodore Goodwill (III) (Commodore/Condor)

Built: Koninklijke Scheldegroep BV, Vlissingen
Launched: 6-11-1995
Dimensions: 126.4 x 21.4 m
Tonnage: 11,166g
Engines: 2 x 6 cyl MaK diesels
Speed: 17.3kt
Passengers: 12
Freight: 1,250 lm
Sister of *Island Commodore* with maiden sailing on 1-3-1996. Hit entrance to La Collette yacht basin on 10-12-2007 during bad weather. Transferred to Condor in 2012. Still in service in 2018.

Condor 1 (Condor)

Built: Rodriguez, Messina, Sicily
Launched: 15-3-1964
Dimensions: 91.5 x 35.1 x 11.9 ft

Tonnage: 127g
Engines: twin screw, V12 Mercedes Benz, 1,350hp
Speed: 37kt
Passengers: 140
PT50 hydrofoil purchased to commence service to replace BR Jersey-France route after closure in 1964. Maiden voyage on 1-5-1964. Served Cherbourg, Granville and St Malo and made crossing to Torquay. Significant internal alterations in 1965/66; suffered mechanical breakdown which curtailed 1996 season from August. Sold in part exchange for *Condor 5* in 06-1976 as *Freccia di Sicilia*. Broken up 7-2003.

Condor 2 (Condor)
Built: Rodriguez, Messina, Sicily
Launched: 1965
Dimensions: 28.7 x 10.7 x 3.5 m
Tonnage: 147g
Engines: twin screw, 2 x Mercedes Benz 12V820DB, 1,350hp
Speed: 37kt
Passengers: 125
PT50 hydrofoil *Freccia Adriatica* chartered from builders to provide extra capacity following demise of Jersey Lines. Operated from 05-1969 for two seasons when charter terminated. Rechartered for 1981 season when Condor 6 returned to builders. Broken up 7-2003.

Condor 3 (Condor)
Built: Rodriguez, Messina, Sicily
Launched: 1971
Dimensions: 28.7 x 10.7 x 3.5 m
Tonnage: 129g
Engines: twin screw, 2 x MTU 493 V12, 1,350hp
Speed: 36kt
Passengers: 136
RHS 140 hydrofoil built to replace *Condor 2* and financed by Nile Steam Ship Company of London. Maiden voyage on 12-4-1971. Traffic outgrew capacity and sold Belt SA in Uruguay in 1980 for River Plate service as *Colonia del Sacramento*. Sank after hitting pontoon at Colonia on 8-11-1987, but not raised for scrapping until 2001.

Condor 4 (Condor)
Built: Cantiere Navaltecnica, Messina, Sicily
Launched: 14-5-1974
Dimensions: 28.7 x 10.7 x 3.3 m
Tonnage: 129g
Engines: twin screw, 12 cyl MTU, 2,700bhp
Speed: 36kt
Passengers: 136
RHS 140 hydrofoil built to meet business expan-

sion, with maiden voyage on 8-6-1974. Operated until end of 1990 season and laid up pending sale on 06-1993 to Hermes Ferries Shipping, Piraeus as *Iptamenos Hermes I*.

Condor 5 (Condor/Commodore)
Built: Cantiere Navaltecnica, Messina, Sicily
Launched: 1976
Dimensions: 31.0 x 12.6 x 3.7 m
Tonnage: 174g
Engines: twin screw, 2 x MTU 652 V12, 1,950hp
Speed: 39kt
Passengers: 180
RHS 160 hydrofoil purchased to replace *Condor I* with maiden voyage on 2-6-1976. Started Condor's Weymouth service in 1987 and operated on route until end of 1991 season. After overhaul allocated to St Malo route for short period in 1992 before being replaced by *Condor 7*. Not part of TNT transaction so passed to Commodore Shipping for sale to Hermes Ferries Shipping, Piraeus as *Iptamenos Hermes III*. Broken up 2004

Condor 6 (Condor)
Built: Westamarin A/S, Mandal, Norway
Launched: 18-4-1980
Dimensions: 31.7 x 9.7 x 1.7 m
Tonnage: 322g
Engines: 2 x Avco Lycoming TF405 gas turbine, 4,000bhp
Speed: 37kt
Passengers: 260
Westamarin W100T catamaran chartered for 1980 season. Maiden voyage on 4-5-1980 but season beset by problems; returned to builders on 23-9-1980.

Condor 7 (Condor)
Built: Cantiere Navaltecnica, Rodriguez, Messina, Sicily
Launched: 1985
Dimensions: 312. x 12.6 x 3.7 m
Tonnage: 208g
Engines: twin screw, 2 x MTU 396 TB83V16, 3,800bhp
Speed: 36kt
Passengers: 200
RHS 160F hydrofoil with maiden voyage on 16-5-1985. Operated the service to Weymouth during the Sealink strike in 10-1986, and initiated the regular service with *Condor 5* in 1987, continuing on this route until arrival of *Condor 9* in 1991. Moved to St Malo route for 1991-93 seasons before being made redundant by pooling arrangement with Channiland in 1994. Sold to Azam Marine & Co Ltd for service from Zanzibar as *Kondor 7*.

Condor 0 (Condor)
Built: Fairey Marineteknik, Singapore
Launched: 1988
Dimensions: 36.3 x 9.4 x 1.3 m
Tonnage: 387g
Engines: 2 x 16cyl MTU 396 TB84, 5,270bhp
Speed: 34kt
Passengers: 300
Marineteknik 36 catamaran purchased for inter-island and St Malo services. Maiden voyage on 17-5-1988. Remained in fleet until 1997 and sold to Rainbow Fast Ferries as *Waterways I* on Great Lakes. Later service in Italy.

Condor 9 (Condor)
Built: Aluminium Shipbuilders, Fareham
Launched: 23-6-1990
Dimensions: 48.7 x 18.4 x 2.0 m
Tonnage: 752g
Engines: 4 x 16cyl MWM
Speed: 35kt
Passengers: 450
Entered service 08-1990 on Weymouth-CI services. Initial services troublesome and quickly withdrawn for modification. Operated until 1993 when replaced by *Condor 10* and *Havelet* acquired from BCIF. Chartered to Viking Line for Helsinki-Tallinn services as *Viking Express* in summer 1994, followed by winter charter in the Caribbean. Ran trips from Torquay in 1995, then Poole based in 1997. Sold to Stetson Navigation as the *Cortez* in 2002 and sailed between La Paz and Topolobampo across Gulf of California.

Condor 10 (Condor)
Built: Incat, Hobart, Tasmania
Launched: 30-9-1992
Dimensions: 77.1 x 26.0 x 4.0 m
Tonnage: 3,240g
Engines: 4 x 16 cyl Ruston 16RK270M diesel
Speed: 39kt
Passengers: 580
Cars: 90
First car-carrying fast ferry used by Condor. InCat hull number 030, delivered from Hobart in 03-1993. Maiden voyage on 1-4-1993 and operated from Weymouth in summer 1993/94, then spent time in New Zealand, and with Viking Line, Stena Line and Holyman Sally. Returned to Condor for St Malo service in 2002.

Condor 11 (Holyman/Condor)
Built: Incat Australia, Hobart, Tasmania
Launched: 1994
Dimensions: 78.3 x 26.0 x 3.4 m
Tonnage: 3,989g
Engines: 4 x 16cyl RK270 Ruston Diesel,

4,320kW
Speed: 32.5kt
Passengers: 674
Car carrying wave-piercing catamaran badly damaged when ran aground on trial on Black Jack Rocks, Tasmania in 1994. Chartered for 1995 season with maiden sailing on 13-5-1995. Moved to Cat-link after 31-10-1995 and re-named *Cat-Link II* for service between Århus and Kalundborg. Sailed between Algeciras and Ceuta as *Euroferrys I* before sale to Egypt in 2004.

Condor 12 (Condor)
Built: Incat, Hobart, Tasmania
Launched: 17-2-1996
Dimensions: 81.1 x 23.0 x 2.1 m
Tonnage: 4,112g
Engines: 4 x 10cyl Ruston diesels, 16,200kW
Speed: 38.7kt
Passengers: 649
Cars: 80
In service on Weymouth-CI route from 8-8-1996 to 30-1-1997. Redeployed to Holyman Ferries as *Holyman Rapide* on Ramsgate-Oost-ende service, and operated Sea Containers' Liverpool-Dublin, Troon-Belfast and Heysham-Belfast services, then Dover-Calais. Sold to Baleària Ferries as *Jamue II* in 06-2006. Still in service in 2018.

Condor Express (Condor)
Built: Incat, Hobart, Tasmania
Launched: 24-11-1996
Dimensions: 86.6 x 26.0 x 3.6 m
Tonnage: 5,005g
Engines: 4 x 20cyl Ruston 20RK270 diesel
Speed: 40kt
Passengers: 776
Cars: 200
Entered service from Weymouth from 31-1-1997 and transferred to Poole from 1-3-1997. Operated final sailing from Weymouth-CI on 23-3-2015. Displaced by *Condor Liberation* and sold in 2015 to Seajets; renamed *Champion Jet 2* for services from Piraeus.

Condor France (Emeraude/Condor)
Built: Marineteknik, Singapore
Launched: 1993
Dimensions: 41.6 x 11.0 m
Tonnage: 585 g
Engines: 2 x 16cyl MTU 396 TE 774L diesels, 5,438bhp
Speed: 34 kt
Passengers: 350
Built for Emeraude Lines as the *St Malo* to serve

the Channel Islands. Grounded off Corbière on 20-4-1995 and offered for sale. Chartered by Condor to replace *Condor 8* and renamed *Condor France*. Operated between 04-1996 and 09-1998 when sold and renamed *Acacia*. Still in service in Dominican Republic in 2018.

Condor Liberation (Condor)
Built: Austal Ships, Fremantle, Australia
Launched: 9-12-2009
Dimensions: 102.0 x 27.4 x 7.6 m
Tonnage: 6,307g
Engines: 3 x MTU 20V 8000 M71L @ 9,100kW
Speed: 35kt
Passengers: 880
Cars: 245
Aluminium 'Auto-Express' trimaran built as a 'stock vessel'. Acquired by Condor in 08-2014 and delivered from Philippines to UK after $6m of modifications, including fitment of bridge wings. Name '*Condor Liberation*' chosen after public competition. Maiden voyage on 27-3-2015. Still in service in 2018.

Condor Rapide (Condor)
Built: Incat, Hobart, Tasmania
Launched: 3-7-1997
Dimensions: 86.6 x 26.0 x 3.6 m
Tonnage: 5,007g
Engines: 4 x 20 cyl Ruston 20RK270 diesels
Speed: 40.5kt
Passengers: 900
Cars: 200
Wave-piercing catamaran initially chartered to Australian fleet as *HMAS Jervis Bay* until 05-2001. Subsequent charters in Italy in 2002 and for SpeedFerries.com as *Speed One* on Dover-Boulogne route 2004-08. Sold to Condor on 26-3-2010 and renamed *Condor Rapide*. Still in service in 2018.

Condor Vitesse (Condor)
Built: Incat, Hobart, Tasmania
Launched: 1997
Dimensions: 86.6 x 26.0 x 3.6 m
Tonnage: 5,005g
Engines: 4 x 20 cyl Ruston 20RK2700 diesel
Speed: 40kt
Passengers: 800
Cars: 200
Wave-piercing catamaran chartered from 1998 and wintered in New Zealand for Tranz Rail in 1999/2000. Operated Poole-Cherbourg service for Brittany Ferries between 2001 and 2004. Sold in 2015 to Seajets and renamed *Champion Jet 1*.

Corbière (CIF/BCIF)
Built: Jos L Meyer, Papenburg
Launched: 23-12-1968
Dimensions: 108.7 x 17.3 x 6.0 m
Tonnage: 4,238g
Engines: 2 x Klockner-Humboldt-Deutz SBV 12M 350 diesel
Speed: 17½kt
Passengers: 1,200
Cars: 240
Built as *Apollo* for Viking Line for Baltic services. Sold to Denmark in 1976 and chartered to Olau Line as *Olau Kent* for Sheerness-Vlissingen route. After further service in Scandinavia chartered to BF as *Benodet* in 03-1984 for Plymouth-Roscoff. Chartered to CIF from 28-3-1985 as *Corbière*, then to BCIF from 10-1986 to 02-1988; returned to BF for Poole-Cherbourg freight operation. Further service as *Apollo* in Scandinavia and Canada. Still in service 2018.

Cornouailles – see Havelet

Countess of Liverpool
Built: Portland
Launched: 1814
Dimensions: 62.1 x 20.1 x 10.2 ft
Tonnage: 105g
Sailing packet on CI service between 22-1-1814 and 07-1827.

Courier/Courrier (NSWSNCo/L&SWR)
Built: Ditchburn & Mare, Blackwall
Competed: 10-1847
Dimensions: 167.0 x 22.5 x 10.6 ft
Tonnage: 314g
Engines: Maudslay, Deptford; 200hp
Speed: 12½kt
Passengers: 265 (42 berths)
Iron paddle steamer, sister of *Express* and *Dispatch*. Named *Courier* on vessel throughout life, although registered as *Courier*. Maiden voyage from Southampton to CI on 12-11-1847. Reboiled in 1852. Relief ship from 1861. Transferred to L&SWR in 1863 and placed on Cherbourg, Honfleur, Le Havre and St Malo routes. Broken up in 1885.

Cuckoo
Built: Wigram & Green, Blackwall
Launched: 1824
Dimensions: 119.6 x 19.8 x 12.6 ft
Tonnage: 234g
Engines: Boulton, Watt & Co;
Wooden paddle steamer *Cinderella* renamed *Cuckoo* in 1837. Withdrawn 1845 and employed

as fishery protection vessel. Wrecked and salvaged in Jersey in 1850.

Cygnus (W&CISPCo)
Built: J Henderson & Sons, Renfrew
Launched: 1854
Dimensions: 182.0 x 21.4 x 9.7 ft
Tonnage: 245g
Engines: McNabb & Clark; 2 cyl, 120 hp
Speed: 11¼kt
Iron paddle steamer, built for North of Europe Steam Navigation Co Harwich-Antwerp service. Chartered by W&CISPCo for Weymouth-CI route, then purchased in 1857. Also acted as relief vessel for Weymouth-Cherbourg route. Re-boilered in 1874 and major overhaul in 1883. Sold to Alfred Tolhurst on takeover by GWR in 1889. Later served for David MacBrayne in Scotland before being wrecked near Isle of Harris in 1896.

Dasher
Built: Chatham Dockyard
Launched: 1837
Dimensions: 120.0 x 21.8 x 13.0 ft
Tonnage: 260 g
Engines: Seaward & Capel, Limehouse; 2 x 50 hp
First steam vessel for Admiralty service from Weymouth. Withdrawn 1845 and employed on fishery protection duties. Broken up 1855.

Deal (SR/BR)
Built: D&W Henderson, Glasgow
Launched: 10-2-1928
Dimensions: 220.5 v 33.6 x 14.1 ft
Tonnage: 688g
Engines: single screw 2 x triple expansion, 165nhp
Speed: 15kt
Passengers: 12
Cargo steamer used as additional vessel during CI produce season from 1935. Assisted in evacuation of civilians from CI in 1940, and provided early services after Liberation from 3-7-1945. Passed to BR in 1948. Scrapped in 06-1963

Devoniun (TS)
Built: Hall Russell & Co Aberdeen
Launched: 04-1964
Dimensions: 71.6 x 14.1 m
Tonnage: 2,104g
Engines: twin screw, 8 cyl Crossly, 2,401bhp
Speed: 15kt
Passengers: 600
Cars: 42
Built as *Hebrides* on Scottish services for David

MacBrayne until acquired by TS on 22-11-1985. Trail run to CI on 5-12-1985 before entering service from Torquay in 05-1986. Sold to Huelin Renouf on 11-4-1990, but laid up from 11-1990 and sold to Monrovia on 24-5-1993. Broken up in 2003.

Diana (L&SWR)
Built: Aitken & Mansell, Glasgow
Launched: 30-11-1876
Dimensions: 232.6 x 28.2 x 14.1 ft
Tonnage: 738g
Engines: single screw, 2 cyl compound invert, 210nhp
Speed: 13½kt
Passengers: 500
First iron screw passenger ship for L&SWR CI service, as dredging work in the ports made her use practical. First mail sailing to CI on 7-4-1877. Two sister ships ordered in 1880 based on success of *Diana*. Boat deck added in 1881. Remained on CI services until 25-7-1890. Converted to triple expansion engines in 1892 and operated on St Malo route. Wrecked and sunk off Cap de la Hague on 21-6-1895.

Dinard (SR/BR)
Built: Wm Denny & Bros, Dumbarton
Launched: 2-5-1924
Dimensions: 325.0 x 41.1 x 16.0 ft
Tonnage: 2,291g
Engines: twin screw, 2 x 2 steam turbines, 433nhp
Speed: 19kt
Passengers: 1,300 (324 1st berths, 118 2nd berths)
First oil fired vessel to be built for SR. Wartime service as hospital ship at Dunkirk, Italy and Normandy. Returned to CI service in 07-1945 but converted to craned car carrier for short sea routes in 1946. To BR on 1-1-1948 and sold in 1959 as first vessel for Viking Line. Scrapped 1970.

Dispatch (NSWSPCo/L&SWR)
Built: Ditchburn & Mare, Blackwall
Completed: 04-1848
Dimensions: 166.7 x 22.1 x 11.6 ft
Tonnage: 149g
Engines: Maudsley, Son & Field; 2 x 1 cyl annular, 200hp
Speed: 13.2kt
Passengers: 259 (40 berths)
Iron paddle steamer, sister of *Courier* and *Express*. Operated initially on Poole-CI service with maiden voyage on 2-5-1848, but transferred to Southampton route after one week. Re-boilered 1852 and new saloon added in

1859. Rescued by *Dasher* when main shaft broke near Corbière on 17-10-1853. Further new boilers and superheating fitted in 1861. To L&SWR in 1863 and switched to other Southampton routes before returning to Southampton-Jersey-Granville service from 1872. Converted to coal hulk in 1881 and scrapped at Garston in 1890.

Dora (L&SWR)
Built: R Napier & Sons, Glasgow
Launched: 2-3-1899
Dimensions: 240.0 x 30.0 x 14.3 ft
Tonnage: 741g
Engines: single screw, 3 cyl triple expansion, 220nhp
Speed: 16kt
Passengers: Berths 140 1st, 60 2nd
First triple expansion on the channel, fitted with electric light, built as improvement to the *Hilda* design. Maiden voyage on 26-5-1889, but soon outclassed by GWR competition and relegated to reserve vessel. Holed on Tasse Rock, Guernsey on 17-9-1892. Hit Balleine Rocks, St Peter Port on 16-5-1893 and towed in by *Lynx*. Replaced by *Vera* in 1898 and sold in 1901 to the IoMSPCo and renamed *Douglas*. Sunk in River Mersey on 16-8-1923 after collision with *Artemesia*.

Dumfries (JSPCo/L&SWR)
Built: Scott & Co, Greenock
Completed: 02-1857
Dimensions: 112.0 x 18.0 x 9.0 ft
Tonnage: 125g
Engines: Scott & Co, Greenock; single screw, 2cyl
Iron paddle steamer built for Dumfries & Solway Firth Company. Sold to JSPCo in 11-1859 for French services. Transfer to L&SWR in 1863 and laid up before use on cargo services to Le Havre and Honfleur. Sold to P McGuffie and wrecked off Killaloe, Ireland in 1873.

Earl Godwin (BR/Sealink/SBF)
Built: Oresundsvarvet A/B, Landskrona
Launched: June 1966
Dimensions: 317.8 x 60 x 18.6 ft
Tonnage: 3,999g
Engines: Klockner-Humboldt-Deutz; twin screw, 4 oil engines, 2 x 12cyl, 2,000bhp
Speed: 18kt
Passengers: 1,000
Cars: 180
Oil burner with ice breaker bow, built as *Svea Drott* for Swedish service prior to charter to BR to relieve *Falaise* in 1974. Purchased in 12-1974

and given extensive refit at Harwich and Holyhead prior to service on CI run from 2-2-1976. Inaugurated Portsmouth service on 8-11-1976. To Sealink UK Ltd in 1979 and SBF in 1984. Struck rocks at St Helier 16-10-1984. Laid up at Falmouth at end of SBF operation then re-opened Weymouth-Cherbourg service on 17-3-1988. Chartered to MMD on 3-1-1989 then laid up prior to sale to Navarama as *Moby Baby* and left Weymouth 17-3-1990. Still in service 2018.

Earl Granville (Sealink/SBF)
Built: Jos L Meyer, Papenburg
Launched: 16-3-1973
Dimensions: 316.5 x 56.6 x 15.1 ft
Tonnage: 4,658g
Engines: Smit-Bolnes; twin screw, 12 cyl oil, 11,600 bhp
Speed: 19kt
Passengers: 1,200
Cars: 260
Built as *Viking IV* for Rederi Sally to operate between Åbo-Mariehamn-Stockholm. Acquired by Williams & Glynn Industrial Leasing for £10m in 1980 and chartered to Sealink for 10 years. Renamed *Earl Granville* 25-8-1980. Extensive £10m rebuild at Jos L Meyer, Papenburg prior to first sailing Portsmouth-CI on 29-3-1981. Fire in boiler whilst south of Isle of Wight on 22-6-1981; collided with ramp in St Helier on 20-7-1981, then suffered further fire on trip to Guernsey. Transferred to SBF on 27-7-1984. Underwent alterations for Starliner service at Ålborg and returned to service on 30-4-1985. After sit-in at end of SBF service in 10-1986 chartered to MOD then resumed Weymouth-Cherbourg route in 1987, Portsmouth-Cherbourg in 1988/9 and covered other SBF routes. Sold on 10-12-1990 to Aegean Pelagos Naftiki Eteria, Piraeus for $9.4m and renamed *Express Olympia*. Broken up 2005 in India.

Earl Harold – see Ailsa Princess

Earl of Chesterfield
Built: Bridport
Launched: 1795
Dimensions: 56.0 x 19.0 x 9.0 ft
Tonnage: 78g
First Port Office packet, operating from Weymouth from 06-1795 until sold in 11-1806.

Earl William (Sealink/SBF)
Built: Kaldnes M/V A/B Tonsberg
Launched: 30-4-1964
Dimensions: 317.8 x 58.2 x 18.6 ft
Tonnage: 3,765g

The *Earl Godwin* in her 1985 Sealink British Ferries colours. (FotoFlite)

Engines: A/B Lindholmens Verv. 2x12cyl, 10,200bhp
Speed: 18.5kt
Passengers: 940
Cars: 180
Launched as *Viking II* for Thoresen Car Ferries' Southampton-Le Havre service. Acquired by Lloyds Leasing for BR in 1977 for £3.5m and re-named *Earl William.* Refitted at cost of £2m. First sailing on Portsmouth route on 16-1-1978 until replaced by *Earl Granville* and moved to Weymouth. Struck La Platte beacon 20-11-1982. To SBF 27-7-1984. Refitted for Starliner service with night pc reduced to 400/day 800. Chartered to Home Office as detention centre in 05-1987, then to SBF Liverpool-Dun Laoghaire route. Route closed 1-1-1990. Sold to Ardonis Shipping as *Pearl William* in July 1992. Sunk on 2-4-2011 whilst under tow from Ch-aguaramas to Venezuela by tug *Icon 1* which collided with drill vessel *Petrosaudi Saturn.*

Elk (BR)
Built: Brooke Marine Ltd, Lowestoft
Launched: 13-4-1959
Dimensions: 228.0 x 39.5 x 13.3 ft
Tonnage: 795g
Engines: Sulzer Bros, Winterthur; twin screw, 6 cyl oil, 1,800bhp
Speed: 14kt
Passengers: 12
Steel cargo vessel built at cost of £408k. First sailing from Southampton on 5-8-1959. Switched to Weymouth in 1960 and operated winter Jersey-St Malo sailings. Undertook last BR sailing from Southampton on 29-9-1972 and was displaced by new container operation from Portsmouth. Final sailing Guernsey-Weymouth on 7-10-1972 then laid up. Sold to Valmas Ship-ping Co and renamed *Nikolas.* Sunk on rocks on Gainnutri Island on 12-2-1976 en route from Livorno to Alexandria.

Ella (L&SWR)
Built: Aitken & Mansell, Glasgow
Launched: 28-5-1881
Dimensions: 235.5 x 29.1 x 14.1 ft
Tonnage: 820g
Engines: J&J Thompson; single screw, 2 cyl compound inverted, 210nhp
Speed: 13½kt
Passengers: 450
Iron steamer built at cost of £28,850, sister of *Diana.* Maiden voyage to Jersey on 30-7-1881. Replaced by *Frederica* in 1890 and used as re-serve ship. Badly damaged losing funnel in storm in 1895 en route from Cherbourg to

Southampton; repair work and new boilers fit-ted by Day, Summers & Co, Southampton in 1896. Collided with *Princess Ena* in Race of Alderney on 24-11-1906. Sold to Shipping Fed-eration in 1919. Broken up 1929.

Esk (Cheeswright)
Built: Smith & Rodger, Govan
Launched: 04-01-1859
Dimensions: 177.0 x 24.4 x 11.9 ft
Tonnage: 349g
Engines: single screw, 2 cyl, 60nhp
Iron steamer initially registered in Leith before acquired by Cheeswright in 1861. Sold to for-eign buyers in 03-1869.

Express (NSWSPCo)
Built: Ditchburn & Mare, Blackwall
Launched: 06-1847
Dimensions: 159.0 x 21.4 x 10.4 ft
Tonnage: 255g
Engines: Maudslay, Deptford, 2 x 1 cyl annular, 180hp
Speed: 12½kt
Passengers: 259 (40 berths)
Iron paddle steamer, sister of *Courier* and *Dis-patch,* completed before company was regis-tered. Engines built for a government steamer but transferred to *Express.* On Le Havre route in 1847 and made first visit to CI on 28-5-1848 to cover refits. Opened Weymouth-CI route from 13-4-1857. Lost on Grunes Houillieres rocks off Corbière on 30-9-1859.

Falaise (SR/BR)
Built: Wm Denny & Bros, Dumbarton
Launched: 25-10-1946
Dimensions: 310.5 x 49.7 x 12.5 ft
Tonnage: 3,710g
Engines: twin screw, 2 x 2 stage Parson's tur-bines, 8,500shp
Speed: 20½kt
Passengers: 940 1st, 510 2nd
Oil fired steamer intended for CI routes but used extensively elsewhere. Inaugural sailing Southampton-St Malo on 14-7-1947 and visited Jersey on weekly sailing from 19-7-1947. To BR on 1-1-1948. Operated cruise programme with visits to CI as well as thrice-weekly Southamp-ton-St Malo route. On Le Havre route from 1952 and occasionally returned to CI services from 1958. Converted to car ferry for Newhaven-Dieppe route in 1964 and switched to Wey-mouth-Jersey service from 1-6-1973 after further conversion work, adding calls in Guernsey from 30-10-1973, with cars craned until installation of linkspan in 1974. Suffered

multiple engine problems and withdrawn on 14-7-1974; scrapped in Spain in early 1975.

Fannie (L&SWR)
Built: Caird & Co, Greenock
Launched: 1859
Dimensions: 231.6 x 26.2 x 13.3 ft
Tonnage: 635g
Engines: 2 cyl simple oscillating, 250nhp
Speed: 12kt
Iron paddle steamer built as the *Orion* for the Bee Company of Glasgow to serve the Lübeck-Kronstadt route in the Baltic. Renamed *Fannie* in 1862 and operated as a blockade-runner in the American Civil War. Returned in 1865 to operate Stranraer-Belfast for the Caledonian Railway. Purchased by L&SWR with *Alice* in 06-1869, primarily for French routes. First visit to CI on 25-6-1870 and re-boilered in 1874. Scrapped in 08-1890.

Fawn (SM&BSSCo)
Built: John Fullerton & Co, Paisley
Launched: 1897
Dimensions: 105.0 x 18.1 x 8.4 ft
Tonnage: 150g
Engines: single screw, 2 cyl, 42RHP
Built for CI-France trade with maiden voyage on 21-7-1897. Also operated on cross-Channel services until sold in 05-1923. Broken up 1951.

Flamer/Fearless
Built: Henry Fletcher Son & Fearnall, Limehouse
Launched: 29-4-1831
Dimensions: 111.0 x 17.0 x 11.4 ft
Tonnage: 165g
Engines: Boulton, Watt & Co; 60hp
Built at cost of £7,190. Renamed *Fearless* in 05-1837. Withdrawn 1839 and converted to survey vessel.

Foam Queen (I) (L&CISCo)
Built: Van Vliet, Nederhardinxveld
Completed: 7-1906
Dimensions: 159.0 x 26.3 x 11.2 ft
Tonnage: 518g
Engines: single screw, 3 cyl, 76nhp
Operated for L&CISCo on London-CI service between 05-1908 and 07-1911.

Foam Queen (II) (L&CISCo)
Built: London & Montrose Shipbuilding & Repair Co, Montrose
Completed: 10-1922
Dimensions: 189.2 x 30.4 x 12.6 ft
Tonnage: 811g
Engines: single screw, 3 cyl, 75nhp

Speed: 9kt
Built as *River Exe* for DR Llewellyn, Merret & Price Ltd in Cardiff. Operated for L&CISCo from 01-1926 until requisitioned and torpedoed off Dundeness Head on 2-11-1943.

Francis Freeling
Built: Portland
Launched: 1809
Dimensions: 57.5 x 19.3 x 9.1 ft
Tonnage: 86g
Sailing packet serving CI from 12-1809 until hit and sunk by Swedish brig off Portland on 6-9-1826 with all hands lost.

Fratton *(SR)*
Built: D&W Henderson & Co. Glasgow
Launched: 18-8-1925
Dimensions: 220.3 x 33.6 x 14.1 ft
Tonnage: 757g
Engines: single screw, 2 x triple expansion, 165nhp
Speed: 15kt
Passengers: 12
Cargo sister of *Haslemere* built at cost of £41,450. Primarily on Le Havre route, but struck Vieux Bank off St Malo on 7-10-1927 and had to be towed back to Southampton by *Haslemere*. Used as a barrage balloon vessel from 1940; sunk by explosion while at anchor in Seine Bay, Normandy on 18-8-1944.

Frederica (L&SWR)
Built: J&G Thompson, Clydebank
Launched: 5-6-1890
Dimensions: 259.0 x 35.1 x 14.1 ft
Tonnage: 1,059g
Engines: twin screw, 2 x triple expansion; 360nhp
Speed: 19kt
Passengers: 712
Sister of *Lydia* and *Stella*. Maiden voyage to CI on 31-7-1890. Allocated to Le Have route in 1894/5 but returned to CI in 1896. Involved in 'race' with *Ibex* off Jersey on 16-4-1897 which saw the latter hit rocks at Noirmontaise. Displaced by *Alberta* in 1900 and moved back to Le Havre service in 1903. Re-boilered by Day, Summers & Co, Southampton in 1904 and funnel lengthened in unsuccessful attempt to utilise lower grade fuel. Funnel shortened and new deck cabin built in 1905. Sold to Turkish Government in 1911 and renamed *Nilufer*. Sunk after hitting a mine off the Bosphorus on 22-11-1914.

Gael (GWR)
Built: Robertson & Co, Greenock

Completed: 05-1867
Dimensions: 211.0 x 23.2 x 10.6 ft
Tonnage: 403g
Engines: Rankin, Blackmore & Co, Greenock; 2 cyl, 150hp
Speed: 16kt
Passengers: Berths 20 1st, 20 2nd
Iron paddle steamer built for Campbeltown & Glasgow Steam Packet Co for day excursions on the Clyde. Purchased by GWR in 04-1884 to replace *South of Ireland* for Weymouth-Cherbourg but route closed on 30-06-1885. Returned to open GWR services from Jersey on 2-7-1899 pending arrival of new fleet. Sold to David MacBrayne in 1891 for Oban services and broken up in 1924.

Galtee More (L&NWR)
Built: Wm Denny & Bros, Dumbarton
Launched: 24-5-1898
Dimensions: 283.0 x 35.1 x 12.9 ft
Tonnage: 1,112g
Engines: twin screw, 2 x 4 cyl triple expansion, 212hp
Speed: 17½kt
Passengers: 900
Built with shallow draught for Holyhead-Greenore service. Substituted for *Ibex* on Weymouth-CI service in 06-1915, and chartered for summer weekend Southampton-Guernsey service in 1919-20. Scrapped 11-1926.

Gazelle (GWR)
Built: Laird Bros, Birkenhead
Launched: 13-6-1889
Dimensions: 235.5 x 27.6 x 13.1 ft
Tonnage: 672g
Engines: twin screw 3 cyl, 1,650ihp
Speed: 16kt
Passengers: 413
Steel steamer built new for CI service as part of order for three vessels, first vessels with triple-expansion engines. Maiden voyage to CI on 8-9-1889. Converted to cargo ship by Cammell Laird in 1908 and used on produce trade from the islands. Wartime service as minesweeper in Mediterranean followed by occasional use as cargo vessel for Guernsey fruit. Sold for scrap 1925.

General Doyle
Built: Looe
Launched: 1803
Dimensions: 57.7 x 19.3 x 9.0 ft
Tonnage: 83g
Sailing cutter operating from Weymouth from 10-1806 until sold in 11-1809.

Grand Turk (CSPCo/NSWSPCo)
Built: R Duncan & Co, Greenock
Launched: 06-1837
Dimensions: 153.3 x 20.2 x 13.0 ft
Tonnage: 369g
Engines: Murdoch, Aitken; 160nhp
Iron paddle steamer, built for Glasgow owners before acquisition by CSPCo for London-Southampton-Weymouth service. Passed to SWSPCo in 1842 for Le Havre route with some calls in CI. Bought by NSWSNCo in 1846 for south coast routes. Chartered to Newbolt Hall & Bros, London in 1849 and 1850 to run in Eastern Mediterranean but returned to operate a Southampton-Guernsey-Morlaix route for a single season from 12-5-1851, before relegated to relief vessel. Scrapped in 1856

Granuaile – see Ulrica

Granville *(L&SWR)*
Built: Blackwall
Launched: 1841
Dimensions: 147.7 x 19.2 x 9.4 ft
Tonnage: 131g
Iron paddle steamer, formerly the *Comet* operating on France-CI routes for French interests. Purchased by Gravesend New Steam Packet Co in 1851, then returned to France as the *Comète* for M Durand of Granville on 20-7-1856. Purchased by L&SWR in 12-1868 for use on Jersey-France services. Sold in 1872 and scrapped in South Wales in 1875.

Great Southern (GWR/GW)
Built: Laird Bros, Birkenhead
Launched: 1902
Dimensions: 275.8 x 36.3 x 15.2 ft
Tonnage: 1,339g
Engines: twin screw, 2 x 4 cyl triple expansion, 433nhp
Speed: 16kt
Passengers: 246 1st, 439 2nd
Steel steamer capable of carrying 500 cattle, built for Milford-Waterford route. Sister of *Great Western II*. Owned by Great Southern & Western Railway, Dublin. Operated to CI from 30-7-1916 to relieve *Ibex* and later offered seasonal cover for cargo and relief sailings. To GW on 1-1-1923. Broken up 1934.

Great Western (I) (GWR)
Built: W Simons & Co, Renfrew
Launched: 1867
Dimensions: 220.4 x 25.2 x 12.4 ft
Tonnage: 447g
Engines: Seaward; 2 cyl compound oscillating,

190hp
Iron paddle steamer built for Ford & Jackson Milford-Cork service. Taken over by GWR in 1872. Operated on Weymouth-Cherbourg service 1878-85, then back to Milford. Chartered to W&CISPCo to replace *Brighton* in 1887. Sold to Nathaniel Miller of Preston in 1890. Broken up 1904.

Great Western (II) (GWR/GW)
Built: Laird Bros, Birkenhead
Launched: 1902
Dimensions: 275.8 x 36.3 x 15.2 ft
Tonnage: 1,225g
Engines: twin screw, 2 x 4 cyl triple expansion, 433nhp
Speed: 16kt
Passengers: 246 1st, 439 2nd
Steel steamer capable of carrying 500 cattle, built for Milford-Waterford route. Sister of *Great Southern*. Owned by Great Southern & Western Railway, Dublin. Operated to CI from 04-1921 and offered seasonal cover for cargo and relief sailings until 1929. To GW on 1-1-1923. Broken up in 1934.

Griffin (L&SWR)
Built: Lawrence Hill & Co, Port Glasgow
Launched: 1858
Dimensions: 155.0 x 20.1 x 11.8 ft
Tonnage: 216g
Engines: single screw, 1 cyl simple, 70hp
Iron cargo steamer built for James Baird, Ayr. Purchased by Ford & Jackson in 1859 for Milford-Waterford service. Purchased by L&SWR in 1865 to inaugurate Honfleur route and fitted with new compound engine and boiler by Day, Summers & Co, Southampton in 1866. Used as winter relief vessel to CI and for cheap cargo service from 1866, operating summer Jersey-France sailings. New compound engine fitted by Day, Summers & Co in 1876. Permanently allocated to Jersey station from 1881 to 1890, then used as cargo vessel. Sold for scrap to J Constant in 1895.

Guernsey (L&SWR)
Built: J & W Dudgeon, London
Completed: 05-1874
Dimensions: 195.5 x 26.0 x 13.4 ft
Tonnage: 545g
Engines: single screw
Speed: 14 kt
Iron single screw cargo and passenger ship for the St Malo service. Limited number of calls in CI from 07-1874 on mail services, and as cargo vessel during potato season. Engines converted to triple expansion and new boiler fitted by Day, Summers & Co, Southampton in 1889. Displaced by new tonnage in 1890 and worked across other routes including Jersey-France routes in summers of 1890, 1893, 1897-99 and 1904-05. Passenger accommodation removed and cargo capacity expanded in 1908. Wrecked off Cap de la Hague on 8-4-1915 whilst sailing from Guernsey to Southampton with loss of 7 crew during wartime blackout.

Guernsey Fisher (BR)
Built: NV Ijsselwerf, Rotterdam
Completed: 12-1971
Dimensions: 269.5 x 39.8 x 12.0 ft
Tonnage: 1,560g
Engines: single screw, 8 cyl oil engine, 1,712bhp
Speed: 13½kt
Built for James Fisher of Barrow and chartered to BR for Southampton-CI container service, serving Guernsey from 6-1-1972. Transferred to Portsmouth under Brit-Comm agreement from 2-10-1972 and mainly worked to Jersey. Displaced by introduction of ro-ro service from 10-1977 and returned to owners. Converted to bulk carrier in 1984 as the *Scafell*. Still operational in 2018 as the *Sveti Jere*.

Hantonia (L&SWR/SR)
Built: Fairfield Shipbuilding, Govan
Launched: 1912
Dimensions: 300.0 x 36.1 x 16.1 ft
Tonnage: 1,560g
Engines: triple screw, 2 x Parson's single reduction geared turbines, 4,950shp
Speed: 19kt
Passengers: 505
Launched as *Louvima*, and renamed *Hantonia* in 1912, sister of *Normannia*. Served as troopship in First World War and passed to SR in 1923, when she replaced damaged *Caesarea* on CI services from 21-7-1923. Allocated to winter Southampton-Jersey-St Malo service from early 1930s. Undertook Second World War evacuation work and chartered to GWR to cover *St Patrick* on Fishguard-Rosslare route in 1941 before being requisitioned. Overhauled by Fairfield Engineering, Govan in 1945 and operated CI service until 03-1947 before returning to Le Havre. Replaced by *Normannia (II)* in 1952 and scrapped at Grays, Essex.

Haslemere (SR/BR)
Built: D&W Henderson & Co, Glasgow
Launched: 22-5-1925
Dimensions: 220.5 v 33.6 x 14.1 ft
Tonnage: 756g

Engines: single screw 2 x triple expansion, 165 nhp
Speed: 15kt
Passengers: 12
Cargo vessel sister of *Deal* and first in the SR fleet allocated to Southampton. Used as a barrage balloon vessel in 1940 and control vessel for Normandy Landings in 1944. First SR arrival in CI after Liberation on 23-6-1945. Struck rocks off Guernsey on 23-11-1945 requiring extensive repair. Collided with *Winchester* in Solent on 2-12-1955. Withdrawn on 7-7-1959 and broken up.

Havelet (BCIF/Condor)

Built: Trondjems Meek Verksted A/S, Norway
Launched: 20-6-1976
Dimensions: 110.0 x 16.5 x 5.2 m
Tonnage: 6,918g
Engines: Semt Pielstick 16PA6V280 diesel, 11,200bhp
Speed: 19kt
Passengers: 500 (560 from 1990)
Cars: 205
Built for BF Plymouth-Roscoff service as *Cornouailles*; latterly employed for Truckline on Poole-Cherbourg route. Chartered by BCIF as cover for *Corbière* refit in 03-1986 and for *Portelet* in 1987. Full charter by BCIF as *Havelet* with maiden call on 10-4-1989 on Poole-CI service. Refitted in 1990 at cost of £2m with extensive internal alterations, expanding passenger capacity. Purchased by CIF on behalf of BCIF. Operated last BCIF sailing on 21-1-1994. Worked for Condor on Weymouth route until 29-10-1996, then laid up. Purchased by Condor as back up vessel on 5-8-1998 to operate as required until arrival of Commodore Clipper in 09-1999. Sold as *Sventi Stefan* to Fortune Overseas Navigation Inc in Montenegro.

Havre (SWSPCo/L&SWR)

Built: Ditchburn & Marne, Blackwall
Launched: 5-4-1856
Dimensions: 184.7 x 24.0 x 14.6 ft
Tonnage: 382g
Engines: Seaward & Capel; 3 cyl, 220hp
Speed: 13½ kt
Passengers: 150
Iron paddle steamer built for Southampton-Le Havre service, sister of *Alliance*. Collided with *Wonder* in 1858. Maiden call in CI on 13-12-1859, but not a regular visitor until 1870. Transferred to L&SWR in 1863. Wrecked on 15-12-1875 on Platte Boue, Little Russel Channel.

HD1 (HDF)

Built: Incat, China
Launched: 1998
Dimensions: 80.1 X 19.0 X 2.2 m
Tonnage: 2,357g
Engines: 4 x Ruston 16RK270
Speed: 47kt
Passengers: 450
Cars: 89
Built as *Afai 08* and renamed *Incat K3* before operating from Miami for Bay Ferries in 1999. Operated in the Caribbean and Mediterranean before overhaul in Gibraltar and ramp trials in CI on 19-2-2007. Maiden voyage Jersey-St Malo on 15-3-2007, but inaugural season suffered from impeller problems and vessel collided with *Commodore Goodwill* on 11-5-2007 and *Condor Express* on 28-7-2008, both in St Helier. Laid up in winter and returned for 2008 season but withdrawn on 7-9-2008 and subsequently sold to Dae A Express Shipping as *Moon Flower*. In service as *Harmony Flower* in Yellow Sea in 2018.

Hilda (L&SWR)

Built: Aitken & Mansell, Glasgow
Launched: 07-1882
Dimensions: 235.5 x 29.1 x 14.2 ft
Tonnage: 822g
Engines: single screw, 2 cyl compound inv, 210nhp
Speed: 14kt
Passengers: 600
Iron single screw steamer built at cost of £33,000, sister of *Ella*. Maiden voyage to CI on 19-1-1883 and remained on route until replaced by *Stella* in 1890 and used as reserve ship. Reboilered by Day, Summers & Co, Southampton in 1893-4 and fitted with electric light. Operated as summer relief and winter service vessel when larger ships were laid up. Wrecked on Pierres des Portes reef, Czembre Island on 18-11-1905 with loss of 128 lives.

Hinchinbrook

Built: Bridport
Launched: 1811
Dimensions: 60.0 x 19.7 x 10.0 ft
Tonnage: 90g
Sailing cutter operating from Weymouth from 07-1811 until wrecked off Alderney in 02-1826.

Hogarth – see Caledonia

Honfleur (L&SWR)

Built: Aitken & Mansell, Glasgow

Launched: 11-1873
Dimensions: 176.4 x 24.1 x 12.4 ft
Tonnage: 410g
Engines: Rait & Lindsay; single screw, 2 cyl simple expansion, 50hp
Iron cargo ship built for Southampton-Le Havre route, sister of *Cherbourg*. Winter relief for CI services including Granville. Saved passengers and crew from *Havre* wreck in 1875. Converted to triple expansion engines and reboiled by J&J Thompson in 1888. Allocated to Jersey station for Granville service 1890-96 until replaced by *Victoria*. Used again between 1907-09. Reboiled in 1907 with old *Alma* boiler. Withdrawn in 1911 and sold to S Galbraith to operate in Turkey. Extensive career thereafter and not scrapped until 2010.

Hythe (SR/BR)
Built: D&W Henderson & Co, Glasgow
Launched: 24-5-1925
Dimensions: 220.6 v 33.6 x 14.1 ft
Tonnage: 685g
Engines: single screw, 2 x triple expansion, 165nhp
Speed: 15kt
Passengers: 12
Cargo vessel sister of *Deal* and *Haslemere*, allocated to Dover station. Operated potato services from CI in 1933-4 and assisted in evacuation of CI in 1940. To BR on 1-1-1948. Joined the Southampton station in 1949 after summer service the previous year. Final sailing from Jersey on 23-8-1955. Broken up 1956.

Ibex (GWR/GW)
Built: Laird Bros, Birkenhead
Launched: 6-6-1891
Dimensions: 265.0 x 32.8 x 14.2 ft
Tonnage: 1,161g
Engines: twin screw, 2 x triple expansion, 299nhp
Speed: 19kt
Passengers: 600 (210 berths)
Steel steamer built for CI service in response to LSWR 'Frederica' class vessels. Hit Noirmontaise Rock on 16-4-1897 during 'race' with L&SWR *Frederica*, returning to service on 207-1897. Hit Platte Fougeres on 5-1-1900 and sank, but was raised in July and returned to service on 23-4-1901. Radio equipment fitted in 1914. Served CI through First World War on thrice weekly sailing pattern. Collided with and sank *Aletta* - cargo vessel on charter to GWR - on 19-9-1917; sank U boat on 18-3-1918. Major refit in 1922 with new shelter deck added. Last sailing from CI on 14-4-1925 and broken up at Sheerness.

Island Commodore (III) (Commodore)
Built: Schelde Koninklijke, Vlissingen, Netherlands
Launched: 4-2-1995
Dimensions: 126.4 x 21.0 x 6.0 m
Tonnage: 11,166g
Engines: 2 x 6 cyl MaK diesels
Speed: 18kt
Passengers: 12
Freight: 1,250lm
Sister to *Commodore Goodwill*. Chartered to Commodore from 19-6-1995 and operated until 26-9-1999. Rebuilt to cable maintenance vessel in 1999 and renamed *Wave Sentinel*. Still in service in 2018.

Island Queen (I) (L&CISCo)
Built: A Vuijk, Capelle a/d Ysel
Completed: 1900
Dimensions: 176.4 x 27.0 x 13.1 ft
Tonnage: 613g
Engines: 3 cyl, 99nhp
Speed: 10kt
Operated to CI between 08-1900 and 08-1913 before being sold to Turkey as *Candiano*. Broken up 1925.

Island Queen (II) (L&CISCo)
Built: Swan Hunter & Wigham Richardson, Sunderland
Completed: 7-1920
Dimensions: 173.5 x 28.1 x 13.5 ft
Tonnage: 689g
Engines: single screw, 3 cyl, 97nhp
Operated for L&CISCo from 12-1920 until 02-1933. Sold to Egypt.

Isle of Guernsey (SR/BR)
Built: Wm Denny & Bros, Dumbarton
Launched: 17-12-1929
Dimensions: 306.0 x 42.1 x 14.4 ft
Tonnage: 2,143g
Engines: twin screw, 2 x 2 Parson's 2 stage srg turbines, 540nhp
Speed: 19½kt
Passengers: 1,400 (154 1st class berths)
Second in the *Isle of Jersey* class for Southampton-CI services. Maiden voyage on 4-4-1930. Extra seating added in 1937. Wartime service as hospital ship at Dunkirk, at Scapa Flow and Normandy Landings in 1944. Re-opened Newhaven-Dieppe route on 15-1-1945 and CI route on 26-6-1945. Major refit before returning to CI service on 23-4-1947. Transferred to BR 1-1-1948. Accommodation improved in 1956. Closed passenger service from Southampton-CI on 13-5-1961 then relief vessel at Weymouth. Broken up 1961.

Isle of Jersey (SR/BR)

Built: Wm Denny & Bros, Dumbarton
Launched: 22-10-1929
Dimensions: 306.0 x 42.1 x 14.4 ft
Tonnage: 2,143g
Engines: twin screw, 2 x 2 Parson's 2 stage srg turbines, 540nhp
Speed: 19½kt
Passengers: 1,400 (154 1st class berths)
First in the *Isle of Jersey* class for Southampton-CI services. Maiden voyage on 12-3-1930. Extra seating added in 1937. Wartime service as hospital ship at Scapa Flow and at Normandy Landings in 1944. Returned to CI service on 10-10-1945. Transferred to BR 1-1-1948 and allocated to Weymouth from 1-1-1956. Accommodation improved in 1956. Struck SE rock of Elizabeth Castle on 7-9-1957. Withdrawn on 21-10-1959 and sold to Mohamed Senussi Giaber of Tripoli for service as a pilgrim ship. Broken up 1963.

Isle of Sark (SR/BR)

Built: Wm Denny & Bros, Dumbarton
Launched: 21-11-1931
Dimensions: 306.0 x 42.1 x 14.4 ft
Tonnage: 2,211g
Engines: twin screw, 2 x 2 Parson's 2 stage srg turbines, 540nhp
Speed: 19½kt
Passengers: 1,400 (154 1st class berths)
Third in the *Isle of Jersey* class for Southampton-CI services. Built with experimental Maier-form bow. Maiden voyage to CI on 18-3-1932. Fitted with first stabilisers in 1934 and extra seating added in 1937. Made final sailing from CI on 28-6-1940 prior to occupation. Wartime service as radar training vessel. After post war refit arrived in CI on 24-6-1946, being fitted with radar. Transferred to BR 1-1-1948. Accommodation improved in 1956. Final sailing on 29-10-1960 and sold for breaking up in 1961.

Isle of Thanet (SR/BR)

Built: Wm Denny & Bros, Dumbarton
Launched: 23-4-1925
Dimensions: 335.0 x 45.1 x 17.1 ft
Tonnage: 2,701g
Engines: twin screw, 2 x 2 srg Parson's compound turbines, 800nhp
Speed: 21kt
Passengers: 1,000 1st, 400 2nd
Built as first oil burner for the Dover services. Operated Southampton-St Malo in 1939. In 1949, and from 1952 to 1958, operated summer Friday night sailing Southampton-Guernsey with daytime return. Broken up 1964.

Ivanhoe

Built: J Scott & Sons, Greenock
Launched: 1820
Dimensions: 103.9 x 16.9 x 11.3 ft
Tonnage: 158g
Engines: Maudsley, Sons & Field; 60hp
Wooden paddle steamer acquired by Government in 1821 and transferred to Weymouth in 1827. Withdrawn in 1837 and moved to London as *Boxer*.

Jersey Fisher (BR)

Built: NV Ijsselwerf, Rotterdam
Completed: 2-1972
Dimensions: 269.5 x 39.8 x 12.0 ft
Tonnage: 829g
Engines: Fairfield Shipbuilding, Govan; single screw, 8 cyl oil, 1,712bhp
Speed: 13½kt
Built for JF and chartered to BR for Southampton-CI container service, serving Jersey from 21-2-1972. Transferred to Portsmouth under Brit-Comm agreement from 2-10-1972 and mainly worked to Jersey. Displaced by introduction of ro-ro service from 10-1977 and chartered to Commodore as *Commodore Challenger* until 3-10-1983.

Juniper (Commodore)

Built: Compagnie Maritime des Chargeurs Reunis SA, France
Completed: 21-1-1977
Dimensions: 109.7 x 11.1 x 5.2 m
Tonnage: 1,575g
Engines: 2 x 9cyl MaK diesels, 6,600bhp
Speed: 16.0kt
Passengers: 12
Freight: 564lm
Chartered from TransEuropa Ferries to launch ro-ro operation from 29-7-1990 but proved unsuitable and replaced by *Commodore Clipper* (IV). Charter terminated on 26-1-1991. Returned in 1994 to cover for repairs to *Norman Commodore* (III).

Kent (CSPCo)

Built: J&G Bauckham, Rotherhithe
Launched: 1829
Dimensions: 125.0 x 17.4 x 10.5 g
Tonnage: 182g
Wooden paddle steamer built to operate on the Thames for the Gravesend and Milton Steam Packet Company. Wrecked in Christchurch Bay in 1842.

L Taurus/Sylbe (TS/BCIF)

Built: Kremer Werft. Elmshorn, Germany
Completed: 1971

Dimensions: 80.7 x 12.9 x 4.2 m
Tonnage: 982g
Engines: Alpha Diesel single screw, 6 cyl;
230bhp
Built as *Bibiana* for Part. Contimar Beteiligungs.
Purchased by P&O in 1975 and operated in
Northern Isles until 1987. Purchased by TS on
17-7-1987 and renamed *L Taurus* and undertook berthing trials in CI in 08-1987. Commenced regular freight service from Poole
under TS Freightliner banner in 09-1987. Purchased by BCIF on 10-4-1990 and renamed
Sylbe in 06-1990. Provided additional freight
capacity but was increasingly laid up. Sold in
1993 and last noted as *M Yuksel* in 2009 in
Moldova.

La Duchesse de Bretagne (BR/JL)
Built: Wm Denny & Bros, Dumbarton
Launched: 7-10-1949
Dimensions: 95.0 x 12.4 x 3.4 m
Tonnage: 2,875g
Engines: 2 x Pametrada single reduction geared
turbines, 19,000shp
Speed: 25kt
Passengers: 1,450
Cars: 25 from 1966
First channel steamer with tripod masts built for
Newhaven-Dieppe route and withdrawn on 18-
9-1966. Purchased by JL in 12-1966 and refitted
in Antwerp to take cars. Inaugural Torquay-CI
sailing on 15-5-1967. Operated for JL until
bankruptcy in 1968 and scrapped in 1970.

La Duchesse de Normandie (GW/BR/JL)
Built: Earle's Shipbuilding & Engineering Co, Hull
Launched: 07-1931
Dimensions: 172.5 x 43.1 x 14.7 ft
Tonnage: 896g
Engines: twin screw, 2 x triple expansion.
261nhp
Speed: 13kt
Passengers 800
Cars; 20
Built as Plymouth tender *Sir Richard Grenville*
for GW, serving as a tender during Second
World War. To BR on 1-1-1948. Withdrawn on
31-10-1963 and acquired by JL, entering service
on 3-5-1964 on inter-island/France routes from
Jersey. Scrapped in 1969 after failure of JL.

Ladybird (HPM/LB&SCR)
Built: Wm Denny & Bros, Dumbarton
Launched: 10-3-1851
Dimensions: 160.0 ft
Tonnage: 353g
Passengers: 101

Speed: 11kt
Operated Shoreham-Jersey service for HP
Maples. Transferred to LB&SCR.

Lady de Saumarez (B&FSNCo/CSPCo/SWSPCo)
Built: Henry Wilmshurst, Millwall
Launched: 12-1835
Dimensions: 131.4 x 21.3 x 12.9 ft
Tonnage: 172 burthen
Engines: Seaward; 90nhp
Wooden Paddle steamer purchased new by
B&FSNCo. Maiden voyage on 5-1-1836; passed
to Commercial Steam Packet Co in 1837 and
SWSPCo in 1842. Displaced by larger vessels
and little used after 1847. Broken up in 1853.

Laura (L&SWR/SR)
Built: Aitken & Mansell, Glasgow
Launched: 20-3-1885
Dimensions: 207.0 x 26.8 x 13.3 ft
Tonnage: 617g
Engines: J&J Thompson; single screw, 2 cyl
compound, 180nhp
Speed: 14kt
Passengers: 400
First steel passenger steamer for L&SWR built as
replacement for *Caesarea* for Southampton-St
Malo route at cost of £23,500. Operated most
Jersey-France summer services from 1891 to
1914 and until closure in 1918/19. Covered
Southampton-CI service during 1916. Reduced
to cargo status in 1922. Passed to SR in 1923.
Replaced by *Ringwood* in 1927 and sold to Ba-
hamas Shipping Co, Nassau. Broken up in 1937.

Liverpool (LG&JSPCo)
Built: Taylor & Farina & Co
Launched: 1830
Dimensions: 137.5 x 22.0 x 14.6 ft
Tonnage: 206 burthen
Engines: 180hp
Wooden paddle steamer owned by Glasgow &
Liverpool Steam Ship Co and chartered for CI-
Southampton-London service with maiden voy-
age from Guernsey on 6-6-1835. London call
dropped and became strong competitor to es-
tablished service. Withdrawn in 08-1835, leaving
many debtors in CI. Subsequently sailed to
Iberia for P&O.

London Queen (I) (L&CISCo)
Built: Van Vliet, Hardinxveld
Completed: 12-1910
Dimensions: 169.5 x 28.1 x 11.7 ft
Tonnage: 599g
Engines: 3 cyl, 75nhp
Passengers: 133

The *Commodore Goodwill* on a very heavily loaded sailing.
(FotoFlite)

Operated on London-CI route from 01-1911 until 11-1925 when struck rocks off Guernsey. Sold to Chile in 1926 as *Risoy*.

London Queen (II) (L&CISCo)
Built: Burntisland Shipbuilding Co
Completed: 2-1933
Dimensions: 201.5 x 30.8 x 14.5 ft
Tonnage: 781g
Engines: single screw, 3 cyl, 129nhp
Operated for L&CISCo from 03-1933 until 07-1946. Sold to British Channel Traders. Broken up 1956.

Lord Beresford (SWSPCo)
Built: William Scott & Sons, Bristol
Completed: 05-1824
Dimensions: 100.8 x 18.1 x 11.8 ft
Tonnage: 81 burthen
Engines: 72hp
Paddle steamer owned by various shareholders. Maiden voyage from CI-Portsmouth on 16-6-1824. Summer only operation, switched to Southampton in 1825. Lengthened by 17ft in 1831/2 and extensively remodeled as passenger ship with new boilers and paddle wheels in 1835/6. Withdrawn due to strong competition shortly thereafter. Later operated Southampton-Falmouth for Falmouth & Southampton Steam Packet Co, and from Swansea. Broken up in 1863.

Lord of the Isles (SWSPCo)
Completed: 23-6-1831
Tonnage: 345g
Engines: 72hp

Lorina (L&SWR/SR)
Built: Wm Denny & Bros, Dumbarton
Launched: 12-8-1918
Dimensions: 299.0 x 36.1 x 14.7 ft
Tonnage: 1,457g
Engines: twin screw, 4 x Parson's single reduction geared turbine
Speed: 19kt
Passengers: 238
Construction began in 1914 but delayed by war. Work re-started for Admiralty in 1918 and converted at Caledon, Dundee to carry 700 troops. Passed to L&SWR in 1920. Maiden voyage to CI on 31-3-1920 but allocated to St Malo service. Passed to SR in 1923 and moved to CI route from 1924. Suffered turbine problems in 1928 and 1929 and relegated to relief work after 1931, including Southampton-Jersey-St Malo from autumn 1935. Grounded off St Helier on 23-10-1935. Served as a troopship at Plymouth in 1939; bombed and beached at Dunkirk on 30-5-1940.

Lune Fisher (BR)
Built: Schpsw, Foxhol
Launched: 1962
Dimensions: 217.5 x 22.8 ft
Tonnage: 1,012g
Chartered by BR from JF for cargo services with first call on 6-4-1963. Operated seasonally in 1964 and then from 17-6-1965 to 31-1-1972 when displaced by new container service. Broken up in 1989.

Lydia (L&SWR)
Built: J&G Thompson, Clydebank
Launched: 16-7-1890
Dimensions: 259.0 x 35.1 x 14.8 ft
Tonnage: 1,059g
Engines: twin screw, 2 x triple expansion; 360 nhp
Speed: 19kt
Passengers: 712
Sister of *Frederica* and *Stella*. Maiden voyage to CI on 6-10-1890. Hit La Rond rock off St Peter Port and holed on 6-5-1891. Caught fire in St Helier on 16-12-1901. Internal modernisation in 1904. Re-boilered in 1909 and allocated to Southampton-Le Havre route in 1910, but also covered CI service. Requisitioned 1915-1919. Surplus in 1921 and sold to Montague Yates for service in the Mediterranean. Broken up 1937.

Lynx (GWR)
Built: Laird Bros, Birkenhead
Launched: 1889
Dimensions: 235.5 x 27.6 x 13.1 ft
Tonnage: 672g
Engines: twin screw, 2 x triple expansion, 184nhp
Speed: 16kt
Passengers: 430
Steel steamer built for CI service as part of order for three vessels, first vessels with triple-expansion engines. Maiden voyage to CI on 4-8-1899. Collided with *Oevelgonne* south of Portland on 5-9-1890. Accommodation improved in 1890 and 1896, but allocated to tender duties at Plymouth from 1903. Converted to cargo ship 1912. Wartime service as *HMS Lynn* followed by occasional use as cargo vessel. Sold for scrap 1925.

Maria (L&SWR)
Built: H Murray & Co, Port Glasgow
Completed: 10-1871
Dimensions: 155.7 x 21.1 x 11.0 ft
Tonnage: 271 g
Engines: single screw, 2 cyl compound, 50rhp
Cargo vessel built for MR Nolan & W Johnston of Liverpool. Acquired by L&SWR in 04-1872 for Honfleur service. Used during produce season from CI. Collided with *Avonomore* off Owers Light and towed back stern-first to Southampton by *Columbia* for repair. Sold on 12-4-1907 to operate in the Black Sea. Broken up in 1927.

May Queen (L&CISCo)
Built: J Meyer, Zaltbommer
Completed: 1900
Dimensions: 137.0 x 23.1 x 8.4 ft
Tonnage: 342g
Engines: 50nhp
Speed: 9½kt
Operated between 7-1900 to 7-1903. Sold to France.

Melmore (GWR)
Built: DJ Dunlop & Co, Port Glasgow
Launched: 1892
Dimensions: 156.2 x 25.8 x 11.3 ft
Tonnage: 412g
Engines: single screw, triple expansion, 96rhp
Speed: 10kt
Steel steamer built as *Melmore* for Earl of Leitrim. Purchased by GWR in 1905 for Irish and CI routes. Operated during potato season from 1905-09. Limited use thereafter and sold on 10-6-1912 to Charles Forbes for abortive treasure-seeking venture. Later operated in British Columbia and Peru. Broken up in 1921.

Meteor
Built: Wm Evans, Rotherhithe
Launched: 1821
Tonnage: 190 g
Engines: Boulton, Watt & Co; 60 hp
Wooden paddle steamer operated from Weymouth from 1828 until wrecked at Portland on 23-2-1830.

Metropolis (C&M)
Built: Joyce & Co, London
Launched: 1857
Overhauled and fitted with new boilers in 1860-61. Wrecked off Jersey 12-2-1861

Monarch (SoESNCo/NSWSNCo)
Built: Rubie & Blaker, Northam
Completed: 03-1837

Dimensions: 137.7 x 21.0 x 13.0 ft
Tonnage: 312g
Wooden paddle steamer for Southampton-Le Havre route from 4-4-1837, winter relief for CI; passed to NSWSN Co in 1846 and operated summer CI service in 1847. Sold in 1848 for £900 to CB Robinson and H Smith for conversion to a square rig sailing ship for service in Australia and New Zealand. Lost in Hobson's Bay, Victoria on 17-7-1867.

Moose (BR)
Built: Brooke Marine Ltd, Lowestoft
Launched: 25-5-1959
Dimensions: 228.0 x 39.5 x 13.3 ft
Tonnage: 795g
Engines: Sulzer Bros, Winterthur, twin screw 2 x 6 cyl oil fired
Speed: 14kt
Passengers: 12
Cargo vessel, sister of *Elk*. Maiden voyage to CI on 16-10-1959.Closed Jersey-France railway service on 19-12-1964. Replaced by Jersey Fisher, but spent 1972 season as car carrier on Weymouth-CI service. Sold in 10-1972 to Valmas Maritime SA as the *Rena*. Subsequent service in Greece.

Norman Commodore – see Pride of Portsmouth

Normandy (I) (L&SWR)
Built: John Ash & Co, Cubitt Town
Launched: 17-6-1863
Dimensions: 210 x 24 x 13 ft
Tonnage: 600g
Engines: J Stewart, Poplar; 2 cyl simple oscillating
Speed: 14kt
Passengers: 400
First iron paddle steamer for L&SWR and first with straight stem, similar to *Brittany*. Maiden sailing to CI on 18-9-1863 and remained allocated to the route. Badly damaged on 17-3-1864 following collision with Holland America Line *Bavaria* in Southampton Water. Sunk after collision with *Mary* on 17-3-1870.

Normandy (II) (LB&SCR/L&SWR)
Built: Earle's Shipbuilding & Engineering Co. Hull
Launched: 12-5-1910
Dimensions: 192 x 29.2 x 14.1 ft
Tonnage: 618g
Engines: single screw, triple expansion, 82rhp
Speed: 14kt
Sister of *Brittany* built for LB&SCR Newhaven-Caen route and transferred to L&SWR on 3-6-

1912. Torpedoed and sunk by *U90* on 25-1-1918 off Cap de La Hague with loss of 32 lives.

Normannia (I) (L&SWR/SR)
Built: Fairfield Shipbuilding & Engineering Co, Govan
Launched: 9-11-1911
Dimensions: 290 x 36 x 15 ft
Tonnage: 1,560g
Engines: triple screw, twin single reduction geared turbines, 4,950shp
Speed: 19kt
Passengers: 300
First passenger steamer of this type. Maiden voyage Southampton-Le Havre on 2-4-1912. Operated as troopship during First World War. Passed to SR in 1923. Made intermittent visits to CI from 1926 covering *Lorina* and *Alberta*. Some winter service on Jersey-St Malo in later 1930s. Allocated to CI route for autumn/winter 1939/40 before call up as troopship. Lost at Dunkirk on 30-5-1940.

Normannia (II) (BR)
Built: Wm Denny & Bros, Dumbarton
Launched: 19-7-1951
Dimensions: 309.1 x 49.7 x 12.5 ft
Tonnage: 3,5423g
Engines: twin screw, 2 x Pametrada geared turbine, 8,000shp
Speed: 19½kt
Passengers: 1,410; 780 1st 630 2nd
Built for Southampton-Le Havre route. Maiden voyage on 3-3-1952. First visit to CI on 13-11-1958 on winter cover with Falaise. Relieved *St Patrick* from Weymouth in winter 1960. Converted to car ferry in 1963/4 for work on short sea routes and replaced *Falaise* on CI winter service in winter 1973/4. Returned the following winter as sole CI vessel and maintained longest unbroken spell of operation on the route. Intermittent visits thereafter until last departure on 6-5-1978. Broken up 1978.

Pembroke (GWR)
Built: Laird Bros, Birkenhead
Launched: 1880
Dimensions: 235.5 x 27.6 x 13.0 ft
Tonnage: 971g
Engines: 2 x 2 cyl compound oscillating
Speed: 14kt
Final paddle steamer for GWR and first with steel hull, built for Irish routes. Suffered major engine failure in 1895 and rebuilt and lengthened by 19ft as twin screw vessel with new boilers for £30,000. Reserve vessel for fleet. Operated as cargo vessel from Guernsey in 06-

1897, but maintained passenger service when *Roebuck* was with drawn. Operated CI service from 1916-1920 and produce services thereafter until 4-7-1925. Broken up 1925.

Pluto
Built: Woolwich Dockyard
Launched: 1831
Dimensions: 135.0 x 24.0 x 11.1 ft
Tonnage: 365g
Engines: Boulton, Watt & Co; 100nhp
Operated for 6 months from 09-1837 until withdrawn in 1838.

Portelet (BCIF)
Built: Cammell Laird & Co, Birkenhead
Launched: 1967
Dimensions: 111.1 x 17.1 x 4.3 m
Tonnage: 6,280g
Engines: Crossley; 2 x 12 cyl four-stroke single-acting diesel
Speed: 19kt
Passengers: 1,200
Cars: 170
Built as the *Lion* for Burns & Laird's Ardrossan-Larne route. Taken over by P&O in 1971 and used on Dover-Boulogne route from 1976. Sold by European Ferries to Marlines as *Baroness M*. Chartered to BCIF in 1987 and 1988 as *Portelet*, initially covering *Corbière* refit, then opening seasonal Weymouth-CI service. Initial operation restricted by DoT due to problems with cabin safety. Full service inaugurated from 24-4-1987. Charter concluded on 2-10-1988 and returned to Mediterranean as *Baroness M*. Broken up in 2004.

Pride of Portsmouth/Norman Commodore (III) (MMD/Commodore)
Built: Ankerlökken Verf, Florö, Norway
Launched: 9-5-1972
Dimensions: 108.3 x 21.5 x 4.9 m
Tonnage: 1,585g
Engines: 2 x 8 cylinder Pielstick 8PC2L diesel, 8,000hp
Speed: 17½kt
Passengers: 12
Freight: 45 trailers
Built as the *Anu* and chartered extensively across Northern Europe before joining Commodore as *Pride of Portsmouth*. Renamed *Norman Commodore (III)*. Badly damaged by fire in December 1993; sank the *Trident IV* on her return to traffic. Final sailing on 7-12-1995. Sold to Finland and renamed *Fjärdvägen* to operate between Långnäs and Nådendal. Still in service in 2018.

Princess Ena (L&SWR/SR)
Built: Gourlay Bros, Dundee
Launched: 25-5-1906
Dimensions: 250.6 x 33.3 x 15.1 ft
Tonnage: 1,198g
Engines: twin screw, 2 x triple expansion, 185nhp
Speed: 16kt
Passengers: 600
Replacement for *Hilda.* Maiden voyage Southampton-St Malo on 16-7-1906. Holed on Paternoster Rock, Jersey on 20-5-1908. Grounded off Isle of Wight near Needles on 10-9-1909. Requisitioned for wartime service and served in North Sea as a Q ship, and in Mediterranean. Passed to SR in 1923. Relief steamer thereafter. Grounded on Minquieres on passage from Jersey to St Malo on 14-8-1923. Caught fire and sank during empty trip from Jersey to St Malo on 3-8-1935.

Purbeck (BCIF/Commodore)
Built: Soc. Nouvelle des At & Ch du Havre
Launched: 13-1-1978
Dimensions: 109.7 x 17.5 x 11.5 m
Tonnage: 2,736g
Engines: 2 MAK 9 M 453 diesels
Speed: 17.2kt
Passengers: 58
Trailers: 64
Built for BF subsidiary Truckline's Poole-Cherbourg service. Lengthened by 15m in 1986. Chartered to BCIF from 1-11-1993 to 21-1-1994 and then to Commodore Portsmouth-CI service from 1994. To Sally Ferries Dartford-Vlissingen service from 19-6-1995. Laid up as *Maria Rosario* in Puerto de la Cruz in 2018.

Reindeer (GWR/GW)
Built: Naval Construction and Armaments Co, Barrow
Launched: 6-3-1897
Dimensions: 280.0 x 34.5 x 16.8 ft
Tonnage: 1,193g
Engines: twin screw triple expansion inclined inboard; 643nhp.
Speed: 20kt
Passengers: 727; 487 1st 240 3rd
Steel steamer built for CI service, sister to *Roebuck.* Maiden crossing CI-Weymouth 3-8-1897. Collided with *Broderick Castle* at Weymouth on 3-9-1897. Requisitioned in 1914 and served in Mediterranean. Collided with and sank Immingham on 6-6-1915 during Gallipoli campaign. Returned to service after refit 02-1920. To GW on 1-1-1923. Shelter deck fitted in 1923. Reserve steamer after 1925 and sold for scrap to TW Ward 1928

Rina (L&SWR/SR)
Built: Ardrossan DD & SB Co, Ardrossan
Completed: 03-1902
Dimensions: 170.0 x 27.1 x 11.4 ft
Tonnage: 548g
Engines: Bow MacLachlan; single screw triple expansion, SR, 3 cyl; 500ihp
Speed: 9½kt
Cargo steamer built as the *Algethi* for RH Penny & Sons, Shoreham. Purchased by L&SWR in 1922 for agricultural cargo and passed to Southern Railway in 1923. Sold to York Line in 1926 and sailed from Italy. Sunk outside Catania in 1941.

Ringwood (SR/BR)
Built: D&W Henderson & Co, Glasgow
Launched: 13-4-1926
Dimensions: 229.6 x 33.6 x 14.2 ft
Tonnage: 755g
Engines: twin screw, 2 x triple expansion, 165nhp
Speed: 15kt
Final vessel in series of cargo builds for SR, with maiden voyage to CI on 18-6-1926. Hit rocks off Grand Jardin Lighthouse, St Malo on 8-10-1927, but able to float off. Specialised in cattle transport after 1927. Attacked by hostile aircraft in St Peter Port on 28-6-1940. Employed as Auxiliary Net Layer at Scapa Flow during Second World War and did not return to CI until 11-6-1946. To BR on 1-1-1948 and replaced by *Elk* after final sailing on 9-10-1959, then scrapped.

Robert Burns (CSPCo/NSWSPCo)
Built: R Duncan & Co
Launched: 1835
Dimensions: 132.1 x 19.4 x 10.5 ft
Tonnage: 309g
Engines: D Napier; 80hp
Built for Largo, Millport & Ayr service. Operated to *CI* from 1837 to 1846.

Roebuck (I) (GWR)
Built: Naval Construction and Armaments Co, Barrow
Launched: 6-3-1897
Dimensions: 280.0 x 34.5 x 16.8 ft
Tonnage: 1,281g
Engines: twin screw 2 x triple expansion; 643nhp
Speed: 21kt
Passengers: 717 (487 1st, 240 3rd)
Built for CI summer service at cost of £55,000, sister of *Reindeer;* maiden voyage to CI on 1-7-1897 but suffered machinery problems. Caught fire and sank at Milford 26-1-1905 and was sub-

sequently raised, ran aground on Kaines Rocks 19-7-1911. Requisitioned in 1914 as *HMS Roedean* and sunk at Scapa Flow 13-1-1915.

Roebuck (II) (GW/BR)

Built: Swan, Hunter & Wigham Richardson, Newcastle
Launched: 24-3-1925
Dimensions: 211.2 x 33.7 x 15.3 ft
Tonnage: 776g
Engines: twin screw, 2 x triple expansion inv; 1,350ihp
Speed: 13kt
Passengers: 12
Cargo vessel for Weymouth services, sister of *Sambur*. Alterations to accommodation in 1928. Wartime service at Dunkirk, as a barrage balloon unit and at Normandy Landings in 1944. Returned to Jersey on 17-10-1945. To BR on 1-1-1948 and remained at Weymouth, but also served Southampton between 1960 and 1963. Withdrawn after last sailing on 27-2-1965 and broken up in 1966.

Rover

Built: West Cowes
Launched: 1789
Dimensions: 53.0 x 18.1 x 8.8 ft
Tonnage: 67g
Sailing cutter, second Post Office packet on the CI route. Operated from Weymouth from 02-1794 until 7-1811.

Rozel *(BCIF)*

Built: Cammell Laird, Birkenhead
Launched: 14-11-1973
Dimensions: 392.1 x 74.2 x 17.0ft
Tonnage: 8,987g
Engines: Stork-Werkspoor; 4 x 8 cyl 8TM410 diesel, 20,400hp
Speed: 21kt
Passengers: 1,300
Cars: 296
Built for Sealink UK Harwich-Hook service as *St Edmund*; requisitioned for Falklands war and purchased by MoD on 16-2-1983 as the *Keren*, then sold in 01-1986 to Cenargo and operated in Mediterranean as *Scirocco*. Chartered by BCIF from 21-2-1989 until 18-1-1992 and renamed *Rozel*. Reverted to *Scirocco* and returned to Mediterranean. Sold in 06-2009 for breaking up in India.

St Briac (SR)

Built: Wm Denny & Bros, Dumbarton
Launched: 2-6-1924
Dimensions: 325.0 x 41.1 x 13.9 ft
Tonnage: 2,202g
Engines: twin screw geared turbines; 5,200 ihp
Speed: 19kt
Passengers: 1,300 (324 1st berths, 118 2nd berths)
Predominantly allocated to the Southampton-Le Havre and St Malo routes, visiting CI on excursions from 1932. Maintained CI service from 23-9-1939. War service from 06-1941 and sunk by a mine off east coast of Scotland on 12-3-1942 with loss of 43 lives.

St Helier (GW/BR)

Built: John Brown & Co, Clydebank
Launched: 23-3-1925
Dimensions: 291.5 x 40.0 x 16.3 ft
Tonnage: 1,885g
Engines: twin screw with 4 x Parsons geared turbines; 819nhp
Speed: 18kt
Passengers: 1,004
New for CI service with maiden voyage on 17-6-1925. Hit pier heads in St Helier on 10-4-1926. Initially twin funneled but reduced to single funnel in 1928. Landing ship in Second World War, including service at Dunkirk and Normandy. Command vessel for liberation of Guernsey on 12-5-1945, but did not return to service until 16-6-1946. To BR on 1-1-1948. Last sailing from CI on 14-9-1960 and broken up at Antwerp.

St Julien (GW/BR)

Built: John Brown & Co, Clydebank
Launched: 24-2-1925
Dimensions: 291.5 x 40.0 x 16.3 ft
Tonnage: 1,885g
Engines: twin screw with 4 x Parsons single reduction geared turbines; 819 nhp
Speed: 18kt
Passengers: 1,004
New for CI service with maiden voyage on 24-5-1925. Initially twin funneled but reduced to single funnel in 1928. Hospital ship in Second World War, including service at Dunkirk and Mediterranean. Returned to CI service on 1-12-1946. To BR on 1-1-1948. Last sailing on 27-9-1960 and broken up in 1961.

St Julien (WMS)

Built: KK Usuki Tekkoso, Usuki, Japan
Launched: 1977
Dimensions: 71.0 x 14.4 m
Tonnage: 1,561g
Engines: twin screw, Niigata diesel, 2,001bhp
Built in Japan as *Emsland* for German interests and purchased by Scandi-Line in 1986 as *Bohus*, then *Lofotferga*. Chartered by WMS as *St Julien*

for Weymouth-CI service with inaugural sailing on 13-5-1989 but re-possessed by owners on 17-10-1989. Later operated for Emeraude Ferries from St Malo in winter 1994-5 as *Elba Nova*.

St Malo (L&SWR)
Built: Aitken & Mansell, Glasgow
Launched: 8-8-1865
Dimensions: 161.0 x 22.2 x 12.1 ft
Tonnage: 301g
Engines: single screw 2 cyl; 120hp
Speed: 12kt
Iron cargo steamer built for Southampton-St Malo service and first screw vessel for L&SWR. Displaced to Normandy routes by *Caesarea*. Re-engined by Day, Summers & Co, Southampton in 1873 and re-boilered in 1885. Provided relief cover for Jersey fleet in 1882-3 and after 1887. Converted to cargo vessel in 1889 and sold to Power Steam Ship Co in 1905 to be scrapped in Holland.

St Patrick (I) (GW)
Built: Alexander Stephens, Linthouse
Launched: 15-1-1930
Dimensions: 281.3 x 41.1 x 16.3 ft
Tonnage: 1,922 g
Engines: Babcock & Wilcox; twin screw single reduction geared turbines, 887nhp
Speed: 18kt
Passengers: 913
Relief vessel for Irish Sea and Channel Island services. Maiden voyage to CI on 18-4-1930 and summer relief vessel thereafter. Hit rocks off Corbière on 5-8-1932 and had to be towed to harbour. Bombed and sunk on passage from Rosslare to Fishguard on 13-6-1941.

St Patrick (II) (GW/BR)
Built: Cammell Laird, Birkenhead
Launched: 20-5-1947
Dimensions: 321.3 x 50.5 x 13.3 ft
Tonnage: 3,482g
Engines: twin screw with 2 x 2 Parson's single reduction geared turbines, 8,500bhp
Speed: 19kt
Passengers: 648 berths
Cars: 25
Owned by Fishguard & Rosslare Railways & Harbour Co until transferred to BR on 17-12-1959. Maiden voyage Weymouth-CI on 4-2-1948. Seasonal Weymouth ship through 1950s and served other routes as relief. Converted to one-class ship in 1961 and used at weekends and for excursions up to end of 1964 season, prior to transfer to Dover with intermittent CI visits thereafter. Sold on 9-3-1972 to Gerasimos S Fe-

touris as *Thermopilae* for service in Greece. Broken up in 1980.

Sambur (GW/BR)
Built: Swan, Hunter & Wigham Richardson, Newcastle
Launched: 9-4-1925
Dimensions: 210.0 x 33.7 x 15.3 ft
Tonnage: 769g
Engines: twin screw, 2 x triple expansion inv; 1,350ihp
Speed: 13kt
Passengers: 12
Cargo vessel for Weymouth services, sister of *Roebuck*. Alterations to accommodation in 1928. Wartime service at Dunkirk, as a barrage balloon unit and at Normandy Landings in 1944. First GWR vessel to sail to Jersey after liberation on 19-9-1945. To BR on 1-1-1948 and remained at Weymouth, but also served Southampton between 1960 and 1963. Withdrawn after last sailing on 29-2-1964 and broken up in 1964.

Sarnia (LJ&GSSNCo)
Built: T&W Pim, Hull
Launched: 1850
Dimensions: 133.5 x 20.0 x 13.0 ft
Tonnage: 265 burthen
Engines: single screw, 40hp
Passengers: 60
Introduced to London-CI route arriving in Guernsey in 11-1850. Disposed of in 1853.

Sarnia (I) (L&SWR)
Built: Cammell Laird & Co, Birkenhead
Launched: 9-7-1910
Dimensions: 296.0 x 39.2 x 15.8 ft
Tonnage: 1,498g
Engines: triple screw, 3 x Parson's direct drive turbines, 4,500 kW
Speed: 20 kt
Passengers: 980
Modified sister of *Caesarea* (II) - only direct drive steamers built for L&SWR. Maiden voyage Southampton-CI on 12-4-1911 but operated summer-only due to heavy fuel consumption. An unsuccessful design, operating to CI in Spring and St Malo in summer. Wartime service as a boarding steamer. Collided with and sank SE&CR *Hythe* off Cape Helles on 29-10-1915. Sunk by *U65* when leaving home port of Alexandria on 12-9-1918.

Sarnia (II) (BR)
Built: Samuel White & Co, Cowes
Launched: 6-9-1960
Dimensions: 322 x 53.7 x 26.8 ft

Tonnage: 4,174g
Engines: twin screw geared turbines; 8,000 shp
Speed: 19½kt
Passengers: 1,290 (110 berths)
First sailing: 17-7-1961
Final traditional steamer for CI service, sister of *Caesarea,* built at cost of £1.5m. Maiden sailing to CI on 16-6-1961. Hit quay in St. Peter Port in 9-12-1961. Winter relief vessel for other BR routes from 1962. Internal improvements in 1971 to add seating for new reservations system. Retained after introduction of ro-ro services as spare vessel, but suffered turbine problems. At 1977 Silver Jubilee Spithead Fleet Review. Final sailing to CI on 10-9-1977. Sold to Supersave Supermarkets for failed duty free venture, then operated in Greece and Egypt. Broken up in 1987.

Scott Harley
Built: Murdock & Murray, Port Glasgow
Completed: 10-1884
Dimensions: 148.3 x 22.6 x 11.1 ft
Tonnage: 379g
Engines: 2 cyl 75hp
Noted on London-CI run from 10-1889 to 11-1897, owned by Cheeswright. Sold to Norway in 1898 as *Barden.* Later sunk by U boat off Fraserburgh on 6-4-1917

Sir Francis Drake
Built: Plymouth
Launched: 1826
Dimensions: 103.7 x 18.7 11.0 ft
Tonnage: 118g
Engines: 70hp
Wooden paddle steamer operated Plymouth service from 1826 to 1862, then sold to London. Caught fire off Grosnez Point in 07-1837.

Sir William Curtis
Built: Hastings
Launched: 1815
Dimensions: 58.4 x 17.7 x 9.0 ft
Tonnage: 75g
Sailing cutter acting as armed scout on relief service. Operated from Weymouth from 06-1816 until 1817.

Southampton (NSWSPCo/L&SWR)
Built: Palmer Bros & Co, Newcastle
Launched: 5-4-1860
Dimensions: 215.5 x 25.4 x 9.0 ft
Tonnage: 585g
Engines: 2 cyl simple oscillating; 200 hp
Speed: 13½kt
Passengers: 300

Clipper-bowed iron paddle steamer with maiden voyage on 13-10-1860. Transferred to L&SWR and overhauled and re-boilered in 1863. Speed increased to 15kt and transferred to Le Havre route. Lengthened by 21ft and re-boilered by Day, Summers & Co, Southampton in 1879-80. Operated on CI routes from 1880 to 1883, then Le Havre route. New engines fitted by Day, Summers & Co, Southampton in 1890. Sold to AF Yarrow as strike breaking accommodation vessel in 1897 and broken up in 1898.

South Western (I) (SWSPCo/NSWSPCo/L&SWR)
Built: Ditchburn & Mare & Co, Blackwall
Launched: 15-5-1843
Dimensions: 143.0 x 18.0 x 10.8 ft
Tonnage: 204g
Engines: Seaward; 2 x 1 cyl, simple vertical, 80hp
Speed: 12kt
First iron hulled steamer for CI service. Maiden voyage Southampton-CI on 31-7-1843. Worked on CI route until end of 1846. On Poole-CI-St Malo service in 1848 and then based in Jersey for French services 1849-51, but initiated Weymouth route in 1850. Relief vessel thereafter. Passed to NSWSPCo in 1847 and the L&SWR in 1862. Sold in 1863 for service in Hong Kong. Lost on Balabec Islands in China Sea on 15-11-1868.

South Western (II) (L&SWR)
Built: J & W Dudgeon, London
Launched: 09-1874
Dimensions: 222.3 x 27.1 x 13.5 ft
Tonnage: 657g
Engines: single screw, 2 cyl compound; 180nhp
Speed: 14kt
Iron cargo vessel, an enlarged version of the *Guernsey.* Maiden voyage to CI on 30-3-1875, but primarily allocated to St Malo route. Engines converted to triple expansion by Day, Summers & Co, Southampton in 1890. Electric light fitted 1906. Operated Jersey-France services in 1904 and 1906. Grounded off Cap de la Hague on 29-4-1915 during wartime blackout conditions. Sunk on 17-3-1918 by *UB59* south of St Catherine's Point with loss of 25 lives.

Stannington
Built: South Shields
Launched: 1871
Dimensions: 127.5 x 21.1 x 10.5 ft
Tonnage: 222g
Engines: 45hp
Noted operating form Maples in 1876, then on London-CI run from 1877 to 19-10-1889. Pur-

chased by Cheeswright in 1878 and sold in 1890.

Staperayder
Built: Henderson, Coulborn & Co, Renfrew
Launched: 3-1866
Dimensions: 115.8 x 22.1 x 12.2 ft
Tonnage: 217g
Operated on London-CI route between 25-5-1868 and 4-6-1889. Owned by C&M, then Cheeswright from 1870. Lengthened in 1874 and 1887. Sold to Monkwearmouth 1890. Broken up 1911.

Stella (L&SWR)
Built: J&G Thompson, Clydebank
Launched: 16-9-1890
Dimensions: 259.0 x 35.1 x 14.8 ft
Tonnage: 1,059g
Engines: twin screw, 2 x triple expansion; 360 nhp
Speed: 19kt
Passengers: 712
Third vessel in the Frederica class, sister of *Frederica* and *Lydia*. Maiden voyage Southampton-CI on 5-11-1890. Cylinder burst leaving St Helier on 24-11-1890, leaving her stranded in Jersey for week. Hit Auquière reef off Casquets during fog on a daylight crossing on 30-3-1899 and sank with loss of 105 lives.

Sylbe – see L Taurus

Transit
(B&FSNCo/CSPCo/SWSPCo/NSWSPCo/L&SWR)
Built: T E Snooks, Orchard Yard, Blackwall
Launched: 1835
Dimensions: 126.0 x 19.6 x 13 ft
Tonnage: 267g
Engines: 1 cyl simple; 80nhp
Wooden paddle steamer built for Southampton-Spain service; passed to CSPCo in 1838. Hit quay wall in Southampton in 1-1838. Used on Southampton-CI service from 1839 and London-CI route from autumn 1839-1841. To SWSPCo in 1842 and first mail carrier for the company but displaced by larger vessels. To NSWSPCo in 1846. Operated cheap boat service from 1851 to 1855. To L&SWR in 1863. Cargo service for L&SWR then converted to coal hulk in Jersey 1869.

Trondenes (IF)
Built: Bolsones Varft, Molde
Launched: 1965
Dimensions: 29.9 x 9.0 x 3.7 m
Tonnage: 233g

Engines: single screw screw, 5 cyl oil; 650 bhp
Passengers: 250
Built fro Norwegian interests and acquired by IF in 1992 and initially operated from Cherbourg to Alderney and Guernsey from 21-7-1992. Weymouth route added from 12-1992 until closure in 7-1993. Sold to Africa in 1994.

Ulrica (L&SWR/SR)
Built: Ailsa Shipbuilding, Troon
Launched: 03-1895
Dimensions: 149.9 x 24.1 x 7.7 ft
Tonnage: 383g
Engines: Muir & Houston; single screw, triple expansion; 75 hp
Speed: 10kt
Cargo steamer built as the *Granuaile* for the Congested Districts Board of Ireland as a cattle carrier. Leased, then sold to L&SWR in 1916 as the *Ulrica*. Maiden voyage to Guernsey on 13-4-1916. Passed to SR in 1923. Holed on the Roustel Rock on 10-3-1923 and reached port waterlogged. Enhanced facilities for carrying of cattle in 1923. Sold to TC Pas for scrap in 1928.

Varangerfjord (CH)
Built: Finnmark Fylkesrederi og & Tuteselskap, Hammerfest
Completed: 06-1990
Dimensions: 38.8 x 9.4 x 1.5 m
Tonnage: 417nt
Engines: 2 x 16cyl MTU, 5,441bhp
Speed: 35½kt
Passengers: 208
Built for seasonal services in Norway. Chartered to CH in 1998 and maiden call in CI on 20-5-1998. Operated from Southampton and Torquay for two seasons until withdrawn in 1999 before further service as an offshore support vessel. Still in service in 2018.

Vena (L&SWR/SR)
Built: Scott & Sons Ltd, Bowling
Launched: 05-1902
Dimensions: 170.4 x 27.2 x 11.4 ft
Tonnage: 555g
Engines: Ross & Duncan, Glasgow; single screw triple expansion; 69rhp
Speed: 12kt
Cargo steamer built as *Clarence* for Joseph Rank Ltd, Hull. Sold to RH Penny & Sons, Shoreham in 1907 as *Algeiba*. Purchased by L&SWR on 9-6-1922 for produce traffic and passed to SR in 1923. Sold to York Line in 1926 and saw service in Morocco. Scrapped 1954.

Vera (L&SWR/SR)
Built: Clydebank Engineering, Clydebank
Launched: 4-7-1898
Dimensions: 270 x 35.1 x 14.4 ft
Tonnage: 1,136g
Engines: twin screw 2 x 4 cyl triple expansion;
254nhp
Speed: 18kt
Built as replacement for *Dora* as relief vessel for
Le Havre and CI routes. Maiden sailing to CI on
27-9-1898. Operated as spare vessel and covered for loss of *Stella* until *Alberta* arrived.
Transferred to Southampton-St Malo route and
altered internally in 1903. Forced draught removed, then re-instated in 1910. Wartime relief
service at Southampton and Weymouth on CI
routes. Sank U boat by gunfire. Overhauled and
re-boilered in 1920 and operated on CI route
until 10-3-1930. Passed to SR in 1923 and re-
opened Jersey-St Malo link in 1932. Replaced by
Brittany in 1933 and sold to TW Ward for scrap
at Pembroke.

Victoria (L&SWR)
Built: J&G Thompson, Clydebank
Launched: 15-6-1896
Dimensions: 220.5 x 28.1 x 16.3 ft
Tonnage: 709g
Engines: twin screw, 2 x triple expansion;
107nhp
Speed: 16kt
Passengers:
Built for Jersey-St Malo service. Maiden voyage
Jersey-Granville-St Malo on 25-7-1896. Based
at Plymouth as tender 1904-1907, returning to
Jersey in 05-1907. Undertook wartime service
as a Q ship 1914-15 before returning to CI serv-
ice in 1915. Requisitioned again in 1918 as Surf II
but peace intervened before required. Surplus,
and sold to James Dredging & Co in 1919 for
service in Turkey. Scrapped in 1937.

Watersprite/Wildfire
Built: Geo Graham, Harwich
Launched: 1826
Dimensions: 107.0 x 17.2 x 11.8 ft
Tonnage: 162g
Engines: Boulton, Watt & Co; 60hp
First steamer to carry mail to CI. Renamed *Wild-
fire* in 1837 and broken up in 1888.

Wave Queen (L&CISCo)
Built: Langeveld en Van Vliet, Nederhardinxveld
Completed: 07-1903
Dimensions: 130.0 x 22.0 x 9.8 ft
Tonnage: 295g
Engines: 2 cyl compound, 50nhp
Speed: 8½kt
Initially named *Gale* but operated as *Wave
Queen* for L&CISCo from 06-1906 to 05-1908.
Scrapped 1934.

Waverley (L&SWR)
Built: A & J Inglis, Glasgow
Launched: 16-5-1865
Dimensions: 222 x 26 x 14 ft
Tonnage: 593g
Engines: 2 cyl simple osc 280nhp;
Speed: 13kt
Iron paddle steamer built for the North British
Railway Silloth-Dublin service and purchased by
L&SWR for CI routes in 08-1868. Maiden voyage
Southampton-CI on 21-12-1868 took two days.
Short period on Le Havre route during Franco-
Prussian War in 1870. Wrecked on Platte Boue
rocks in Little Russel Channel on 5-6-1873.

Whitstable (SR/BR)
Built: D&W Henderson, Renfrew, Glasgow
Launched: 16-8-1925
Dimensions: 229.6 x 33.6 x 41.1 ft
Tonnage: 687g
Engines: single screw, 2 x triple expansion;
165nhp
Speed: 15kt
Passengers: 12
Cargo vessel for Dover routes. Assisted during
civilian evacuation of CI in 6-1940. Restored
services from Southampton from 14-7-1945
until 4-1947. To BR on 1-1-1948; returned to
Southampton station from 5-1948 until 5-1947
then moved to Weymouth. Last sailing from CI
on 25-3-1959 and scrapped in 4-1959.

Winchester (SR/BR)
Built: Wm Denny & Bros, Dumbarton
Launched: 21-3-1947
Dimensions: 251.5 x 27.8 x 12.8 ft
Tonnage: 1,149g
Engines: Sulzer; twin screw, 5 cyl oil; 3,000bhp
Speed: 15kt
Passengers: 10
Built at cost of £215,154 to replace war losses.
Maiden voyage Southampton-CI on 1-12-1947.
To BR on 1-1-1948. Collided with *Haslemere* in
Solent on 2-12-1955, sustaining bow damage.
Allocated to Weymouth to replace *Roebuck*
from 1-3-1965. Hit and damaged Roustel Bea-
con off Guernsey on 25-2-1970. Displaced by
containerisation project and sold in 04-1971 to
Allied Finance SA, Athens for Greek service. Bro-
ken up in Greece on 05-1988.

Wolf (L&SWR)
Built: Robert Napier, Govan
Launched: 1863
Dimensions: 242.7 x 27.2 x 13.8 ft
Tonnage: 728g
Engines: 2 cyl compounded; 310hp
Speed: 15kt
Passengers: 150 berths
Iron paddle steamer built for G&J Burns' Glasgow-Belfast service. Sunk in Belfast Lough 16-10-1867, but raised and repaired in 1868. Purchased by L&SWR on 10-4-1871 and allocated to St Malo route. Engines compounded by Rait & Lindsay of Glasgow in 1873. On Le Havre route from 1874 to 1894. Hit and damaged by *Alliance* in 1890. Re-boilered in 1891. Replaced by *Alliance* and became a seamen's hospital and quarantine ship in 1896 before being sold for scrap to JJ King, Garston in 1900.

Wonder (SWSPCo/NSWSPCo/L&SWR)
Built: Ditchburn & Mare, Blackwall
Launched: 09-1844
Dimensions: 158.0 x 20.6 x 10.1 ft
Tonnage: 251g
Engines: Seaward & Capel; 3 cyl atmospheric vertical boiler, 160hp
Speed: 14kt
Passengers: 180
Iron paddle steamer employed on CI service from 3-5-1845. Passed to NSWSPCo in 1847. New boiler in 1848 and allocated to Le Havre route. Relief vessel from 1856. Damaged in collision with *Havre* in 1858. Transferred to the L&SWR in 1862. Re-boilered in 1864 and employed on Jersey-France route latterly for cargo service. Scrapped 1874.

The *Caledonian Princess* arriving at Weymouth. *(Miles Cowsill)*

Bibliography

Arnott A (2010): Southampton – Gateway to the World

Atkins T (2014): Great Western Docks & Marine

Beale G (2001): The Weymouth Harbour Tramway in the steam era

Breeze G (1988): The Papenburg Sisters

Couling D 1982): Wrecked on the Channel Islands

Cowsill M (1989): British Channel Island Ferries

Cowsill M (1990): Earl William Classic Car Ferry 1964-1990

Cowsill M (1995): Ferries of Portsmouth and the Solent

Cowsill M (2006): Fishguard – Rosslare 1906-2006

Cowsill M & Hendy J (1995): The Sealink Years

Coysh V (TSG* 1976): Island Steam Packets

Crosby A (2011): Titanic – The Channel Island Connections

Cruikshank C (1975): The German Occupation of the Channel Islands

Danielson R (2007): Railway Ships and Packet Ports

David JM (TSG* 1954): Early Channel Island Steamers 1823-1840

Dendy Marshall CF (1963): The History of the Southern Railway

Denton T & Leach N (2010): Lighthouses of England; The South Coast

Duckworth CLD & Langmuir GE (1968): Railway and other Steamers

Farr G (1967): West Country Passenger Steamers

Faulkner JN & Williams RA (1988): The London & South Western Railway in the
    Twentieth Century

Graseman C & McLachlan GWP (1939): English Channel Packet Boats

Greenway A (1981): A Century of Cross Channel Passenger Steamers

Greenway A (2014): Cross Channel & Short Sea Ferries

Haresnape B (1982): Sealink

Haws D (1993): Merchant Fleets: Britain's Railway Steamers; Western & Southern
    Companies + French & Stena

Haws D (1993): Merchant Fleets: Britain's Railway Steamers; Eastern & North West-
    ern Companies + Zeeland & Stena

Henderson R (1997): Crossing the Channel

Hendy J, Merrigan J & Peter B (2015): Sealink and before

Jackson B L (2002): Weymouth to the Channel Islands - A Great Western Shipping
    History

Jordan S (1998): Ferry Services of the London, Brighton & South Coast Railway

Le Scelleur K (1985): Channel Islands' Railway Steamers

Le Scelleur K (1997): Commodore Shipping: The First Half Century 1947-1997

Lucking JH (1971): The Great Western at Weymouth

Lucking JJ (1986): The Weymouth Harbour Tramway

MacDermot E T (1964): History of the Great Western Railway vol. 1 1833-1863

MacDermot E T (1964): History of the Great Western Railway vol. 2 1863 -1921

Mayne R (1971): Mail Ships of the Channel Islands

McLoughlin R (1997): The Sea was their Fortune

Mitchell A (1866 – reprint 2014): Diary of a Trip to Jersey and Guernsey

Mullay A J (2008): Railway Ships at War

Nock O S (1967): History of the Great Western Railway vol 3 1923-1947

O'Brien FT Capt (1973): Early Solent Steamers

Ovenden J & Shayer D (1999): The Wreck of the Stella

Ovenden J & Shayer D (2014): Shipwrecks of the Channel Islands

Robins N (1999): Turbine Steamers of the British Isles

Rousham S (1992): Maritime Guernsey

Searle B (2010): Weymouth Ferries: The Rise and Fall of a Port

Sharp EW (TSG* 1959): The Harbours and Shipping of Guernsey at the turn of the 19th Century

Sharp EW (TSG* 1967): Wrecks in the Bailiwick of Guernsey

Sharp EW (TSG* 1967): The evolution of St. Peter Port Harbour

Sharp EW (1986): Lighthouses of the Channel Islands

Shayer D (TSG* 1981): The Loss of the Stella

Stevens J & Jee N (1987): The Channel Islands

Trotter JMY (TSG* 1950): Early Guernsey Postal History

Vaughan A (1985): Grime and Glory; Tales of the Great Western 1892-1947

Williams C (2000): From Sail to Steam; Studies in the Nineteenth Century History of the Channel Islands

Williams RA (1968): The London & South Western Railway Vol 1: The Formative Years

Williams RA (1973): The London & South Western Railway Vol 2: Growth and Con-solidation

Winser J de S (1994): British Cross-Channel Railway Passenger Ships

Winser J de S (1999): BEF Ships before and after Dunkirk

*Transactions of the Société Guernesiaise

Magazines and Newspapers

Back Track

Ferry & Cruise Review

Journal of the Jersey Maritime Museum

Railway Magazine

Railway and Travel Monthly

Sea Breezes

Sealink News

Ships Monthly

Transactions of the Société Guernesiaise

Acknowledgements

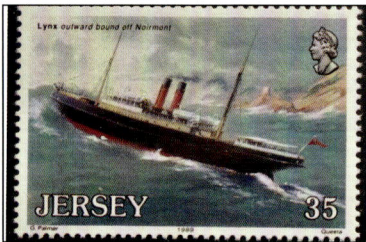

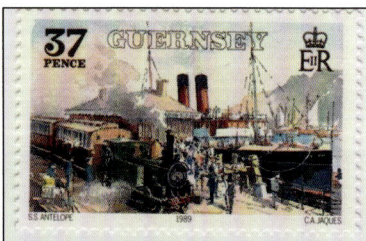

I joined Sealink at Portsmouth as Operations Manager shortly before privatisation in 1984, and was Freight Manager for the Channel Islands and Cherbourg services during the period of competition with Channel Island Ferries. Experiencing the 'merger' at first hand I joined British Channel Island Ferries as Sales Manager and helped establish the new company. Later, whilst with P&O European Ferries, I was part of the bid team that sought to win the contract in 1998. I have tried to avoid any bias in my recollection and perspective on these key periods of recent history.

During my time with Sealink and British Channel Island Ferries I was privileged to share many journeys to the Islands with a group of highly professional masters and their crews, who gave freely of their knowledge and experience. I worked ashore with dedicated teams in both companies, who consistently endeavoured to make the best of the situation that often-distant forces dealt them. It was a tragedy that so much experience was lost at the end of the Sealink era. This was truly a watershed for the Island services.

The early history of shipping services to the Channel Islands has been well documented, and this narrative is an attempt to bring that account up to date. It was fortunate that publication of Kevin Le Scelleur's work coincided with my time with Sealink and kindled an interest in the complex sequence of events that make up this story. I acknowledge the particular value of his work, and that of J.M. David, Duncan Haws and John Lucking in the preparation of this book. A glance at the bibliography will guide the reader towards further works of interest.

I am grateful to Miles Cowsill for the original concept for the book and his confidence and design skills in bringing this into print. I have received help and support from Mel Bradley, Andrew Cooke, James Dann, John Downs, Ambrose Greenway, John Hendy, Dave Hocquard, Darren Holdaway, George Holland, Martin Miller, Kevin Mitchell, Bridget Yabsley, the staff of the Priaulx Library in Guernsey and Société Jerseaise in Jersey, Guernsey Post Ltd, Jersey Post Ltd, the National Newspaper library, the National Archives and Southampton City Museums. The Castle Cornet Maritime Museum in Guernsey and the Maritime Museum in Jersey are essential destinations for anyone interested in this story.

My wife Christina patiently tolerated my disappearances to 'work on the book' and I am, as always, humbled by her loving support.

Any errors are, of course, my sole responsibility.